# Quicksilver Capital

# Quicksilver
# Capital

*How the Rapid Movement of
Wealth Has Changed the World*

Richard B. McKenzie
Dwight R. Lee

THE FREE PRESS
*A Division of Macmillan, Inc.*
NEW YORK
Collier Macmillan Canada
TORONTO
Maxwell Macmillan International
NEW YORK   OXFORD   SINGAPORE   SYDNEY

The Free Press
A Division of Macmillan, Inc.
866 Third Avenue, New York, N.Y. 10022

Collier Macmillan Canada, Inc.
1200 Eglinton Avenue East
Suite 200
Don Mills, Ontario M3C 3N1

Printed in the United States of America

printing number
1 2 3 4 5 6 7 8 9 10

**Library of Congress Cataloging-in-Publication Data**

McKenzie, Richard B.
    Quicksilver capital: how the rapid movement of wealth has changed
the world / Richard B. McKenzie, Dwight R. Lee.
        p.     cm.
    Includes bibliographical references and index.
    ISBN 0–02–920535–2
    1. Capital movements—Political aspects.   2. Foreign investments—
Political aspects.   3. Finance, International—Political aspects.
4. International trade—Political aspects.   5. International
economic relations.   6. Monetary policy.   7. Fiscal policy.
I. Lee, Dwight R.   II. Title.
HG3891.M42     1991
332'.042—dc20                                           90–22477
                                                            CIP

*For Vaclav Klaus*

# Contents

# Preface

Governor James Florio of New Jersey and Governor Ray Mabus of Mississippi hold their high offices under dramatically different economic and social settings. New Jersey is second from the top in individual income, while Mississippi is dead last.

However, as news reports of the last year attest, these governors face practically the same recurring dilemma. Their states have increasing pressing needs in the face of constant revenue short-falls. They want additional revenue to meet easily documented social and educational needs, but they understand that tax increases anger citizens and businesses.

The good citizens of New Jersey no longer have to read their governor's lips. He doubled the income tax rates for his state's wealthiest taxpayers in 1990—albeit grudgingly. His once soaring political popularity immediately took a nosedive, the result of which meant that in mid-1990 "a mere 17 percent of New Jersey's voters have a kind word to say about their governor to opinion pollsters."[1]

Governor Mabus sought to escape boosting taxes in the most painless way he could think of, by offering Mississippians a chance to play games, the lottery. Even though he wants desperately to be known as the South's "education governor" who will help pull poor Mississippians up by their collective bootstraps, Mabus refused in 1990 to seek a tax increase when his lottery proposal was turned down by the state legislature. He could hear the rumblings in Trenton as easily as those in Hattiesburg.

Although they took opposite fiscal courses, Florio and Mabus' fiscal deliberations were driven by the same two political fears—one old and one new. The old political fear—the one that has always been endemic to public life—is the grief the governors must take from their constituents, who may turn to someone else in the next election, when they contemplate "revenue enhancement," the current euphemism for a tax hike. The new fear—the one they do not yet know how to handle very well—is the prospect that in response to a tax increase citizens will take themselves, their earning power, or their capital elsewhere, to a more hospitable tax climate.

This latter threat which faces Florio and Mabus is the exact same one confronting all other state governors and, for that matter, all world leaders, from New Zealand, Turkey, and France to the United States.

Until recently, the prospects that people might move their capital or themselves in response to taxes did not have to be given much thought by political leaders, simply because people could then not move except at great expense. People and capital were largely captive of the political decisions made with great deliberation in the halls of the world's legislatures or parliaments. The politics of tax decisions had to be considered carefully, but the economics of tax decisions could be ignored.

Today, technology permits people and their capital to be far more fugitive, far more capable of bounding over government borders—far more like quicksilver—slippery, elusive, and hard to contain and control. As never before, political leaders must be concerned that their efforts to raise tax rates in their own jurisdictions will mean that other leaders in adjoining or even far-flung governments, who have not touched their tax rates, will enjoy revenue increases.

"Damned if I do; damned if I don't" must be what Florio and Mabus, and all of their contemporary political cohorts, mutter when they look in the mirror each and every morning. The sad truth is that they are damned to govern in a world of severe economic constraints that political leaders in earlier times never thought much about. The evidence continues to mount that people, capital, jobs, and incomes gravitate toward those government jurisdictions with the most favorable fiscal and regulatory environments.[2]

Much has been written and said about the "competitiveness" of businesses, especially American businesses, and the stress it has exerted in business leaders. Without any question, over the past decade businesses have had to meet serious competitive challenges from both foreign and domestic sources. Because their economic survival has been at stake, they have had to go with the flow of the global market and restructure and revitalize their internal operations to meet global standards.

Little has been made about the "competitiveness" of governments. Nonetheless, the competitive struggles faced by governments in the new world economy are no less important, and perhaps even more so, than the struggles faced by businesses. *Quicksilver Capital*, seeking to fill the void, is about the global economic forces that are dramatically shaping and restructuring governments and their policies.

Our central argument can be outlined with relative ease. The increased mobility of capital, coupled with the growing economic integration of national economies, has dramatically expanded the scope and intensity of competitive markets. This growth in business competitiveness has necessarily forced governments into a competitive struggle for the world's human and physical capital base. As a consequence, governments have lost much of the monopoly power that undergirded their growth in earlier decades. World governments have had to compete against one another by seeking more efficient policies in order to lure and retain the physical and human capital that is now so crucial to modern production processes and to the tax bases on which governments depend.

In general, governments have been forced to lower tax rates, deregulate industries, and privatize services in order that the productive facilities within their borders can remain competitive on a world scale. Governments at all levels—local, state, and national—have lost the vestiges of unchecked economic sovereignty. That is the source of much of Governors Florio and Mabus' fiscal frustrations. And it is at the heart of the theory of competitive governments that we develop in this book

We understand that our views will be controversial. We have confronted controversy for the four years over which this volume has taken shape. But then unfolding events, especially in the Soviet Union and Eastern Europe, during those four years have served only to fortify our position.

In the best spirit of the "market for competing ideas," *Quicksilver Capital* is intended to spark a debate over how government policies are formulated in an economy that is progressively more global. Governments are not completely autonomous, self-controlling social institutions in which only politically devised, formal constitutional precepts constrain policy choices. On the contrary, governments are constrained by economic forces that, to a significant degree, exist outside of political systems, regardless of their conservative or liberal stripes. These exogenous economic forces have changed, giving rise to changes in direction for government policies.

Our argument explains why world competitive forces will continue to work for improvements in the efficiency of government, whether in the provision of income relief or building bridges, and for the elimination of many government programs that are just downright wasteful or are designed to pad the pockets of the not-so-disadvantaged. We suggest that the world forces at work on governments will ultimately free resources for doing many of the basic things that governments have forsaken such as taking care of the truly disadvantaged and keeping our streets safe and clean.

Much was written in the late 1980s about America's lost hegemony in the world's political and economic arenas. The facts of the debate have been misinterpreted and misunderstood. Nonetheless, many proponents of the decline thesis—including Paul Kennedy, Robert Reich, and, most recently, Kevin Phillips—have assumed that America can regain its position of world leadership by the federal government reasserting its will to manage the economy.[3] Critics of federal policy reversals in the 1980s have written eloquently about the need for managed trade and managed industrial structure and growing government subsidies and taxes to match government's growing responsibilities. From the perspective of this book, such a policy course is a throwback to the 1960s romantic model of government and is anticompetitive and totally out of sync with world economic forces. It will only ensure America's economic decline.

In the new world economy, greatness will come to people and companies—not so much to countries and governments—who are resourceful, inventive, and competitive. That is to say, greatness will come to those people who are free and able to take responsibility for their own welfare, not those who are constrained by government regulations, subsidies, and taxes. Greatness will come to Americans—or Japanese or Brazilians or Italians—but only to the extent that their governments create an environment in which they can freely express their resourcefulness, inventiveness, and competitiveness with the minimum degree of interference. In this regard, "America's greatness" will hinge not on a return to government principles widely accepted two decades ago, but to those that were dominant two centuries ago.

The goods news, we believe, is that governments, not just in the United States but around the world, are increasingly going to act *as if* they are guided by the principles of the limited state and by the forces of global competition that render it impossible for them to act otherwise. That is the lesson to be learned from our reexamination of modern world history and government policies.

# Acknowledgments

We accept responsibility for the overall direction, scope, and content of our analysis, but we must share the credit for many of the insights that we include. Fortunately, this work is a joint product with our reviewers and critics, almost all of whom bolstered our arguments and prevented us from saying some things that, on reflection, were misdirected. We are especially indebted to the participants of an academic symposium organized around an early draft of the book in August 1989 and sponsored by the Liberty Fund of Indianapolis. These valued participants, collaborators, and critics were Stuart Butler, James Child, Keith Crisco, John Fund, George Gilder, the late Burton Gray, Paul Heyne, W. W. Hill, Vaclav Klaus, Peter Kotauczek, Kenneth MacKenzie, Walter Nord, Robert Poole, Alvin Rabushka, Albert Zlabinger, Robert Tollison, and Rufus Waters.

We are also indebted to colleagues around the country who took the time to talk with us about our theme and read all or part of the manuscript. They include Warren Brookes, Rex Cottle, Tyler Cowen, James Kau, Hugh Macaulay, Clark Nardinelli, George Selgin, Alan Reynolds, William Shughart, Richard Timberlake, Myles Wallace, Larry White, Clinton Whitehurst, Keith Womer, and Bruce Yandle. Tyler Cowen's extensive suggestions for improvement in the manuscript were especially helpful. In an article for the *National Journal* concerned with the theme of the book captured in a paper written by one of the authors for the Cato Institute, economic columnist Jonathan Rauch inadvertently gave us the title for the book. We appreciate his turn of words, which vividly captures the essence of our argument. We are also indebted to Ed Crane and David Boaz at the Cato Institute for their willingness to publish one of our early papers that developed the book's theme.

We cannot overlook our editors who vastly improved the correctness and clarity of our prose, including Carolyn Foster and Karen McKenzie. We owe a special debt of thanks to Peter Dougherty, who in his role as acquisitions editor at The Free Press gave considerable direction to the final organization of the book. Rossanne Schwalenberg and Kristin Johnson helped a great deal in managing all aspects of the project.

We acknowledge the considerable support that the John M. Olin Foundation provided for the project from 1987 through 1990. We are deeply indebted to the Olin Board of Directors for supporting a research project that several years ago appeared to be far more controversial and speculative than it does today.

Finally, we acknowledge the support of the Hearin/Hess endowment in the University of Mississippi's College of Business that supported Richard McKenzie's research, of the Ramsey endowment in the University of Georgia's College of Business, and of the Philip M. McKenna Foundation that supported Dwight Lee's research during parts of the last four years. Our working relationship with Kenneth Chilton, Melinda Warren, and Murray Weidenbaum at the Center for the Study of American Business at Washington University in St. Louis has provided us with an invaluable forum for developing, disseminating, and "test marketing" major elements of the book's thesis.

For reasons that will become apparent in the first few pages of Chapter 1, we are pleased to dedicate this book to Vaclav Klaus and the "velvet revolution" that he helped guide.

Richard McKenzie
Oxford, MS

Dwight Lee
Athens, GA

*September 1990*

Quicksilver Capital

# 1

# Government's Dilemma in a Competitive World Economy

In the future, we will vote more frequently with our feet. If politicians try to boss us, brainworkers will go away and telecommunicate from Tahiti. Countries that choose to have too high a level of government expenditure or too fussy regulations will be residually inhabited mainly by dummies.

*Norman Macrae*[1]
Editor, *The Economist*

WE met the Czech economist Vaclav Klaus in August 1989 at a small academic symposium held in North Carolina. The purpose of the symposium was to bring together thinkers from around the world to debate the argument of this book: That the recent revolution in computer and information technology has enabled firms to move assets around the world at the touch of a button. It has also caused an explosion of competition not only among businesses, but among national governments seeking to attract new business and to keep existing business within their borders. This competition has forced government to reduce tax rates, spending, and regulations and to lower trade barriers. The resulting loss of fiscal and regulatory power has put a severe crimp in the very ability of these governments to govern.

All the attendees were distinguished in their own right, but Dr. Klaus's attendance was special—and it became even more special as world events unfolded the following fall and winter.

Vaclav Klaus was, at the time, employed in the Ministry of Economics in Czechoslovakia. He was, of course, from a Communist state and could speak eloquently, from firsthand experience, about the East's obliviousness to international economic forces in making economic decisions. Allegiance to Communist ideology and centralized planning of the economy were the only forces that seemed to matter back in his home country, even if the people were, in the process, being impoverished. Governments don't compete for resources; they control them. That was the message he had been taught but never wanted to accept.

Coming to the symposium was not easy for Vaclav, certainly not as easy as it was for the attendees from Western countries. Foreign travel was strictly controlled by the Czechoslovak government, and Vaclav was persona non grata in his home country. He had been fired in 1970 from one government post for having dismissed John Kenneth Galbraith as a "social critic," rather than an economist, in his antistatist essays for *The Czech Encyclopedia of Economics*. He was regarded as a counterrevolutionary.[2]

Vaclav was finally allowed to attend, although he spent months getting approval. He was a scholar, unassuming and affable, but he was genuinely skeptical about our argument that technology-driven reductions in transportation and communication costs were diminishing the sovereignty of governments everywhere. He listened quietly and patiently for the first day or so to those in attendance as they talked about how the tiny microchip, the heart of the personal computer, had, by freeing the movement of capital, enfranchised firms and people while weakening the state. And he listened carefully as the participants attributed the economic boom of the 1980s to this rapid movement of money and other assets—this quicksilver capital— that had been nourished by the Thatcher and Reagan tax cuts. The optimistic tenor of the discussion ran counter to his own experience.

Of course, Vaclav was aware of some of the economically inspired political crises afoot in the Soviet bloc. He knew that Hungarian Communists had approved free elections after they had dumped their leader, János Kádár, in May 1988. Furthermore, he was aware that opposition groups in Poland, led by the once-outlawed Solidarity trade union, had trounced the Communists in the Senate election the previous June, winning ninety-nine of the one hundred seats. Nevertheless, Vaclav insisted that he saw no clear signs at the time of the symposium, again early August 1989, that non-Communists in Poland would be given a meaningful political say in running the country.

On several occasions he cautioned with exceptional politeness (given that he must have believed that the other participants were off their intellectual rockers) that the much-touted revolution had not come to his country and was unlikely to come at any time in the near future.

The diehards in the group, however, stressed that an important, previously unrecognized economic phenomenon was unfolding on a worldwide scale. Countries—mainly non-Communist countries—were jumping over each other seeking to lower their tax rates, deregulate industries, and reduce the economic influence of their governments. These unfolding changes were not isolated. Rather, they covered the globe, spanned the ideological spectrum from capitalism to socialism to state communism, and were linked by underlying economic forces that had been set loose by technological changes. Several of the participants predicted that even the extraordinary power of Communist governments would, by the end of the century, begin to fall prey to these forces.

As several of the other participants pointed out, the Soviet Union's Mikhail Gorbachev was then showing the way for "new thinking" for communism—which, to a significant degree, appeared to be clever rationalizations to make market economics compatible with Marxian teachings. Indeed, the "new thinking" was mandated by the ubiquitous domestic and international economic forces at work in the rest of the world, or so several of us maintained. There must be ties, we pointed out, that linked world events, because the new thinking was much the same in many countries—for Reagan, Thatcher, and Gorbachev. Quicksilver capital was at work on a global scale.

Vaclav Klaus could only shake his head.

He was not alone among the participants in his reluctance to accept this idea. He was, however, in a position to insist more forcefully than others that technology in general, and computer power in particular, was important in his country, but for reasons in direct opposition to those being invoked at the meeting. Officials in Communist countries were only inclined to think in terms of how such power could be employed to maintain and elevate the state's economic controls. In practical terms, computer power was viewed as a new means of supplanting individual decision making and making central planning more effective and less costly—more, not less, pervasive and authoritarian.

Vaclav warned that we were not thinking like the loyal Communist planners he knew. Technology could facilitate the "rationalization" of resources to achieve the government's production and income goals and could extend the constraining economic reach of the state. Though he shared with us the hope that fueled our heady discussions, he contended that instead of quicksilver as a metaphor for modern technology, computers were more like the steel at the core of the state's guns, a hard and fixed tool that could be used for greater and more effective control. Computers enabled the state to track people and their incomes with greater facility and to solve the numerous problems associated with the central planning of the national economy.

## The Dominoes of Eastern Europe

We parted after several days of talk, willing to think that we had been too daring in our assessment of the diminution of government power. After all, Vaclav lived literally on the boundary that separated his desire to dismantle the power of his own government from the reality of that vast power, which he understood must be faced squarely on his return. His personal testimony could not be summarily dismissed.

Nonetheless, Vaclav's conservatism and his repeated cautions notwithstanding, our rewriting of the book was made very difficult in the fall and winter of 1989. Events in Eastern Europe quickly overtook our every revision:

• In late August, Communist members of the Peasant and Democratic parties in Poland defected from the Communist ranks and agreed to join in the formation of a government led by Solidarity. Gorbachev encouraged the rest of the Communist leadership, most importantly, Poland's General Wojciech Jaruzelski, to support the Solidarity-led government. A form of democracy broke out in Poland, much to everyone's disbelief. The introduction of free enterprise into the corroding Polish economy became a question of "how," not "if."

• In August 1989, Hungarian Communists faced an unpleasant political dilemma. In 1968 the government had signed a treaty with East Germany that required each government to prevent the other's citizens from crossing into a third country without permission. How-ever, in January 1989 Hungary had signed a thirty-five-nation human rights agreement in Vienna that obligated the signing governments not to prevent travel abroad and not to force refugees to return home. That treaty made the fence along the Hungary/Austria border superflu-ous, resulting in its being torn down when the spring thaw permitted. East Germans began one-way treks on what were advertised as holi-days but were really getaways. The "vacationers" who continued to slip into the West, often in the dark of night, used Hungary only as a way station in their flight.

On August 31, Gyula Horn, Hungary's foreign minister, avowed that Hungary could not become East Germany's holding pen and offered unobstructed and open passage for East Germans to West Germany through Austria. Photographs of trains and buses packed with fleeing and rejoicing East German refugees were seen around the world.

• The massive outflow of refugees forced a split in the ranks of the East German Communists. On October 9, 1989, Leipzig was an armed camp, with Communist troops—including fighting units of the "Stasi," the much-feared state security police—poised to quell the growing demonstrations, in Erich Honecker's words, "by any means." The guns, however, were never fired that day because Le-ipzig's Communist party leaders, again with Gorbachev's tacit backing, pledged to the assembled crowds that they would permit, and even encourage, a "free exchange of opinions about the continuation of socialism in our country." Shortly thereafter, on October 18, the ailing Honecker was replaced by reformer Egon Krenz, who—because he was judged to be too close to his predecessors—was later, also replaced.

With East Germany's means of production—workers—moving to West Germany by way of Hungary, and with little or no means available to East Germany to stop the outflow, the Berlin Wall became in effect an irrelevant symbol, a dike as porous as the natural limestone that went into its concrete. The Berlin Wall, which Honecker had declared the previous January would last for another century, was torn down with hammers and, when they were unavailable, literally with the fingernails of West *and* East Germans in full view of the world's television cameras.

• For three decades before 1989, Bulgaria had been renowned not so much for its adherence to communism as for its acceptance of "Zhivkovism"—that is, state-sponsored corruption, racism, and gangsterism fostered by Communist party boss and government leader Todor Zhivkov. Nevertheless, in October 1989, Zhivkov, then seventy-eight, fell victim to what amounted to a palace coup led by foreign minister Petar Mladenov.

• The political dominoes kept falling. In November 1989, 25,000 young Czechs, mainly students, demonstrated in Prague's Wenceslas Square for free expression, free elections, and free markets. The unarmed students were encircled by units of riot police and the Red Berets, an antiterrorist squad, and were clubbed until blood covered much of Narodni Street. The brutal treatment, however, only incited the Czechs into what has since been dubbed the "velvet revolution," the daily outpouring of hundreds of thousands of citizens into Wenceslas Square demanding individual freedom, a meaningful democracy, and the resignation of the then Communist government headed by Miroslav Stepan and Milos Jakes. After the country was virtually shut down by a nationwide strike, and with calls for peaceful change coming from Moscow, the Communist leadership capitulated to prodemocracy forces on November 26, giving in to the demonstrators' principal demand: that the Communist party give up its monopoly political position and admit non-Communists to the government.

• No turn of political events in Eastern Europe was more bloody than that in Romania. Nicolae Ceauşescu, the leader there for twenty-four years, was not about to give up his Stalinist management style without a fight—which he got. The upheaval began in earnest on December 14 with a demonstration in the border town of Timisoara by supporters of a Lutheran minister who was being deported for preaching prodemocracy sermons. When profreedom, prodemocracy demonstrators refused to retreat from their demonstration at the minister's church, on December 17 Ceauşescu personally gave the order to shoot—a decision that brought even more Romanians into the streets, mainly because hundreds of citizens were slaughtered.

The following day Ceauşescu called for a progovernment demonstration in Bucharest, but much to his surprise, he was met with calls for freedom and democracy from opposition leaders among the assembled crowd. Ceauşescu had to withdraw from the podium, dazed by his inability to silence the dissidents with oratory and the implied threat of force. On December 22 the "Securitate," the dictator's secret police, opened fire on the Bucharest demonstrators, and Ceauşescu's defense minister was executed for failure to transmit Ceauşescu's personal orders to shoot the demonstrators in Timisoara. In the end the army apparently grew weary of killing fellow citizens and sided with the rebels. Nicolae and Elena Ceauşescu were themselves captured, after seeking to escape by helicopter from the rooftop of their palace, and executed on Christmas Day.

## The Outbreak of Freedom

All in all hordes of people in several Eastern European countries took to the streets in the fall of 1989 demanding that state controls on their lives be drastically reduced. Freedom began breaking out everywhere. Free markets were exalted in writing—by Russians, Poles, Hungarians, Romanians, Czechs, East Germans, and Bulgarians. Former Moscow Communist boss Boris Yeltzin dared to tour the United States, declaring at every opportunity that Marxism was a nice ideal but in practice was dead. Western conservatives delighted in observing that the only remaining true Communists appeared to be in American universities.

During a few fateful months in late 1989, the central political question being raised in the West shifted from one of how the Soviet Union would make the transition to a more market-based economy, which had never before been raised as a serious question, to one of how long the Soviet Union might last as a unified republic. Soviet Communists from the Baltic republics, most notably Lithuania, started declaring their independence of the leadership in Moscow. In an apparent effort to calm growing dissent, in February 1990 the Central Committee in Moscow consented to waive its monopolistic political stranglehold on the country, allowing for—of all things—competitive politics. Shortly thereafter in March, the Soviet Congress approved a new constitution that allowed for "citizen property" (a Communist euphemism for the long-spurned capitalistic notion of "private ownership") in businesses, including manufacturing facilities.

These remarkable events, however, were preceded by what was for us a poignant twist of fate. Just before Christmas Vaclav Klaus was named the new minister of finance in Czechoslovakia.

For all our academic prognosticating about the influence of capital mobility and government power, we wish we could have predicted the political upheaval in Eastern Europe of 1989. But we, along with everyone else, were caught totally off guard by the rapidity of change.

Nevertheless, we were delighted to see Vaclav capture the spirit of the moment when he wrote, with another Czech economist, in the *Financial Times*, "We should seek a new social contract—without it we cannot go forward."[3] He later identified that what he meant by the new social contract was nothing short of a reversion to a market economy. He proposed to start the reform process by allowing state companies to sell shares to their employees, permitting Czech citizens to start companies of whatever size they chose, allowing foreign investors to own 100 percent of Czech companies, and slashing away at the state budget by cutting business subsidies by 15 percent.[4] Quite a switch for a country that only months earlier was arresting people for suggesting such reforms.

## The Determining Forces

The press has been replete with explanations for the political turnarounds in Eastern Europe and for the changes taking place in the United States, Great Britain, and other countries. Some commentators have relied on the obvious explanation, the "great man" theory of history.[5] These commentators often point to the strategic importance of the elections of Margaret Thatcher and Ronald Reagan and, most recently, the elevation of Mikhail Gorbachev—and, by extension, the emergence of Lech Walesa, Vaclav Havel, and the other heroes of Eastern Europe in support of this theory. These leaders do indeed possess unusual charisma, vision, and political will. We would be the first to grant that leadership changes of this order can often explain much about government behavior. However, we hardly think that changes in government leadership alone enabled the world in the 1980s to stand witness to the extraordinary political events that cut across divergent political systems and were orchestrated in the name of greater individual freedom and efficiency in government policies.

Others have argued that the failures of aggressive democratic socialism in the West and state communism in the East have forced the changes that have taken place.[6] Without much question, governments in the East and the West have demonstrated pervasive failure in the past in their unchecked efforts to solve private problems through collective means.[7] However, these failures are hardly news to people who lived through the 1960s and 1970s.

Pointing to government leadership changes and government failures simply begs an important question: Why did world leaders from divergent political ideologies but with similar pressing policy concerns rise to the top of their governments at more or less the same time? Our answer is straightforward: Economic forces have been at work on established political regimes and have changed them drastically. By the 1970s modern technological developments were having profound affects on the ability of governments to make independent decisions.

First: These developments made capital as slithery and as elusive as quicksilver, and the growing transnational mobility of capital forced world governments to become competitors for the globe's expanding capital base—by cutting tax rates, curbing unnecessary and wasteful expenditures, eliminating inefficient regulations, and renouncing all the trappings of state central planning.

Information and knowledge have been forged into capital. Information—now no more physical than electrical blips on a computer disk or tape—remains fluid, easily converted to electromagnetic fields, and difficult to contain in any one place and stands ready to leap whole continents via satellites.

Knowledge, for instance, of how specialized subsystems of plants work together has replaced steel as the critical tie that binds many production processes. Such knowledge, which economists call "human capital," has necessarily become a relatively-more-important source of economic power and income.

People—human capital personified—can walk away from oppressive government policies more easily than ever before. East Germany saw its human capital steal away to its more prosperous neighbor. Mainland China is watching a similar, although more measured, exodus from Hong Kong. It must be noted that the spread of human capital through education has given far more people a greater political stake in protecting their capital from political abuse from the workings of governments. In short, liberalizing governments have made their constituents capitalists, who now have an intrinsic interest in protecting the value of their assets and who have the ability do so by moving away from oppressive and ineffectual regimes.

Second: Modern technological developments have increased the sophistication and complexity of production, thereby undermining the ability of any individual to understand the intricacies of entire production processes, much less whole segments of the economy. As a consequence government leaders have had to decentralize economic decision making—that is, give up on grand designs to "plan" large segments of their national economies.

The confluence of mass demonstrations in the Soviet Union and Eastern Europe for the simultaneous creation of free and competitive democracies and free and competitive markets is, to us, no accident of history. Democracies and markets distribute power across entire populations, thereby preventing tyrants and bullies from monopolizing and abusing it for their own gain. Also, democracies and markets have always been means of ensuring that decision-making authority is relegated downward to those best able to make the decisions, those who have the necessary information on people's preferences and abilities.

Today the economic and political decision-making locus must, as never before, reside with individuals. Government leaders *cannot* know all that their constituents know and, therefore, *cannot* know all that they need to know in order to manage their societies—from the center. In none-too-blunt terms, technology has rendered government officials unable to exert the same degree of control over their subjects and to govern effectively using the same strategies as their predecessors.

Third: The modern-day technoelectronic revolution is also fostering, as never before, a rapid integration of formerly independent national economies. The integration of economic activities is, of course, fusing the political and economic interests of people around the world. In the wake of world economic integration, nationalistic tendencies of governments to formulate tax and regulatory policies that help domestic economies at the expense of foreign economies must also wane.

The distinction between "us" and "them" has simply become muddled. Domestic interests have become tied progressively to foreign interests, and foreign interests in policies adopted in the domestic political arena have expanded to the point that foreign interests now lobby effectively against legislation—which has been dubbed "beggar-thy-[foreign] neighbor" legislation—designed to improve the welfare of domestic at the expense of foreign residents. A result of the more evenly balanced competing political forces in domestic politics has been a reduction in the capacity of governments everywhere to regulate and tax with a clear sense of purpose.

No wonder protectionists are no longer as effective in controlling trade as they were in the past. The national interest is simply not as clearly defined as it once was, and while protection still has its special-interest appeal, the issue of who is being protected from whom and for what national purpose is not one that can be easily answered by policymakers.

The "great men" who now walk the world's stage are products of their age, not the other way around. Governments needed leaders who recognized the need to get competitive by restructuring economic incentives and disincentives. This is hardly the whole picture, but it is the background that has been obscured by day-to-day political events.

## The Containment of All Economic Power Centers

Technology is, of course, containing the capacity of *all* economic power centers—not just governments—to set output and prices and select the quality of goods and services provided. Such power centers include domestic and multinational corporations and labor unions. Corporations in any given industry must now compete, to a greater degree than ever, with many other companies throughout the world. Labor unions must now compete with workers around the world and are understandably worried about the extent to which low-wage labor in foreign countries undermines their bargaining position. Given the ease with which markets can be created and invaded by rivals, all these groups must restructure themselves to cope not only with present competitors but also with potential competitors, many of whom may now operate in other markets and can move around to exploit untapped profitable opportunities.

By increasing the ease with which information flows among people, the new technology has greatly expanded competition. And greater competition has forced firms to adopt the new technology and, in many instances, to alter the internal nature of their operations.

The firm has long been useful because it enables people to work together with relative ease in mutually productive endeavors. In the past, when communicating at a great distance was difficult, people had to be in close proximity to get things done. Personal contact was then the best way to maintain the constant and necessary interchange of information. With communication, transportation, and transaction costs high, hierarchical firm structures based on commands were the preferred and most efficient way to organize enterprises.

Now, by touching a few keys and for the cost of a telephone call, modern managers can, via satellites, send millions of bits of crucial information on design specifications, production costs, or schedules to virtually any point on the globe at almost the speed of light. Such transmissions can lead to a shifting of the world's physical capital stock (or the use of it) across national boundaries. In doing so, modern managers can escape many government controls. And, in doing so, these modern managers are forcing legislators to think carefully about the economic, as well as the political, constraints they impose on their citizens.

## The Government Dilemma

Modern governments, like other economic power centers, sit astride the horns of a dilemma of no modest consequence. They have an understandable desire to preserve the good old days, when more stationary and internationally isolated economies gave them more power. But the new reality is that the quicksilver capital of the global economy cannot be easily fettered. Governments must respond to this new reality with "new thinking," to use Gorbachev's phrase, and must concede to the implied threats of quicksilver capital in much the same way that the Eastern German government responded to the exodus of its citizens, or they can relegate their countries to the backwaters of the world economy, as China has chosen to do for now.

Accordingly, government leaders have had to think more like executives caught up in competition for consumers' dollars. They have had to think more in terms of cutting the "prices"—that is, the taxes and regulatory costs—they charge their citizens and in terms of providing greater value for the tax dollars they collect. More and more, they have had to respond to demands of political interests groups for special privileges and protections with the lament that government's fiscal and regulatory hands are tied and that it must keep the nation's policies competitive with those in other countries.

## Changing Government Strategies

Thus, the fortuitous changes for Vaclav Klaus and his fellow East Europeans are part and parcel of an unfolding world drama. Some of the measures governments have been employing to compete indicate the direction in which these changes are going and frame the challenges that will continue to confront nations as their economies become further entwined.

Former President Ronald Reagan's admonitions that we need to get the federal government "off the backs and out of the wallets of Americans" succinctly captured the new approach to governing adopted by leaders as widely different as Margaret Thatcher in Great Britain and Mikhail Gorbachev in the Soviet Union.

Whereas governments once expanded relentlessly, they now expand only with great caution. The watchwords of the 1960s and much of the 1970s were *nationalization* and *regulation*. Now the slogans are *privatization* and *deregulation*, despite the difficulties surrounding the saving and loan debacle.

In earlier decades opponents of government subsidies and transfer payments could expect no more than to temper increases in tax rates and in their governments' spending tendencies. In the 1980s they came to expect tax rate decreases and contractions in the relative, if not absolute, spending proclivities of their governments. The effects of taxes on incentives became a guiding concern in policy discussions not because of Reagan but because incentives became important—to governments in their efforts to be competitive. Two decades ago most citizens presumed that important social goals had to be met by governments. Now they are no longer convinced that this must be the case. Government's role is being constricted, and much is being done to privatize remaining government activities—that is, to enlist private enterprise in the achievement of such diverse government services as garbage collection, welfare payments, maintenance of prisons, and highway and airport development.

Signs now abound that national leaders, Gorbachev and Bush in particular, have realized that aside for the oil rich areas of the Middle East and elsewhere, much of the world's surface no longer means what it once did to national power and prestige. Unless used with inspiration and careful thought, land is just so much dirt that must be defended, at great cost, with possibly few attendant benefits. The computer chip—which, in terms of market value, is 2 percent sand and 98 percent brains—illustrates, figuratively but vividly, the collapse in relative importance of the productive value of land per se and its implication for competitive government policies.

Japan has demonstrated to those leaders who find understanding abstract transnational economic trends difficult that control over large expanses of land, and the raw materials that go with the land, is no longer necessary or even very important to becoming a great and economically powerful nation. Japan has also emphatically shown other world leaders that the "national economy" is no longer defined by old land-based borders. Through international trade and investments, the "national economy" of Japan (and most other countries) is more like a fluid that washes around the world than it is like land that is fixed in place.

Hong Kong has shown how great wealth can be created from virtually nothing, on a tiny island in what used to be a remote part of the Pacific. That vibrant island is also in the process of alerting world leaders to the fact that, when suppression (in this case, from mainland China's takeover scheduled for 1997) threatens economic and political stability, wealth and productive capacity can slip away more easily than they were created. The current Hong Kong "brain drain," spurred by the June 1989 massacre of students in Beijing's Tiananmen Square, may leave China in 1997 with the 2 percent of the microchip that has no value without the other 98 percent.

However, the same forces at work on nations' tax rates and spending proclivities were also at work on their military posturing, forcing them—particularly the Soviet Union—to consider the advantages of calling off the Cold War and bringing the troops and tanks home.

## Competing Visions

Many observers have recognized that current technological trends have created a global market. In fact, the national media has been replete with such commentaries, so much so that the phrase *global markets* has become trite. However, some of these critics—especially in the United States—have assessed the consequences and policy implications of the trends in a discouraging light.[8]

In the early 1980s, academic institutions around the United States and policy circles in Washington buzzed with concern over "capital flight," meaning the way capital is draining out of the United States and other Western capitalistic countries and thereby, supposedly, sapping their economic vigor.[9] We were warned then by these critics that capital flight had "shifted the fulcrum of bargaining power in favor of capital to an unprecedented degree" and, as a consequence, had pitted workers of the world against one another in a perverse Marxian-style struggle for wages and salaries.[10] Through so-called downsizing and out-sourcing, major companies had become "hollow corporations," or shells of their former selves, since they supposedly no longer produced anything of intrinsic worth.

These critics worried that the result of capital mobility was no less than the disarming of organized labor, which took place with the blessings and encouragement of the Reagan administration. The growth in capital mobility combined with Reagan's unbending conservative ideology—his failure to expand social infrastructure expenditures and his reckless reduction in tax rates for the rich, or so we were told—ensured a "great U-turn" on the road to economic progress.[11] Unless quickly reversed through new and expansive government industrial programs, we were told, the country's "economic illusion" would result in a continuing decline in its "hegemony," if not termination in a catastrophic "day of reckoning" or "crash."[12]

Many of these writers warned that world technological trends needed to be opposed by new, innovative government policies, mainly "industrial policies" designed to "pick winners" and "ease the pain of losers."[13] These critics have from the start suggested that the U.S. government in particular must take action to impede further capital flight and redirect the flow of capital both across regions of the country and in and out of the country. One of these critics has argued that under the banner of "Team America"—a phrase designed to suggest that the United States is in a competitive struggle for world economic leadership—the government should be delegated broad new discretionary powers in the development of the nation's research agenda and should play a major role in firms' investment, disinvestment, and reinvestment decisions through the creation of tripartite councils that would include representatives from labor, management, and government. Furthermore, workers' jobs should be protected from capital flight via plant-closing restrictions and more government encouragement for unionization and by giving worker and community representatives voting rights on major management decisions.

Where capital flight should not be restricted, as determined by the tripartite councils, government should retrain and maintain the displaced workers. In effect, this policy advocate recommends that American enterprises become "owned and controlled by all their employees (rather than solely by their overleveraged executives, per the latest fashion in corporate finance)."[14] If all else fails, government policymakers must, we are told, recognize the prospects of capital flight and "wisely" invest limited resources in the education of people, not industries per se (on the assumption that physical capital is far more mobile than human capital). All these new government ventures would, of course, be financed by much higher tax rates, applied mainly to those citizens with "princely incomes."[15]

Here we do not wish to challenge such policy proposals on ideological grounds.[16] Instead, we maintain that advocates of industrial policies have simply misinterpreted the consequences of the technological trends they have so accurately identified. We contend that, as opposed to fortifying the need for more government expenditures and regulations and higher taxes, these trends have undermined the very capacity of government to do what these policy reformers recommend. The relevant challenge is that of shifting resources away from political control and back into the productive sectors of the economy through tax reform, deregulation, and reduced tariffs.[17]

Our goal in documenting the remarkable acceleration of capital mobility, and the consequent rise of competitive government, is not to appeal to politicians to find new ways of controlling it, but to appeal to people to take account of the freedom and opportunity afforded by this quicksilver capital. From the student in the algebra class to the worker on the factory floor to the executive in the office, the global economy means new challenges. But therein lies opportunity. And this opportunity will be the source of greatness for nations as peoples, not as governments.

## The Challenge of the Nineties

The world will likely be beset for a long time to come by governments holding enormous power to tax and regulate. We hardly expect the problems of government waste, inefficiency, and corruption to evaporate soon. The quality and cost-effectiveness of many government services will probably leave much to be desired for decades. Governments will continue to flirt with the imposition of additional regulations of one sort or another.

At the same time, the point of this book is that theory and historical evidence now appear to be reinforcing one another in demonstrating that growth in the enormous power of government is being checked by fundamental economic forces that transcend national boundaries. Governments have become weaker, at least relatively, and will surely become weaker yet, and for good reason. But the new trend in government economic leverage can mean that governments become leaner and more effective in doing many of the things that their constituencies want them to do. In this regard, governments will become more like businesses—led by the "invisible hand" of competition to policies that are more socially and economically productive.

# 2

# From Captive Capital to Quicksilver Capital

## *A Short History of Technology and Its Influence on Modern Government*

---

In acquiring new productive forces men change their modes of production, and in changing their mode of production, their manner of gaining a living, they change all their institutions.

---

*Karl Marx*[1]

THE first words of this book were typed on a plane cruising at thirty-three thousand feet. The computer in use was about the size of a small box of detergent and weighed about the same but had the internal memory of the entire computer center of the University of Maryland when one of the authors was a graduate student there more than two decades ago. The computer disks the author now carried in his jacket pocket had sufficient storage capacity to hold all the business records of a modest-size firm.

Yet any such observation about the small size but great power of modern computers is remarkable only because it is no longer astounding. What is astounding, however, is that the computing power that can fit on a lap and be used high in the sky represents a threat to the sovereignty of governments around the world, perniciously totalitarian as well as plain inefficient.

17

No one worries that anyone armed with a lap-top computer
will plot the overthrow of any particular government. That isn't the
point. On the contrary, the lap-top enables firms to move capital—
not only money or financial capital but information—across borders
at lightning speed. As a consequence, it can remove this capital
from the grasp of the taxing and regulating power of punitive governments. The lap-top represents a peril to government power precisely
because it, along with so many other similar technological wonders,
makes governments relatively less valuable, even as objects of overthrow. If governments are less powerful, people have fewer incentives
to control them or to extract favors from those who run them.

Admittedly, much capital, particularly in the form of factories
and workers, is still difficult to move or altogether immobile. Much
economic activity continues to take place within the confines of national boundaries. Accordingly, government control over capital, national economies, and, for that matter, people has hardly disappeared.
To see that patently obvious point, all we need do is note that government expenditures in real-dollar terms have continued to rise in the
United States in spite of the professed efforts of the Reagan administration to "slash" the federal budget.

At the same time, government growth is certainly waning relative
to the size of the national economy. Rhetoric is changing too. The
trends are evident in the collapse of the Eastern European governments and in the expanding view in the West that government cannot
be the solution to all social ills. Political leaders now know that governments must contain themselves and become more prudent and efficient.

The reasons for these changes can be found by exploring the
standard historical arguments regarding the impact of technological
developments on politics. The leading schools of modern political
economy—Marxist, conservative, and liberal—have traditionally held
that technology increases the size of government and its influence
on the lives of citizens. While these schools of thought have been
valuable in helping us understand the nature of modern society,
they have been appropriate primarily in explaining the past, from
the late nineteenth century until the 1960s, when much capital was
highly immobile and captive. Since then we have seen a radical
change in the nature of technology itself.

Nevertheless, only by understanding how past thinkers have
conceived of the effect of technology on political economy can we

really appreciate the implications of the lap-top for our lives today. One of the more important of these thinkers was none other than Karl Marx.

## Steam-Mill Society and Industrial Capitalism: Karl Marx Interprets the Industrial Revolution

Marxism is founded squarely on a seductively simple and appealing view of history.[2] According to Marx, who wrote during the Industrial Revolution and was more interested in discussing the process of economic change than the then current state of the economy, the historical development of economies proceeds in a stepwise progression from feudalism to capitalism to socialism and then, ultimately, to communism. The driving force is a "dialectic," which Friedrich Engels, Marx's longtime friend and collaborator, characterized as "nothing more than the science of the general laws of motion and development of Nature, human society and thought," but which may be more usefully described as the interplay of technological and institutional forces, with each responding to the changes in the other.[3]

Marx reasoned that people would understandably develop institutions to accommodate the existing "mode of production," or technology. As indicated by this chapter's epigraph, he wrote that changes in "modes of production" lead to changes in all societal institutions: "The windmill gives you society with the feudal lord; the steam-mill society with the industrial capitalist."[4]

However, Marx reasoned that while institutions remain relatively fixed over long periods of time, technology continues to evolve, due in part to the dialectical process—the disruption of old ideas or modes of production (the thesis) with new ideas or new modes of production (the antithesis), and the eventual replacement of both with even higher ideas or modes of production (the synthesis). Marx predicted that each new mode of production, or technology, would have its own set of unique political institutions that would be created either by evolution or revolution.

Under capitalism, Marx maintained, technological advancement is accelerated because of competitive pressures to minimize costs and prices and because of the capitalists' natural drive to exploit labor—that is, pay workers less than the value of their production— and to reinvest labor's "surplus value."[5] The capitalists' ability to exploit labor is eased by the presumed connection between wages and population growth developed by Thomas Robert Malthus in his *Essay on the Principle of Population,* first published in 1798. If wages, for any reason, rise above the subsistence level, then workers will have more children, which means that eventually the labor supply will expand and drive wages back down to the subsistence level.

If workers are exploited and if capitalists cannot themselves find ways of spending the workers' surplus value on consumption goods, which Marx believed they would not, then capitalists must invest or else have to endure a recession or depression inspired by inadequate demand. These downturns did occur from time to time, and Marx believed they would become more severe with time, leading to progressively more destructive depressions. He argued further that new investment would advance technology, that is, lead to improvements in design and productivity, reductions in production costs, and growth in the economy's capital base.

However, Marx believed that along the way workers would become slaves of the very capital they produced. They would become impoverished materially and would cease to thrive as human beings because they would be forced into "lifelong repetition of one and the same trivial operation," and each would be "reduced to the mere fragment of a man."[6] Accordingly, workers would be alienated from the economic system of which they were a crucial part and to which they contributed so much productive value.

Sooner or later, Marx warned, contradictions between political institutions and the modes of production, forged by underlying technological forces, would appear: "At a certain stage of their development the material forces of production in society come in conflict with the existing relations of production. . . . From forms of development of the forces of production these relations turn into their fetters. Then comes the period of social revolution."[7] In a more modern formulation of the Marxian theory, socialist economist Oskar Lange argues,

> Thus the capitalist system seems to face an unescapable dilemma: holding back technical progress leads, through the exhaustion of profitable investment opportunities, to a state of chronic unemployment which can be remedied only by a policy of public investments on an ever-increasing scale, while a continuance of technical progress leads to instability due to the policy of protecting the value of old investments. . . .

It seems to us that the tendency to maintain the value of old investments can be removed successfully only by the abolition of private enterprise and of the private ownership of capital and natural resources, at least in those industries where such tendency prevail.[8]

The emergence of capitalism from feudalism was, in other words, dependent on the evolution of technology and the resulting tension between people and their institutions and among classes that, eventually, were released in revolution. Similarly, the emergence of socialism from capitalism, and then the communist state, would require the playing out of capitalistic forces that cause the development of the necessary capital base to support government's extensive redistributive policies under socialism, grounded in the dictum From Each According to Ability and to Each According to Need.[9] This, in turn, would give rise to a new set of social "contradictions" required for political change. A widespread worker revolution, not just a coup led by a few disgruntled leaders, would be necessary to break the hold that the capitalists have on all industrial property and to create a people's republic in which the means of production would be owned by everyone in a classless society.

Despite the appeal of Marx's argument, there is much about Marxism to criticize.[10] He was obviously way off base when he deduced that capitalism would emerge directly from feudal society. Feudalism in Europe ended around 1500, while capitalism was not reasonably well developed for another three hundred years.[11] He was also wrong in predicting that continued exploitation of labor and the socialist revolution were inevitable under capitalism. As opposed to workers' wages being perennially held to the subsistence level, real wages in capitalist economies have continued to rise, reaching contemporary levels that could not have been predicted from the strictures of Marx's technological dialectic.

Furthermore, Marxist revolutions, when they have occurred, have rarely been led by the discontented proletariate, but rather by intellectual, military, or political leaders who have eventually elevated themselves to the status of the new bourgeoisie. As we have seen in China, the USSR, Cuba, and Nicaragua, the power of the state has hardly withered as a direct consequence of communist revolutions. Generally, under Communist regimes, the state has become more powerful, dictatorial, less benevolent, and hostile to egalitarian goals (except among the governed whose incomes tend to be equalized, not between the governed and those who govern whose incomes are bolstered with special buying privileges). And institutional change has generally tended to remain an evolutionary—as distinct from revolutionary—process, just like technology.

Finally, technological development has not proved to be the mindless and reckless historical process, detached from economic incentives, that Marx seemed to think it was. Real people have always worked to improve technology, and these people have been motivated by many considerations. Some of these motivations are purely economic in nature, but some are also related simply to the quest for knowledge for knowledge's sake.[12] However, there remains an important element of truth in the Marxian analysis—that political institutions are grounded to a meaningful degree in technology. But Marx's most daring and questionable claim is related directly to the point. Marx argued that the linkage between these technological forces and governmental institutions moves exclusively and inextricably in one direction, leading to the much-heralded communist utopia. In his view, there is no chance that technology can reverse the dialectic—that is, undercut the steadily increasing power of the state. It's on to communism, period.

The success and spread of democratic capitalism in the twentieth century, culminating in the elections of Margaret Thatcher and Ronald Reagan, both of whom cut government power in their respective countries, must be construed by contemporary Marxists as a huge political aberration in the long march of history toward more powerful socialist states. Modern-day Marxists would be hard pressed to explain the collapse of communism in Eastern Europe. This is so, at least in part, because the power of microtechnology to influence the capacity of governments to tax and regulate far surpassed Marx's wildest dreams.

## Leviathan by Other Means: The Early-Twentieth-Century Lament That Capitalism Leads to Bigger Government

Early-twentieth-century conservative thinkers Joseph Schumpeter and Friedrich Hayek rejected most Marxian tenets but agreed with Marx that the technological engine of capitalism would produce bigger and more influential governments—this despite their fervent hope, and that of their followers, that it not be so. Marx's vision of capitalism's effect on institutions is only slightly more stark than Joseph Schumpeter's. Schumpeter, an Austrian émigré who wrote his economic treatises from Harvard beginning in the early thirties, worried that capitalism's creative capacity would ironically also be its undoing.[13] Schumpeter recognized that capitalism has built-in incentives for people to innovate, to use technology to create new products and ways of doing things, and—more importantly to his thesis—to destroy old products and ways of doing things. This "process of Creative Destruction," to use Schumpeter's words, might well have brought about an electorate prepared to replace the free flow of economic and social changes under the chronic instability of capitalism with extensive government impediments to innovation that offer the hope of greater security.[14] Without much question, the economic energy of capitalism that breeds devotees also invigorates the system's critics, who fervently believe that economic life should be guided by more humane objectives other than profits—job and income security, for example.

At about the same time that Professor Schumpeter was working on his magnum opus, *Capitalism, Socialism, and Democracy*, Nobel laureate F. A. Hayek was recording his own grave concern that countries around the world were, in the 1930s and 1940s, moving along what he called in his book *The Road to Serfdom*, through incremental changes in the scope and authority of government.[15] National, centrally controlled economies were then the order of the day, as in Soviet Russia, Nazi Germany, Great Britain, and to a lesser extent, the United States. While Professor Hayek was convinced that in most of these countries few people could agree on a centrally determined economic plan for an entire society, he concluded that various majorities might be able to agree, as they had in separate political actions, on individual controls for differing segments of the economy.[16] Hayek maintained that these various controls would inevitably be inconsistent, contradictory, unstable, and destructive and would therefore give rise to democratic demands for more extensive, and more centralized, government controls. He feared that modern Western democracies might follow fascist Germany and Italy and Communist Russia down the road toward a loss of individual freedom due to the increased meddling of the government in the economy.

Many contemporary conservatives, while lamenting the existing trend toward larger government, see this trend as the inevitable result of the interplay of political and economic forces and therefore as fairly fixed. They also doubt that this trend can be reversed. As did Vaclav Klaus before the 1989 revolution in his country, many conservatives have regarded modern technological developments—the laptop included—as toys that can be readily employed by political operatives to extend the economic and political control of governments. For example, political scientist Aaron Wildavsky, advocate of a balanced budget/tax limitation amendment to the U.S. Constitution, made this thoughtful point in the late 1970s: "Modern technology has undermined these Madisonian principles [that government fiscal powers will be checked by competing 'factions,' or interest groups]." As he notes, "It is far easier and cheaper for people to get together than he [Madison] could have imagined. Groups aiming at this process of differentiation show no signs of stopping. All around the western world, articulation of interest increases with size of population, frequency of interaction, and growth of government, which makes it worthwhile to get together."[17] Furthermore, governments have the necessary power to impose their will on their constituencies and to buy the technological toys to use in controlling their constituencies. But if this is so, why is the growth of government on the wane?

## The State as the Solution: J. K. Galbraith and Liberalism

Modern liberals and social democrats happily accept the inevitability of the large welfare state predicted by Marx, Schumpeter, and Hayek. And they agree with Marxists that economic development results from the interplay of technological and social/institutional forces (although they may not believe that change occurs strictly by way of the Marxian dialectic). Because of ongoing technological developments, liberals fear that workers and consumers have become progressively more susceptible to exploitation by capitalists, especially those capitalists who own and run large corporations, single-mindedly pursue profits, and have allegiance to no particular country. At the same time, they believe that national economies have become more and more controlled by capitalists.

Liberals generally argue that modern technological developments continue to spawn economies of scale.[18] Such economies have driven firms to become larger and larger economic power centers and to span the globe as multinationals. These megacorporations are often viewed by liberals as having more economic clout than many of the world's governments. This is the case because the capitalists in large corporations, which form the core of the "new industrial state," as former Harvard economist John Kenneth Galbraith labeled it in the sixties, are not effectively controlled by their stockholders and hold the reins on substantial amounts of flight capital—that is, money, plant, and equipment that can be shipped around the globe with orders from corporate headquarters.[19] As a consequence liberals believe that unless citizens take corrective political action at the national and even world levels, workers and world governments stand at the mercy of the multinationals, which have the capacity to pit worker groups in different countries against one another for their business, to impose their production interests on citizens through advertising, and to subvert domestic political processes to achieve corporate and not national goals.[20]

The growth of industrial power, however, begets a neutralizing force, or "countervailing power." As Galbraith observed more than three decades ago: "The long trend toward concentration of industrial enterprise in the hands of a relatively few firms has brought into existence not only strong sellers, as economists have supposed, but also strong buyers as they have failed to see. The two develop together, not in precise step but in such a manner that there can be no doubt that the one is in response to the other."[21]

From the liberal perspective, governments have an obligation to be big in order to engage in socially productive activities; to take advantage of economies of scale and scope for the purpose of eliminating duplication and waste produced by small competing governments; and to encourage and even subsidize the development of socially responsible countervailing power groups (for example, farmers, through the development of agricultural cartels) that can then bargain more effectively with large corporations.

Furthermore, some liberals argue that national planning is necessary to co-opt the de facto planning of existing private power centers: "Controls are made necessary because planning has replaced the market system. That is to say that the firm and the union have assumed the decisive power in setting prices and wages. This means that the decision no longer lies with the market and thus with the public."[22]

Many liberals would have governments come to the rescue of its citizens and offer political protection from the free flow of domestic and international economic forces, being driven extensively by technologically based economies of scale. In their view, governments should encourage unionization and legislate "worker rights to their jobs," minimum wages, mandated fringe benefits, managed international trade, and an array of industrial policies that would make everyone a part of "Team America" (or "Team France" or "Team Germany," by extension) noted in the first chapter.[23]

These measures are designed to spread the role of democratic votes in the economy. The three major economic power centers that emerge from the liberal dialectic—governments, unions, and businesses—would resolve firm and national economic problems through the creation of so-called workplace democracies within firms and "tripartite councils" within industrial regions of the country, also mentioned in the first chapter.[24] In workplace democracies, workers and community representatives would be given voting rights on managerial decisions within firms. Among other assigned duties, tripartite councils would allocate capital within regions. A national tripartite council would allocate capital among regions of the country.

The economic and political influence of large corporations would be diluted by these new democratic institutions that, unlike markets, will not be guided by "greed and fear."[25] According to many liberals, the emergence of the expansive welfare state is only a matter of time. Governments will again begin to exert themselves once the flaws in mindless, current conservative policies are revealed through years of experience. As Harvard business professor Robert Reich puts it:

> With the liberal resurgence will come a new appreciation of the importance to society of loyalty, collaboration, civic virtue, and responsibility to future generations. . . . Resurgent liberals will adopt a different set of organizing principles. Avarice will be discouraged (there will be no shame, for example, in enacting a very high marginal tax rate on princely incomes). The pain and fear of economic dislocation will be eased (through extended unemployment insurance, job training coupled with day care, health insurance for the unemployed and working poor, and similar programs). American enterprises will become owned and controlled by all their employees (rather than solely by their overleveraged executives, per the latest fashion in corporate finance).[26]

The liberal dialectic will eventually undercut the political base of the George Bushes and Margaret Thatchers of the world and lead to the elevation of "better people." These "better" political leaders will inevitably convert business firms into "social agents" of the state, a transformation that will make government control of the economy not only more complete but also more efficient.[27]

Liberals, in other words, have long recognized the power of capital mobility. However, so-called flight capital has not been viewed as a force to be accommodated by more competitive public policies. Rather, liberals regard it as a force that must be overpowered and neutralized by more expansive and invasive government.

## The Public-Choice Perspective

Like Marxists, conservatives, and liberals who see technologically driven capital mobility as enlarging the power of government, economists and political scientists who subscribe to public-choice theory, which is the application of economic principles to political issues, also see government adding to its stock of power.[28] This vision of government growth has a dialectic quality because it identifies an interplay of economic and political forces that will ultimately constrain private economic activity in favor of government growth. For example, farmers, cable companies, and truckers alike have interests in obtaining government subsidies and restrictions on competition in their industries in order to ensure that their prices and profits can be raised. Members of Congress, on the other hand, can supply the industry restrictions—at a price, of course, paid in the form of campaign contributions and supplements to members' incomes.[29] Technology has expanded the ability of industrial groups to lobby Congress for the needed market restrictions and to subvert the interest of the general electorate.

Unlike their earlier fellow conservatives, who lamented the inevitable growth of government, public-choice theorists such as James Buchanan, Gordon Tullock, and others see the possibility of controlling this growth through constitutional limitations but claim that this line of defense has turned to Swiss cheese.[30] They lament that constitutional restrictions on what government can and cannot do in the economy have largely collapsed or have failed to check the expansion of governments.[31] For example, public-choice economists complain that governments' taxing authority is now virtually unbounded.[32] Property rights have regularly been violated through the proliferation of regulations and have been usurped everywhere without just compensation as required under the Takings Clause of the Constitution.[33]

Not too many decades ago, government spending may have been checked by informal fiscal rules. For example, before the Keynesian justification for budget deficits was accepted by policymakers, budget deficits were discouraged by unwritten fiscal norms that equated budget deficits with irresponsible political behavior. But, given the string of federal deficits of over $100 billion, such fiscal norms have obviously broken down. Through deficit spending, government has acquired the capacity to spend beyond the limits the public would permit by the imposition of higher taxes.[34]

Now that governments have grown more powerful, so say public choice experts, they can be expected to continue to grow because of their own mistakes and the considerable resources at their command. Past efforts by governments to plan or, in other ways, to control economic activity have led to policy failures, but such policy failures have only given rise to political demands for more government controls to correct the failures.[35] For example, efforts by Congress to control the prices of selected crops have led the federal government to pay farmers not to produce. Building regulations and rent controls have given birth to federal and state subsidies for new residential construction. Failed efforts to fine-tune the macroeconomy have led to more detailed controls on industries in the form of import restrictions and export subsidies.

Democracies continue to run amok, the public-choice theorists tell us. Changing majorities within the electorate and Congress continue to push the dialectic along. For example, members of controlling majorities, or even controlling minorities (for instance, the elderly), gain by way of government-provided benefits (Social Security and Medicare) at the expense of all other citizens.[36] The success of some interest groups in gaining political favors at the expense of the general population has forced the proliferation of other interest groups that organize to obtain their share of the largesse and to avoid paying the burden of government benefits passed out to other groups.[37] As a consequence, "antiprotectionists" (for example, foreign exporters and domestic retailers and consumers) have organized political lobbies to fight the trade restrictions proposed by the "protectionists" (for example, textile manufacturers). Groups of young people have organized to countervail against the political efforts of the elderly lobby, pressing for lower elderly benefits and social security taxes.

Public-choice theorists tell us that the policy-making process has been gradually encumbered by interest-group politics, a trend that has been aggravated by technology, as suggested earlier by Aaron Wildavsky. Technology—computers, copiers, and telephones—has increased the capacity of people to coalesce behind organizations that seek private gain via public means, the result of which, according to University of Maryland economist Mancur Olson, has been ever-increasing demands for government aid to this or that group and ultimately an anchor on economic growth.[38] The government delivery system has become encrusted with bureaucrats who have an incentive to push for government expansion, have a stranglehold on government purse strings (especially since they are primarily responsible for drawing up budget proposals), and determine the cost-effectiveness of government programs.[39] Under the "public-choice dialectic," government growth, for all practical purposes, feeds upon itself.

Hence, as Geoffrey Brennan and James Buchanan have lamented, given the past expansion of governments, only continued government growth can be expected unless additional formal, external, constitutional checks are imposed on governments.[40] If left to its own internal momentum, the political process cannot be expected to reverse the course of government growth, primarily because the political power groups that brought about that growth will work as diligently to protect their favored positions as they worked to achieve them. This is the case even though the country may, on balance, be worse off by the continuation of the status quo.

Public-choice theorists reason that the general public's interest in effecting meaningful improvement in government policies will not motivate the electorate to take corrective action through normal political channels. Individual voters do not have sufficient private incentive to become well informed about the array of pressing public issues, much less make the extensive cost-benefit calculations necessary to determine if government programs are being efficiently developed.[41] They all, or practically all, will remain free riders, content to sit back and let their government extend its control.[42]

The *Wall Street Journal* echoed the public-choice thinkers when its editors worried in early 1990 about the prospects for meaningful economic reform in Eastern Europe: "If there is anything to learn from the Swedish model it is that once the state is thoroughly embedded in the economic mechanism of a country, it's all but impossible to diminish its role, let alone eliminate it."[43]

Some public-choice theorists recommend new amendments to the U.S. Constitution to reduce the scope and size of the influence of government on the economy. Such proposed amendments include a reaffirmation of the rights of private ownership that cannot again be abridged by government, imposition of limits on the growth of the money stock, a mandate that government budgets be balanced, and a limitation on government expenditures tied to a fixed percent of national income.

Those who hold the traditional public-choice perspective must, like the Marxians and liberals, see the Thatcher and Reagan era as a historical aberration that will probably be nullified, given enough time. Their reasoning, however, is dramatically different.

According to these thinkers, the governmental institutional setting, meaning the extant constitutional precepts within which the political process works and which determine the long-term direction of government policies, has not been materially changed. Recommended fiscal, regulatory, and monetary constitutional amendments have not been adopted. Politics continues to be conducted more or less as usual, with few remaining limits on issues that can be decided by majority votes of Congress or state legislatures. Interest groups continue to proliferate.

The same public-choice theorists also see government programs as replete with growing "rents"—profits to be had from investment in the manipulation of the political process (for example, subsidies granted farmers). So-called rent seekers have every bit as much incentive to ferret out government rents in the 1990s as they had in earlier decades. Public-choice theorists might fear that because the presidential guard was changed at the White House in 1988, the United States is no longer blessed with the ideological rigidity of Ronald Reagan, which might have been a useful but temporary substitute for constitutional checks on government power. These theorists worry that Margaret Thatcher will soon fall from political grace. In the 1990s national capitals remain centers in which legislators are at liberty to sell off rights to government privileges, in the form of programs, regulations, international trade restrictions, and transfers, to the highest bidders.

Reagan and Thatcher may or may not have abated the growth of government, but any success they may have had will be no more enduring than they are, or so public-choice theorists might reason. The ongoing unbalanced political jousting between interest groups with intense interest in legislation and the oblivious, free-riding private citizens with few incentives to pay close attention to what their legislators are doing will inevitably result in a return of government growth, expanded regulation of those industries that have remained regulated, and reregulation of those industries that have been deregulated.

Some public-choice theorists even worry that proposed constitutional reform will not break the stranglehold that interest-group politics has on the nation. The rent seekers who have clogged the political process will also have their noses under the "constitutional tent" (where new, presumably more restrictive amendments will be developed and adopted), ready and willing to warp the constitutional choices to their own narrow advantages. Indeed, the rent seekers may be more active in constitutional choices than they have been in policy choices, mainly because constitutional amendments have large long-term payoffs. Because of the substantial payoffs, the (constitutional) rent seekers should be willing to spend more on political maneuvering than they would be willing to spend in the workaday world of everyday politics, where policies can be easily reversed.[44]

A select group of public-choice pessimists even contends that the stranglehold of interest-group politics on the economy may only be broken—and then temporarily—by some large-scale catastrophe, like a major war or earthquake.[45] As Mancur Olson has shown in the case of Japan, a war can disrupt the economy and government operations so badly that the rent seekers lose their favored positions in the political power structure. As a consequence the economy may be freed of extensive regulations—for a while—which means that the country can once again grow with the outbreak of competition— but only for a relatively short period. Regrettably, public-choice theorists argue, the rent seekers will eventually return to the struggle for political favors—that is, various forms of protection from internal and external competitors—and the economy will sooner or later begin to suffer from an expanding public sector (and Japan's "economic miracle" will soon be capped by interest-group politics).

## Accounting for Change: From Large-Firm Technologies to the Microchip

We disagree with the outlook for government growth articulated by the twentieth-century thinkers covered in this chapter. However, our prognosis is not molded by a different ideological temperament. Hardly. Ideology has little or nothing to do with our expectations. Rather, we suggest that the theories of Marx, Schumpeter, Galbraith, Olson, Buchanan, and others may have been reasonable theories for the times but that the changing nature of technology has made them obsolete. Instead of steam mills, theories of institutional change need to account for the lap-top—better yet, for the microchip inside the lap-top. They need to reconsider how the new technology is limiting government's capacity to adopt all the social policies that liberals have applauded and conservatives have condemned.

Public-choice theory emerged as an identifiable academic discipline in the 1960s. During its formative years, the Kennedy administration was intent on using Keynesian macroeconomic theory and the public's purse as means of "getting the country moving again"; that is, reducing unemployment and increasing economic stability and growth. The Johnson administration followed with the War on Poverty

and an assault on racial discrimination and other social ills identified
then by the media. The U.S. government and those of other Western
democracies did appear to be growing without constraint. Governments at virtually all levels were then expanding both in real-dollar
terms and as a percentage of domestic income. The accelerating
growth of the U.S. government under the supposedly conservative
Nixon administration appeared to validate the apparent inability of
democracies to repress the snowballing effects of interest-group politics, deduced from public-choice theory.

Perhaps public-choice economists then had good reason to write
at length about the coming "Leviathan" government (in reference
to Thomas Hobbes's all-powerful state) and to fear that nineteenth-
century English historian Thomas Babington Macaulay might soon
be proved right:

> It is plain that your government will never be able to restrain a distressed
> and discontented majority. For with you the majority is the government,
> and has the rich, who are always a minority, absolutely at its mercy.
> The day will come, when in the State of New York a multitude of
> people, none of whom have more than half a breakfast, or expect to
> have more than half a dinner, will choose a legislature. Is it possible
> to doubt what sort of legislature will be chosen? On the one side is
> the statesman preaching patience, respect for vested rights, strict obedi-
> ence of public faith. On the other is a demagogue ranting about the
> tyranny of capitalists and usurers, and asking why anybody should
> be permitted to drink champagne and to ride in a carriage. Which of
> the two candidates is likely to be preferred by a working man?[46]

In short, in the 1960s and 1970s, new long-term and binding constitutional restrictions may have appeared to public-choice theorists to
be the only reasonable way of tempering government expansion.

Similarly, the Marxian dialectic (followed by the less-radical
liberal dialectic) may not have been totally incorrect during its formative stage, given that the elements of the theory emerged in the
middle of the nineteenth century from classical economic theory.
Industry did appear to be developing in a manner that would make
control of capital relatively easy for governments. A major hallmark
of the Industrial Revolution was the widespread and growing use of
capital—plant and equipment—that permitted people to harness non-
human and nonanimal sources of energy. Water and steam power
became important means of dramatically expanding production because they supplemented the energy expended by workers, horses,
and oxen, and capital was needed to convert water and steam power

into productive power. Since the Industrial Revolution, people have become progressively more productive not only because they have tapped alternative energy sources but also because they have made improvements in the methods—capital—employed in the energy-tapping and -conversion processes.

In the early stages of the Industrial Revolution and continuing through, perhaps, the first half of this century, production was generally (but, of course, not always) beset by escalating economies of scale. Understandably, with large firms producing an expanding share of domestic output, Professor Galbraith's concern about the growing economic power of the "new industrial state" struck a popular chord, as evidenced by the robust sales of his book. By the 1960s conglomerates and multinational corporations received substantial media and scholarly attention.

What has been overlooked by virtually everyone in conventional discussions of scale economies is their impact on the capacity of governments to tax and regulate. In the process of reducing per-unit cost, scale economies over the decades have tended to increase the amount of capital used in industries and, often, to concentrate that capital geographically. As a general tendency, much industrial development of economies in the past resulted in larger and larger plants being concentrated around some critically important resource and/or near major markets.

The expansion and concentration of capital has important consequences for government power. First, the capital can be readily taxed and regulated by government. To the extent that large concentrations of plant and equipment are massive, tied to some critically important resource, and geographically immobile, governments may look upon such assets in much the same way that energy companies look upon prospective oil fields: as something to be tapped—or rather, in the case of governments, taxed. Oil fields cannot move, obviously. As a consequence, the energy firms have considerable power over them: They can drain them dry.

Plants and equipment, no matter how large, are obviously never as immovable as oil fields. However, relatively immobile plants and equipment, and the people they employ, do, in varying degrees, share a fate: They are subject to exploitation. It should be no wonder that Galbraith, and others, described modern firms as dinosaurs lumbering across the economic landscape and, at the same time, felt confident that calls for more government controls, taxes, and expenditures would be taken seriously.

Seeing plants and equipment grow in size, Marx must have

reasoned that capitalism was doing a terrific job of producing the fixed capital base that, at some point, could be taxed extensively by a future revolutionary socialist government. But the crucial mistake he (and liberals who followed in his intellectual footsteps) made is to assume that technology would continue to develop the way it appeared to be developing during much of the nineteenth century, meaning that more captive capital would be created.

Marxians and liberals must have rejoiced at the growth and power of mainframe computers. Mainframe computers were big and powerful and could be afforded and used efficiently only by very large businesses *and* by very large governments. They failed to anticipate the coming of the lap-top and its power to free competitive resources—money, information, and other assets—from national boundaries.

Public-choice theorists, on the other hand, have recognized that governments are not constrained solely by constitutional precepts, as important as they may be. They are also constrained by economic forces that are extensively shaped by the underlying technology. However, they, like the Marxians, have overlooked the fact that capital mobility has greatly increased, tightening the economic controls on governments.

A new dialectic is afoot. While the trend toward scale economies continued for decades after Marx made his revolutionary claims, it is now equally clear that crucial technological trends shifted during this century from captive to quicksilver capital, thus subverting the explanatory power of the Marxian, liberal, and conservative dialectics. Modern technological developments have had the effect of making the government's tax base less captive and more fugitive. The shifts in technological trends are apparent in historical data and anecdotal evidence that are reviewed in the next chapter. But the lap-top in use at thirty-three thousand feet speaks volumes about the fleeting capacity of government to maintain control over its subjects.

# 3

# Economics, Meet Electronics

*The Technology of Decreasing Scale*

---

At the turn of this century, we created
economic value by moving ore by rail from
the Mesabi Range down to Pittsburgh, where
it was joined with coal to produce steel.
Today, economic value is created by moving
data, analyses and insights from one location
to another through ever more sophisticated
electronic means. Economic production
continues to serve human needs and values.
But the products serving those needs are
becoming progressively impalpable.

---

*Alan Greenspan*[1]
Chairman, Federal Reserve
Board of Governors

NEWSCASTS beamed from around the globe confirm daily
the fact that we live in a global economy. Because so much business
is now conducted on a world scale, government, which relies on
business for its capital base, must adapt. Government institutions
are adjusting, albeit reluctantly. If Marx were alive today, he would
understand but also be taken aback. *Our* contemporary mode of production, built on a stunning new technology, has reduced the required
scale of operation for many businesses, enabling them to disperse
their activity to the corners of the earth.

35

Both Karl Marx and John Kenneth Galbraith, though separated by a century of technological developments, agreed that the conduct of business and government policy-making are inevitably guided by growing economies of scale (or even "superscale"). Technology breeds size, and size breeds growth in government.

While others embellished Marx's and Galbraith's views, a funny thing happened on the way to escalating government growth. Technology changed. The scale of production began to shrink, resulting in "economies of *decreasing* scale." This change is reverberating from the shop floor through the stock exchange through the legislative chamber. Our intention in this chapter is not simply to document this change—our readers see its various manifestations in all facets of their lives—but rather to demonstrate how the forces comprising it have reinforced each other to create a new political and economic synthesis.

## Scale Economies in Manufacturing

Trends in scale economies are nowhere more clear-cut than in manufacturing, because reliable data covering much of this century are available on the number of manufacturing firms and their production and employment.

### *Production in Manufacturing*

Preliminary data on average-size production facilities in manufacturing reveal that in the period between 1899, the earliest year for which consistent data are available, and 1982, real value added to goods produced in U.S. manufacturing firms multiplied many times over (measured in 1982 dollars), from $58 billion in 1899 to $824 billion in 1982. However, the real value added declined from $932 billion in 1977 to $824 billion in 1982. This decline reflects a combination of two forces—the recession in the early 1980s, and the fact that U.S. manufacturers now import more of their materials and parts from foreign suppliers, spurred by the appreciation of the dollar in the late 1970s and early 1980s.[2] Whether U.S. plants are on average adding more or less value to manufactured goods is debatable. What appears to be certain is that the much-heralded economies of large-scale production are dissipating in a wide array of industries. A growing share of the nation's plants are adding more value with fewer workers, square feet of floor space, and bricks and mortar—facts that loosen the ties that bind many of them to their current locations.

*Employment in Manufacturing*

The average size of manufacturing plants, measured by employment, underwent something of a U-turn during the second and third quarters of this century. The number of production workers per manufacturing establishment rose from approximately twenty-two in 1899 to fifty-one in 1937, after which a gradual, irregular decline in average size set in. By 1982 the average manufacturing establishment employed slightly fewer than thirty-five workers (a decline, most of which ensued after 1967, of 32 percent from the 1937 peak).

Predictably, the average-size plant (measured by employment) relative to total U.S. employment fell even more dramatically. This is so because total manufacturing employment remained more or less constant, at about 20 million in the 1960s, 1970s, and 1980s, at the same time that total U.S. employment continued to rise. Between 1950 and 1988, total U.S. employment practically doubled, meaning that each manufacturing plant was, on average, not only becoming smaller in terms of absolute employment but also in terms of its relative importance to the country's total employment.

Historical trends could have been reversed since 1982, the last year for which adequate data on manufacturing establishments and employment are, at this writing, available from the same data source. However, other detailed studies, using alternative data sources and methods of analysis, indicate that, if anything, the trend toward smaller production units has continued and may have accelerated.

As is widely recognized, the service sector of the economy has continued to expand in terms of employment. While the consequences of that trend have been grossly misinterpreted, with many commentators mistakenly suggesting that the rise of service sector employment has reduced worker wages,[3] it is clear to all partisans in the debate that service-sector firms tend to be smaller than goods-sector firms, which means that small firms dominate the most rapidly expanding sector of the economy. Small firms are, therefore, tending to expand in relative importance within economies, especially advanced ones.[4] However, small firms are also expanding their share of establishments (or plants and places of doing business) and employment in the manufacturing sector across the majority (at least 80 percent) of major industry categories. According to the Small Business Administration, between 1980 and 1986, small firms' share of all manufacturing establishments expanded by .5 percent while their share of employment expanded by 3.9 percent.[5]

In a study employing Dun & Bradstreet files (which track firm

births and deaths and their resulting employment gains and losses),
David Birch deduced that between 1981 and 1985, small firms with
from one to nineteen employees were responsible for upward of 82
percent of the net employment change in the United States[6] (see
Table 3.1). Large companies, those with more than five thousand
employees, lost nearly 14 percent of their employees in the same
period. Birch concluded that "Galbraith and others who think that
big business is the American economy don't seem to realize fully
that the bubbly, yeasty, creative segment is the small businesses
segment. Moreover, most American workers can be found in their
employ."[7] While Professor Birch's data, by themselves, do not speak
directly to the issue of trends over the past decade or so, they certainly
suggest that the number of small firms cannot continue to increase
and be responsible for the vast majority of jobs created without there
also being a shift toward smaller production units.[8]

TABLE 3.1   Net Job Creation by Size of All Enterprises, 1981–1985

| Enterprise Size (number of employees) | Net of Expansions (number of employees) | Net of Starts (number of employees) | Overall Net Job Creation (number of employees) | Percentage of Net |
|---|---|---|---|---|
| 1–19 | 2,600.2 | 790.5 | 1,809.7 | 82.0 |
| 20–99 | 1,867.2 | 1,263.7 | 603.5 | 27.3 |
| 100–499 | 1,264.2 | 1,230.4 | 33.8 | 1.5 |
| 500–4,999 | 1,099.6 | 1,040.7 | 58.9 | 2.7 |
| 5,000 + | 993.8 | 1,291.5 | −297.7 | −13.8 |
| Total | 7,824.9 | 5,616.7 | 2.208.2 | 100.0 |

Source: David L. Birch, *Job Creation in America* (New York: Free Press, 1987), p. 14.
Sum of numbers in columns do not always equal totals because of rounding.

In addition, survey evidence indicates that many large firms,
in an effort to become more efficient and competitive, are cutting
out plants and reducing the overall size of their production units
(also known as downsizing), eliminating middle management levels
(or "demassing"), decentralizing operations, and forming strategic
partnerships (productive alliances with suppliers and buyers or even
competitors) in order to gain a competitive advantage. For example,
one 1988 survey found that 35 percent of more than one thousand
chief executive officers (CEOs) interviewed reported that their companies had downsized over the preceding year, with an average reduction

in the work force of 150; and 50 percent of the executives expected the downsizing process to continue.[9] The downsizing trend continued at a slightly faster pace in 1989, with 39 percent of the survey respondents reporting that they had downsized, with an average reduction of 162 workers. Only 10 percent of the moves to downsize were the result of corporate mergers.[10]

And, it should be added, many of the downsizing efforts are by no means minor. Between 1981 and 1989, General Electric reduced its work force by a fourth, from 405,000 to 298,000, partly by sales and swaps of divisions but also by layoffs. Virginia Power did something in 1989 that was virtually unthinkable in the electricity business prior to the 1980s: It eliminated nearly 1,000 jobs from its payroll of 13,500.[11]

Brookings Institution economist Robert Crandall has found that the average-size manufacturing unit across virtually all manufacturing industries decreased between 1958 and 1982.[12] In general Crandall found that firms with fewer than 100 employees maintained approximately the same employment share in the 1958–82 period; however, all firms with fewer than 1,000 workers increased their employment share from 69.5 percent in 1958 to 74.8 percent in 1982.[13] This means that firms with more than 1,000 workers must have lost employment share in the 1958–82 period.[14] In addition, sophisticated technology, which leads to greater specialization of effort, can be expected to cause many small firms to come into being. These firms, in turn, will spread the overhead costs of their specialized knowledge in providing services to other firms. The cost of this specialized knowledge is just too much for many firms to replicate within internal departments.

*Changes in Organizational Forms*
Still other forces are contributing to the increased efficiency and flexibility of firms. Downsizing has been abetted because firms have been able to buy more of their materials, parts, and services from outside suppliers through what has been called out-sourcing. Indeed, many companies have encouraged out-sourcing by seeking to improve the efficiency of their internal bureaus. They converted them into profit centers, giving each the responsibility and authority to obtain needed parts and services at the lowest possible cost and best quality, whether inside or outside the parent firms. According to a 1988 survey conducted by the American Electronics Association, 41 percent of the corporate planners surveyed intended to increase their out-sourc-

ing, whereas only 18 percent intended to reduce it.[15] Still another factor contributing to downsizing is that firms have increased their capacity and speed of delivery by pooling their resources to exploit emerging opportunities.[16]

At the company level, the ongoing restructuring process has caused the loss of many jobs and threatened many remaining employees. According to one management researcher, the competitive threat to Kodak's continued prosperity, if not survival, in the growing international photography industry caused its new management team, appointed in the middle of 1983, to accept painful changes in the size of the company:

> By year's end [1983] Kodak eliminated eleven thousand jobs; by 1986, Kodak thinned top management ranks by 25 percent, and reduced the domestic workforce by 8 percent—moves that symbolized the end of Kodak's century-old reputation as a bastion of lifetime employment. Between 1983 and 1986 Kodak also shut its famed "Mother Lab" in Rochester, where 651 employees had handled problem film that photo-finishers in the field could not. Accompanying the restructuring were other efforts to reduce expenses, from not emptying wastebaskets every night to a major quality control campaign aimed at lowering manufacturing waste by more than 10 percent.[17]

Kodak has since contracted out its personal computer operations to Businessland, Inc., and has hired IBM to establish and operate its data-processing center. In 1989 the company was looking into the prospects of hiring an outside firm to run its software and telecommunications operations. Kodak had come to the conclusion that it had to reduce the complexity of its operations by farming out work to specialists; that it was in the photographic-products business, not in the business of maintaining its computer centers and other ancillary business services; and that it wanted to deal with computer companies the same way it dealt with the utility companies.[18]

In short, the growing competitiveness and sophistication of modern production has forced firms to be more cost- and quality-conscious, to experiment with new organizational forms, to be less tied to old internal sources of supply for parts and services, and to have less concern for the national origins of parts and services.

## The Miniaturization of Capital

Modern microelectronics began with the development of the transistor by Bell Laboratories just after World War II and was accelerated in the late 1950s with the development of the integrated circuit, which permitted the packing of a ever-larger number of transistors onto a given circuit board.[19] As former Secretary of the Treasury (now CEO of Unysis) Michael Blumenthal has pointed out:

> Through miniaturization it has been possible, on the average, to double the number of transistors on one tiny chip each year since [1947]—with dramatic implications for performance and, above all, cost. As a result one random-access memory chip can today accommodate as many as one million bits, which is 125,000 separate characters of information, on a device no bigger than a fingernail and at a tiny fraction of the earlier cost.[20]

Ironically, Blumenthal's description of the computer chip's capacity was out of date by the time it was published in 1987. In early 1990 a computer chip encompassing ten million transistors could perform electronic operations in as fast as four billionths of a second.[21] However, that chip was expected to be obsolete by 1991.[22] In the late 1990s the speed of a state-of-the-art chip packed with a billion transistors is likely to rise to one electronic operation every two hundred trillionths of a second.[23]

The resulting expansion of the computation capacities of computers has been nothing short of astounding. In 1961 only thirty-four thousand arithmetic operations per second could be handled by one computer (and a very large one at that). Just two decades later in 1981, eight hundred million arithmetic operations per second could be performed by a single computer. Microprocessors now permit combinations of varied features and functions for memory and logic processes, and the technology of microprocessors has developed so rapidly that currently *each* microprocessor (not an entire computer, which may incorporate a number of microprocessors) can handle up to twenty million instructions per second. Such technological advancements in computers have resulted in a 90 percent reduction in computing costs in the past two decades.[24] The cost savings have been possible mainly because of the competitiveness (or openness) of the industry and because a principal ingredient—apart from new ideas—of microchips is common sand. Thus, as George Gilder has pointed out:

> Unlike oil, however, which is a material extracted from sand, semiconductor circuitry is written on sand and its substance is ideas. . . . All these devices [CD-ROM, floppy disk, 35-millimeter film, or videocassette] cost a few dollars to make in volume and all ultimately sell

for the value of their contents—the images and ideas they bear. A
memory chip sells for a couple of dollars; a microprocessor that costs
about the same amount to make may sell for as much as an ounce of
gold. A blank CD-ROM also costs a couple of dollars, but it contains
the operating system for a new IBM mainframe. . . . In the microcosm,
the message remains far more important than the medium.[25]

The expansion in the storage capacities of computers has been
no less dramatic than the expansion in computing power. Today,
ten billion bits of information can be stored on a disc no larger than
a phonograph record. This means that "the entire contents of the
Library of Congress can be stored in a cabinet hardly bigger than a
medium-sized medicine chest."[26]

The technological advancements in microelectronics are most
evident, and personalized, in progress made in office calculators and
personal computers. Back in what now appear to be the modern
dark ages of electronics, perhaps no farther back than the early 1960s,
office calculating machines were truly what they were called—"machines"—that is, bundles of gears and other movable parts that made
lots of noise and were essentially as "dumb" as the person punching
the keys. The better calculators had to be plugged into a electric
power grid just to add two and two, much less multiply two by two
or find the trend in a series of numbers, a highly labor-intensive
task.

The transition from mechanical to hand-held calculators and
then to calculators embedded in watches (with added functions) speaks
volumes about the ongoing miniaturization of capital in capitalism.
A typical office calculator of the early 1960s may have been about
the size and weight of an equally clumsy office typewriter. The first
electronic calculator (which performed only the four basic arithmetic
functions) appeared in the mid-1960s and weighed as "little" as eight
pounds. The first hand-held calculator, which surfaced on U.S. markets in 1969, was much smaller than its electronic predecessor but
still weighed in at 4.5 pounds, was as large as an oversized paperback
book, still had only four functions (addition, subtraction, multiplica-
tion, and division)—and cost more than thirteen hundred dollars (measured in 1990 dollars).

Once the integrated circuit was developed and applied widely
in the early 1970s, the weight and prices of calculators dropped precipitously at the same time that their power and functions escalated.
Today, one has to want far more than the basic functions to spend

more than a few dollars. And for under forty dollars, a watch that includes a multifunction calculator (as well as a daybook and chronograph) can be purchased. The actual size of modern calculators appears to be limited more by the size of the finger pushing the buttons than by existing electronic technology.

Computers, of course, have followed much the same miniaturization path, principally because computers are nothing more than calculators with added power, programming capacity, and flexibility. In 1946 the first computer was developed at the University of Pennsylvania: "It weighed 30 tons, utilized 18,000 vacuum tubes, stood two stories high and covered 15,000 square feet. It cost many millions."[27] Many of the major universities in the United States purchased their first mainframe computers in the early 1960s. These first computers filled a suite of offices but had only a meager 8K of random-access memory (RAM). In the early 1990s the same computing power could easily be replicated with a calculator the size of a business card. Indeed, because of the growth in off-the-shelf programs, desktop computers have become far more useful and productive for many business and research purposes than their mainframe ancestors of the early 1970s. These programs have vastly increased the power of the computer owners by enabling them to do complicated statistical, graphics, accounting, and drafting tasks with a few relatively simple instructions.

In 1981 there were only 2.1 million (single-user) personal computers in the country, approximately 35 percent of which were in homes. By 1986 the number of personal computers had expanded sixteenfold to 32.5 million.[28]

Without much question, many of these computers were bought for fun and games and many have been rarely used; however, many have always been work stations. The growing use of computers for serious business purposes is probably indicated by the expanding use of modems, as well as add-in boards and other devices. In 1981 only 8.5 percent of the personal computers had modems. In 1986 the percentage of computers with modems had increased more than two and a half times, to 22.2 percent.

What is interesting about current technological trends is that there appears to be no end to the miniaturization process. In 1987 desktop computers based on the Intel 386 microprocessor "were 90 times more cost effective than mainframes. Mainframes remained valuable for rapid and repeated disk access and transaction processing for banks and airlines. But small computers were barging in everywhere else."[29] By 1988 one lap-top had broken the five-pound barrier; and by 1989, two companies had introduced computers—appropriately called "palmtops"—that weighed in at about a pound, one of which could slide into the vest pocket of a sport coat.[30] By 1990, six-pound lap-tops, like one author's now-primitive package, were moving up to 286 microprocessors and adding 20MB hard-disk drives along with much-more-readable screens.

Computer power can be expected to expand virtually exponentially for the foreseeable future, at the same time that the size and cost of computers continues to contract.[31] Experts in the field have predicted that sometime during the 1990s, the central processing units of today's "supercomputers" will have been miniaturized to the point that they can be used in lap-tops.[32]

## The Miniaturization of Production

The changes in the power of computers are important in themselves. So much modern production is dependent upon what can be done on computers, and computer technology plays such an important role in other production processes.

But modern technology is drastically reducing the size of equipment in many other industries, causing dramatic contractions in production costs. For example, metal-fabricating plants used to require large numbers of workers and long production runs in order to maximize efficiency. Maximum efficiency can now be achieved with six machines and six people. The floor space for some "flexible manufacturing systems" has been reduced by 60 percent.[33] In the case of one machine tool company, Okuma Machinery Works Ltd. of Japan, flexible manufacturing reduced the number of machine tools from eight to four, the number of processes from three to one, and the number of workers from ten to two. It increased machine utilization from 50 to 75 percent, expanded factory availability from sixteen to twenty-four hours, and lowered the necessary lead time from six days to one.[34]

In textile production, modern textile looms—called air-jet looms—are up to 50 percent larger than their fly-shuttle predecessors. However, air-jet looms are from four to seven times more productive in terms of yards of cloth produced per minute than their older fly-shuttle counterparts. This means that one air-jet loom reduces the floor space required to produce the same amount of fabric by at least two-thirds.[35]

What is also remarkable about the new manufacturing technology is that the length of the runs necessary to achieve maximum efficiency in many production processes has also been greatly reduced. Specialized magazines and newspapers with very limited circulations have proliferated with the computerization of publication processes that have in a growing number of cases have become, virtually, one-person operations.[36]

With the aid of CAD/CAM (for "computer-aided-design" and "computer-aided-manufacturing") programs, engineers and architects can individually complete, and then revise repeatedly, designs that in the past took teams of draftsmen. McGraw-Hill has developed a computerized printing process for university textbooks that allows professors to design their own class texts from a menu of available chapters that are held on a computer. McGraw-Hill will print individualized texts for classes with as few as ten students. And because customers can phone orders for computers with detailed specifications that are transmitted immediately to the assembly line, one Texas computer manufacturer has informally made Mass Production in Runs of One its slogan, but such a slogan is applicable to a growing array of firms. In a survey of aerospace and related high-precision industries, more than 8 percent of the production batches were of size one, and 38 percent were of size sixteen or less.[37] The Allen Bradley Company is capable of switching among its 725 electrical control products in an average of six seconds.[38] With CAD/CAM programs, engineers at General Motors were able to change over their equipment from producing 1988 models to 1989 models over a single weekend,[39] and the Lockheed Corporation was inspired to redefine worker responsibilities and adopt a team approach and was able to reduce the time spent redesigning and manufacturing its sheet metal parts from fifty-two to two days.[40]

When production becomes smaller, plant size shrinks. But established plants have not been exempted from the miniaturization process. Existing plants are being divided up into separate units. For example, Jacobs Manufacturing Company, the world's largest producers of chucks for drills, used to have in its Clemson, South Carolina, plant one long production line that covered the entire plant floor. It took six weeks for a piece of metal to be converted into a chuck through Jacob's production and assembly process. By buying new machines, Jacobs was able to divide its Clemson plant into six production "cells," each of which can produce a complete chuck. With the new production arrangement, the company has been able to reduce its production time to three days and, at the same time, fill larger orders.[41]

The move toward greater output with less floor space has been so rapid that a major North Carolina textile firm bought two existing textile plants in 1987 with the idea that it would need the additional space to accommodate its expanding sales. However, in spite of sales exceeding company expectations, the plants were still unused in 1990 because the firm had been able to increase sufficiently the productivity of operating plants to meet the expanding demand.

The United States is producing a far greater real-dollar value of goods and services than it did at the turn of the century, but this is the case not because the actual weight or volume of goods such as grain, cotton, ore, coal, steel, or cement has expanded on a per capita basis.[42] The miniaturization process has actually reduced the volume of international trade as measured in terms of weight per dollar value of goods and services shipped in and out of the United States. Between 1967 and the first half of 1988, the pounds per real dollar of U.S. exports fell by 43 percent, or an average of 2.3 percent per year. The pounds per real dollar of U.S. imports fell during the 1967–88 period by substantially more, an average of 3.1 percent per year.[43]

Naturally, the computed average plant size hides diversity of business changes in the United States and elsewhere. Not all plants and firms are getting smaller. Economies of scale still exist for a number of industries. Japanese banks, in particular, have grown dramatically in terms of deposits and loans over the last three decades. Many semiconductor firms, such as Texas Instrument or IBM, are large international firms, and they need to be large in order to do the necessary research and market chips as a new form of commodity. Not all equipment has become miniaturized. Electric power plants and shopping malls are as big, if not bigger, than ever. The late 1970s and 1980s stood witness to the fourth merger wave of the twentieth century. Takeovers, which have produced more spinoffs than megacompanies, have mushroomed as financial entrepreneurs have discovered profitable opportunities in changing management styles, in restructuring organizations, and in the tax benefits of more highly leveraging companies.[44]

Such observations, however, do not change the fact that the downsizing and miniaturization process underway is now more widespread than ever, and for several good reasons. A hundred years ago business had to be conducted practically at arm's length. Eyes were one of the best methods of monitoring people's productive behavior, to ensure that business commitments were met.

Voice was the best method of communicating and of consummating deals between employers and employees, producers and suppliers, and producers and customers. Mail was available but slow. The telegraph was available but expensive and often inconvenient. The telephone had been invented (in 1877) but was far too expensive to be in widespread use.

People simply needed to be in close contact in order to be heard and to enable their business activities could be monitored. As a consequence the complexity and size of organizational structures of businesses had to reflect the technological limitations on communications and monitoring. The locations of businesses were equally restricted by the size and scope of the market, which was also limited by the technology of communication and monitoring.

As mail, telegraph, and telephone systems improved, economies of scale could be tapped, larger numbers of employees could be communicated with and monitored, and mass selling on a national scale became more and more practical. The market power of local monopolies was dissipated as firms from all parts of the country began to invade each other's markets.[45] At the same time, however, competition across many (but not all) national boundaries was still limited by the cost of communication and travel.

Over the past two decades the world has literally undergone a communication revolution. Between 1960 and 1980, the number of ocean cable systems increased fivefold. Communications satellites were only a dream in 1960, but six U.S. communications satellites were in use by 1982, each capable of carrying many times the transmissions of a single previous oceanic cable system. The number of satellites that will be sent up in 1990 will probably exceed the total number that were in space in 1982.

In the 1960s microwave transmission of calls began to replace transmission by copper wires. Today, if they so choose, companies— for example, K mart—can bypass the telephone companies and to create their own communication systems (called VSATs) with the aide of ever-smaller satellite dishes. Today fiber-optic (or glass) wires, which use light for transmission of electrical signals, have begun to replace microwave dishes in transmission, and in the 1980s the transmission capacity of fibre systems was doubling every year.[46]

In the United States in 1960 there were 66 million telephones in a highly regulated, centralized telephone network. In 1982, the last year before the breakup of AT&T and the elimination of AT&T's monopoly on the telephone market, there were 151 million telephones. Now, because of greater competition among telephone suppliers, telephones have proliferated to the point that an accurate count of their number is no longer available.[47] Even if a count of telephones were available, its meaning would no longer be clear, simply because many telephones have become small computers with many more features than they had just a few years ago; and, of course, the range of telephone services has greatly expanded.[48]

Because of cost reductions and service expansions, telephone use in the United States has escalated. The number of average daily local calls was 273 million in 1960, 717 million in 1980, and 1.4 billion in 1986. The average number of daily long distance calls increased 12-fold in the 1960–1986 period, from 12 million a day in 1960 to 153 million a day in 1986.[49] The actual amount of time Americans have been talking on the phone has escalated in recent years. While the U.S. population grew only 7 percent between 1980 and 1987, the time Americans spent on the telephone expanded by 24 percent, or from slightly more than 3 trillion minutes in 1980 to slightly under 3.8 trillion minutes in 1987.[50]

Although the number of overseas calls has always been small by comparison to domestic calls, they increased by far more than domestic local and long-distance calls in the 1960–86 period. International calls from the United States increased 145 times, from a meager 3.3 million a year in 1960 to 478 million a year in 1986. All told, the opportunity for increased local, long-distance, and international calls has greatly increased the variety of connections people have established for undertaking more complicated business transactions and has greatly expanded the scope and complexity of markets. In so doing, communications technology has made the task of controlling markets vastly more complicated, because there are more people involved in a wider area, under more governments, and undertaking more complex business because more-specialized talent can be tapped.

Of course, the standard telephone jack is no longer limited to voice communications. The jack has become an outlet to the world for computers, video cameras, and fax machines. Through the standard telephone jack, voice, video, numbers, words, and pictures can be transmitted to virtually all parts of the world. Already many people can talk on the same line and at the same time that they make fax transmissions. The transmission of more media of communications at the same time on the same line awaits the standardization of the "integrated services digital network" (ISDN), which would permit the transmission of "digitized voice, PC, video, telex, facsimile and other services . . . simultaneously over two independent channels on an existing transmission medium."[51] With standardization of networks, the equipment costs will be reduced, since modems (which convert digitized computer information to an analogue of telephone networks) will no longer be necessary. "Ultimately, it should be possible for almost any information-processing equipment to be put on line just by plugging it into a standard jack. The major overall benefit is increased user access to the sources now available."[52] Markets will then become even more complex than they currently are.

In the late 1980s the communication world stood witness to what was dubbed the "faxplosion," or a dramatic expansion of sales of fax machines that permit the scanning and transmission of any document by telephone wires.[53] In early 1988 there were approximately two million fax machines in the hands of people in businesses, governments, and private homes—or about one for every 125 people in the country. However, sales of fax machines were then booming. More than four hundred thousand fax machines were sold in 1987 (many of them installed for less than one thousand dollars). And given expected price decreases, annual sales of such technological wonders by 1988 had more than doubled their 1987 level.[54] Use of fax machines can be expected to rise exponentially to the number of machine sales, since owners will then have more places to send more messages. Sometime in the 1990s fax machines will probably be as common in homes as microwave ovens are today.

## The Economic Consequences of Technology

Computers and advanced communications have changed whole industries and created new ones, not the least of which are space and biotechnology. However, the confluence of changes in several crucial technologies wrought to whole economies have been far more profound. The mutually reinforcing technological forces we have identified have caused a break with past trends and have given rise to a quantum leap in the competitiveness of businesspeople around the world. The new technology has made vital information, including data on prices and alternative sources and characteristics of supply, available to more people simultaneously. One no longer has to be in New York, Tokyo, or London in order to operate effectively in major markets. To that extent, transactions can be made at lower costs. Furthermore, this cheaper information, available almost instantaneously, enables managers to choose from a greater variety of production outlets—far beyond arm's length and out of sight, even in several governmental jurisdictions.

Five decades ago, University of Chicago economist and law professor Ronald Coase argued brilliantly that firms exist to reduce "transaction costs."[55] That is, while market transactions require participating parties to incur the necessary costs of searching out and of consummating deals, sometimes, through time-consuming bargaining processes, the firm as a hierarchical structure substituted commands, through a chain of management levels, for bargaining. Firms thus forswore the benefits of obtaining competitive sources of supply of needed services—for example, accounting or marketing services from the market. But things changed. Since markets have been made cheaper by improved technology and enhanced global competition, firms have been forced to embrace transactions with outside suppliers and alter their hierarchical structures. This shift in incentives is driving the out-sourcing and decentralization discussed earlier in this chapter. In other words, the new technology has spawned the development of smaller firms. It has increased the complexity of the economy by forcing the growth in the number of these firms and the economic linkages among them. And it has pushed the frontier of business activity right into our living rooms.

### Home Production

Computers and advanced communications have converted tens of millions of U.S. homes to potential "electronic cottage" status. Reported estimates of the number of people currently working in the electronic cottage industry in the United States vary widely, from a few hundred thousand to 10 or even more than 20 million.[56] However, one of the most frequently cited estimates of home-based workers has been made by the Bureau of Labor Statistics (BLS). The BLS figures that in 1987 approximately 5 million men and 4 million women worked for commercial ends at home eight or more hours a week. A majority of those 9 million workers appeared to be putting in unpaid overtime hours. Still, 1.9 million Americans, two-thirds of whom are women, worked exclusively at home, and not just in cleaning and child-care services.[57]

Regardless of the current count of home-based workers, the number is at least large enough to justify three new trade associations: the Association of Electronic Cottages, the National Alliance of Home-Based Businesswomen, and the National Association for the Cottage

Industry.[58] Problems abound with home-based work: Workers understandably worry about being cut off from colleagues, and firms worry that computer linkages to their employees' homes run security risks.[59] Nevertheless, in spite of numerous and widespread legal barriers to starting and expanding home-based industries, virtually everyone agrees that the trend toward greater "home production" will likely escalate as larger firms increase out-sourcing services to external vendors, including home producers, and to encourage their workers to stay at home and remain linked to their central offices via telephone wires and computers.[60]

In addition to reducing commuting time and providing a convenience for employees, especially mothers of young children, home-based production also has reduced the need for expansive, centralized offices and plants. For example, Pacific Bell of San Francisco closed three such small offices in 1987 when it allowed eighteen of its employees to telecommunicate from home.[61] Again, the economy has been made far more complex because technology has greatly expanded the ways by which business can be conducted.

*The Global Office*
Of course, the benefits of telecommunication are not restricted to homes. Telecommuting allows firms to shift work out of centralized offices in high-priced, high-rise downtown buildings to smaller, lower-cost offices in the suburbs or rural areas.[62] In short, the computer has once again facilitated the breaking up of production units and the spreading of work among a vastly greater number of production and resource outlets. Furthermore, many former reasons for keeping capital in any particular place have evaporated with the expansion in the ability of people to communicate from virtually any point on the globe—even previously inaccessible points, for example, remote mountaintops, lakes, and islands.[63]

The new buzz word in office automation is the "global office," an expression that suggests, correctly, that office work need not be done in the same country, let alone the same building. New York Life Insurance Company provides an example of how and why the global office works. Because of shortages of skilled office workers, high turnover rates, and high wages in the United States to process its insurance claims, New York Life has shifted its claims works to Ireland, a country beset by high unemployment but blessed with well-educated workers.

An insurance claim that is received at a post office box at Kennedy

International Airport in New York City on any given day is put on a 6 P.M. flight to Ireland, arriving early the next morning. The claim is then driven sixty miles to New York Life's Castle Island office, where it is processed within seven days and then transmitted back to the United States via a transatlantic lease line to a computer at New York Life's service center in Clinton, New Jersey. Overnight, depending on whether the claim requires payment, a check is drawn or a letter of explanation is written.[64] New York Life likes its new arrangement, since the cost of processing claims is 20 percent lower in Ireland than in the United States.[65]

Ireland and a host of other countries are actively promoting the concept of the global office, and the promotion is paying off. Also in Ireland McGraw-Hill processes its journal subscription renewals and Travelers Insurance Company writes its software. But the global office is hardly limited to Ireland. American Airlines employs more than a thousand workers in Barbados to enter data into its computers.[66] To these and other similarly situated countries, the potential of a globalized service economy is far more attractive than a globalized manufacturing economy. Governments, too, are also actively promoting the global office in the hope that their workers will get some of the business and that they—the governments—will be able to siphon off some of the revenues in taxes. With computers, a great deal more information—from design specifications to production schedules to financial reports to legal briefs—can be produced faster and more cheaply. With modern telecommunications, information can be made available, simultaneously if necessary, to more people in more places at lower cost.

With the growing ability to downsize production units and to spread out production among numerous locations, and with the greater capacity to seek alternative sources of supplies and alternative outlets for the goods and services produced, businesses must avail themselves of a broader array of information in order to remain competitive. Accordingly, information of various kinds—sources and prices of supplies, production specifications and costs, feasibility studies, and reports on successes and failures—has acquired a greater economic value. As a consequence entrepreneurs have understandably diverted resources into the acquisition of information, which they now must consider as a capital asset because it is at least as salable as the physical capital in their plants and offices and as mobile as electricity and radio waves.

*Brainpower as Capital*

But as important as information is, one other form of capital has become probably even more crucial to modern production: brainpower, the ingredient needed to produce the information capital—the designs, production schedules, financial monitoring reports, and legal briefs. When increased productivity is dependent on improved design, then the brains that conceive the improved designs—the new ideas—must be viewed as a fundamental form of capital in the new world economy, much as land was crucial to agrarian economies and steel, to industrial economies.

The growth in the relative importance of brains in production processes is clear, in part, from the relative decline of manufacturing employment, which encompasses many routine jobs, as a percentage of employment. Between 1960 and 1980, employment in manufacturing fell from 31 to 22 percent of total employment in the United States, and then dropped to 18 percent of the labor force in 1989. By contrast, according to one recent study, the number of people who do intelligent work and produce information—the so-called brainworkers—rose from 42 to 53 percent of the labor force between 1960 and 1980.[67] The importance of brains as capital is also reflected in the recent dramatic growth in pay of college graduates, when compared with high school graduates. According to economists Kevin Murphy and Finis Welch, in 1979 college graduates in the United States earned 32 percent more than high school graduates. However, by 1986, the education earnings gap had more than doubled, to 69 percent.[68]

One of the more interesting features of capital in the form of land or machinery made from steel is that they have to be rooted in place in order to be actively engaged in production, and they cannot be used simultaneously in different locations. Given modern communications, however, brainworkers can conduct their business from virtually anywhere. Clearly the most notable feature of brainpower and information as capital assets is their easy convertibility into electronic impulses. As a consequence they are the most mobile of all capital: They fit the description of "quicksilver" as no other forms of capital can. This characteristic makes them—but especially brainpower—two of the most difficult forms of capital for governments, corporations, or unions to contain and exploit.

Brainpower and information hardly constitute the kind of capital base that Marx envisioned. In his writings he predicted the eventual uprising of the proletariat, virtually all of whom were engaged in sweat labor. This is the type of resource the state finds easy to control because it is easily measured and monitored.

Expansive governments have lost a portion of their control over economic activity for the same reason that expansive corporations and unions have. Overblown governments, corporations, and unions were capable of organizing and controlling, through centralized command structures, workers using their brawn, but none has ever been very good at controlling, by way of direct commands, workers using their brains. Brainworkers deal in concepts that are manipulated, to a great degree, inside the head, which means that the substance of the work is not so easily measured, and it is difficult to determine when work is and is not being done. Economists have always argued that the quantity bought of anything is inversely affected by the price. The greater the price, the lower the quantity purchased, and vice versa. Similarly, the greater difficulty of controlling brainwork implies a higher cost of control via commands, and therefore less control being exercised by governments or any other economic power center.

### The Exponential Expansion of Economic Possibilities

Any given increase in the speed of movement and communication—or reduction in the attendant costs of movement and communication—vastly increases opportunities for expanding product lines and the complexity of production. The Caterpillar Corporation reports that its billion-dollar modernization program resulted in a doubling of the number of its products.[69] Managers at 3M and Rubbermaid now have rules that 25 or 30 percent of their sales must come from products introduced in the last five years.[70] Of course, greater speed can also expand exponentially the potential for economic contacts and relationships, for finding production cost savings, and for increasing the complexity of production. The result is a much more competitive world economy.

Consider: The tenfold increase in the average speed of travel from 4 miles per hour in 1800 to 40 miles per hour in the early 1970s increased by a factor of 100 the land area that could be covered in a given amount of time. This is because the area that can be covered in an hour at a speed of four miles per hour is equal to the area of a circle with a radius of 4 miles, or 53 square miles. The area that can be covered in an hour at 40 miles an hour is exactly

100 times greater, or 5,300 square miles. If people are distributed evenly over the area of the concentric circles, say, 4 people in the smaller, inner circle and 400 people in the larger circle, then the number of possible interacting pairs of people grows from 6 (at 4 miles an hour) to 79,800 (at 40 miles per hour). With the possibility of people moving at an even faster pace today—or, for that matter, accomplishing the same objective by telecommunicating—with the size of the relevant circle covering the globe and its more-than-5-billion inhabitants, the number of interacting pairs reaches astronomical levels.[71]

## The Growing Competitiveness of Business

With computers not much bigger than this book, individual entrepreneurs, working alone or in companies, have become tremendously powerful—but only in the very limited sense that they have access to their counterparts throughout the world. The power in entrepreneurs' hands, however, is not a power to command or coerce others, to be the business counterpart of the bygone slave owners or tyrants or even the so-called robber barons of the nineteenth century. Those people are becoming an "endangered" business species. Rather, the power of the modern entrepreneur is the power to become a productive force competing with roving company resources. His or her power is to move decisively in terms of how and where things are produced.

The control each entrepreneur exercises over others is extensively limited and contained by the fact that others have much the same opportunity to compete for resources and customers. As opposed to controlling others, each entrepreneur must appeal, to a degree never before imagined, to others' best interests by offering products and services on the best terms possible. This dynamic competition among businesspeople has meant that governments have had to forgo their former privileged monopoly positions in the selection of policies.

With the expansion of the market to a world scale, the prospects for collusive agreements that overpower market competition have dimmed considerably. There are simply more actual and potential competitors for businesses to contend with. As never before, they must be at all times in search of the most cost-effective production location on the globe, taking advantage of the best technology and organizational form, or else lose to someone else someplace else on the globe who can more easily invade their markets no matter where they are located. As never before, firms must be footloose, flexible, and ready to adapt at the slightest provocation.

Because modern technology *permits* greater capital mobility, greater dispersion of plants and equipment, greater reliance on markets, and more effective communications, competition is heightened. The resulting competitive forces *demand* that the new technology be employed. And the confluence of several new technologies—which have reduced the cost of collecting, organizing, and communicating data, of product design and development, and of flexible manufacturing—has caused many firms to dispense with past marginal adjustments in production techniques and to reorganize and reorient old production processes in dramatic ways.[72] As one business reporter has observed, the confluence of several technologies has induced many firms to accept another rule of change: "To get these benefits, you probably have to redesign the way you do business, changing everything from procurement to quality control."[73]

The new global competitiveness also means that workers must join with management to ensure that the firm's products can remain competitive on a world scale by holding productivity and labor costs to the best (and lowest) of world standards. As we said at the start, local standards of efficient production are no longer relevant. World standards are. That's why Ford began telling us in the 1980s that quality was "Job 1."

The publicly held corporation, suggests Harvard economist Michael Jensen, has been a cornerstone of economic development in the United States for more than a century: "Its genius is rooted in its capacity to spread financial risk over the diversified portfolios of millions of individuals and institutions and to allow investors to customize risk to their unique circumstances and predilections."[74] However, Jensen notes that the benefits of the corporate organizational form have always been limited by the lack of incentive managers have had to invest corporate assets to maximize stockholder wealth. The dispersion of ownership reduces the incentive of individual stockholders to monitor the investment strategies of corporate officers, to replace unsuccessful managers, and "to force managers to disgorge cash rather than spend it on empire-building projects with low or negative returns, bloated staffs, indulgent perquisites, and organizational inefficiencies."[75] Given the weak control links between stockholders and their agents at the company headquarters, it is altogether understandable that corporate managers came to be viewed as national power brokers. They had considerable discretion to employ and redeploy corporate assets.

Now, however, with the growth in domestic and international competition and in new organizational forms, which Jensen calls "LBO Associations,"[76] the power of the corporate managers is beginning to break down. These LBO associations—a prominent example is Kohlberg Kravis Roberts—have constrained corporate managers with pay tied more closely to stockholder wealth and with heavy debt burdens incurred in leveraged buyouts that force managers to pay out their cash flows so that they will not be wasted on managers' pet projects and so that investors, not corporate managers, can redeploy corporate earnings. In addition, because of their sizable stakes in their bought-out companies, the partners in LBO associations have strong incentives to monitor the progress of their companies in meeting global competition.

Similarly, legislators and policymakers at all levels of government have had to become concerned with how their policies affect business competitiveness and, hence, their ability to extract their revenues from the income stream generated from business. Legislators know that their policies can and will be readily monitored by the footloose capitalists whose fortunes can change with slight upward or downward adjustments in tax rates and regulations. And, like many corporate managers, legislators have had their discretion constricted by rising debt and interest burdens.

In the 1980s *competitiveness* did not become a favorite buzzword in Washington, London, and other capitals because it was a nice intellectual idea. Competitiveness was forced on policymakers who only very reluctantly paid heed. Somewhat belatedly they realized that their policies could impede the competitiveness of their businesses only at their own cost.

In short, Professor Galbraith's theory of countervailing power, outlined in the last chapter, may prove more correct than Galbraith himself—and certainly more than his critics—recognized. He maintained that government power would rise concomitant with the power of large business enterprises, more or less as a neutralizing force. He offered no reason why his theory should not work in reverse. If it does, the demise of business power through the development of truly global competitive markets should cause countervailing powers of government to recede as naturally as they arose when the power of business was expanding.

### Global Financial Markets and Physical Capital Mobility

The type of capital we have discussed throughout this chapter has been *real* capital: productive resources such as plant and equipment, information, and brainpower. But the kind of capital the man on the street thinks of as investment capital, or *finance* capital—stocks, bonds, and commercial paper—qualifies for discussion as well.

Until now we have directed our attention to the mobility of real capital simply because the growth in such productive resources ultimately determines the basic health of most economies. This is what nations need if they are to grow and prosper. But the world's financial markets are playing an increasingly critical role in spurring competitive enterprise and undermining the power of governments by allowing investment throughout the world.

The global financial markets have fueled investments in two ways. First, these markets have exploded, diversified, and become more complete. Financial markets now offer a larger variety of securities from an expanding array of companies, both domestic and foreign. Investors are no longer restricted to buying securities in a relatively small number of domestic companies from a limited number of domestic stock exchanges. Domestic residents can buy foreign stocks and bonds as easily as they can buy domestic ones. The availability of a broader range of securities has increased the overall level of purchases of financial assets and the mobility of wealth held in these various different financial forms. There are now simply more options from which investors can choose.

Furthermore, investment professionals have been exceedingly creative at inventing new financial assets. So-called electronic switches, which permit immediate transfer of funds across financial markets in different countries, were developed just thirty years ago. The first money market funds, which permit individual investors, in effect, to employ financial experts to develop their diversified portfolios, were developed as late as 1970. Futures, options, security credits, index future contracts, financial futures, warrant zero-coupon bonds, and high-yield bonds are just several of the newly invented financial instruments. This expanding menu of securities, available from a growing list of international companies and governments, has encouraged financial investment and eased the difficulty of moving funds among markets in different countries.

Technological developments have enhanced the international mobility of financial assets far more than the mobility of most real capital, particularly plants and equipment. Like information and brain-power, financial assets can be converted into electrical impulses and moved along cables as easily as electricity powers kitchen appliances, and these electrical impulses can jump national boundaries by way of satellite transmissions with no more difficulty than do television pictures.

The effects of the international transmissions of financial assets have been critically important to the continuing prosperity of national economies, because such electronic flows eventually affect the alloca-tion of the nations' real capital bases. Savings can be pooled and moved with relative ease to nations where they earn the highest rate of return, and those same funds can usually be pulled out with equal ease from countries where the rates of return are, for whatever reason, not competitive. This helps to explain the consistently high investment in liberal democracies and the atrophy of planned econo-mies.

The free flow of information across national boundaries has made it easier for people to invest over long distances. The resulting invest-ment activity has accelerated the integration of the world's financial markets. This, in turn, has increased the liquidity of global capital and thereby reduced the risk of investing abroad. These international financial flows may not appear to hold any surpassing importance beyond their own face value. (After all, money is money.) They can be thought of as representing mere "paper entrepreneurship," to use Robert Reich's pejorative phrase. But Reich is wrong. The residual importance of financial flows is that they now command the world's real goods and resources. The financial assets denominated in dollars or yen or lire that are moved from one locale to another will cause a portion of the world's real capital stock to follow. The people who acquire the different currencies then have the purchasing power to command movement—by barge, tanker, cable, or plane—of the real resources.

Information, such as work orders and supply sources, can be bought with financial capital flows and shipped by the same technology that moves the financial assets, and with no more difficulty. Though other physical capital—plants and equipment—may not be moved with the same ease, it is not invulnerable to accelerated financial flows. In fact, plants have had to become more adaptable and equip-ment more mobile largely to serve the commands of this quicksilver capital. In short, these various forms of capital mobility reinforce each other as technology supercharges them.

Political leaders must now pay attention to the growing mobility of financial capital because so many countries are in debt up to their bureaucratic necks. Shifts in the international flow of funds can change national interest rates and government fortunes. The resulting change in government interest payments can change domestic government spending on other established government programs, as well the discretionary authority of governments to spend any increase in revenue.

Furthermore, international flows of financial assets are important because the actual movement—or just the threat of movement—of financial capital can spell trouble or comfort for the future economic development of countries, when real resources follow the financial flows. When domestic residents start investing abroad or when foreigner investors in the domestic economy start withdrawing their financial capital, political leaders must realize that the country's resources will be the next to go as the country's currency is devalued on international money markets and foreigners then begin to buy up the country's real resources (which can leave the country as exports).

These financial markets can now quickly capitalize the economic value of suggested or enacted policy changes, and they accomplish this feat within a relatively short period of time after the changes are announced, or even tossed out as a trial balloon. Market reactions to policy pronouncements have become almost instantaneous opinion polls among people who count not just because they were called by pollsters, but rather because they called their brokers with their economic futures in mind.

The world's central bankers know that in their public pronouncements they must watch their words carefully. They are highly powerful government official, but also highly constrained. Any suggestion that they may make hinting that they intend to increase or slow the rate of growth in the money supply can cause money markets to reel as world investors interpret their comments by anticipating changes in interest rates. In early 1990 U.S. Federal Reserve Chairman Alan Greenspan suggested that he did not foresee a recession in the near future. The markets interpreted his comments as an indication that the Fed would not ease money growth. Hence, interest rates would not fall. As a consequence, stock and bond prices immediately fell.

President George Bush learned how international financial markets constrain public policy discussions shortly after his election in 1988. In December 1988, President-elect Bush made an offhand remark intimating only the possibility that his administration might go back on his often-cited campaign pledge, "Read my lips. *No new taxes!*" International financial markets went into a minor tailspin as investors tried to move their assets out of dollars. The value of the dollar on international money markets fell within hours of Bush's comments, which forced the president-elect to announce he had been misinterpreted and to reaffirm his original no-new-tax pledge.

In the fall and winter of 1989, Communist governments in Eastern Europe collapsed, signaling a potential revival of those economies and opening up a whole new array of profitable investment opportunities in the Eastern Bloc countries for Western entrepreneurs. Long-term interest rates around the world began to rise in late 1989 and early 1990 partly because the world's savings pool began to be redirected toward the Eastern Bloc countries. Even if world governments wanted to stop the redirection of the asset flows, there was really not much they could do, simply because of the size and diversity of world financial markets and the limited effects of actions taken by individual governments or groups of governments.[77]

## The Evolving Economy

Historians such as Fernand Braudel have shown that the world economy has been continuously transformed over centuries and the mobility of capital has steadily played a role in determining the sovereignty of governments.[78] We stress this point in order to avoid misinterpretation. We have not tried to argue that the world has been subjected to a sudden break in the way business is done.

"Economies of decreasing scale" have emerged gradually and do not as yet apply to all industries. Much capital has gotten smaller and become more mobile—gradually. The cost of transportation and communication has been lowered, firms have restructured themselves to become more flexible and to accommodate changing policy conditions, informational and brainpower have begun to take on more important production roles, and individuals have acquired more power to produce and compete—all very gradually. The data show that at least a couple of these trends—in particular, cost reductions in transportation and communications—started as early as the last century.

Nevertheless, all these identified trends were in full force by the 1970s, and they all appeared to be accelerating and compounding the effects of one another by the 1980s. The world economy emerged in the 1980s dramatically different from what it was a few decades before. The process by which the transformation occurred may have been gradual, but by the 1980s the confluences of the forces—with their evolutionary, compounding effects—suddenly became patently evident to even casual observers.

We agree with public-choice theorists who maintain that interest groups seeking to extract rents by lobbying governments monopoly economic powers for the achievement of private ends will continue to do so. The only problem with the theory is that technologically driven competitive forces dissipated many of the rents over which governments traditionally had complete control—that is, rents produced by stationary capital.

Capital mobility forced policymakers, who are not known for being on top, much less ahead, of world trends, to see that a quantum leap in world economic activity occurred. To them, Competitiveness (with a capital C) became a movement to embrace. However, the "C-word" meant that policymakers had fewer policy options. A more competitive world for business meant a more competitive world for governments.

In the quotation that heads this chapter, Federal Reserve Chairman Greenspan took note of the essential changes in the world when he observed the products that serve human needs and values are far more "impalpable" than they were at the turn of the century. Norman Macrae, editor of *The Economist*, ended a 1987 talk by putting his finger on the relevance of the impalpability of much modern production: "In the future, we will vote more frequently with our feet. If politicians try to boss us, brainworkers will go away and telecommunicate from Tahiti. Countries that choose to have too high a level of government expenditure or too fussy regulations will be residually inhabited mainly by dummies."[79] That observation, which appears to have eluded Marx, is food for much thought for modern-day government officials.

# 4

# Workers of the World
# Unite—At Last!

Where are the pins for the connectors made?
Well, they have to be machined in
Switzerland. Where are the connectors put
together? In Germany. There are thousands
of companies . . . in America, completely
off the scan of the honchos who watch the
trends. They are the little folks who've
figured out, because they are there where
the rubber meets the road, where to
manufacture. The longer I am out of
bureaucracy, the more thrilled I am to find
all of these niche players I never would have
had the opportunity to meet who are making
a buck and wearing their Rolexes. They're
not interested in the balance of payments
and global problems. They are interested in
making products and selling them.

*Walter Wriston*[1]
Former CEO, Citicorp

If he revisited the world today, Marx would undoubtedly
marvel at the profound reversal of scale that technologies have undergone since the invention of the microchip, and he would be dismayed
by the subsequent emergence of today's intricately integrated and
dynamic markets. But maybe he would have some second thoughts

about the human value of removing capitalism. After all, nowhere has the system had a more dramatic effect on the lives of workers, and people in general, than in his native Western Europe.

Wracked by two monstrous world wars in this century, the countries of Western Europe emerged from the second of these conflicts in 1945 with a victory over nazism and a system of liberal democracy but, at least in the economic realm, little else. With some assistance from the United States, Western European countries rebuilt their economies, reconnected old commercial links among each other, and forged constructive new ones. While this economic integration, best represented by the European Common Market organized in 1957, evolved steadily through the first several postwar decades, its pace was quickened impressively by the accelerating influence of capital mobility witnessed since the early seventies. Only now, in the nineties, with the emergence of a full-fledged European Economic Community, can we see in clear focus the miraculous influence the postwar mushrooming of international forces has had on the old world, and how this old world is reshaping the new. Workers of the world—indeed, their economies—have in fact been united to a degree, and in a manner, that Marx never anticipated. And while governments are playing a crucial part in the reshaping of Europe, their role is largely one of enabling the integration to proceed, not preventing it. This triumph has been one of people, not bureaucrats.

## Sovereignty Lost

The U.S. economy, like those of Western Europe, has become increasingly open to international forces that are, to one degree or another, beyond its political control. As the United States has become better integrated into the world economy, domestic fiscal and regulatory policies are being guided more by international economic forces and less by domestic political constraints. Politics, in other words, is having to yield to economics to such an extent that fundamental structural changes are now evident.

Some critics worry that national governments must regain control over their economies.[2] Some even fear that many foreign businesses that have moved into the relatively open U.S. economy have "hidden agendas, including the destruction of American competitors and the acquisition of American technology."[3] If American policymakers fail to meet the foreign "challenge," then "the threat of losing a measure of political and economic sovereignty becomes a real possibility."[4]

But this presumed threat has become the new reality for national governments not only in the United States but in most other countries, as is manifestly clear in Western Europe. The source of this "threat" to political sovereignty does not stem, as was so often the case in the past, from an army assembling just over the border. Rather, it comes from a quiet, unnoticed source—from the many people whose lives have become fully integrated through their business and consumption activities with the rest of the world, and from others who have been internationalized to a lesser extent but whose lives are no longer fully bound, as in the past, by accidents of birth and geography, to the countries they call home.

Furthermore, there is every reason to believe that current trends will continue—that more people will begin to live internationalized lives and that the economic powers of governments will continue to succumb to the rising tide of global competition of which these people partake. This loss of control sustained by government is borne out not only by the facts of a changing global economy but by the ways in which nations and their citizens are redefining their interests.

## The Growing Ambiguity of The National Interest

The "national interest," once a unifying banner, no longer elicits automatic accord among citizens of many nations. Indeed, an appeal to national interest has become, to a greater extent than ever, a means of stirring up domestic political conflict between proponents of competing economic interests. The growing problem is to define whose interest is reflective of *the* national interest. Citizens now have economic and social ties to countries other than their own.

People have always defined nationalities, to one degree or another, by reference to their place of birth, their culture, their history, and their faith—but also by reference to the source of their well-being. And their well-being now emanates from many other countries. A Tennessean who works, say, for Honda, listens to a Sony Walkman, and works on a Toshiba computer is, in some ways, as closely connected to the economic interests of people in Osaka as to people in New Jersey or Alabama. Many people in the United States today have only a scant idea of how little of their work is truly "American." While it is clear that nationalism in many of its cultural manifestations shows no sign of abating in the world, it is equally clear and ironic that the economic interest of individuals is and will become increasingly international. This fact has frustrating implications for government leaders as they try to steer their ships of state.

Whereas in an earlier era dependence gradually replaced independence in commentaries on relationships among nations, dependence is now rapidly giving way to interdependence. This twist of phrase has more than metaphorical content. Both independence and dependence imply an element of governmental power to control the economic fates of the people. Interdependence has forced a loss of governmental leverage, particularly at the nation-state level. Prime ministers and presidents can simply no longer set policies without anticipating the influence of external forces on the outcomes of those policies. Indeed, the growing frequency of calls for international cooperation and coordination in managing monetary, fiscal, and trade policies stands as a testimonial to the more constrained environments that policymakers face.[5]

The obvious questions flowing from the acceptance of international interdependence as a constraining force on governmental powers are: How much interdependence exists among nations? How fast is this interdependence developing? When will the move toward interdependence end? The first step in answering these questions is to learn how this growing interdependence specifically affects governments attempting to act on their own—that is, to tax, spend, and regulate the citizens and firms in their own jurisdictions.

## The Growth in International Trade

The most obvious way of describing the openness of an economy is simply in terms of changes in its volume of international trade—that is, exports and imports—over time. For the United States, the growth of exports and imports of goods and services since World War II has been dramatic. In 1947 exports and imports of goods and services were, respectively, $82.3 million and $39.9 billion (in terms of 1982 prices). By 1989 exports had grown to $597.6 billion—a more-than sevenfold increase in constant (1982) dollar terms. Imports had grown far more, by sixteenfold, to $643.9 billion (leaving a trade deficit of $56.3 billion).

Throughout the postwar period, international trade has expanded more rapidly than domestic production, meaning that international trade has become a progressively larger percentage of GNP. In 1947 U.S. exports and imports of goods and services represented 7.7 and 3.7 percent of GNP, respectively. Throughout the 1950s exports remained at less than 6 percent of GNP. However, by 1980, exports as a percentage of GNP more than doubled, to 12.2 percent. After U.S. exports as a percent of GNP fell for several years in the 1980s (partly because of relatively strong growth in GNP), exports in 1989 represented 14.4 percent of GNP. On the other hand, imports as a percentage of GNP climbed rapidly after 1982, reaching 15.5 percent of GNP in 1989.[6]

Many of the internationally traded goods may have been, by some criteria, nonessential. For example, imported party favors bought in the United States often carry the label "Made in Hong Kong." At the same time, many of the traded goods represented real increasing dependence of sectors of the U.S. economy on the world economy. In 1960 the United States imported 89 percent of its manganese, 74 percent of its bauxite, 66 percent of its cobalt, 46 percent of its zinc, and 32 percent of its tungsten. By 1983 all of the import percentages of these materials had risen—manganese to 98, bauxite and cobalt to 96, zinc to 66, and tungsten to 39 percent.[7]

Europeans have traditionally been far more dependent on international trade than has the United States. This is so because of the small sizes of the European countries (or the large size of the U.S. market). Nonetheless the dependence of European countries on international trade grew substantially during the 1960–86 period.[8] Exports by all European members of the Organisation for Economic Cooperation and Development (OECD-Europe) stood at $277.4 billion (U.S. dollars, measured at the 1980 price level and exchange rates) in 1960.[9] By 1986 their collective exports had grown to $1,248.1 billion (in constant-dollar and exchange-rate terms), a greater than fourfold increase.[10] Imports amounted to $284 billion in 1960 and $1,228 billion in 1986.

Real exports and imports of OECD-Europe also expanded relative to domestic production. In 1960 both imports and exports were 16 to 17 percent of the countries' combined gross domestic product (GDP). By 1986 exports and imports were, respectively, 31.2 percent and 30.8 percent of the GDP of OECD-Europe.

Even Japan has become more dependent on international trade. Japanese exports continued along an upward trend throughout most of the years between 1960 and 1986, growing from $13.9 billion to $209.2 billion (measured in U.S. dollars and at the 1980 price level and exchange rate). Japanese imports also grew in real terms throughout most of the period, from $24.5 billion in 1960 to $177.5 billion (again, at the 1980 price level and exchange rate). However, it needs to be noted that Japanese imports grew more slowly in the 1980s than in the 1960s or 1970s, possibly because the newly acquired dollars were being used to buy more foreign assets.

Japan's exports also grew relative to its GDP—from 5.6 percent of GDP in 1960 to 15.9 percent in 1986 (down from 17.2 percent in 1984 and 1985). Japanese imports, on the other hand, have grown more slowly than GDP since the mid-1970s. In 1960 Japanese imports amounted to 9.9 percent of GDP. By 1974, Japanese imports represented 17.8 percent of Japanese GDP. The percentage generally trended downward thereafter, reaching 13.5 percent in 1986.

## International Investment Flows

The openness and integration of world economies can also be assessed, to a limited extent, by the flow of international investments. International investments represent a willingness of entrepreneurs to risk their capital to the jurisdictions of foreign governments. Such investments also represent a dependence on foreign economies for the security of the investments deployed and for a flow of income that, in turn, depends on the efficient working of foreign economies.

Greater international investment can reflect a host of economic considerations, not least of which is greater profitability from extending the geographical range of investments. However, greater profitability may be attributable to lower costs of transporting capital and the goods and services produced from the capital, lower costs of communications (or of keeping in contact with the operation of foreign capital), greater ease of capital repatriation, greater government stability or reduced threats of expropriation, and greater stability in exchange rates. In general, the lower the costs of international investments, the greater the volume—and the greater the mutual dependence, or interdependence, of economies.

Of course, the growth and spread of financial markets can also explain much international investment. Financial markets not only permit the raising of funds, but also the disposal of foreign investment. Financial markets, in effect, make capital more liquid and, to that extent, reduce the risk associated with foreign investments. In addition the unification of nationalities through the use of a common language also helps the deployment of capital in foreign countries. The fact that English has become the "language of commerce" has, no doubt, increased the willingness of Americans to invest abroad and foreigners to invest in the United States.

The facts of foreign investment are relatively strong in favor of greater interdependence. In 1960 U.S. residents invested slightly more than $7 billion abroad (measured in 1982 prices).[11] By 1970 their foreign investment rate had more than doubled (in constant-dollar terms) to just above $15 billion. In 1988 Americans' foreign investments (after falling by more than 25 percent since 1986, partially attributable to the continuing economic recovery) were close to 4.4 times their 1970 level. Foreigners' investments in the United States expanded even more rapidly in constant dollars, rising from just under $4 billion in 1960 to more than $10 billion in 1970 and to $176.9 billion in 1988.

For most of the 1960–88 period, capital inflows and outflows were on the rise relative to GNP. Capital inflows swelled from 0.5 percent of GNP in 1960 to 4.5 percent in 1988. Capital outflows, on the other hand, started off at 0.8 percent in 1960, rose to 3.8 percent of GNP in 1982, and then fell to 1.7 percent of GNP in 1988 (again, attributable to the continuing economic recovery in the United States, which made investment relatively more profitable).

The somewhat erratic year-to-year changes in investment flows resulted in a steady buildup of U.S. assets abroad and of foreign assets in the United States. In total, in 1960 Americans owned $434 billion (measured in 1986 prices and exchange rates) in foreign assets (stocks, bonds, real estate, manufacturing facilities, equipment, and so on). By 1988 their aggregate real foreign investments had nearly tripled, to $1.2 trillion. Of this 1988 total, U.S. citizens held 74 percent, or $927 billion, in portfolio assets (securities and bank accounts). The remainder, $327 billion, was direct foreign investment (plants, equipment, banks, and real estate).

Foreigners' total investments in the United States increased in a more dramatic fashion, rising from $280 billion in 1970 in constant (1986) dollar terms to more than $1.6 trillion in 1988, 78 percent ($1.4 trillion) in portfolio assets and 12 percent ($297 billion) in direct investments.[12] As commentators are fond of stressing, the United States, through 1984, was the world's leading "creditor nation" (meaning its aggregate investments abroad exceeded the sum total of investments of foreigners). However, in 1985, it had achieved the status of the world's leading "debtor nation." Total foreign investments in the United States in 1987 exceeded total U.S. investments abroad by $378 billion. The following year the difference between U.S. assets abroad and foreign assets in the United States swelled by 40 percent, to $533 billion in 1988.[13]

Whether the shift from the status of creditor to debtor nation (if in fact the United States *has* become a debtor nation, when the value of U.S. foreign investments are properly valued in current dollars) represents a benefit or bane to the U.S. economy is not particularly important to the central theme of this book. What is important is the magnitude of the capital interdependence of the

U.S. economy with the rest of the world. By 1987 foreigners owned more than 6 percent of all fixed tangible property in the country, including 10 percent of the U.S. manufacturing capacity (with a total investment of $91 billion).[14]

According to another study, "By the end of 1986, Japanese corporations had at least a 50 percent stake in 489 U.S. assembly or production companies, 118 of which were begun that year. In the United States today, the Japanese have six automobile assembly and manufacturing plants in construction or operation, as well as 150 automobile parts suppliers."[15] Four of the nation's largest chemical companies, half of the nation's cement industry, and a sizable segment of the country's financial industry are all owned by foreigners. Indeed, familiar company names are now controlled or owned outright by foreigners: CBS Records (Japanese), Hardee's (Canadian), Brooks Brothers (British), Doubleday (German), Viking Press (British), Smith & Wesson (British), A&P (German), Grand Union (French), Food Lion (Belgian), and Carnation (Swiss).[16] As two concerned analysts have recently noted,

> An American can buy Chicken-of-the-Sea tuna (owned by an Indonesian company) from A&P (Britain) or dresses from Bonwit Teller (Canada) with a credit card from Marine Midland Bank (Hong Kong). She may drive a Plymouth Laser (Japan), fill up at a Texaco station (Saudi Arabia), read a Doubleday book (West Germany), swig a Lone Star beer (Australia), and listen to Willie Nelson on CBS Records (Japan).[17]

Furthermore, in 1987 foreigners owned one-third of the commercial property in Washington, D.C., one-fifth of the commercial property in Manhattan; nearly 50 percent of the commercial property in Los Angeles; and almost 40 percent of the commercial property in Houston.[18] Foreigners also owned 12.5 million acres of land, most of it in ten states (Maine, Texas, California, Oregon, Louisiana, Georgia, New Mexico, Florida, Colorado, and Washington).[19] And foreign direct economic interest in the United States was on the rise, both in absolute real terms and relative to national production.[20] The rise of capital flows among other foreign countries has been on par with—and, on occasion, has substantially superceded—the rise of capital flows between the United States and foreign countries.

Consider the data on direct investment flows (excluding portfolio investments) for selected countries in table 4.1. The outflow of direct investment from the United States rose fivefold in current-dollar terms between 1967 and 1984; at the same time the inflow of direct investment rose more than sixteen times. Between 1967 and 1984, the rise in the outflow of direct investment from all of European countries was on par with the rise from the United States. The rise in the direct investment inflow to European countries was approximately sixfold. Both the rise in the inflow to and outflow from Japan and the outflow from Canada were substantially greater than those for the United States and Europe. For all countries covered by the survey, direct investment inflows and outflows expanded by about sixfold between 1967 and 1984. In general, over the period covered by the table, the United States accounted for a smaller percentage of all outflow of direct investment and received a greater share of the inflow of direct investment.

TABLE 4.1   Inward and Outward Foreign Direct Investment for Selected Countries, 1967 and 1984

| | Outward Investment | | | | Inward Investment | | | |
|---|---|---|---|---|---|---|---|---|
| | In billions of dollars | | Percentage of world foreign direct investment abroad | | In billions of dollars | | Percentage of world foreign direct investment received | |
| | 1967 | 1984 | 1967 | 1984 | 1967 | 1984 | 1967 | 1984 |
| United States | 56.6 | 238.0 | 50 | 40 | 9.9 | 164.6 | 9 | 27 |
| Europe | 45.1 | 265.0 | 40 | 44 | 31.4 | 182.7 | 30 | 30 |
| Japan | 1.5 | 37.9 | 1 | 6 | 0.6 | 4.5 | 1 | 1 |
| Canada | 3.7 | 31.6 | 3 | 5 | 19.2 | 61.9 | 18 | 10 |
| Developing countries | 3.0 | 18.2 | 3 | 3 | 32.2 | 153.9 | 31 | 26 |
| All countries | 112.3 | 600.0 | 100 | 100 | 105.4 | 602.6 | 100 | 100 |

Source: Office of Trade and Investment Analysis, U.S. Department of Commerce, unpublished data, May 1988, as reported in Linda M. Spencer, *American Assets: An Examination of Foreign Investment in the United States* (Arlington, Va.: Congressional Economic Leadership Institute, 1988), p. 17.

The growing integration of world economies might also be assessed with reference to the tendency of capital flows to narrow the

rates of return on investment among nations. If capital is more mobile—everything else being equal—then rates of return on investment
within nations should narrow. If, for example, the rate of return in
West Germany is higher than the United States, then capital can
be expected to flow from the United States to West Germany, lowering
the rate of return on capital in West Germany and increasing the
rate of return on capital in the United States. The evidence on the
extent to which capital flows close the rates of return is mixed, at
the very least.[21] Several researchers have found no obvious closing
of the gaps in rates of return.[22] At the same time, researchers cannot
be certain whether the gaps are *narrower* than they would have been
otherwise, given all the changing political and economic factors that
confuse the statistical picture. What appears to be true is that there
is sufficient capital mobility to ensure that "one country's macroeconomic policies can sometimes have an appreciable impact on other
countries."[23]

## Other Measures of Openness and Integration

Trade in consumption and capital goods (and services) has, no
doubt, been facilitated by reductions in national barriers to trade
and capital movements and by cost reductions in transportation and
communications. Through the 1960s the United States and almost
all European countries had extensive controls on capital movements,
including exchange controls, limitations on foreign interest in domestic
firms to discourage takeovers and achieve national security objectives,
special reporting and approval requirements for foreign investments,
and special taxes on foreign investments. Many still do, but a substantial number of the most restrictive controls have been eliminated.[24]
Furthermore, while much trade, especially between the United States
and the rest of the world, has been progressively obstructed in the
1980s by the imposition of nontariff barriers (quotas and "voluntary
export restraint" agreements on, for example, automobiles and steel),
many tariff barriers have been eliminated through various rounds of
tariff reductions. As a result, the average "tariff wall" was steadily
lowered through the 1950s, 1960s, and 1970s.[25]

The dramatic growth in world trade and international capital
flows, even in the 1980s, reveals that any recent reversal of past
trends toward reductions in trade and capital barriers has not fully

offset the opposing trend toward world integration. The so-called neomercantilist (or modern-day protectionist) movement is, at best, only marginally slowing the pace of world integration.[26]

The pace of economic integration has quickened for standard economic reasons, not the least of which is the reduction in the cost to individuals and firms of developing and maintaining foreign connections. Not many decades ago, movements of goods and people across national boundaries were difficult and required great sacrifice. In 1937, for example, the price of an airline ticket between the West Coast of the United States and Japan was $12,725 (measured in 1986 dollars). By 1973 the price of a flight of comparable distance, at faster speeds and with improved services, was down to $1,860. By 1985, the constant-dollar cost had fallen another 50 percent, to $930.[27] Between 1937 and 1984, the price of a transpacific flight fell from more than 300 percent of annual per capita disposable income to less than 8 percent of annual per capita disposable income.

As a result of air-fare reductions, faster speeds, and more convenient flights, the volume of international travel increased substantially: from 27.6 billion revenue-passenger miles in 1970 to 64.4 billion revenue-passenger miles in 1986. The increase in average plane speeds in international travel from 149 miles per hour in 1944 to 493 miles per hour in 1986, without question, reduced the total cost of air travel (which includes the ticket price plus the wages foregone by the travelers while in the planes) by a greater percentage than indicated by the reductions in the air fares.[28] The increase in speeds probably also had the effect of reducing the perceived size of the globe by more than a third and, to that extent, increasing the ease of entering far-distant countries.

The dramatic reductions in the cost of international telephone calls clearly added to the openness of world economies. People could, in effect, cross national boundaries and become participants in other economies by electrical impulses, first by way of cables and then by way of satellites. (In the process, the need for emigration was made less pressing and the impact of immigration restrictions less onerous.) The number of international telephone calls rose from 3.3 million in 1960, to 23.4 million in 1970, to 199.6 million in 1980, and to 478 million in 1986.[29] Because of the trend toward cross-border data flows, international data circuits in the late 1980s expanded by 40 percent a year, a rate that was then expected to lead to a 22 to 40 percent reduction in line charges by 1996.[30] In much the same way, reductions in the real cost of postal services and increases in the availability of private overnight delivery services have also added to the openness, and the accompanying integration, of national economies.

## Implications of the Data

Although incomplete and often inaccurate, available measures of the growing openness of national economies in general and the U.S. economy in particular must change people's perception of the world and alter political forces within individual countries. At the most basic level of analysis, the available data on openness offer a different perspective on production within a country. In general the data indicate that over the last four decades or so, a progressively smaller share of domestic production in the United States and many other countries around the world was directly attributable to resources owned and controlled by domestic residents. More and more of each country's production was occurring abroad and was being done at the behest of foreign owners. More and more production of each country's so-called domestic output was resulting from strategic alliances, stakeholder alliances, joint ventures, or cross-country consortiums of suppliers and buyers and even of competitors in different countries, although multiple-firm production arrangements were also blossoming within domestic economies.[31] Such strategic (international) partnering gave rise in 1987 alone to eight thousand visits by U.S. employees of Ford Motor Company to Japan.[32] In short, production capacities, and even many traditional company identities, were gradually being blended on a worldwide basis, with an accompanying blurring of the concepts of national production levels. There is every reason to expect these trends to continue.

### Measuring U.S. Economic Prowess

Concern has been expressed that U.S. manufacturing output—produced within the official national boundaries—has declined as a percentage of world manufacturing output since the end of World War II.[33] However, this does not mean that the underlying U.S. economy is eroding. On the contrary, U.S. manufacturing output in terms of real dollars and volume has continued to rise. In addition, according to Kenichi Ohmae, managing director of McKinsey & Company in Japan, "trade figures do not prove a loss of U.S. prowess," meaning its manufacturing capability on a worldwide scale.[34] This is true because many U.S. firms that move abroad export goods back to the United States and sell in the foreign markets where they have located, expanding the world market served by U.S. manufacturing firms. In fact, Ohmae reports that

> the U.S. share of manufacturing goods exported from *other* countries is increasing. It was 13 percent in 1977, 14 percent in 1983, and 15 percent in 1985. . . . America's share of all manufacturing jobs in the U.S., Japan, Europe and the newly industrializing countries was 27 percent in 1960. It reached 30 percent in 1980, and was still 30 percent in 1986.[35]

In 1985 American firms producing in Japan sold more than $53 billion of goods and services to the Japanese, an amount that exceeded the U.S. trade deficit with Japan that year.[36] Similarly, in 1986 U.S. affiliates of foreign firms imported more than $124 billion of goods and services into the United States and exported just under $51 billion.[37]

Many people are fully aware that manufacturing jobs in the United States have declined as a share of total U.S. domestic employment. At the same time, the U.S. share of manufacturing employment in the United States, Japan, Europe, and newly industrializing countries increased between 1960 and 1980, rising from 27 percent in 1960 to 30 percent in 1980. The U.S. share of world manufacturing employment was still 30 percent in 1986.[38]

The concept of domestic production is obviously blurred by the integration of world markets. Approximately half of all U.S. imports and exports are actually internal firm transactions, between U.S.–based parent firms and their foreign affiliates. As Murray Weidenbaum notes, Unisys exemplifies developments in integration of firms on a world scale:

> Half of its sales are overseas, covering more than 100 advanced and developing nations. The company uses components produced in virtually every continent, and its financing is worldwide. The company is simultaneously a customer of—and supplier to—Fujitsu, Hitachi, IBM, Honeywell, Phillips and Siemens. Together these companies (headquartered in five different nations on three continents) engage in joint ventures, serve as sources for each other, share output and compete.[39]

In an 1989 interview for *Fortune* magazine on the economy in the 1990s, former Citicorp CEO Walter Wriston noted that he is now employed by a little company in Connecticut whose sales of connectors and cables total $300 million in a "good year."[40] He then asked, "Where are the pins for the connectors made?" The short answer is that they are made on a world scale. Similarly, Corning Glass gets half its profits from joint ventures, and two-thirds of the joint ventures are with foreign firms, including Samsung in South Korea, Ciba-Geigy in Switzerland, and Asahi Glass in Japan.[41] In other words, it is no longer clear whether the output of U.S. corporations abroad (using foreign workers, land, and capital) is any more foreign (or nondomestic) than domestic production that uses foreign-produced robots (or any other form of imported equipment and parts that are produced or assembled offshore). By the same token, it is equally unclear whether goods produced within American borders with the aid of American labor, but using components produced at various points on the globe, are American or foreign. What is clear, however, is that now as never before, more than the economic interests of nationals within given borders are at stake when individual countries, including the United States, determine their domestic policies.

*Countervailing Political Forces*
The broadening of interests represented in domestic political processes and the growing uncertainty over economic ties should be expected to affect democracies in several important direct and indirect ways. The direct means are more or less obvious. Many domestic voters will, no doubt, identify with the economic interests of their foreign sources of supply, jobs, sales, and incomes, and will vote accordingly. In 1986 nearly three million Americans (or 3 percent of the labor force) worked for U.S. affiliates of foreign-owned companies,[42] and an untold number of other American workers' jobs depended on orders from U.S. affiliates. These foreign owners should be expected to call upon their constituents in domestic political battles. Indeed, as Senator Lloyd Bentsen (D., Texas.) is reported to have said, "You get an immediate reaction when you introduce a piece of legislation that affects these foreign investors in the United States. They just don't stop at the Washington level. You hear from their distributors and contractors back home right away."[43] Measured by jobs alone, the political opposition to protectionist measures could be formidable because there are a lot of votes out there.[44]

All the jobs, sales, and incomes tied directly or indirectly to the international economy can affect domestic political agendas in many vital ways. For example, because the United States exports so much of its agricultural production, U.S. farmers have an economic interest in policies that increase the openness of foreign markets. Similarly, U.S. retailers, who buy much of their apparel goods from abroad, have an interest in keeping U.S. markets open to textile and apparel trade.

Many of these foreign political forces can be expected to moderate, if not always neutralize, domestic political forces seeking protection. One of the most interesting political phenomena of the 1980s was the emergence of the so-called antiprotection movements (political forces opposed to protection from foreign imports). According to researchers who have begun to study opposition to these movements, the most effective antiprotection groups include multinational corporations, exporters, retailers, and foreign direct investors.[45]

American manufacturing interests have historically had an understandable disdain for rises in the value of the dollar on international money markets. Such exchange rate changes have increased the attractiveness of imports by reducing their prices in U.S. markets and have reduced the attractiveness of U.S. exports by increasing their prices in foreign markets. As a consequence U.S. manufacturers have had as strong an interest in propping up the value of foreign currencies—yen, marks, or whatever—in terms of dollars on international markets as they have had in protective tariffs and quotas.

In the early-to-mid-1980s, when the international value of the dollar was rising, Caterpillar, Inc., led a broad-based industry lobbying effort to bring its value down and thereby increase U.S. exports (and Caterpillar sales in foreign markets) and discourage foreign imports (and increase Caterpillar sales in the U.S. market). Its political efforts paid off, leading in 1985 to the Plaza Agreement among industrialized countries to seek a reduction in the value of the dollar.

When the dollar began to rise in the late 1980s, Caterpillar sought once again to enlist federal help to bring it down. However, much had changed over four or five years. Other American industries had invested heavily abroad and had begun to export manufactured goods back to the United States, and to the rest of the world, from their foreign bases. The appreciation of the dollar, in other words, no longer harmed the market position of so many American manufacturers. Indeed, the appreciation of the dollar meant that many American firms with foreign production facilities could increase their sales (and profits) in the U.S. market.

As a consequence, in early 1990, Caterpillar was finding it far more difficult than in the early 1980s to enlist the cooperation of other American industrial interests in its lobbying efforts to bring the value of the dollar down. Caterpillar's chief lobbyist even lamented in the press, "There aren't a whole lot of folks getting concerned" about the rising yen-price of the dollar.[46] In other words, the growing integration of the global economy had eliminated yet another policy area in which, in the past, governments were able to move with far greater unity of purpose, speed, and decisiveness.

### Growth in Political Complexity

As should be expected, the growth in economic integration has also forced greater political integration through indirect means. It has increased the number of competing interest groups—what James Madison called "factions"—operating within the domestic political arena.[47]

The globalization of markets has, in effect, diluted the political power of many but (of course) not all domestic groups. Foreign citizens and their firms have increased their efforts to manipulate each other's political outcomes. Martin and Susan Tolchin lament a trend they should have expected: In 1984 wholly-owned foreign firms spent, through political action committees (PACs), more than a million dollars on congressional campaigns, and more than one hundred foreign PACs were active in the 1986 election.[48]

Just like their domestic counterparts, foreign firms have been actively seeking to change U.S. tax laws to their advantage and to obtain state and federal subsidies to create jobs and increase America's capital base. At the same time, American firms have sought to manipulate the policies of foreign governments, and American governments have sought to attract foreign capital to the states, by using a variety of subsidy and tax-abatement schemes. In 1986 forty states had foreign offices, all competing for foreign capital.[49] Naturally, foreign firms have followed their domestic counterparts in pitting national governments and state governments within nations against one another in a competitive bidding process for capital and the accompanying job-creating capacities. Naturally, too, in the process of entering the domestic bidding process, foreign firms have reduced the privileged monopolistic position of domestic firms for various forms of government largess.

To the extent that political expenditures are effective, the integration of the economic and political realms on a world scale should also cause a relative, if not absolute, reduction in the importance of strictly democratic forces in determining political outcomes. This is true because foreign firms do not have direct access to votes. They must influence or sway votes mostly by economic means. One of these is to increase contributions to existing representatives; another means is the threat to move capital, production, and jobs elsewhere. In an open, integrated world economy, such threats cannot be dismissed by domestic political forces. This is especially true when products and production processes are highly technical and sophisticated and when a major share of the value added by capital is more attributable to the incorporated technology—which can be moved readily at modest or low cost—than to the physical assets.

Of course, the political consequences of foreign direct and indirect influences will not all be positive. Many foreign owners of domestic capital of textile mills, for example, will be just as interested in continued protection from textile imports as are owners of domestic firms. Japanese-based automobile manufacturers definitely have an understandable preference for quotas over tariffs if automobile imports into U.S. markets are restricted. The quotas enable them to raise their prices in the protected markets, whereas tariffs force them to accept lower prices (after deducting the tariff).

### Reduced Restrictions on International Trade
There are three reasons we should expect the integration of markets, on balance, to lead to less restriction on international trade, to lower taxes, and to fewer inefficient government regulations. First, foreign connections will raise the importance of open trade to a larger number of domestic voters. For instance, domestic apparel workers will be likely to understand that their jobs and livelihoods depend on cheap textile products imported from abroad. The result should be marginally fewer trade and capital barriers and marginally lower trade barriers when they do exist.

Second, there is less certainty on the part of American voters than in the past that their economic interests lie squarely with the economic interests of a well-defined geographical area (the fifty states) and specific group of people (all other Americans). As regionalism and nationalism exert less influence, fewer Americans will be interested in restricting trade and more will be interested in finding ways of opening the economy further (and responding to international economic forces in general).

Third, foreign interests are likely to be far less rigidly bound (for cultural or nationalistic reasons) to their country of residence. They are, therefore, likely to be more mobile and responsive to ineffective or costly domestic policies than to domestic interests.

This potential greater mobility of capital (as distinct from the actual quantity of capital that moves across national borders) is likely to represent a threat to governments. With greater foreign interests in the domestic economy, governments must fear, to a greater extent than otherwise, that domestic policies that are not cost-effective will drive existing foreign capital out of the country and will discourage the investment of additional capital. These points are central to our conceptual arguments covered in the following two chapters.

## Sovereignty Lost, Opportunity Gained

In this chapter, we have relied extensively on conventional measures of world economic activity. These statistical sources tell us much about the extent of the openness of domestic economies, especially the U.S. economy, and of the resulting world integration, but they hardly describe the full extent of the changes occurring in the world. This is because there are many qualitative changes in the way people do business that are not, and cannot be, captured in conventional data.

Many people think globally today. They plot their business strategies differently, and they work differently—as never before, with an eye toward what their competitors around the globe may or may not be doing. They have been internationalized, not just in what they do and consume but in the fact that they think no more about calling a client in Madrid than they may once have thought about contacting a client in Youngstown. They are literally tuned in and turned on to the global economy. Those who are not now will be soon, because they will have to compete with those who are. Governments will surely have to cope with growing hordes of people who have little economic allegiance except to the concept of meeting competition on a world scale. Such people represent a check on the power of domestic governments because nationalism no longer exerts the same economic force that it once did.

Senator Lloyd Bentsen does not share our optimistic appraisal of the domestic consequences of economic integration. He fears that Americans—in particular, members of Congress—have been "selling America on the cheap."[50] He does not worry alone. Nationally syndicated columnist Jack Anderson asks, "Why are our political leaders abetting the buyout of America? I believe foreign investment has become a narcotic, and the politicians have become addicted. . . . The politicians have got this country so deep in hock to foreign interests that they can't face the withdrawal pains—which might include risks to their own political futures."[51] Susan and Martin Tolchin are understandably concerned that American policymakers meet the foreign challenge, or else "the threat of losing a measure of political and economic sovereignty becomes a real possibility."[52]

"A measure of political and economic sovereignty" has already been lost, however, and there appears to be no way that it can be fully recaptured. The very fact that so many policy critics suggest that the government must respond to the foreign investment threat suggests the extent to which control over domestic policies is no longer in the hands of domestic policymakers. In no small way, that control has been exported and diffused throughout the world.

Government officials and policy commentators may in years to come talk and write a great deal about recapturing the lost sovereignty through various international cooperative schemes. However, such efforts will run upstream against the mounting forces of integration and competitive markets for businesses—and for governments. That has been the central theme of this chapter (and book), captured with incisiveness by Walter Wriston,

> Borders that were once the cause of wars are now becoming porous. Money moves over, around and through them with the speed of light. The flows of capital are now in the range of 30 to 50 times greater than world trade. The world's capital market that moves along this electronic highway goes where it is wanted and it stays where it is well-treated. This is why there was no crowding out [due to the federal deficit], this is why foreign capital comes and stays in the U.S. As long as our free-market system permits and delivers an acceptable rate of return on investment in an environment of political stability that is competitive with other areas of investment, the capital will keep coming.[53]

In the future, governments will probably learn a valuable lesson about markets continuously taught in the past to private firms: Cartels do not work very well or last very long. To suppress competition, private firms have a natural stake in cartelizing their markets through various cooperative and coordinating schemes. From time to time, groups of firms within industries have set production quotas or divided their markets with the intention of raising the prices and profits of all cartel members.

The problem cartel members have faced emerges precisely from the goal of the cartel, which is to achieve greater profits at reduced cost to each member. Once the cartel creates monopoly profits, each firm has an incentive to break with the cartel in order to raise its profits even more (at the expense of all other members). The greater the number of members, the greater the incentive for each firm to cheat.[54] When all concede to this incentive to cheat, the cartel collapses, and competitive prices and production levels are reestablished. The moral of most private cartels is that they don't work effectively for very long, especially when many firms, operating under divergent cost and demand conditions, are involved.[55]

In their quest to recapture their lost control, governments will naturally think in terms of cartelizing their own "government markets" (following, perhaps, the path charted by the Organization of Petroleum Exporting Countries [OPEC]). In such circumstances they will invariably face the same dilemma as do private cartels. All governments may have an incentive to collude in (or to cooperate and coordinate) their policies, with the intent of raising their tax and regulatory prices (for whatever political or economic goals they may have in mind).

However, much like private firms, too, governments have divergent cost and demand conditions, and each has an incentive, based on the desire to increase the benefits going to constituents in its particular country—to cheat on any restrictive international cartel agreement. Each government can reason that a unified movement to raise taxes or regulation can make all governments (as distinct from countries) better off. Nonetheless, once the government cartel is organized, each country can reason that its own tax base (and benefits derived from it) can be expanded by shifting, in overt and covert ways, to more competitive policies. The crucial problem governments will be likely to face in maintaining their policy cartels is made more difficult by the sheer number of governments around the world and the great variety of policy devices for overtly and covertly circumventing cartel rules.

The moral of the government cartel: It may work in certain places and for limited periods of time (OPEC worked for several years), but cartels lose much of their impact over time. This is not to say that some government cooperation and coordination with the intent of regaining lost monopoly power will never occur. Governments do have the power of coercion, and a relatively small number of governments now dominate the world economy. However, cartelization is likely to be a continuing struggle from which many governments can be expected to withdraw. In the end government efforts to cartelize the international policy process will probably offset only partially the emerging economic forces that are now beginning to suppress the power of national politics.

Nevertheless, it appears that global entrepreneurs and workers of the world will take steps to ensure that the growth in the power of governments will continue to wane. On their side, world entrepreneurs have strong personal economic incentives—unmatched by governments' bureaucratic incentives—to improve their competitive positions by remaining lean and mean, ready to jump jurisdictions in response to the slightest policy provocation. In the past entrepreneurs were handicapped by their inability to actually move their assets and to stay in touch with their investments in distant lands. They were reluctant to cross cultural boundaries that often went with national borders. However, such problems are nowhere as important as they once were. Entrepreneurs have the technology to move decisively in a world that has become much more of a whole. Indeed, they must move decisively around the world, like it or not, because of the growing intensity of competition on a world scale.

# 5

# The Empire Cuts Back

*From Coercive Government to Competitive Government*

---

The fact was that in Europe there were always some princes and local lords willing to tolerate merchants and their ways even when others plundered and expelled them; and, as the record shows, oppressed Jewish traders, ruined Flemish textile workers, persecuted Huguenots, moved on and took their expertise with them. A Rhineland baron who overtaxed commercial travelers would find that the trade routes had gone elsewhere, and with it his revenues. A monarch who repudiated his debts would have immense difficulties raising a loan when the next war threatened and funds were quickly needed to equip his armies and fleets.

---

*Paul Kennedy*[1]

YALE historian Paul Kennedy recently achieved international prominence for his book *The Rise and Fall of the Great Powers*, in which he identified America's decline as a world power.[2] While we and others disagree with his assessment that America has declined *relatively* in the world economy—we judge that all governments have lost power—we concur with a major point he made in the book: Mobile capital has historically been attracted to competitive govern-

84

ments, and governments, in turn, have nurtured the growth and mobility of commerce.[3] Kennedy specifies this relationship smartly in the words quoted above.

We explain in this chapter how our theory of competitive governments, founded on the mobility of capital and people, has had an honorable tradition in much political and economic thought that predates Kennedy. We also show how the growing complexity of modern economies, fueled by technology and the quicksilver acceleration of capital in the past twenty years, has forced governments to relinquish their dreams of centralized planning and has moved them to decentralize decision-making and become ever-more competitive in their policy selections and therefore more efficient. In this and following chapters we marshal evidence that supports the themes we have developed thus far—the reversal of the direction of technological growth, the explosive integration of global economic forces, and the unraveling of the forces of national economic interests—to show that many contemporary governments are, each in its distinctive way, beginning to emulate the behavior of Kennedy's competitive princes and local lords. These national governments are competing to attract mobile capital and are adapting to global markets to reduce the task of government to manageable proportions. This new synthesis of market and government forces is a development Marx never anticipated. However, what he and his intellectual offspring missed has not eluded other scholars on whose theoretical framework we depend and in whose work we see the distant origins of today's revolutionary changes.

## Capital Mobility and Competitive Governments in Western Political Economy

Scottish economist Adam Smith has long been known for his support of free markets and opposition to government intervention in markets.[4] Nevertheless Smith recognized that governments must have fundamental roles in society—namely, the definition and enforcement of property rights, the administration of justice, and the provision of public goods that would not be adequately provided by private entrepreneurs. At the same time, he, like so many of his followers, believed that government's powers must be strictly circumscribed, or else they might be misused and abused. And he appears to have understood that government powers are constrained by the mobility of capital. In his discussion of tax policy toward land and financial capital, he cautioned:

Land is a subject which cannot be removed, whereas stock easily may. The proprietor of land is necessarily a citizen of the particular country in which his estate lies. The proprietor of stock is properly a citizen of the world, and is not necessarily attached to any particular country. He would be apt to abandon the country in which he was exposed to a vexatious inquisition, in order to be assessed to a burdensome tax, and would remove his stock to some other country where he could either carry on his business, or enjoy his fortune at his ease. By removing his stock he would put an end to all the industry which it had maintained in the country which he left. Stock cultivates land; stock employs labour. A tax which tended to drive away stock from any particular country, would so far tend to dry up every source of revenue, both to the sovereign and to the society.[5]

Similarly, the Founding Fathers, many of whom had read Smith's *Wealth of Nations*, also recognized the constraining influence of economic forces on democratic politics.[6] The political forces opposed to the adoption of the U.S. Constitution, called the "antifederalists," included patriots who were more concerned than the Founders about the uncontrollable powers of a strong federal government.[7] The antifederalists worried that special interests would have undue power in the nation's capital. James Madison, one of the drafters of the Constitution, responded by acknowledging that he shared such fears but that the influence of "factions" would be greatly weakened,[8] if not neutralized, in the national government by competition among the factions:

The influence of the factious leaders may kindle a flame within their particular states but will be unable to spread a general conflagration through the other states. . . . A rage for paper money, for an abolition of debts, for an equal division of property, or for any other improper or wicked project, will be less apt to pervade the whole body of the Union than a particular member of it.[9]

The large number of factions at the national level, in other words, would make it difficult for majorities to form around intrusive federal legislation and would amount to a safeguard of the rights of minorities or majorities.

The Founders also sought to ensure that the federal government would be restrained by the economic forces they thought would be intrinsic to their governmental scheme, which they tagged a "compound republic," to describe the multiplicity of government units under the federal umbrella whose authority had strictly defined boundaries. The Founders reasoned that if the federal government were strictly limited, both by constitutional limitations on what it could and could not do and by the delegation of much governmental responsibilities to state and local governments, then individual human, political, and economic rights would be fortified against governmental abuse.[10]

Adhering to commonly accepted market principles of their day, the Founders also figured that competition among governments at the state and local levels would cap much government growth.[11] In selecting their policies, state and local governments would have to worry about the loss of their tax revenue bases, because people could "vote with their feet," or move to more congenial governmental venues.

Professor Vincent Ostrom has reworked the politicoeconomic theory of the Founding Fathers for modern audiences, emphasizing the concept and value of "competing governments."[12] Professor Ostrom argues that the Founders sought to fortify their political constitution with "competitive control" of state and local policies by ensuring, to a degree, their continued independence of one another. Hence, given intergovernmental competition for people and capital, state and local tax and regulatory policies would be restrained and, as a consequence, would be even more efficient and effective than otherwise. And it is worth noting that in the United States, tax rates at the federal level (where people, real capital, and financial assets are least mobile) are now higher than at the state level (where mobility is greater), and that tax rates at the state level are higher than at the local level (where mobility is typically highest).[13]

Modern public-choice economists have developed more formal models of the Founders' basic, intuitive model of the way governments are prone to work. These modern theorists also conclude that governments should, within limits, be expected to react to competition, or its absence, much like firms.[14] That is to say, pressed by the prospect of people "voting with their feet," governments should be expected to constrain their tax increases and to offer better, more efficient services.

## The Demand for and Supply of Government

Economists Geoffrey Brennan and James Buchanan have gone one step farther and have formalized a model of governmental behavior that, very likely, would have been highly congenial to Smith's and the Founders' way of thinking. Brennan and Buchanan have argued that democratic governments face demand and supply constraints, much like any private-market monopolist.[15]

Rightfully, a private-market monopolist, or single seller of a good or service, is recognized for its market power; but, it must be emphasized, the monopolist's market power is not unlimited. In order to maximize profits, a monopolist must realize that it faces a demand for its products that restrains its ability to raise its price. That is to say, the quantity sold will fall with an increase in price. Any monopolist must know that at some point a price hike will result in lower total revenues and that the price can be raised only so far before the reduction in its revenues, due to the curtailment of sales, exceeds the reduction in its costs. This means that at some point as price is increased profits will fall.

Most governments have traditionally not been thought of as being in the business of selling goods and services for a "price." This may be so because governments cannot always be concerned with choosing the profit-maximizing price and output levels. Many of the goods and services governments provide—such as national defense, police protection, and environmental programs—cannot be sold for a price. People benefit from such goods and services regardless of whether they pay. It is this fact, according to Brennan and Buchanan, as well as almost all other public-choice economists, that justifies granting governments the coercive power to tax in order to obtain the revenue needed to finance their activities. And given the power to tax, governments obviously do not have to be as concerned as private monopolists do with the public's demand for particular goods and services.

Nevertheless, according the Brennan/Buchanan model, governments do have a need for people to live (and to hold their assets, financial and real capital) within their respective jurisdictions and to earn incomes that are taxable. Additionally, it must be acknowledged that people have a demand for living and running their businesses in particular governmental jurisdictions, and that governments must cope with the demands of their citizens to earn livelihoods in their jurisdictions. Granted, people's demands for living and working in any governmental jurisdiction are founded on many considerations, not least of which are accidents of birth, cultural background, and earning potential (which can be said of the demand for almost any good or service bought in private markets). Still, their decision to enter and/or remain in any particular jurisdiction can be influenced to a meaningful degree by government policies—most prominently tax and regulatory policies.

Brennan and Buchanan argue that taxes (and regulations) amount to "prices" government charges for the right of residence. Of course, just like private-market prices, higher taxes (and regulatory costs) can reduce the net long-run benefits from hard work and can reduce the inclination of citizens to work, save, and prosper in the future in their particular government jurisdiction. Higher taxes (and regulatory costs) can also marginally reduce people's inclination to stay put.

In short, governments are just like their counterparts in private markets in one important respect: They face a demand constraint. The major difference between government and the private firm is that, in the case of government, the relevant demand is the willingness and ability of residents to live and earn their incomes (from which governments extract tax revenues) in a given jurisdiction.

How high any given government can push its taxes and regulation costs, regardless of how democratic its decision-making process is, depends crucially on people's responsiveness to the "tax price" that is charged (or on what economists technically call the "elasticity of demand"). And people's responsiveness to politically imposed tax-price changes depends upon their ability to escape the tax prices— that is, to move from taxable to nontaxable activities and/or from their current governmental jurisdiction to others.

Just like the private-market firm that has a degree of monopoly power, a government can only charge so much in the way of "tax prices" and "regulatory prices." It is quite possible for a government to charge "too much," in the sense that its tax and regulatory prices drive out so many people and their income-generating assets that total tax collections are reduced and the ability of the government to carry out desired social functions is impaired.

Furthermore, given the overall constraints on governmental powers implied in the Brennan/Buchanan model, tradeoffs among policy tools abound. If, for example, the government seeks to raise its tax prices in the form of tax rates on earned incomes, it must concede something in the way of less-demanding regulatory prices. An increase in taxes, without any offsetting decrease in regulatory costs, can drive capital and tax revenues away, making everyone in the country (or jurisdiction) worse off.

Obviously, as we have acknowledged, economic forces are not

all that matter in democracies. The constitutional rules of democracies—including the U.S. requirement that legislation must be passed by majority votes in both houses of Congress and signed by the president—can limit the tax and regulatory proclivities of governments. However, the essential point of the Brennan/Buchanan model is not disturbed by such an observation. Within the existing democratic constraints, economic forces—comprised by the capacity of citizens to move themselves and their assets elsewhere to alternative, competing governments—impose an additional, supplemental, or "auxiliary" (to use Madison's word), but nontrivial restraint on the policies that will be adopted.

It follows, as Brennan and Buchanan note in passing, that the more mobile capital and people are, the more responsive they can be to any given level of or change in tax rates (the more elastic their demands for living in any given government jurisdictions will be), and the more restrained governments must be in raising their taxes and regulations. We add that technology has increased people's responsiveness to tax-price changes (their elasticity of demand), the result of which should be more-competitive government policies. Our model of competitive governments has been implicitly, if not explicitly, assumed in many previous historical studies of government policies, one of the most notable recent being Paul Kennedy's.

## Competitive Provision of Property Rights in Western History

Economic historians Douglass North and Robert Thomas made much the same argument as Kennedy's, only years before, specifying the role of capital mobility in the rise of free Western society.[16] Working independently, North identified the vital role played by landed nobles who extended property rights to merchants and traders in return for revenues.[17] North sees the extension of property as a primary explanation for economic progress since the Late Middle Ages.[18]

North knew that feudalism was grounded in the cost of military protection of large landmasses by the powerful nobles. The Roman Empire, after all, had collapsed partly because the cost of maintaining its military force had become too great. And while he was aware that military power was crucial in determining the sizes of manors, North realized that the costs to the nobles of protecting their serfs and other property mitigated this military power: "As the number of inhabitants protected by the lord grew, however, the distance of farmed lands from the castle increased and eventually led to rising

costs of protection. . . . The 'efficient' size of the manor was determined at the point where the marginal cost of providing protection
equaled the value of the lord's share of the marginal product of
labor (that is, the tax)."[19]

This shift from a military to an economic source of power resulted
in the proliferation of a multitude of competing manors that, according
to North, then imposed a check on the extent to which the lords
could exploit their serfs through reneging on their bargains with the
serfs—protection in exchange for taxes. As North notes, labor became
scarce during this the period and, more importantly, "Lords were
frequently in competition for serfs and, accordingly, unlikely to return
a runaway serf. Therefore, the lord had an incentive to abide by
the contractual arrangement embedded in the custom of the manor
and to interpret them with 'restraint.' If he failed to do so, his serfs
might break the contract by fleeing the manor."[20]

Furthermore, the competition among manors and, later, among
the newly formed cities, escalated with the growth in the population
that fueled the "frontier movement," or the expansion of people
into unsettled areas. As population grew and spread, the increased
gains from trade reduced the costs of doing business (which North
and other economists call "transaction costs"). Landed lords, who
were often strapped for funds to maintain their military forces, began
to compete with each other by offering improved protection to merchants and traders through the extension of property rights under a
more settled body of land and commercial laws in England, Burgundy,
Champagne, France, as well as elsewhere in Western Europe: "Everywhere kings and princes were guaranteeing (for a fee) safe conduct
to traveling merchants, protecting alien merchants and providing them
with exclusive trading privileges, enforcing the judgments of commercial courts, and granting or delegating property rights to the burgeoning
towns."[21]

Of course, the kings and lords also sought to raise revenues by
devising and maintaining the local monopoly privileges of guilds to
protect local artisans, but their efforts to do so were often hampered
by the limited intergovernmental competition that prevailed at the
time, which the Hanseatic League sought to suppress: "Despite repeated efforts to regulate maximum wages, competition among land-
lords led to increasingly liberal terms for tenants as well as to rising
wages; as a consequence, the master-servant aspect of serfdom gave
way to recognition of copyhold rights and an end to servile obligations,
although it was not until 1666 in England that they were legally
swept away."[22]

Professor North goes on to note that Europe between 1300 and 1650 was characterized by cycles of wars, falling wages, widespread upheaval, and religious conflict, and that property rights were always subject to usurpation. When Charles VII assumed the French throne in 1422, his country was a nation-state in name only. A major portion of the country was controlled by the British, "marauding bands of unpaid soldiers preyed upon the countryside, and the great nobles engaged in seemingly endless squabbles."[23] Even though Charles was constantly pressed for additional revenues to reestablish law and order throughout the country, North reports, "The amounts that he could ask for and expect to receive were limited by the levels of taxation in competing English-occupied France and Burgundy."[24] Nonetheless, by offering the prospects of legally protected property rights, Charles was able to unify the country with effective police protection.

At the same time, his elimination of much competition among rival cities through the centralization of government powers within France enabled the nation-state to grow: "With a reduction in the power of external and internal rivals, the crown increased its ability to exact income from its constituents but was constrained by the cost of measuring wealth and income which were predominantly de-rived from local and regional production and trade."[25] Hence, in search of more revenues, the French nation-state began selling off exclusive local monopoly rights to the local guilds for a cut of the profits, all of which resulted in tax revenues increasing by twenty-twofold between 1470 and 1540.[26]

Spain adopted many of the same practices as did France—high rates of taxation, monopoly privileges, and property confiscation.[27] As a consequence economic growth in both France and Spain lan-guished. The Dutch and English, however, did not follow suit, al-though the Tudors in England tried. Indeed, the Dutch and English employed policies that encouraged trade: much lower taxes and fewer restrictions—many of which were effectively not enforced—on trade and commerce. The result was that trade and commerce flourished in the Netherlands and England. Professor North attributes the rela-tive success of economic development in the Netherlands and England to the creation and protection of private property rights.[28] It was emergence of these property rights that enabled modern democratic governments throughout the world to maintain order and encourage citizens to pursue economic well-being. What is curious is that Profes-sor North repeatedly points out the dependence of the Dutch and English on international trade but apparently overlooks that it may have been this international dependence that caused the Dutch and British to adopt the efficient policies, including the defense of private property, low tax rates, and patent laws, that he identifies as a major source of the relative success of their economies.

## Polanyi's Views on Haute Finance

Social philosopher Karl Polanyi, who, like Marx, fervently maintained that market economies would eventually self-destruct, argued that during the nineteenth century international financial forces were essential in circumscribing the political and military powers of European countries.[29] Indirectly the growing financial interdependence of countries during the nineteenth century ensured that there were no "general wars" for one of the longest stretches in history, the one hundred years between 1815 and 1914. In Polanyi's words, "The secret of the successful maintenance of general peace lay undoubtedly in the position, organization, and techniques of international finance."[30] Bankers financed both governments and private industry, at home and abroad, contributing a major fuel for the Industrial Revolution. This new so-called haute finance was independent of any government but indirectly influenced the policies of all governments. The international flow of funds became important to the governments themselves, especially those that borrowed heavily, and to the economic development of their countries. Financiers would counsel their governments that peace would be good for business, the national economy, and the government treasury. In addition, writes Polanyi, international finance had a more sobering indirect effect on policies. Financial flows, or the threat of them,

> acted as a powerful moderator in the councils and policies of a number of smaller sovereign states. Loans, and the renewal of loans, hinged upon credit, and credit upon good behavior. Since, under constitutional government (unconstitutional ones were severely frowned upon), behavior is reflected in the budget and the external value of the currency cannot be detached from the appreciation of the budget, debtor governments were well advised to watch their exchanges carefully and to avoid policies which might reflect upon the soundness of the budgetary position.[31]

Economic interests within countries favored policies that ensured peace because so much international trade, and hence the health of the domestic economies, depended on the international flow of funds and on the real resources that always tended to follow them.

The one-hundred-year peace ultimately broke down in 1914 because, according to Polanyi, the artificially contrived international economy, and the political world built on it, was utopian and could not continue to be "self-regulating," as Adam Smith said markets could be. The peace also broke down for political reasons, because "the Concert of Europe, that loose federation of independent powers [that were politically neutralizing one another in the name of private gain from peace], was finally replaced by two hostile power groupings."[32] Unfortunately, "Colonial rivalry and competition [among governments] for exotic markets became acute," facts that exacerbated long-standing hostilities between the two prevailing national groups.[33]

Because of rapidly rising domestic inflation rates, which contributed to the demise of the gold standard prior to World War I, the international economic system threatened to collapse, which resulted in a "cellular" process setting in: By the 1920s and 1930s, "nations found themselves separated from their neighbors, as by a chasm, while at the same time the various strata of the population were affected in entirely different and often opposite ways. The intellectual middle class was literally pauperized; financial sharks heaped up revolting fortunes. A factor of incalculable integrating and disintegrating force had entered the scene."[34]

Polanyi's hypothesized "great transformation" developed as national governments began to grow in the 1930s on the international seedbed of economic instability and in response to the disintegration of the international economy into "cellular" nations with less economic interdependence. From our perspective the cellular nature of the world can mean that nations had reacquired some monopoly power, which, as history shows, they exploited for several decades to follow.

## Baechler on Capitalism and Political Anarchy

French historian Jean Baechler begins his explanation of the origins of capitalism in the West from the Late Middle Ages with the familiar axiom that "all power tends toward the absolute."[35] He then adds, as we would, that "if [power] is not absolute, this is because some kind of limitation has come into play."[36] He cites the church and the "social elites" who are not beholden to the state as powerful restraints on the state's power. More important, Baechler takes the same path as Kennedy, North, and Thomas and suggests that capitalism developed in the West because of the fortuitous circumstance of "political pluralism"—independent states that permitted the shift of resources within the "homogeneity of cultural space" or what he also refers to as a "cultural whole." In short, Baechler emphasizes, *The expansion of capitalism owes its origins and its raison d'etre to political anarchy.*[37]

The broad Western cultural whole afforded entrepreneurs considerable latitude to conduct their affairs, meaning they were blessed with alternative, competitive national outlets for their investments. These entrepreneurs put "pressures on the State to take measures that were favorable to them," which can be interpreted to mean that with political competition economic liberties were broadened and the national economies, and capitalism, flourished.[38] Baechler fortifies his basic hypothesis with reference to the experience of Byzantium from the seventh through the eleventh century. Byzantium never experienced political pluralism, only extensive state controls, and capitalism never flourished there.[39] However, imperial China was a dramatically different case. Whenever imperial China was politically divided, which it was at the end of the Tang and during the Sung period, or from the second half of the eighth to the thirteenth century, "a victory of provincial particularism would enable economic activities to spring to life," mainly because the "provincial particularism" included the relaxation of centralized government controls on the separate economies.[40]

Similarly, capitalism flourished in Japan partially because of its own brand of political pluralism or, rather, "dualism," installed as early as the sixth century, in the form of one central government surrounded by multiple principalities. However, the emperor, or *tenno*, at the head of the central government had no meaningful economic power and he (like the central government he represented) was hardly more than a "symbol of cultural unity." Japan prospered because of that cultural unity, which grew with interprovincial trade and the continuing "dispersal of power among rival principalities."[41]

## A Revised Interpretation of the Rise and Fall of Mercantilism

Several public-choice economists, most prominently Barry Basinger, Robert Ekelund, and Robert Tollison, have reexamined the economic origins and demise of mercantilism, the system of extensive state controls imposed by states on the economies of Europe from roughly 1500 to 1776, and have found that conventional explanations that emphasize the desire to hoard gold may be misleading.[42] Traditionally, historians and economists have contended that mercantilism was rooted in nationalism, or the drive of the state and its citizens to increase their countries' wealth, which was closely identified with their gold holdings.

In contrast, Basinger, Ekelund, and Tollison maintain that mercantilist policies were the political consequences of rent-seeking special interest groups, concerned not so much about national wealth as their own private gain, enhanced by government-supported restrictions on market competition. This new theory of mercantilism overlaps our own model of competing governments in several important respects.

First, these three economists reason that "prior to the centralization of authority [in fifteenth-century Europe under monarchs], rent seekers had to deal with a multitude of feudal rulers, which made the costs of negotiating and enforcing exclusive [monopolistic production and trading] rights relatively higher."[43] They show that the more costly the rent seeking, the less the rent seeking and the fewer the government-backed market controls (for example, import restrictions) that would result.[44] Under feudalism entrepreneurs were too fearful that they would pay a great deal to the feudal lords for their favored restrictions and then not obtain sufficient benefits. This was so because the restrictions covered a relatively small area and because restrictions in one principality could easily drive trade elsewhere.

Similarly, these writers discovered that mercantilism did not break down in the late eighteenth century because of an upsurge of popular opposition to the economic costs of controls per se or because of the publication of Adam Smith's *Wealth of Nations*, which explained the folly of mercantilist controls. On the contrary, mercantilism dissolved, according to Basinger, Ekelund, and Tollison, because political authority was shifted from monarchs toward representative democracies and parliaments: "The costs of lobbying a representative body are higher than the costs of lobbying a unified monarchy for monopoly charters because there are more decision makers rather than one. . . . [W]e would therefore expect to see a decline of government interference in the economy because of the higher costs."[45]

In the case of England, there was an additional problem for the would-be rent seekers: "There was an important jurisdictional competition between the common law courts and those supporting the king's interest."[46] Any monopoly restriction granted by the king might be, and often was, nullified by the common-law courts. As a result, the rent seekers were hesitant to make the political investment required to obtain the restrictions.

We see this rent-seeking reinterpretation of mercantilism as offering historical support to our own theory of competing governments. First, it holds that extensive mercantilist controls only arose when many competing governments were eliminated. In this regard the historical evidence provided on the origins of extensive government controls corroborates modern econometric studies that have found that government consolidation leads to more extensive government influence in the economy. Second, this mercantilist theory suggests that competitive politics, which is a form of decentralization of government power among competing government leaders, leads to fewer government controls over economic activity and that competing governments, in the limited form of overlapping court jurisdictions, also lead to fewer economic restrictions.

However, aside from suggesting that members of parliaments began to covet the ability of the monarchs to sell off newly created market restrictions, this revised view of mercantilism does not explain fully why political power shifted from monarchs to parliaments. We argue that these monarchical economies had simply become inefficient and uncompetitive in the eighteenth century due to growing international trade, capital mobility, and economic integration at the national nation-state level.

## Modern Government Competitiveness: Econometric Evidence

If the historical studies we have cited provide one stream of evidence to support the relation between capital mobility and competitive markets, composed of entrepreneurs of governments, another persuasive source of evidence is the federal, multilevel government structure of the United States. However, a word of caution is in order. By reporting data on relative tax rates of the three levels of government in the United States in the studies we are about to cite, with no adjustments for the influence of other forces, we are certainly attributing more power to government competitiveness than is warranted. We are the first to recognize that these other forces, such as the need for more government services at the various levels, have just as certainly influenced the structure of these governments.

No matter. The studies that follow have employed statistical techniques for sorting out the role of competitiveness from other factors
and help us to better grasp the strategies by which governments are
reshaping themselves in response to market forces.

The econometric literature that tests the theory of competitive
government policies has grown dramatically over the past two decades,
and much of it demonstrates that when citizens have the opportunity
to move from one jurisdiction to another, as they do in the United
States, competition among governments for these people and their
capital will tend to improve government services and contain government costs.

Studies undertaken since the mid-1970s by Richard Cebula
and others on local American governments show that people have
moved to municipalities that supply more cost-effective nonwelfare
public services. They have also left, albeit less consistently, municipalities with relatively higher tax rates.[47]

The theory of competitive governments implies that in an effort
to avoid undue levels and costs of government services approved
by local majorities with different preferences, people will tend to
move and sort themselves among government jurisdictions. People
with, say, above-average incomes may sort themselves among local
governments by income because they want to live among other people
with similar backgrounds and interests and, therefore, are interested
in similar types and levels of local government services and because
they may want to avoid being taxed for the benefit of lower-income
groups.

The end result of this sorting process should be greater homogeneity by income in groups of people living in different municipalities. Between 1950 and 1970, people's ability to move did indeed
increase. In the case of the municipalities within Los Angeles County,
the results of the increased mobility were as expected. While income
disparity remained high across the whole of Los Angeles County,
the incomes of people living within particular government jurisdictions
within the county became more homogeneous.[48] Similar results have
been found by other researchers who explore the effects of citizen
migration in alternative collections of governments—for example,
voter migration among multiple school districts and between central
cities and their suburban areas.[49]

How does all this sorting of citizens by migration among local
government jurisdictions affect local government policies and the
quality and cost of their services? Robert Deacon studied the expendi-

tures made by sixty-four cities within the Los Angeles area on police and street maintenance in the early 1970s.[50] Some of these cities contracted out their police and street maintenance services to other cities or private firms, while the rest bought their services from their own internal government departments. The former group availed themselves of more competition in the provision of police and street maintenance services than did the latter. As expected, Deacon found that after adjusting for municipal differences (like population and mean income), those cities that contracted out services had police costs of only 58 percent those of cities that did not contract out. Their street maintenance costs were 70 percent the costs of non-contracting-out cities. Furthermore, the overall total expenditures of the contracting-out cities were also significantly less, equal to 86 percent those of the non-contracting-out cities. The message from the Deacon study is obvious: Competition with other cities or private firms tends to make local governments more efficient, a point that has been confirmed by other studies.[51]

Economists have traditionally argued that restrictions on entry into markets—which, until deregulation in 1978, existed in the U.S. airline industry—grant the existing firms in those markets a degree of monopoly power; that is, the ability to restrict output, maintain prices, and collect profits that are higher than competitive levels. Such firms do not have to worry about potential rivals coming into the market, because the latter cannot do so except possibly at dangerously high cost. With the elimination of entry restrictions, we would expect prices to fall, which did in fact occur in the U.S. airline industry.[52]

If our theory of competing governments is correct, these points should also apply to governments as well as markets.[53] That is, restrictions on entry into the government should grant existing governments a degree of monopoly power, which they should attempt to exploit. Economists Dolores Martin and Richard Wagner observed in a 1978 study that the state of California imposed severe limitations on the ability of its citizens to break away from existing local government entities and to incorporate as new local governments.[54] Martin and Wagner found that after adjusting for differences among areas, the California "government entry restriction" led to higher costs for local government services, and higher taxes. They discovered that when the existing government competitors were unchallenged, they did what came naturally: They restricted services but raised taxes. The researchers concluded: "Competition where it exists [has] the same salutary effect on efficiency that competition among firms does."[55] This point has been confirmed by subsequent studies of the competitiveness of local governments.[56]

Consider another aspect of possible local government competition: School districts in the United States depend on tax revenues to provide a public service within specified jurisdictions, and they have a degree of monopoly power that can be enhanced through consolidations. They have gone through a consolidation binge since the beginning of World War II. Between 1940 and 1988, the number of school districts declined dramatically from more than 117,000 to fewer than 16,000. Why?

Many of these consolidations were proposed on the grounds that they would achieve economies of scale, which would result in cost savings. However, a number of studies have found that significant diseconomies of scale occur when school districts reach about 2,000 students.[57] Two researchers have found that student achievement levels go down when school district size goes up,[58] and another has found that the number of administrators tends to rise faster with consolidation of districts than does the number of students, which caused him to conclude that school districts have consolidated simply to increase and exploit their own monopoly power.[59]

More generally, researchers have argued that the growth of different governments within a particular country can be expected to be limited by the form of those governments embraced by the country in question. The more competitive the structure, the more constrained the growth, or so one would expect. The federal government structure embraced by the United States is one prominent form of competitive government structure that should limit government growth. Comparative studies show that it does: A federalist government structure tends to throttle the growth of governments, everything else being equal.[60]

## Taxing Decisions: Competitive Governments Respond to Capital Mobility

Increased capital mobility has enabled citizens and businesses to respond more readily and with greater ease to tax or regulatory price hikes and has allowed them to move themselves and their assets to other jurisdictions where tax prices are lower. Hence, as our theory goes in its simplest form, whenever a government jurisdiction raises taxes or regulations, capital will depart and the jurisdiction's income will decrease.

To see this more clearly, consider the following example: A government that charges a tax of 30 percent may believe its national tax base and tax collections to be secure so long as people find movement difficult (or costly), in spite of the fact that other governments charge 20 percent. However, if people become highly mobile and are able to move assets easily (or at less cost) to government jurisdictions that charge lower rates, the government charging 30 percent has to fear that at least a part of its income base will move and that its total tax collections will fall.[61] It must consider giving its citizens greater value in services for the dollars collected in taxes, lowering its tax price, and attracting even more capital from other governments.

Before the recent increase in capital mobility, our hypothetical government may rightfully have figured that a tax reduction from 30 to 25 percent of income would lead to an inflow of people and capital and would thereby raise aggregate national income from $1 to $1.1 trillion, resulting in a reduction in tax collections from $300 to $275 billion. However, with the enhancement of mobility, the inflow of people and capital could be great enough to raise expected national income to $1.3 trillion and to raise total tax collections to $325 billion.

Obviously, our example proves nothing about the actual behavior of governments. However, the central point, which the example merely illustrates, is not dependent upon the particulars of the examples. Simply stated, greater capital mobility incorporates a nontrivial, potentially powerful inducement for governments to at least consider lowering their tax prices. Ongoing improvements in capital mobility would therefore make the inducement irresistible to *some* governments interested in raising their citizens' aggregate income and their own tax collections. Just like competitors in private markets, individual governments must also fear that if they do not lower their tax prices in light of greater capital mobility, other governments will.

In other words, enhanced capital mobility threatens governments with a "damned if I do, damned if I don't" predicament, whose net effect is a greater likelihood of these governments lowering their tax prices. When this greater likelihood translates into actual tax reductions (which we think has happened, given the evidence assembled in following chapters), the tax prices with the greatest impact on mobile capital are those that are most affected. This means reductions in the high marginal tax rates on incomes generated from capital both physical and human. To offset the revenue effects of lower marginal tax rates on top incomes, governments often change the progressivity of their tax rate structure, or flatten it out, raising the marginal tax rates on the lower income brackets.[62]

While recent changes in the tax code of the United States and many other countries around the world have been caused by myriad factors, it is interesting to note that real-world tax-code changes observed notably by Vito Tanzi, the late Joseph Pechman, and Alan Reynolds are consistent with the theory of competing governments.[63] Many policy analysts have conjectured that flatter tax codes in the United States have mirrored the ideology of Ronald Reagan and Margaret Thatcher. We can only emphasize that enhanced capital mobility certainly preceded the Reagan/Thatcher supply-side tax policies and perhaps caused these leaders to find sympathetic support in their respective countries for the tax strategies they pursued.

### Economic Complexity: Hayek and Sowell on Government Competitiveness

A recurring theme in the life's work of Nobel laureate Friedrich Hayek is captured in the truly simple but easily overlooked observation that bears directly on the need for governments to compete:

> Knowledge exists only as the knowledge of individuals. It is not much better than a metaphor to speak of the knowledge of society as a whole. The sum of the knowledge of all the individuals exists nowhere as an integrated whole. The great problem is how we can all profit from this knowledge, which exists only dispersed as the separate, partial, and sometimes conflicting beliefs of all men.[64]

That "knowledge exists nowhere as an integrated whole" is the bane of centralized governments. This is so because these governments, by necessity, rely on collective decision-making. To govern effectively, government decision makers must seek to centralize this information that is necessarily and broadly dispersed. In order to make policy, these decision makers must then pretend that the information they have assembled is an accurate representation of the dispersed knowledge from which it flows, which it can never be.

Regrettably for these governments, their officers can deal only with so many facts and comprehend only so many technical, political, and economic relationships. Governments have only limited resources at their disposal for gathering information, organizing and analyzing it, extracting conclusions from their analyses, and administering the state.

The problem of dispersed information does not mean that centralized governments cannot govern at all. Obviously they do govern. It does mean, however, that the effectiveness of these governments will necessarily be impaired by the size and scope of the polity and economy they are attempting to govern. Reinterpreted, Hayek's basic point is that the more complex the economy and the more centralized the government, the more information relevant to decisions will be ignored when those decisions are made. Given their limited resources for centralized administration, these governments attempt to manage broad sectors of the population by describing them according to such abstract categories as "average attributes," "central tendencies," "large firms," "basic industries." For all their arbitrary imperfections, these abstract categories at least enable such governments to get a handle on the task of governing.

By imposing environmental or plant-closing restrictions on large firms—such as those with more than one hundred workers—government officials are able in this instance to reduce the problem of directing the country's labor relations to manageable levels. By classifying goods and services within broad categories—drugs, for example—and by imposing rules on their use regardless of popular preference, those same officials ease the problems inherent in managing a consumer economy. No governments have worked harder at centralized administration, or failed more miserably, than those of the Communist countries. The Soviet Union and many other centrally planned economies know all the problems associated with over-zealous central administration: They go by the names of *retarded economic growth, stagnant technological development, product shortages,* and *misallocation of resources.* As economist Thomas Sowell observed in extending Professor Hayek's basic point:

> The limitations and distortions of articulation revolve around the simple fact that third-party central planners cannot know what users want. . . . It is not merely the enormous amount of data that exceeds the capacity of the human mind. Conceivably, this data can be stored in a computer with sufficient capacity. The real problem is that the knowledge needed is knowledge of *subjective patterns of trade-offs that are*

*nowhere articulated*, not even to the individual himself. . . . There is
no way for such information to be fed into a computer, when no one
has such information in the first place.[65]

Unfortunately for government officials, when technology increases
the sophistication and complexity of production techniques and goods
and multiplies the number and variety of services, the "subjective
patterns of trade-offs that are nowhere articulated" become even
less accessible to central authorities.

However government planners solve their decision-making problems, added complexity in the production and consumption of goods
and services makes it even more unlikely that they can make decisions
that increase, rather than decrease, the collective well-being. There
is a paradox here that was fully recognized by Professor Hayek, who
noted prophetically:

> The more men know, the smaller the share of all that knowledge
> becomes that any one mind can absorb. The more civilized we become,
> the more relatively ignorant must each individual [including each gov-
> ernment worker] be of the facts on which the working of his civilization
> depends. The very division of knowledge increases the necessary igno-
> rance of the individual of most of this knowledge.[66]

The information demands of growing complexity cause private
decision makers to reduce their own information requirements by
dividing up production and consumption tasks, which invariably
means that the "information of the whole" can never be controlled
by any one person and is held ever more broadly in small parts by
everyone.[67] In our modern integrated, electronically connected world
economy, the information of the whole is necessarily spread throughout the world and its more than five billion inhabitants, and no single
government—not even a superpower—controls directly more than a
small fraction of the world's population.

Inevitably, growing complexity in production and consumption,
and the resulting economic integration, reduces the capacity of government planners to make tolerably acceptable (not to mention efficient)
decisions and to retain their centralized control. Interested in securing
revenues from their economies, and faced with growing complexity
of products and markets, these governments are under pressure to
decentralize decision-making, which means relinquishing some measure of control to lower-level governments, spinning off activities to

private producers, and simply not trying to do as much and letting those who have the requisite information take charge of their lives and economies.

The full force of our position need not be accepted in order to appreciate the basic proposition: If modern technological developments cause economies to rely on more specialized, sophisticated, and complicated knowledge spread over a greater number of people, central governments must, at some point, become relatively less important in their economies. Central government powers should be delegated to a greater number of lower-level governments, and there we should expect greater competition among the larger number of governmental units. The growing complexity of production reinforces the growing mobility of capital and economic integration of economies in forcing governments to carry out their functions more efficiently—and more competitively—with less reliance on centralized collective decision-making and more reliance on decentralized individual decision-making. Growing economic complexity simply makes reliance on markets all the more productive and likely.

## Modern Mercantilists and Competitive Governments

Just as the rise of international trade in the eighteenth century squelched the rent-seeking mercantilists of that time and produced a wave of free democratic capitalism, today's capital mobility is undercutting the modern mercantilists on Capitol Hill and in Westminster. Competitive constraints on governments amount to constraints on what people can do through their governments. Much government mischief comes from special-interest groups whose advocates are disproportionally represented in the halls of legislatures. Modern technology, on which growing capital mobility is founded, has checked the influence of such interest groups in two principal ways. First, as public choice economist Mancur Olson has argued, special interest groups thrive in eras of political stability mainly because they can make their investments in developing and fortifying their political contacts and in seeing installed government programs (from farm subsidies to import quotas) that earn rents for their groups' membership.[68] Olson was right to point out that, although devastating in many obvious ways, wars and natural catastrophes harbor the potential for at least beneficial side effects for society: They can undercut the political and economic systems so badly that they destroy the value of past investments, both in real property and political contacts, and can break the stranglehold that interest groups have on the political process and therefore the domestic economy. Olson, however, failed to realize that technology, although less dramatic than a war or an earthquake, could just as assuredly break the political grips of interest groups. Technology can give rise to new methods and sources of competition that were not envisioned when special-interest government programs were past. For example, when Congress gave the post office a monopoly on first-class mail, it probably never thought about the prospects of competition springing from overnight air delivery services and fax machines.

In addition Olson does not appear to have realized that technological improvements can undermine the balance of existing political forces by creating more viable political interest groups, thus moving us toward the fulfillment of the Madisonian vision of government being constrained by the multitude of "factions," or special-interest groups. As did Olson, Madison saw the ability of organized interest groups to capture government privileges, but he also saw competition among the factions as a limitation on the ultimate influence of each faction. Technology is abetting this competition and is moving the world toward, in Baechler's words, one homogeneous "cultural space" within which people can move much more freely.

While it is no doubt true that in the past the political power of any one interest group has, to some extent, come at the expense of a reduction in the political power of other interest groups, to a larger degree the political success of organized interest groups has come at the expense of the unorganized public. Having diverse interests and being geographically dispersed, the public has found it far more costly in the past to organize for the purpose of speaking with one clear political voice in opposition to special interest groups on policies that cost more than they are worth. As a consequence, a relatively small number of dairy farmers, for example, have been able to pass laws that legally restrict the supply of milk and increase dairy prices and profits—and reduce the purchasing power of the public's incomes.

While it will always be less costly for a relatively small and unified group with a common interest to organize for political action than it will be for the general public to do so, technologies that are becoming widely available are reducing this cost gap. With fax machines, computer networking, teleconferencing, and desktop publishing, the cost of organizing any size group has been reduced. But by allowing large, diverse groups to organize at all, the new technology has dramatically lowered, relatively speaking, the organizing costs of large groups relative to that of small, single-interest groups which have always been able to organize. And, of course, to be effective, the general public does not have to be as well organized in opposition to special-interest legislation as the narrow special-interest group has to be in support of that legislation. The general public has a massive number of votes on its side.

In short, technology has enhanced the relative political weight of the general interest of the larger voting public, vis a vis all of the various narrow concerns of special interest lobbies. Hedrick Smith recognized the growing problems faced by traditional Washington-based interest groups when in 1988 he wrote:

> Old-breed lobbying . . . thrives on an aura of influence, a promise of the inside track, the hint of priceless contacts. . . . The new-breed game reflects the organized changes in American politics and the institutional changes in Congress. Its medium is mass marketing; its style is packaging issues; its hallmark is wholesale lobbying. New Breed lobbying borrows heavily from the techniques of the political campaigns, with their slick P.R., television advertising, orchestrated coalitions, targeted mass mailings, and their crowd of activists.[69]

Naturally, well-organized interests will often effectively exploit the opportunities offered by the new technology to engage in "new-breed" lobbying for purposes that expand government programs and increase the scope of government waste. On balance, however, new-breed lobbying has forced greater restraint in government. The technology on which new-breed lobbying is based is already highly democratizing in the sense that it is becoming increasingly available to all interest groups, including those in remote places in the country, not just those that are well situated in Washington. A fax machine is likely to be more important to an interest group in Bozeman, Montana than one in Washington simply because the interest group in Bozeman does not have the option of walking to Capitol Hill and talking directly with members of Congress.

Accordingly, interest groups that are economically harmed by bills designed to help another group can quickly find out about the potential harm, even though they may not be in Washington, and can more effectively countervail than they once could against the proponents of the legislation. In other words, the new technology expands the number of factions in politics and increases the likelihood that the influence of the factions will be offsetting, as Madison thought they would be.

There are other important reasons why technology and capital mobility have undermined the power of governments to respond to even the most well-heeled, unscrupulous factions. Faced with a more responsive citizenry and more elastic demands for the services of governments, governments are now less able to respond to special-interest political demands, even when accompanied by political contributions and bribes. Inefficient policies that reflect favoritism—such as import quotas for steel that drive up the domestic price of steel—will be reflected in an erosion of the capital base by those groups who do not get the political favors and, as a consequence, must suffer the tax costs of the political favors granted others—such as the steel-using industries in the domestic economy that are forced by worldwide competition to move their plants abroad.

Given the potential for capital flight, interest groups now reason that, more than ever, their own members will in the long run suffer at least some of the consequences of their own politically-induced market inefficiencies or redistributive policies. Policies that are designed to benefit a particular interest will tend to drive away those groups that are harmed (through taxes or market restrictions), leaving the special-interest groups that have engineered the harmful policies to suffer a greater share, if not all, of the costs.

To the extent that the costs of political mischief are borne by the perpetrators, and to the extent that politicians themselves are harmed by yielding to the demands of interest groups, the political process should be less encumbered, if certainly not completely unencumbered, by political maneuvering for private gain—rent seeking. Interest groups are now less able and willing to bribe or pay off, directly or indirectly, politicians or, what may be much the same thing, to make contributions to political campaigns for special legislative favors.[70] Political bribes, payoffs, kickbacks, and contributions are simply less productive. The contraction of rent seeking in a relative, if not absolute, sense should, at some point, deplete resources tied up in redistributive and predatory efforts within the political process. The rent-seeking pressure on the political process to expand government activities should be reduced, resulting in a suppressed growth of government.[71]

Relatively more resources will then become available for the private production of goods and services. The net consequence of the suppression of rent seeking by worldwide competitive forces implies a slower growth in the relative size of government—if not a retrenchment of the relative size of government in the economy.

Government itself is now growing more slowly in absolute real terms, and the private sector of the economy, with more resources to work with, may grow relatively more rapidly in real terms.[72]

## Subverting Coercion; Supporting Competition

Governments around the world continue to maintain considerable economic clout. More than 40 percent of the national production of the United States is run through government at some level. Several governments in Europe are conduits for more than half of their domestic production. Nothing we have written is intended to deny these obvious facts.

Our analysis relates chiefly to what is happening at the margin to the powers of government to tax and to grow relative to the entire economy. We have sought to make one simple overriding point. Ongoing international competitive forces—predicated to a significant degree on technological developments that are increasing capital mobility and the economic complexity of production and consumption—should be expected to constrain the fiscal and regulatory powers of government and thereby make government more competitive. This does not mean that future growth in many governments is ruled out. What it does mean is that, whatever its past status, the power to grow through political means alone has been moderated. Where governments continue to grow, their growth rate will be slowed by world economic forces. For some governments under some conditions, growth may be altogether capped; in the future (when capital mobility has reached an advanced stage), growth of some governments may actually be reversed.[73]

The prospect of an actual decline in government may be a highly optimistic outlook, although some governments' influence in their economies has already begun to recede. The deregulation and privatization movement that spans Western *and* Eastern economies is ample testimonial to the decline in government power and authority. The shifts toward freer markets in almost all former Communist countries dramatizes the power of the technological forces we have identified to undermine the capacity of governments to control and manage their economies.

As we have said, suppression of a government's economic powers can easily extend beyond that government's fiscal powers. Indeed, everything said about tax powers can be applied, in principle, to government regulatory powers. Both tax and regulatory powers of governments impose costs on human and physical capital—to a lesser or greater extent and with lesser or greater visibility. Capital can be induced to migrate in response to all imposed costs that are not offset by demonstrated service benefits, regardless of their source, whether by regulations or by taxes. As a consequence capital mobility also circumscribe and suppress the regulatory powers of governments.[74] For this reason we believe it is no coincidence that the deregulatory and tax reform movements emerged more or less together in the 1970s.

Furthermore, governments, faced with tightening economic constraints, now try to circumvent those constraints by the substitution of covert methods of taxation for overt methods. Initially governments have, in effect, imposed taxes by regulations, to the extent that such regulations obscure or obfuscate the costs of government objectives. More specifically, they have sought to achieve political objectives for, say, workers by requiring firms to provide "mandated benefits" (for example, health insurance) instead of trying to provide them through higher taxes and an expanded government bureaucracy.

Finally, it is no surprise to us that the worldwide movement to privatize government services has accompanied the worldwide deregulatory and tax reform movements. Strapped for additional revenues to finance expanded services and confronted with the growing complexity of governing a more sophisticated economy, governments must pull back and spin off inefficient, loss-generating government services and must do more effectively those things that can attract and retain the capital base governments need in order to generate their revenues.

## Tiananmen Square Revisited

The year 1989 brought the impact of the new technological dialectic, and its limited consequences for government power, home to television watchers and political leaders around the globe in a most ironic way. In May of that year, more than a million students demonstrated in Tiananmen Square in central Beijing, China. They openly flouted Premier Li Peng's threats to bring in troops—and the world watched it all in vivid color on television.

Surely China's leaders would have preferred to quell the demonstrations in the old-fashioned way, secretly. The leaders obviously preferred to keep the rest of the country in the dark concerning events in Tiananmen Square through traditional controls on the press, and they tried to orchestrate the news blackout. However, by 1989 technology was easily able to penetrate the news controls. Many foreign broadcasts, both television and radio, of events in Tiananmen Square could be picked up in China. Chinese students and relatives in the United States and elsewhere kept their friends and family members back home partially informed through repeated phone calls and faxes of news articles from papers outside China. In the words of editors at the *Wall Street Journal:*

> Telecommunications now ensures that huge populations of people find out quickly what works and what fails. In our time, it has let them learn and believe that democratic markets work and that totalitarian socialism fails. . . . For much of this century, when markets were developing, they could get away with totalitarian brutalism as a form of government. The distance between the world's competing political forces was large economically, but still close enough in some relative sense to allow the Communist bloc leadership of the Soviet Union and China to exercise significant world power and influence.
>
> Now that is waning. Because the West created extraordinary innovations in telecommunications and computer-driven technologies, all of its activities—the production and distribution of goods, services and information—have begun to occur at an exponentially more rapid rate. The countries that are plugged in are pulling away; those that aren't are falling behind. . . .
>
> Whether its leaders want it or not, China was globalized last week. The integrating network of political economies is a system that requires the free flow of opinions as much as it does the free flow of financial transactions.[75]

The unfolding events in China made that point, which is central to our argument, perfectly clear. Shortly after the *Wall Street Journal* ran the just-cited editorial, Chinese troops literally blew away many of the demonstrating students. At least 800, and maybe several thousand, students were killed. Several student leaders were summarily arrested and executed, all within a matter of a couple of weeks.

Governments, such as in Beijing, still have the guns and authority for control, which can be used for good and bad purposes. Our point is not that they cannot use them at all. Rather, our message is that governments must now use their guns and authority more tentatively and with greater reserve. As never before, China is dependent on outside capital, technology, and management skills. That dependency means that Chinese leaders have had to endure the residual effects of the Tiananmen Square demonstrations far longer they would have liked and had to be far less barbaric than they have been in past episodes of domestic unrest. China's leaders have also had to suffer a turnaround in the willingness of investors around the world to do business in their country. In 1988 the world's capitalists were all eagerly knocking on China's economic doors, wanting to get a foothold in the massive Chinese market and fill the void left by the lack of domestic financial capital. In the last half of 1989, after the Tiananmen Square massacre, China was closing down planned development projects—for example, a $2 billion iron mill, power plant, and improvements in the telephone system in Jiangsu province, the country's "showcase" coastal manufacturing center—for lack of foreign investment. With the killings the cost of foreign capital rose precipitously, adding hundreds of millions of dollars to the cost of important projects.[76]

We are not so naive as to think that the Chinese leaders will suddenly shed all their old ways of governance. However, the turnaround in investors' attitudes must certainly be forcing the country's leaders to think more earnestly about more civil ways of dealing with internal dissent. In this least competitive of regimes, we can at least hope that capital mobility will make leaders think twice about future coercive actions. This is the singular legacy of the rise of competitive governments in the West.

# 6

# The Invisible Hand of Global Competition Contains the Visible Hand of Government Fiscal and Regulatory Powers

Countries, like companies, must compete in producing the most value at the lowest possible cost. Taxes are an important part of the cost of production, as well as the cost of living. Since people have to produce more in order to earn more, a tax system which penalizes added income will also penalize added output. It is relatively insignificant whether taxes are direct or indirect, corporate or personal. Capital and labor bear all taxes, either through lower incomes or higher prices. . . . Any country in which the marginal cost of government is not competitive will experience a loss of both real capital (a capital outflow) and human capital (a "brain drain").[1]

*Alan Reynolds*
Senior Economist,
Hudson Institute

ECONOMISTS argue that competition coordinates the behavior of market rivals—that in their efforts to serve their own private goals, buyers and sellers seek to outmaneuver all others in their markets. The result of competition is a form of "spontaneous order" characterized by relentless pressures to allocate resources into those activities in which they generate the most value.

Nevertheless, at all times the economic interests of buyers and sellers remain in conflict. Buyers seek more of the desired goods and preferred services on the most favorable terms. Similarly, sellers seek to maximize sales on the most favorable terms. The exact terms of the market exchanges—which include but are not limited to prices—are determined by the competitors in search of the best available deals. As if by an "invisible hand," to use Adam Smith's characterization, resources and goods and services are developed, made, and moved by way of exchanges to where they are more useful.[2]

Competition in private markets is easily understood. This is so mainly because it is easy to imagine buyers and sellers operating in close proximity of one another—each trying to outdo one another and each possessing little or no monopoly power to control market outcomes. Participants must, in effect, "go with the flow" of market forces—they must compete.

Understanding the same kind of competition among world governments is more difficult, however, principally because governments are known to be sovereign—a characteristic not normally associated with competitors. Governments fit the mold of geographically isolated monopolies, and often very powerful ones at that. Governments have distinct boundaries, harbor the coercive power of taxation, and define their own policies with all the ostensible trappings of political independence.

Nonetheless, as economists have long recognized, the power of competitors to control events in their markets can never be gauged in absolute terms. General Motors may be very large absolutely, but GM still has to compete, because of its competitors in the markets as well as potential competitors threatening to enter its markets. GM's absolute size is always threatened by what its smaller rivals are willing and able to do to become larger at GM's expense. And GM's size remains threatened to the extent that its customers and suppliers (including GM shareholders who supply capital and workers who supply labor) are mobile, meaning they can invest and work elsewhere. In establishing its strategies, GM must at least implicitly consider the mobility of its customers and suppliers.

We make these introductory remarks regarding private competitors like GM in order to drive home a point about the ways in which competitive market forces influence government behavior. Governments may be much more powerful than the businesses that operate within their jurisdictions. But at the same time, governments' power is circumscribed by the mobility of the human and physical capital within their jurisdictions, just as businesses' power is constrained by the mobility of their suppliers and customers.

Governments cannot ignore the economic consequences of growing mobility just as GM cannot ignore them. In modern times most governments may not have to fear a loss of territory (except in the rare instances of succession), but they do have to fear a loss of their economies, now more than ever dependent on resources other than so much turf. Not only must governments be concerned about the ability of people to move their bodies, their brains, and their business abroad, they must now worry about mobility in a less-traditional sense: Advanced technology has made it easier for people to move their resources from the aboveground to the underground economy through illegal tax evasion, from the taxed to the untaxed economy through perfectly legal tax avoidance, from capital goods to consumer goods. In effect this means that governments must now compete not only with other national economies, but with other whole economies that can spring up within their own territories and can remain out of sight and beyond the grasp of tax collectors. As a result we now see governments acting more like market rivals in their struggle to retain and expand their capital bases. We see them selecting policies more strategically—that is, with greater concern for the international consequences of their actions, with more care, with less abandon, with greater concern for economic efficiency, and with a longer-term view.

The absolute growth or size of the budgets of governments will not necessarily contract. After all, governments might grow to accommodate the needs of more citizens and expanding economies. However, the growth of governments relative to their economies is waning in the advent of growing competitiveness.

## Comparative Economic Policies: The Data and Their Limitations

In this chapter we direct our analysis toward the actual competitive economic policies adopted in countries around the world. Here we direct our analysis toward the fiscal and regulatory records of

the major industrial countries other than the United States and the
Soviet Union, which we consider separately in following chapters.

However, like most data, these data are inherently limited.
They do not measure all dimensions of the changes in governments'
influence in their respective economies.

For example, government expenditures can be used to buy goods
and services, ranging from desks to garbage trucks, produced in the
private sector. The economic cost of government in such instances
may then be limited, more or less, to the sum of such expenditures.
On the other hand, government expenditures can also be used to
coerce or induce additional private expenditures. For instance, regulatory expenditures on the creation and policing of noise-pollution standards divert resources from serving people's private objectives to
serving legislated governmental ends. Firms' expenditures on govern-
ment-mandated noise abatement and all similar regulations represent
a nontrivial component of the total cost of government. However,
these costs are very difficult to measure, given the fact that they
may be spread among workers and owners who may suffer lower
wages and returns on investment and higher prices on the goods
and services they buy. A part of the total costs may also be borne
by consumers, through higher prices.

In addition, because laws and budgetary priorities change, movements in the levels of real expenditures over time may mask changes
in the *composition* of government expenditures—and, thereby, changes
in required private sector expenditures to meet government regulations. Regrettably, no single statistic summarizes the total influence
or cost of government in the economy. At best the evidence on the
indirect costs of government expenditures and regulations is spotty.
By the same token, the size and growth rate of underground economies
in different countries vary, which means that the rate of growth of
total government influence in the total domestic economy (including
the underground and aboveground economies) may only be roughly
indicated by the available data. Such unknown factors call, of course,
for caution in the interpretation of the data.

Accordingly, statistics can only suggest tendencies. For that reason alone, the analysis we shall present is decidedly preliminary.
Nevertheless, the figures are instructive. The weight of the evidence,
at the very least, favors the view that governmental growth in many
countries is no longer escalating. Indeed, as we shall see in this
and the next two chapters, in many countries, including the United

States, the pace of governmental growth has been slowing, if not stagnating, for almost a decade.

We begin our analysis by reviewing the expenditure and tax records of members of the OECD. Later we consider the available evidence on the growing competitiveness of less-developed countries around the world.

## Expenditure Records of OECD Governments

Trends of government outlays in major industrial countries around the world are very similar to each other. Consider table 6.1 and figure 6.1. Table 6.1 includes annual data from 1966 to 1987 on government outlays as a percentage of the gross domestic products (GDP, as computed by the OECD) for all OECD countries.[3] Figure 6.1 (see pp. 120 and 121) plots the percentages reported in table 6.1 for selected countries.

The basic thesis of this book cannot be better illustrated than by examining what has happened in Japan. Outlays in Japan peaked in 1984 at 34.1 percent of GDP, only to fall (slightly) to 32.7 percent by 1985 and then to rise slightly, back to 33.2 percent in 1987 (the last year for which the necessary data are available). However, what is most important in the case of Japan is that the rate of growth in the percentages began to slow several years before 1984, possibly as far back as the early-to-mid-1970s.

The trend in percentages for West Germany is also especially noteworthy. The curve has been more or less flat, since the mid-1970s, moving between 46 and 50 percent.

In the United Kingdom the trend has been flat (or moved ever so slightly downward in the early 1980s), declining from 47.7 percent in 1981 to 43.2 percent in 1987. More important, the overall trend between, say, 1975 and 1987 is decidedly flatter than the trend between 1966 and 1975.

Outlays in Canada as a percentage of GDP were virtually flat, ranging between 46 to 48 percent, between 1982 and 1987. Because of the obvious jump in government outlays as a percentage of GDP between 1981 and 1982 (probably due in part to the country's recession), the data for Canada are not clear. At the same time, a roughly drawn curve through all points on the graph might well have a decreasing slope, which would imply a decreasing rate of growth.

The percentages for Australia and all smaller European countries

TABLE 6.1  Total Outlays of OECD Governments as Percentage of GDP, 1966–1987

| | 1966 | 1967 | 1968 | 1969 | 1970 | 1971 | 1972 | 1973 | 1974 | 1975 | 1976 | 1977 | 1978 | 1979 | 1980 | 1981 | 1982 | 1983 | 1984 | 1985 | 1986 | 1987 |
|---|---|---|---|---|---|---|---|---|---|---|---|---|---|---|---|---|---|---|---|---|---|---|
| United States | 28.5 | 30.5 | 30.7 | 30.4 | 31.6 | 31.6 | 31.3 | 30.6 | 32.2 | 34.6 | 33.4 | 32.2 | 31.6 | 31.7 | 33.7 | 34.1 | 36.5 | 36.9 | 35.8 | 36.7 | 36.9 | 36.7 |
| Japan | 19.1 | 18.2 | 19.2 | 18.9 | 19.4 | 20.9 | 22.1 | 22.4 | 24.5 | 27.3 | 27.7 | 29.0 | 30.5 | 31.6 | 32.6 | 33.5 | 33.7 | 34.1 | 33.2 | 32.7 | 33.1 | 33.2 |
| Germany | 36.7 | 38.6 | 38.6 | 39.1 | 38.6 | 40.1 | 40.8 | 41.5 | 44.6 | 48.0 | 47.9 | 48.0 | 48.6 | 47.6 | 48.3 | 49.2 | 49.4 | 48.3 | 48.0 | 47.5 | 46.9 | 46.8 |
| France | 38.5 | 39.0 | 40.3 | 39.6 | 38.5 | 38.1 | 38.3 | 38.3 | 39.3 | 43.4 | 43.9 | 43.7 | 44.6 | 45.0 | 46.1 | 48.7 | 50.4 | 51.4 | 52.1 | 52.2 | 51.8 | 51.8 |
| Italy | 34.3 | 33.7 | 34.7 | 34.2 | 34.2 | 36.6 | 38.6 | 37.8 | 37.9 | 43.2 | 42.2 | 42.5 | 46.1 | 45.5 | 41.9 | 45.8 | 47.4 | 48.6 | 49.3 | 50.8 | 50.9 | 50.7 |
| United Kingdom | 35.3 | 38.2 | 39.1 | 41.1 | 38.8 | 38.1 | 39.3 | 40.4 | 44.9 | 46.6 | 46.3 | 43.8 | 43.3 | 42.7 | 44.9 | 47.7 | 47.1 | 46.9 | 47.5 | 46.2 | 45.5 | 43.2 |
| Canada | 29.5 | 31.5 | 32.4 | 32.7 | 34.8 | 36.1 | 36.6 | 35.4 | 36.8 | 40.1 | 39.1 | 40.1 | 40.3 | 39.0 | 40.5 | 41.5 | 46.6 | 47.2 | 46.8 | 47.1 | 46.4 | 45.6 |
| Total of above countries | 30.2 | 31.6 | 31.9 | 31.7 | 32.3 | 32.7 | 32.9 | 32.6 | 34.5 | 37.7 | 36.8 | 36.2 | 36.5 | 37.0 | 38.4 | 38.9 | 40.4 | 40.5 | 39.5 | 39.7 | 40.0 | 40.0 |
| Austria | 38.3 | 40.5 | 40.6 | 40.3 | 39.2 | 39.7 | 39.8 | 41.3 | 41.9 | 46.1 | 46.9 | 46.8 | 49.7 | 48.9 | 48.9 | 50.3 | 50.9 | 51.2 | 50.8 | 51.7 | 52.4 | 52.5 |
| Belgium | 33.5 | 36.3 | 36.3 | 36.1 | 36.5 | 38.0 | 38.8 | 39.1 | 39.4 | 46.1 | 44.9 | 46.4 | 47.8 | 49.3 | 50.7 | 55.3 | 55.5 | 55.4 | 55.4 | 51.7 | 53.5 | 52.3 |
| Denmark | 31.7 | 34.3 | 36.3 | 36.3 | 40.2 | 43.0 | 42.6 | 42.1 | 45.9 | 48.2 | 47.8 | 48.9 | 50.6 | 53.2 | 56.2 | 59.8 | 61.2 | 61.6 | 60.3 | 59.3 | 56.0 | 58.3 |
| Finland | 32.0 | 32.9 | 32.8 | 31.2 | 30.5 | 32.0 | 32.4 | 31.0 | 32.0 | 36.1 | 37.1 | 38.3 | 37.8 | 36.7 | 36.6 | 37.4 | 39.0 | 40.2 | 39.7 | 41.4 | 41.9 | 42.0 |
| Greece[a] | 21.5 | 23.6 | 23.5 | 22.5 | 22.4 | 22.8 | 22.0 | 21.1 | 25.0 | 26.7 | 27.4 | 29.0 | 29.9 | 29.7 | 30.5 | 35.9 | 37.0 | 38.2 | 40.2 | 43.7 | 42.1 | 43.0 |
| Iceland | 28.4 | 32.2 | 33.8 | 30.2 | 30.7 | 33.5 | 34.3 | 36.7 | 38.2 | 38.5 | 33.2 | 32.8 | 32.9 | 33.4 | 32.2 | 32.8 | 34.1 | 35.8 | 32.0 | 34.4 | 36.7 | 33.3 |
| Ireland | 33.6 | 34.8 | 35.2 | 36.6 | 39.6 | 40.5 | 38.8 | 39.0 | 43.0 | 46.5 | 46.0 | 43.7 | 44.3 | 46.8 | 50.8 | 52.5 | 55.3 | 55.3 | 53.3 | 54.5 | 54.7 | ;; |
| Luxembourg | 35.0 | 37.5 | 37.3 | 34.1 | 33.1 | 36.8 | 37.2 | 36.1 | 35.6 | 48.5 | 49.2 | 51.9 | 51.3 | 52.5 | 54.8 | 58.5 | 55.8 | 55.1 | 51.8 | 51.1 | 51.7 | ;; |
| Netherlands | 40.7 | 42.5 | 43.9 | 44.4 | 43.9 | 45.0 | 45.6 | 45.8 | 47.9 | 52.8 | 52.9 | 53.0 | 54.4 | 55.8 | 57.5 | 59.7 | 61.2 | 62.2 | 61.0 | 59.7 | 59.4 | 60.1 |
| Norway | 34.8 | 36.4 | 37.9 | 39.9 | 41.0 | 43.0 | 44.6 | 44.6 | 44.6 | 46.2 | 48.1 | 49.6 | 51.8 | 50.4 | 48.3 | 47.9 | 48.3 | 48.4 | 46.3 | 45.6 | 49.9 | 51.6 |
| Portugal | 20.3 | 20.9 | 20.9 | 20.9 | 21.6 | 21.3 | 22.7 | 21.3 | 24.7 | 30.3 | 35.1 | 35.2 | 36.4 | 36.2 | 25.9 | 43.9 | 43.0 | 47.9 | 44.4 | 43.4 | 43.9 | ;; |
| Spain | 19.5 | 21.0 | 21.3 | 21.7 | 22.2 | 23.6 | 23.2 | 23.0 | 23.1 | 24.7 | 26.0 | 27.5 | 29.3 | 30.5 | 32.9 | 35.6 | 37.5 | 38.8 | 39.3 | 42.1 | 41.7 | |
| Sweden | 38.3 | 40.2 | 42.8 | 43.2 | 43.3 | 45.3 | 46.2 | 44.7 | 48.1 | 48.9 | 51.7 | 57.5 | 59.2 | 60.7 | 61.6 | 64.6 | 66.6 | 66.2 | 63.5 | 64.6 | 63.6 | 59.9 |
| Switzerland[a] | 20.1 | 20.4 | 20.7 | 21.8 | 21.3 | 21.9 | 21.9 | 24.2 | 25.5 | 28.7 | 30.2 | 30.4 | 30.2 | 29.9 | 29.3 | 28.9 | 30.1 | 30.9 | 31.4 | 31.0 | 30.5 | 30.1 |
| Turkey | 20.6 | 21.0 | 21.9 | 23.1 | 21.9 | 22.1 | 22.5 | ;; | | | | | | | | | | | | | | |
| Total smaller European countries | 30.2 | 31.6 | 32.8 | 33.1 | 33.5 | 34.9 | 35.0 | 35.5 | 36.9 | 40.1 | 41.5 | 43.0 | 44.1 | 44.6 | 45.5 | 48.0 | 48.9 | 49.7 | 48.9 | 49.5 | 49.2 | 50.7 |
| Australia | 24.7 | 25.4 | 24.1 | 24.1 | 26.8 | 27.5 | 27.1 | 27.7 | 31.6 | 33.6 | 34.1 | 35.2 | 34.2 | 33.4 | 33.8 | 34.6 | 37.1 | 37.5 | 38.5 | 38.5 | 37.9 | 35.8 |
| New Zealand | ;; | ;; | ;; | ;; | ;; | ;; | ;; | ;; | ;; | ;; | ;; | ;; | ;; | ;; | ;; | ;; | ;; | ;; | ;; | ;; | ;; | ;; |
| Total smaller countries | 29.4 | 30.7 | 31.5 | 31.8 | 32.6 | 33.8 | 33.9 | 34.3 | 36.1 | 39.2 | 40.3 | 42.0 | 42.8 | 43.2 | 44.0 | 45.8 | 47.1 | 47.7 | 47.1 | 47.8 | 47.7 | 48.4 |
| Total OECD | 30.1 | 31.5 | 31.9 | 31.7 | 32.3 | 32.9 | 33.1 | 32.9 | 34.8 | 38.0 | 37.3 | 37.1 | 37.5 | 38.0 | 39.3 | 39.9 | 41.3 | 41.4 | 40.4 | 40.7 | 41.0 | 40.9 |
| Four major European countries | 36.4 | 37.7 | 38.6 | 38.7 | 37.8 | 38.5 | 39.5 | 39.8 | 42.1 | 45.9 | 45.5 | 45.1 | 45.8 | 45.6 | 45.8 | 48.1 | 48.7 | 48.8 | 49.2 | 49.1 | 48.8 | 48.3 |
| OECD-Europe | 34.6 | 35.9 | 36.9 | 37.0 | 36.6 | 37.4 | 38.1 | 38.5 | 40.5 | 44.1 | 44.2 | 44.4 | 45.2 | 45.2 | 45.7 | 48.0 | 48.8 | 49.1 | 49.1 | 49.2 | 48.9 | 48.9 |
| EEC | 35.1 | 36.4 | 37.4 | 37.4 | 36.9 | 37.7 | 38.5 | 38.7 | 40.7 | 44.5 | 44.3 | 44.3 | 45.1 | 45.1 | 45.7 | 48.2 | 49.0 | 49.3 | 49.4 | 49.5 | 49.1 | 49.2 |
| Total OECD less the United States | 31.7 | 32.5 | 33.1 | 33.0 | 33.0 | 34.0 | 34.4 | 34.5 | 36.5 | 40.1 | 40.0 | 40.3 | 40.9 | 41.4 | 42.3 | 43.6 | 44.6 | 44.7 | 44.2 | 44.1 | 43.7 | 43.4 |

Note: The percentages for each group of countries are calculated from the total GDP and total outlays of government for the group, with both aggregates expressed in U.S. dollars at current exchange rates.
Percentages for country groups exclude countries for which no data are shown in the table.
Total outlays of government mainly consist of current disbursements plus gross capital formation.
[a] Only current disbursements.

Source: OECD, OECD Economic Outlook (December 1989), p. 179.

combined follow much the same path for government outlays as those observed in many of the other countries we have already highlighted: Growth in government outlays as a fraction of GDP for Australia and these smaller European countries appears to have declined, albeit gradually and slightly, since the mid-1970s.

France and Italy have been sidestepped for the one important reason that, of the major OECD countries, they are notable for *not* tempering the growth in their outlays as a percentage of GDP.[4] There is *slight* evidence of some moderation in growth, but it is indeed slight. The steepness in respective growth paths for France and Italy, even into the 1980s, causes us to worry that growth-rate declines, if detectable, may be temporary.

## Tax Policies

Real public expenditures constitute the ultimate "tax" on the private sector. This is true because, while public expenditures may yield benefits, they actually divert resources away from private uses. If all governments within a country spend $1 trillion, then $1 trillion of resources will be unavailable to the private sector and a corresponding quantity of final private goods and services will not be produced. Public expenditures must be financed; taxation is only one of several methods of financing them. Deficits and money creation are two prominent alternative financing methods. Ultimately, no matter how government expenditures are financed, citizens bear the costs.

Nonetheless tax policy is important because different taxes have different consequences for the economy. Taxes can distribute and redistribute the overall burden of government expenditures, and taxes can add to or subtract from the overall efficiency, or cost, of government. They can also affect the future growth of the economy. Accordingly, countries can compete for their needed current and future human and physical capital bases by the adoption of specific tax policies.

Apparently, as evident in the review of the global tax-reform movement that follows, many governments around the world are taking note of past marginal tax-rate reductions in the United States and are responding accordingly. Thus, in several cases, major governments are making their tax policies more competitive, more like U.S. policies. At the same time the U.S. tax-code changes have not always predated changes in the tax codes of other countries.

FIGURE 6.1  Total Government Outlays in Selected Countries as
Percentage of GDP, 1966–1987

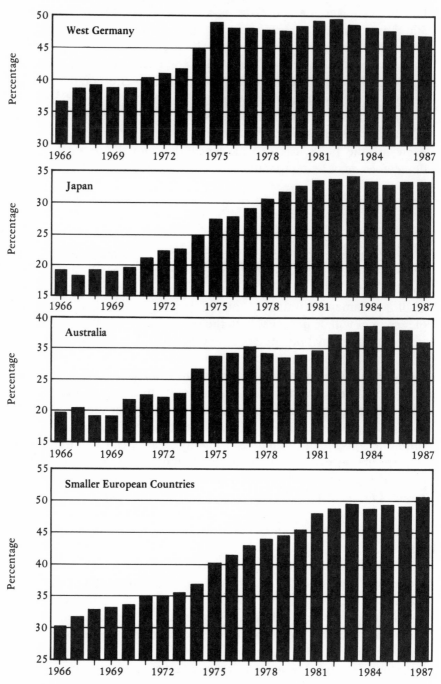

Source: OECD, *OECD Economic Outlook* (December 1989), p. 179.

FIGURE 6.1 (*continued*)

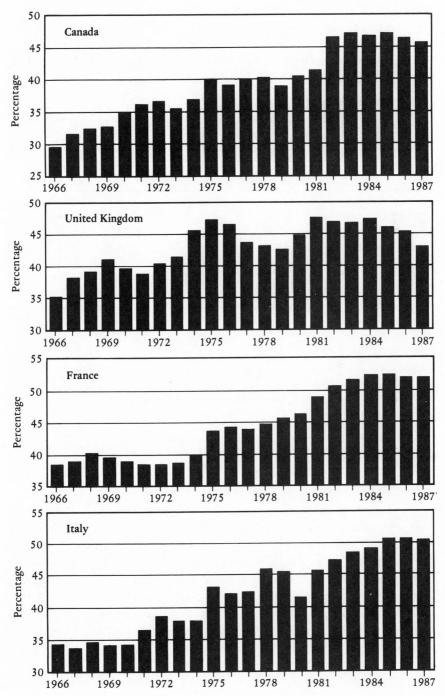

Consider table 6.2, which contains the findings of a country-by-country survey undertaken by Vito Tanzi, an economist with the International Monetary Fund.[5] Table 6.2 reports the changes in the range of marginal tax rates imposed by the national governments in ten major countries between 1985 and 1986 (or later years, depending on when the new lower marginal tax rates became effective).

TABLE 6.2   Recent and Proposed Changes in Lowest and Highest Personal Income Tax Rates (Percentages)

| Country | Tax Rates in 1985 | Tax Rates in 1986 or Later |
| --- | --- | --- |
| Australia | 30–60 | 24–49 (from 1987) |
| Denmark[a] | 50–73 | 50–68 (from 1987) |
| France | 5–65 | 5–50 (from 1988) |
| West Germany | 22–56 | 19–53 (from 1990) |
| Ireland | 35–65 | 35–58 (from 1986) |
| Italy | 18–65 | 11–56 (from 1988) |
| Japan | 10.5–70 | 10–50 (from 1988) |
| New Zealand | 20–66 | 15–48 (from 1986) |
| United Kingdom[b] | 30–60 | 27–60 (from 1987) |
| United States[c] | 11–50 | 15–28 (from 1988) |
| Average | 23–63 | 21–52 |

[a] Includes tax to primary and county authorities and church tax.

[b] Up to 1979 the top tax rate had been 83 percent for earned income and 98 percent on investment income.

[c] The table is presented as given in the above below. However, the highest marginal tax rate was actually 33 percent in 1988 for a range of high income.

Source: Vito Tanzi, "The Response of Other Industrial Countries to the U.S. Tax Reform Act," *National Tax Journal* September 1987), p. 344.

Rate reductions are evident in all countries included in the surveys, except the United Kingdom. The lack of rate reductions in the United Kingdom is actually a result of the time period covered by the table. Between 1979 and 1985 the United Kingdom lowered its highest marginal tax rates on earned income from 83 to 60 percent, and on investment income from 98 to 83.[6] In addition, in the late 1980s the Thatcher government lowered the highest marginal tax rate on personal income to 40 percent and reduced the top marginal rate on corporate income to 35 percent (with companies with taxable profits of less than £750,000 paying an even lower rate).[7]

Australia lowered its top marginal rate from 60 percent in 1985 to 49 percent in 1987.[8] (This means that between 1985 and 1987, the percentage of additional income that could be kept after taxes from top-income earners rose from 40 to 51 percent, an increase in share of nearly 28 percent). Similarly, Denmark reduced its top rate from 73 percent in 1985 to 68 percent in 1987; France, from 65 percent in 1985 to 50 percent in 1988; and West Germany, from 56 percent in 1985 to 53 percent in 1990. Japan reduced its highest marginal tax rate more than any other country except the United States; the rate for Japan was reduced from 70 percent in 1985 to 50 percent in 1988. Overall, the nine countries listed in the table reduced their highest tax rates by more than 17 percent, from an average of 63 percent in 1985 to 52 percent after 1985.

The listed countries, on average, lowered their lowest marginal tax rates by about half the percentage reduction in their highest marginal tax rates. However, the reduction in the taxation of low-income earners may have been reduced by more than is indicated by the table. This is the case because a higher percentage of income may have been exempted from taxation.[9] A major reason given by Tanzi for the disparity in reductions between the high and low tax bracket is the potential for greater revenue loss when reductions are made at the lower end of the progressive tax schedule.[10]

However, we stress that lowering top rates more than bottom rates is consistent with the view expressed in chapter 5 that many of the rate reductions were designed to flatten the tax schedules in response to greater capital mobility. Rate reductions were enacted to improve incentives to work and invest in human and physical capital, to reduce tax avoidance and evasion, and to move out of the underground economy.[11]

The reductions in personal income tax rates have frequently been accompanied by reductions in corporate income tax rates. Nine of the ten listed countries either had, at the time of the survey, made tax-rate reductions on corporate income or had plans to reduce the tax rate.[12]

In another recent tax project, the late Joseph Pechman, an economist who did research at the Brookings Institution, summarized the findings of a number of Brookings tax researchers.[13] These data, which apply to combined national and local taxes for 1984–90, are reported in table 6.3. For top-income earners, when all national and local taxes, before and after reform, are tallied and computed as a percentage of income, Dr. Pechman observed that by 1990 "most countries will reduce individual income-tax rates, particularly in the top brackets, and compress the number of brackets. In this respect, they will be following the lead of the United States, although no country expects to emulate the reduction of twenty-two percentage points in the top U.S. federal tax rate (from 50 percent to 28 percent)."[14]

TABLE 6.3   Top Individual Income Tax Rates, 1984–1990[a]

| Country | 1984 | 1985 | 1986 | 1987 | 1988 | 1989[b] | 1990[b] |
|---|---|---|---|---|---|---|---|
| Sweden[c] | 82 | 80 | 80 | 77 | 75 | 75 | 75 |
| Denmark | 73 | 73 | 73 | 68 | 68 | 68 | 68 |
| France | 65 | 65 | 58 | 58 | 57 | 57 | 57 |
| Netherlands[d] | 72 | 72 | 72 | 72 | 70 | 70 | 70 |
| United Kingdom | 60 | 60 | 60 | 60 | 60 | 60 | 60 |
| West Germany | 56 | 56 | 56 | 56 | 56 | 56 | 53 |
| Italy[d,e] | 65 | 62 | 62 | 62 | 60 | 60 | 60 |
| Canada[e,f] | 51 | 52 | 55 | 53 | 45 | 45 | 45 |
| Australia | 60 | 60 | 55 | 49 | 49 | 49 | 49 |
| United States[e] | 55 | 55 | 55 | 43 | 33 | 33 | 33 |
| Japan | 88 | 88 | 88 | 88 | 76 | 76 | 76 |

[a] Combined national and local tax rates.
[b] Assumes no unscheduled changes in current tax provisions unless otherwise indicated.
[c] Assumes a local tax rate of 30 percent.
[d] Assumes that proposed reforms will be enacted.
[e] Takes no account the deductibility of local tax when calculating national tax.
[f] Assumes the Ontario provincial tax rate and includes federal and provincial surtaxes.
Source: Joseph A. Pechman, "Introduction," *World Tax Reform: A Progress Report*, ed. Joseph A. Pechman (Washington, D.C.: Brookings Institution, 1988), p. 4, who extracted the data from other papers in the conference proceedings, supplemented by various official government publications.

The actual percentage reductions are not as great in table 6.3 as in table 6.2 because of the influence of nonnational tax policies. However, we observe significant reductions in the combined tax rates of all countries, again excluding the United Kingdom. Except for the United States, Japan has lowered its overall top tax rates by the greatest number of percentage points, twelve. In table 6.3, the reduction in the average top marginal tax rate for all countries listed, other than the United States, is approximately 9 percent, from an average top rate of 67.2 percent in 1984 to 61.3 percent in 1990.

Dr. Pechman also found that seven out of the eleven countries covered by the survey reported in table 6.3 either had lowered their combined national and local top marginal rates on corporate income or would have lowered them by 1990.[15] France lowered its corporate income tax rate from 50 percent in 1984 to 42 percent in 1988 and thereafter; the Netherlands, from 43 percent in 1986 to 42 percent thereafter; the United Kingdom, from 45 percent in 1984 to 35 percent after 1985; West Germany, from 56 percent in 1989 to 50 percent thereafter; Canada, from 53 percent in 1986 to 44 percent after 1989;[16] the United States, from 51 percent in 1986 to 39 percent in 1988; and Japan, from 53 percent in 1986 to 52 percent thereafter. Sweden has not changed its corporate tax rate, and three countries have increased their tax rates: Denmark, from 40 percent in 1984 to 50 percent thereafter; Italy, from 36 percent in 1984 to 46 percent thereafter; and Australia, from 46 percent in 1986 to 49 percent thereafter.[17]

In general Dr. Pechman concluded that tax reform was motivated by three considerations: first, widespread recognition of the disincentive effects of high marginal tax rates;[18] second, the inefficiencies and many misguided incentives of many tax deductions, the elimination of which was generally accompanied by a broadening of the countries' tax bases; and, third, "fear of flight of capital to other countries."[19] The tax-reform movement may also have been motivated by desires to simplify the tax systems. However, aside from reducing the number of brackets (hardly a major simplification for most tax preparers), progress toward simpler tax systems has been slow at best.

The worldwide tax-reform movement has not accomplished everything implied in the hypotheses developed in our earlier chapters. Crosscurrents are evident in tax policies—some taxes rise while others fall. For most countries, given their deficit problems, the net effect of the crosscurrents is a negligible reduction in revenues.

Nonetheless, among the United States' principal trading partners, competition among tax systems has been contagious. Countries do appear to be interested in seeking new ways to minimize the distorting influence of their tax codes. Though we might like to assume that such reform movements are totally motivated by policymakers' efforts to be "good guys," we are suspicious of such an assumption. We wonder why policymakers have taken so much interest lately in the efficiency attributes of their respective tax systems. As Dr. Tanzi notes, the incentive effects of tax rates were not a particularly hot issue in the 1950s and 1960s.[20] By far, the macroeconomic and equity consequences were the dominant considerations in tax policy between 1950 and 1970. To see these points more clearly, consider what individual countries accomplished under the banner of tax reform.

### Tax Reform, Country by Country

A country-by-country description of tax reform helps render a more accurate picture of the exact nature and economic foundations of the reforms in the above surveys. We suggest that the more detailed findings of the individual studies undergirding Pechman's summary tables support the view that in the 1980s the pressure to be more competitive in the global economy was a factor in the reform.

Admittedly, the end result of most tax-reform efforts in most OECD countries, combined with changes in national income growth and in other sources of government revenues, has been that total government receipts as a percentage of GDP have continued to rise through the 1980s, a point that is evident from scanning the detailed data in table 6.4. The marked slowing of growth in receipts as a percent of GDP in West Germany, the United Kingdom, and Canada is easily observed. The growth in the receipts as a share of GDP in Japan, France, Italy, and Australia may or may not have slowed. The growth of the combined receipt share for the smaller European countries, however, appears to have been largely unchecked.

However, it must be kept in mind that tax revenues as a share of GDP are not direct policy instruments but rather derivatives of the interplay of tax and expenditure policies on the one hand and national production and income on the other.[21] Total receipts may rise because a government may intentionally seek more revenue through higher (or, for many supply-siders, lower) tax rates. The greater receipts may, of course, be used to expand expenditures, but they may also be used to reduce the budget deficit, with government expenditures as a percentage of GDP holding steady or falling.

In addition total receipts may rise as a percent of GDP because tax policy changes have reduced incentives to evade and avoid tax payments and may have increased incentives to increase earned (and taxable) income. Finally total receipts (as distinct from tax revenues) may rise because of government's greater reliance on market-determined user charges, which, if they supplant taxes, may improve the efficiency of people's purchases. For all these reasons, close attention must be paid to the particular fiscal intentions of different governments.

#### Australia

Before tax reform in 1986, the average wage earner in Australia faced a dramatically escalating marginal tax rate—one that more than dou-

TABLE 6.4  Total Receipts of OECD Governments as Percentage of GDP, 1966–1987

| | 1966 | 1967 | 1968 | 1969 | 1970 | 1971 | 1972 | 1973 | 1974 | 1975 | 1976 | 1977 | 1978 | 1979 | 1980 | 1981 | 1982 | 1983 | 1984 | 1985 | 1986 | 1987 |
|---|---|---|---|---|---|---|---|---|---|---|---|---|---|---|---|---|---|---|---|---|---|---|
| United States | 26.7 | 27.1 | 28.7 | 29.9 | 28.9 | 28.2 | 29.3 | 29.6 | 30.3 | 28.8 | 29.5 | 29.7 | 29.9 | 30.5 | 30.8 | 31.6 | 31.1 | 30.7 | 30.7 | 31.2 | 31.3 | 32.0 |
| Japan | 19.1 | 19.3 | 19.6 | 19.7 | 20.6 | 21.6 | 21.5 | 22.5 | 24.5 | 24.0 | 23.6 | 24.7 | 24.5 | 26.3 | 27.6 | 29.1 | 29.5 | 29.8 | 30.4 | 31.2 | 31.5 | 33.2 |
| Germany | 36.1 | 36.7 | 37.8 | 39.3 | 38.3 | 39.4 | 39.8 | 42.2 | 42.7 | 42.7 | 44.0 | 45.0 | 44.7 | 44.4 | 44.7 | 44.8 | 45.4 | 45.1 | 45.3 | 45.6 | 44.9 | 44.4 |
| France | 38.4 | 38.2 | 38.8 | 39.8 | 38.3 | 37.6 | 37.8 | 40.4 | 42.7 | 39.7 | 41.8 | 45.1 | 44.7 | 44.4 | 44.7 | 45.1 | 45.4 | 45.1 | 47.6 | 47.6 | 47.1 | 47.6 |
| Italy | 30.1 | 31.0 | 31.6 | 30.7 | 30.4 | 31.1 | 30.9 | 30.4 | 30.6 | 31.2 | 32.9 | 34.3 | 36.0 | 35.7 | 33.1 | 34.1 | 35.9 | 37.7 | 37.4 | 38.0 | 39.0 | 39.3 |
| United Kingdom | 34.3 | 36.2 | 37.6 | 39.5 | 40.2 | 38.4 | 36.4 | 35.8 | 39.8 | 40.5 | 40.0 | 39.1 | 37.7 | 38.2 | 40.1 | 42.4 | 43.0 | 42.3 | 42.3 | 42.3 | 41.5 | 40.7 |
| Canada | 28.8 | 30.3 | 31.5 | 33.5 | 34.2 | 34.7 | 35.2 | 34.9 | 36.2 | 36.1 | 35.8 | 36.1 | 36.2 | 35.5 | 36.2 | 38.5 | 39.1 | 38.7 | 38.7 | 38.5 | 39.4 | 39.5 |
| Total of above countries | 28.7 | 29.2 | 30.3 | 31.3 | 30.7 | 30.5 | 31.0 | 31.5 | 32.6 | 32.2 | 32.6 | 32.9 | 32.8 | 33.9 | 34.6 | 35.0 | 35.0 | 34.7 | 34.5 | 34.9 | 35.3 | 36.2 |
| Austria | 39.3 | 39.1 | 38.9 | 39.6 | 39.7 | 40.5 | 41.2 | 41.9 | 42.5 | 42.9 | 42.4 | 43.7 | 46.2 | 45.8 | 46.4 | 47.8 | 46.7 | 46.4 | 47.5 | 48.5 | 47.9 | 47.6 |
| Belgium | 32.4 | 33.2 | 33.8 | 34.3 | 35.2 | 35.7 | 35.5 | 36.4 | 37.7 | 40.4 | 40.1 | 41.6 | 42.4 | 43.1 | 42.7 | 43.4 | 45.2 | 44.6 | 45.7 | 46.0 | 45.1 | 45.4 |
| Denmark | 33.5 | 34.1 | 36.9 | 37.2 | 41.7 | 46.4 | 45.9 | 46.8 | 48.4 | 46.1 | 46.9 | 47.6 | 49.6 | 50.8 | 52.2 | 52.1 | 51.2 | 53.6 | 55.5 | 56.5 | 58.6 | 59.5 |
| Finland | 32.8 | 34.6 | 34.8 | 33.8 | 34.1 | 35.7 | 35.4 | 36.0 | 35.7 | 37.8 | 41.0 | 40.4 | 38.0 | 36.0 | 35.8 | 37.4 | 37.2 | 37.4 | 38.9 | 40.3 | 41.5 | 39.6 |
| Greece | 25.3 | 26.2 | 27.3 | 27.2 | 26.8 | 26.6 | 26.6 | 25.4 | 27.0 | 27.4 | 29.5 | 29.9 | 30.1 | 30.6 | 30.5 | 29.1 | 32.3 | 33.6 | 34.8 | 34.6 | 35.6 | 37.2 |
| Iceland | 31.0 | 33.6 | 33.5 | 30.3 | 30.9 | 32.6 | 34.5 | 36.6 | 34.7 | 34.6 | 33.4 | 31.8 | 32.1 | 33.5 | 33.3 | 33.8 | 35.5 | 33.4 | 33.9 | 32.5 | 32.2 | 32.2 |
| Ireland | 30.0 | 30.6 | 31.0 | 31.6 | 35.3 | 36.3 | 36.3 | 34.5 | 35.2 | 34.6 | 37.9 | 36.4 | 35.2 | 35.9 | 38.8 | 39.6 | 41.5 | 43.2 | 43.3 | 43.1 | 43.4 | — |
| Luxembourg | 35.8 | 35.7 | 34.5 | 34.3 | 35.4 | 38.4 | 38.5 | 39.0 | 40.2 | 48.6 | 50.3 | 54.2 | 55.2 | 52.1 | 53.3 | 53.8 | 53.8 | 56.2 | 54.2 | 55.3 | 53.6 | 53.3 |
| Netherlands | 39.2 | 40.6 | 42.4 | 43.2 | 42.0 | 43.3 | 44.5 | 45.9 | 47.0 | 49.2 | 49.5 | 50.5 | 50.9 | 51.4 | 52.8 | 53.5 | 53.8 | 55.3 | 54.1 | 54.3 | 52.9 | 54.2 |
| Norway | 38.3 | 40.5 | 41.1 | 46.7 | 43.5 | 46.6 | 48.4 | 48.7 | 48.5 | 48.7 | 49.8 | 50.0 | 50.8 | 53.2 | 53.2 | 51.8 | 51.9 | 51.8 | 53.0 | 55.1 | 54.6 | — |
| Portugal | 20.8 | 21.0 | 21.5 | 22.5 | 24.3 | 23.5 | 23.4 | 22.7 | 23.0 | 24.8 | 28.1 | 30.5 | 29.5 | 30.0 | 31.4 | 33.3 | 35.4 | 37.8 | 37.3 | 35.9 | 37.6 | — |
| Spain | 19.4 | 21.4 | 21.2 | 21.9 | 22.5 | 22.6 | 23.0 | 23.7 | 22.8 | 24.3 | 25.3 | 26.5 | 27.1 | 28.4 | 29.7 | 31.2 | 31.4 | 33.5 | 33.2 | 34.5 | 35.0 | — |
| Sweden | 41.3 | 42.7 | 45.7 | 46.7 | 46.6 | 49.4 | 49.5 | 47.7 | 48.8 | 50.5 | 55.1 | 58.0 | 57.5 | 56.4 | 56.6 | 58.3 | 58.9 | 59.9 | 59.6 | 59.5 | 61.6 | 62.7 |
| Switzerland | 24.1 | 24.2 | 25.3 | 26.4 | 26.5 | 26.2 | 26.4 | 28.8 | 29.7 | 32.1 | 33.9 | 33.7 | 33.8 | 33.1 | 32.8 | 32.8 | 33.3 | 33.9 | 34.7 | 34.4 | 35.0 | 34.5 |
| Turkey | 19.9 | 22.1 | 21.8 | 23.8 | 23.7 | 23.7 | 27.1 | | | | | | | | | | | | | | | |
| Total smaller European countries | 31.1 | 32.3 | 33.4 | 34.1 | 34.8 | 36.0 | 36.3 | 37.2 | 37.6 | 39.2 | 40.8 | 41.8 | 42.0 | 41.9 | 42.7 | 43.4 | 43.6 | 44.8 | 45.2 | 45.7 | 45.9 | 48.9 |
| Australia | 25.3 | 26.1 | 25.7 | 26.5 | 26.6 | 27.3 | 25.2 | 26.7 | 28.5 | 29.1 | 29.9 | 30.3 | 29.1 | 29.8 | 30.7 | 31.9 | 32.4 | 31.7 | 33.2 | 33.6 | 34.4 | 34.2 |
| New Zealand | | | | | | | | | | | | | | | | | | | | | | |
| Total smaller countries | 30.3 | 31.4 | 32.3 | 33.0 | 33.6 | 34.8 | 34.8 | 35.5 | 36.1 | 37.6 | 39.1 | 40.3 | 40.3 | 40.4 | 41.2 | 41.6 | 41.8 | 42.6 | 43.0 | 43.8 | 44.4 | 46.7 |
| Total OECD | 28.9 | 29.5 | 30.6 | 31.5 | 31.1 | 31.1 | 31.5 | 32.1 | 33.2 | 33.1 | 33.7 | 34.1 | 34.0 | 34.9 | 35.6 | 35.9 | 36.0 | 35.7 | 35.6 | 36.0 | 36.5 | 37.3 |
| Four major European countries | 35.2 | 36.0 | 36.9 | 37.9 | 37.3 | 37.2 | 37.0 | 37.8 | 39.0 | 39.6 | 40.9 | 41.2 | 41.0 | 41.3 | 41.5 | 42.3 | 43.1 | 43.4 | 43.6 | 43.8 | 43.5 | 43.3 |
| OECD Europe | 34.0 | 34.9 | 35.8 | 36.7 | 36.5 | 36.9 | 36.8 | 37.6 | 38.5 | 39.4 | 40.8 | 41.4 | 41.4 | 41.5 | 41.9 | 42.7 | 43.3 | 43.8 | 44.1 | 44.4 | 44.2 | 44.7 |
| EEC | 34.1 | 34.9 | 35.9 | 36.8 | 36.5 | 36.6 | 36.4 | 37.2 | 38.2 | 38.9 | 40.2 | 40.7 | 40.8 | 41.0 | 41.4 | 42.1 | 42.9 | 43.5 | 43.6 | 43.9 | 43.7 | 44.3 |
| Total OECD less the United States | 31.2 | 31.9 | 32.4 | 33.1 | 33.1 | 33.6 | 33.2 | 33.8 | 35.1 | 35.7 | 36.4 | 36.9 | 36.4 | 37.4 | 38.2 | 38.7 | 39.3 | 39.4 | 39.5 | 39.9 | 39.8 | 40.5 |

Note: The percentages for each group of countries are calculated from the total GDP and current receipts of government for the group, with both aggregates expressed in U.S. dollars at current exchange rates.
Percentages for country groups exclude countries for which no data are shown in the table.
*Current receipts of government* mainly consist of direct and indirect taxes, and social security contributions paid by employers and employees.
Source: OECD, *OECD Economic Outlook* (December 1989), p. 180.

bled, rising from 19 to 46 percent between 1935 and 1985. In addition, just before reform, the top marginal rate applied to all income above 1.5 times the average earnings, whereas thirty years before, the top rate had not applied until income reached 18 times the average earnings.[22] As a consequence tax avoidance and evasion became something of a major growth industry, with fringe benefits representing a progressively larger percentage of people's (especially executives') pay and with anecdotal evidence indicating that the underground economy was, in the words of Michael Porter and Christopher Trengove, economists with Monash University in Australia, "alive and well in those sectors of the economy to which it is particularly suited."[23]

Australian tax reform in 1986 has been characterized as a "mixed bag."[24] It resulted in lower marginal rates and a broader taxable-income base, mainly by taxing fringe benefits and by eliminating the deductibility of entertainment expenses and expenditures on water conservation.[25] The corporate income tax was raised, but the double taxation of corporate income (first, as corporate income and then as personal income through the distribution of dividends) was largely eliminated by so-called imputation (the process of reducing personal income taxes of individual stockholders by some percentage of the corporate taxes paid by their companies).

In general tax reform in Australia was not intended to be "revenue-neutral." Through reform, however, the Australian Treasury expected to lose $3.1 billion, or 4 percent of its total revenue, which amounted to 1.1 percent of GDP.[26] The reason for the revenue loss is interesting, given the thrust of our argument. On international money markets, Australian currency, before reform, had seriously depreciated. Fearing that Australian unions would seek wage adjustments to compensate for the inflationary impact of the currency depreciation, the national government struck a deal. In exchange for a two-percentage-point reduction in union wage demands, the national government agreed to reduce taxes by an equivalent amount. In order to make progress in reducing the budget deficit in the face of revenue loss, government expenditures were reduced from 29.7 percent of GDP in 1984–85 to 26.8 percent in 1987.[27]

In short, fiscal reform was induced, partially at least, by concern for a dwindling taxable-income base and by international considerations. For example, an Australian official noted that "the inevitable increase in tax rates [during the thirty years prior to the 1986 reform movement] promoted, during the 1970s, tax avoidance and evasion—

practices that exacerbated legislative and judicial narrowing of the tax base, leading, equally inevitably, to disrespect for the system."[28]

Genuine concern about the competitiveness of the new higher corporate tax rate prevails: "While such a rate was not out of line then [1986] with the developed world generally (the United Kingdom being the exception), the rest of the world has not stood still, and Australia's rate is now toward the upper end of the spectrum."[29] At the same time, the Australians do not appear to have realized fully that they are in a competitive world. The economy still appears encumbered by heavy taxation and by extensive controls, so much so that the deal the government struck with its unions in 1986 did not halt the depreciation of the Australian dollar. As a consequence of persistently high tax rates, the top 5 percent of income earners in the country pay a smaller share of the country's income taxes than do their opposite numbers in the United States and in the United Kingdom.[30]

## Canada

Tax reform in Canada has been a long-term project. It began in 1972 when the top marginal tax rate (for combined federal and provincial rates) was reduced from 80 percent on income over $1.3 million (in 1987 dollars) to about 61 percent on taxable income over $190,000 (in 1987 dollars). Tax reform continued in 1982 when the top rate was lowered to just over 50 percent on taxable income over $65,000 (in 1987 dollars). Nonetheless, the Canadian tax system in the mid-1980s was at least as complex as that of the United States. In addition to all the complications added by tax deductions and exemptions for computing personal and corporate income, the Canadian system had the added complexities of a federal sales tax levied on manufactured goods (as well as provincial retail sales taxes). Because of variations in application to different goods and services, this federal sales tax was characterized as an "administrative nightmare"[31] and was estimated to subject "net exports to a 3 percent tax, which is a nontrivial perverse feature."[32]

Tax reform in Canada was motivated by many considerations, not the least of which was the desire to achieve greater efficiency, equity, and simplicity in the tax code.[33] In addition, tax reform, accompanied by rate reductions, was fully compatible with the general goals of the government elected in 1984: to bring about a "less intrusive role for government in the private economy."[34] However, it is understandable that reform in Canada, probably more so than in any other country, was necessitated by tax reform in the United States. According to two officials of the Canadian Department of Finance,

> A situation in which statutory corporate tax rates were higher in Canada than in the United States, besides influencing longer-run competitiveness of business activity in Canada, could be expected to inspire arrangements by multinational firms to direct income to the lower tax jurisdiction and expenses to the country with a higher tax rate. Any significant statutory rate differential could thus seriously threaten corporate income tax revenues. *The sharp reduction in statutory corporate tax rates in the United States virtually forced some reduction in Canadian statutory rates.*
>
> Similarly, a situation in which average personal income tax rates were much higher than rates in the United States would tend to put Canadian businesses . . . at a disadvantage in obtaining key people. [emphasis added][35]

The Canadians were given some breathing room in pushing rates down because the United States had in its 1986 tax-reform effort pushed up rates on new investment (via the elimination of accelerated depreciation and the investment tax credit provisions).[36] Yet, following the U.S. lead, Canada proceeded to lower marginal rates (more at the upper than at the lower end of the income spectrum) and broaden the tax base, the net effect of which was a slight reduction of total tax revenues.[37] In 1988, in order to bring their tax code more in line with that of the United States, Canadians flattened their tax-rate schedule and reduced the number of brackets from ten to three, lowering the highest marginal tax rate from 34 to 29 percent. They also eliminated the investment tax credit and reduced the acceleration of depreciation, which the United States had done two years earlier.[38]

The Canadian government has been evaluating alternative methods of replacing its national sales tax, the most prominent of which is the VAT (a value-added tax imposed at each stage of production). Of course, such a tax would have the effect of further flattening the average tax rates paid by the different income brackets. This might induce efficiencies in the allocation of resources within Canada, make Canadian products more competitive on world markets, and increase the attractiveness of investment. "In a world of increasing international economic integration," a VAT would have an added advantage, according to its supporting officials in the Canadian Department of Finance: "It avoids the imposition of any competitive disadvantages on domestic producers."[39]

*Denmark*

The announced objective of the 1985 tax-reform movement in Denmark, scheduled to take effect in 1987, "was to discourage tax speculation, encourage private saving, lower the marginal tax rate of taxation, improve the conditions of families with children, and provide a more equitable distribution of the tax burden by making allowance for low-income taxpayers."[40] Such objectives sound noble, and they are especially praiseworthy for a country that has one of the highest tax burdens of all industrial countries.[41] As a consequence of these tax burdens, Denmark has a real problem creating capital and trying to dissuade investors from paying more attention to the tax consequences of their projects (called "tax speculation") than to the productive attributes of their projects. However, the success of tax reform in Denmark has been modest at best.

Tax reform began in Denmark with a progressive marginal tax rate at an initial rate of 50 percent. When coupled with two surtaxes on higher income, the high marginal tax rate could run up to 73 percent. The chief accomplishment of reform was to reduce the high marginal tax rate on personal income to 68 percent and on interest income to 56 percent.[42] However, in Denmark, when the total reform package is considered, tax reform may be more apparent than real. The income tax base has been partially broadened by including the incomes of charitable organizations, and the corporate income tax rate has been raised from 40 to 50 percent. Total tax revenues increased in 1987 because of the tax-rate adjustments on personal and corporate incomes and the broadening of the income base.[43]

To help families the Danes provided an annual tax-free subsidy for all children under the age of eighteen living in Denmark. This subsidy of Kr2,500 and included in the tax-reform package, may have encouraged the Danes to have more children. Yet it is doubtful that such a tax stimulated investment and production. A newspaper commentator may not have been exaggerating all that much when he suggested, "The Danes apparently never understood what capitalism is about. Their Viking forefathers got wealthy by robbing abroad. Today Denmark maintains its wealth by borrowing abroad. The principle is really the same: The Danes like wealth but they do not create it."[44] In the end, the Danes may find they have done little to achieve their noble objectives of reducing "tax speculation" (which implies a form of resource mobility). "The increase in the corporate income tax rate," writes a Danish businessman, "will almost surely worsen the competitiveness of Danish business and make it harder to attract foreign investments."[45]

*France*

Tax reform in France during the 1970s and early 1980s amounted to tax-rate increases, especially in social security taxes. These taxes needed to be raised to accommodate escalating pension and health expenditures driven up by an aging French population and by all the "free" health services.[46] By 1985 total taxes in France equaled almost 46 percent of GDP.[47]

To finance the expanding government expenditures, the social security tax for the average wage earner was raised in 1987 to 57.4 percent of gross wages (40.6 percent imposed on employers and 16.8 percent imposed on employees). For the aggregate tax burden, the slight regressiveness of the social security tax was partially offset by the highly progressive individual income tax rates, which had ranged from marginal rates of 5 to 65 percent in 1986.[48]

Although progressive, the individual income tax system has been responsible for only a relatively small share of total French tax collections (equaling only 13 percent of total revenue).[49] This is the case mainly because social security taxes and a general tax credit of 28 percent of gross wages is deducted in calculating taxable income, against which the progressive tax schedule is applied. The result of these deductions for determining taxable income is that in France half the taxpayers pay no individual income taxes and a large share of the remaining taxpayers pay very low income taxes.[50]

Not much has been accomplished in reducing French tax rates in the 1980s. However, what may be impressive about recent tax policy in France is the reversal in the previous upward trend in tax rates. When the left coalition government took office in 1981, the top marginal tax rate was increased from 60 to 65 percent, and a "wealth tax" was enacted—a tax intended solely as redistributive, to be paid by only the richest people on their accumulated "large fortunes." The wealth tax was repealed in 1986, only to be proposed again in 1988.[51]

However, according to one government official, "The shortcomings of a high tax burden and high marginal rates became more and more obvious, *especially in the context of growing international competition*" (italics added).[52] In 1985 taxes were reduced by 1 percent of GDP; the elimination of an additional social security surtax and a reduction in individual income taxes accounted for one-fourth of this decrease. The corporate income tax rate was lowered in 1986 from 50 to 45 percent on undistributed corporate profits, supposedly because of a growing public awareness of the need to maintain "the profitability of business enterprise."[53] Since 1986 the corporate income-tax rate has been further reduced to 42 percent and extended to all profits. Finally, the top marginal tax rate has been reduced from 72.4 to 56.8 percent, and the wealth tax has been eliminated. The VAT tax was also reduced on certain products, and the payroll tax has been progressively lowered. Still, with increases in social security contributions and indirect taxes, France retains the distinction of having the highest tax burden of the major OECD countries.[54]

With full European unification set for 1992, France, like all other members of the European Economic Community, faces the problems of the "harmonization" of tax policies. Harmonization will probably call for additional tax-rate cuts in France, given the country's relatively high tax burden. As recognized by Édouard Balladur, France's finance minister from 1986 to 1988, in 1992 France will be likely to have the highest tax rates in Europe: "That means that if we want to join Europe and have a chance and not be penalized in the single market, we have to be able to lower considerably all our taxes."[55]

## West Germany

Official supporters of tax reform in West Germany do not mince words in articulating the economic basis of their reforms:

> The Federal Republic of Germany is internationally open, and its economy is highly interdependent with the world economy. It must, therefore, keep in line with international developments in shaping its tax laws. . . . Economic developments and tax reforms in other countries tend, furthermore, to affect German tax policies as a consequence of international interdependence. Thus the recent U.S. tax reform was and is carefully studied by German tax politicians.[56]

Accordingly, after watching the progress of tax reform in the United States, West Germany began a three-step tax-reform plan to be completed by 1990. In 1986 the Tax Reduction Law reduced income taxes by DM11 billion, an amount equal to .6 percent of GDP. The national government in 1988 reduced taxes further by DM13.7 billion, or .65 percent of GDP—reducing marginal rates and increasing the personal exemption, the education deduction, and the special depreciation allowance accorded small businesses. The tax reduction in 1990 is expected to be DM39.2 billion, significantly larger than the previous two reductions combined. The 1990 cut in tax revenue will be the result of further reductions in individual income tax rates, and a reduction in the corporate tax rate on retained earnings from 56 to 50 percent.[57]

We have already noted that total German government expenditures have remained more or less stable as a share of GDP since the mid-1970s. West Germans appear to be dedicated to maintaining that trend, if not to redirecting it decidedly downward. A broadening of the tax base, principally through the elimination of various tax preferences, and withholding on interest income, will cover a large share of the projected tax-revenue losses. However, half of the DM39.2 billion tax reduction for 1990 is expected to be "financed" by reductions in expenditure increases (causing the increase in government expenditures to be less than the growth in the national economy).

As is true of other countries, a portion of the so-called tax reduction in West Germany actually offsets past inflation-induced tax increases. What makes the German tax cut significant is that it is accompanied by a determined effort to control the real tax on the German economy—government expenditures. In addition the national government appears to be responding strongly to international forces (in spite of domestic political opposition due to sluggish growth and high unemployment in West Germany in the late 1980s). At the same time, a major debate over tax policy in the late 1980s appeared to be over whether the reform goals could be moved forward to 1989, not over the reform planned for 1990.[58]

Proponents of more tax reform stress that tax cuts are needed to compensate for the highly regulated German economy, which is clogged with red tape, highly restrictive hiring and firing laws, and limitations on shop-opening hours. The extensive regulations are apparently contributing to a highly developed underground economy, which has been estimated to be as much as 10 percent of GDP.[59] The continued regulation of the German financial markets, when other capital markets around the world are being freed of government constraints, and the withholding of taxes on interest income were, apparently, giving rise in the late 1980s to a nontrivial amount of capital flight.[60]

*Italy*

We noted earlier that growth of government in Italy, as a share of GDP, appears to have gone unchecked by international forces through the late 1980s. The same can be said of Italian tax policies. Italy's apparent motivation for initiating reforms and lowering marginal tax rates has been to offset partially the effects of "bracket creep" caused by significant inflation in the 1980s, to increase revenues, and to dampen excessive domestic demand that threatens to lead to higher inflation rates.[61] In 1988 the tax benefits of lowered personal income tax rates were outweighed by greater restrictions on the evaluation of assets, a speedup of corporate income tax payments, and an increase in the VAT—all of which caused Italian tax revenues to rise slightly as a percentage of GDP.[62] The greater revenue collections were designed to reduce domestic demand and inflation and, thereby, terminate a depreciation of the lira on international money markets.

How much weight can be given to official tax-law changes in Italy is uncertain. Italians are internationally renowned for their capacity to avoid and evade the tax authorities. According to one study, the declared income on Italian tax returns in 1984 amounted to only 50.2 percent of the estimated total income of its citizens.[63] The tax authorities must contend with the prospects of greater tax-base erosion from expanded tax avoidance and tax evasion (which are, as we have noted, forms of resource mobility that we suspect will rise). Critics have little faith that the tax-collection system can be significantly improved.[64] Perhaps the inability of the Italians to "get their tax act together" is one of the country's great hopes for continued economic development in the competitive world economy.

At the same time the Italian government appears ready to return control of an increasing share of Italian industry back to market forces and, in the words of the Italian minister of industry, "to remove many bureaucratic headaches and obstacles that still confront companies operating in Italy, introduce competitiveness in public services, promote a new flow of foreign and domestic investments and stimulate small- and medium-sized industry."[65] Like all the other countries in Europe, Italy must face the prospects of the increased competition among industries and governments that will spring from the unification of Europe in 1992.

## Japan

The 1985 tax-reform movement in Japan appears to have been motivated by four major considerations.[66] First, Japanese policymakers were concerned that the steep and growing progressiveness of the tax code was distorting incentives. In the 1960s and 1970s, marginal tax rates rose from a range of 20 to 55 percent to a range of 10 to 75 percent. Indeed, the maximum marginal rate, including local taxes, broached 93 percent.[67]

Second, the inequality in Japanese incomes had greatly narrowed since immediately after World War II; the tax code needed, or so it was argued, to be adjusted to reflect the new income distribution (and correct the waning usefulness of the tax system as a means of redistributing income).[68]

Third, given Japan's high savings rate, the existing tax exemptions for savings were no longer viewed as productive and were also causing criticism abroad (mainly because the high savings rate might be holding down Japanese imports, particularly from the United States).[69]

Finally, and more to the point, because Japan is heavily dependent on foreign trade, it cannot ignore tax-reform movements abroad. As an official of the Japanese Ministry of Finance argued:

> In the present world, the domestic economies are so closely interrelated that Japan cannot be immune to the international environment. Large differences in tax burdens among countries are likely to produce distortions not only in international trade but also in the domestic economy. *Active corporations may consider avoiding heavy tax burdens by moving their place of business to countries where taxes are lower.* Such a development could make the Japanese economy less dynamic, if not actually depressed [italics added].[70]

The major reform that took effect in 1987 significantly reduced the marginal personal income tax rates at both the national and local levels, and reduced total national income tax collections by an amount equaling .8 percent of GDP.[71] The income bracket to which the lowest marginal rate, 10.5 percent, was applied increased threefold. In effect, reform meant that two-thirds of all Japanese wage earners would be taxed at only 10.5 percent.[72] And virtually all workers could anticipate never facing a marginal tax rate of more than 15 percent.[73]

The reform reduced the national corporate income tax from 43.3 to 37.5 percent over a three-year period. Because of local corporate taxes, the overall reduction in corporate income tax would not be as large as the national rate reduction.[74] What is significant about the corporate rate reductions, as small as they were, is that they came on the heels of repeated increases in the corporate tax rate during the 1960s and 1970s.[75] As a consequence, through their corporate income tax, the Japanese have generated more tax revenue as a percentage of GDP (6 percent) than any other industrial countries except Denmark and Luxembourg.[76] The personal and corporate tax-rate reductions were partially offset through a substantial contraction of tax-exempt savings.[77]

Apparently the Japanese have felt a continuing need to make their tax system more competitive, given reforms in the United States.[78] In late 1988 the Takeshita government engineered the passage of another tax bill that dropped the top national marginal income tax rate from 60 to 50 percent and the top local income tax rate from 16 to 15 percent. The top corporate income tax rate was also lowered from 42 to 27.5 percent, and excise taxes on liquor, automobiles, electrical appliances, and luggage were decreased from the 20 percent range to a uniform 3 percent. Japan's Economic Planning Agency estimated that the 1988 tax-reform bill would reduce total personal and corporate income tax collections in 1989 by the equivalent of $46 billion.[79]

### The Netherlands

The future of tax reform in the Netherlands is constrained by one important fact: "The high rates of taxes and contributions are the result of government spending and an excessive social security system. When the public sector siphons off approximately two-thirds of national income, as it does in the Netherlands, taxes and contributions must be high."[80] Apparently, the high tax rates have inspired an immensely complex tax code, perhaps more complicated than that of the United States.[81]

Nonetheless the complexity of the tax system, coupled with growing tax fraud and evasion, has given rise to plans for modest reforms by 1990. The main feature of the reform will be an integration of social security contributions with the personal income tax code. In 1990 the starting marginal rate will be 40 percent (10 percent for personal income taxes and 30 percent for social security taxes), and the top rate will be 70 percent.[82] Approximately 80 to 88 percent of Dutch workers will face a "flat tax" at the initial marginal rate. However, they will also pay an additional 20 percent of their wages to their "employee insurance programs," meaning that the vast majority of Dutch workers, after reform, will face a marginal tax rate of 60 percent. However, many workers may receive a minor rate reduction, given the higher rate in the reform code.[83]

About the only expected benefit of tax reform in the Netherlands is tax simplification. Because of growing public restlessness with the high tax burden, one Dutch official says, "It is possible to speak about a tax cut of the highest tax rates to 60 percent without being called a dreamer."[84]

### New Zealand

Tax reform in New Zealand is part and parcel of so-called Rogernomics—the economic policies of Roger Douglas, an avowed socialist who became finance minister when the Labour government took over in 1984. Like Ronald Reagan, Douglas was (until he stepped down in 1988) an ardent advocate of less reliance on government programs, greater deregulation of private industries, and more privatization of government services. More important, Douglas had the political will to get many of his proposed reforms enacted.[85] Under his leadership the New Zealand government deregulated its financial markets; eliminated the minimum wage; reduced interest, export, and import controls; lowered agricultural and business subsidies; and put $14 billion worth of government assets up for sale, partially to lower the budget deficit.[86]

The Labour government appears to have accepted, at least while Douglas was finance minister, all major tenets of supply-side economics. As we have noted before, supply-siders maintain that many government activities, including tax collections, provide the wrong incentives for economic growth and development. Accordingly, while equity concerns were said to be a major rhetorical impetus for reform, efficiency appears to have been the central force.[87] New Zealand's high marginal tax rates, which reached 66 percent when Douglas was appointed, encouraged tax evasion and avoidance, discouraged work and saving, and diverted much-needed professional talents into playing tax games with investments.[88] In seeking to reconcile his policies with his socialist ideology, Finance Minister Douglas noted:

> The reason [for our policies], in fact, is very simple. It is because this government is more interested in ends than it is in means. We are hungry for results and not obsessed with process. There is nothing *socialistic* about high inflation, nor about high levels of foreign debt, about an economy which does not grow for a decade and a half, about unemployment rising from nil to 6 percent of the labour force in a decade. And there is nothing socialistic about waste and inefficiencies in state sector and protected industries, nor in a tax system which encourages speculation at the expense of production.[89]

Reform in New Zealand has been similar to reforms elsewhere around the world. Marginal tax rates were reduced from a range of

20 to 66 percent of personal income in 1985 to a range of 15 to 48 percent in 1986. However, in order to make up for lost revenues, the tax base was broadened and a form of the VAT, called the "goods and services tax," was introduced in 1986 at 10 percent. In addition the corporate income tax rate was raised from 45 to 48 percent, an increase that was adopted in anticipation of the full imputation of corporate income taxes between 1988 and 1989.[90] The net impact of the tax reforms has been that total tax revenues rose from 31 percent of GDP in 1984 to 38 percent in 1988. The government's critics charge that New Zealand's sluggish—and, at times, zero—growth can be credited to the breadth of reforms under Rogernomics, which caused excessive economic disruptions.[91]

Douglas responded in 1988 to his critics by arguing that reforms had not been broad and deep enough, and by proposing to lower marginal tax rates further. After first seeking a totally flat personal income tax rate of 24 percent in 1987 and being rebuffed politically, he returned to the tax-reform podium in 1988 with a proposed rate reduction that included only two steps: 24 and 33 percent (this proposal, if enacted, would reduce the highest marginal rate to exactly one-half the highest rate in effect when he assumed office). The anticipated revenue loss would be partially offset by a proposed 2.5 percent increase in the VAT.[92]

The combination of lower marginal tax rates and higher VAT tends to flatten the overall tax burden as a percentage of income, meaning that the tax payments of low-income groups may increase. At the same time, we suppose that Douglas would argue that the economic fate of low-income groups will be determined by his entire reform package—which includes tax reforms that may increase (low-income) tax payments but will also result in (low-income) consumers having lower product prices attributable to fewer government intrusions in the economy. The totality of the reform package, Douglas argued, harbors the prospect of greater future growth. His major problem may have been that the benefits of the reforms may not be realized for a number of years to come, probably not until after the next election.[93]

*Sweden*

Ranked by tax burden in the first half of the 1980s, Sweden topped the list of major industrial countries (and probably all other countries). In 1985 its total taxes were 50.5 percent of GDP. After tax reform the top marginal tax in 1988 was 75 percent, down from the top marginal rate of 82 percent in 1984.[94] As in the Netherlands, what can be accomplished through tax reform is limited by the size of the public sector. The public sector in Sweden claims a higher share of GDP expenditures than in any other industrial country, more than 60 percent of GDP in 1985 (see table 6.1).

Tax reform in Sweden appears to have been motivated by six factors. First, a sizable percentage of the voting public objected to the high marginal tax rates. Almost half the public faced marginal tax rates higher than 50 percent. (The marginal tax rate exceeded 100 percent in some cases.) The 1983–85 tax reform reduced marginal rates by up to 20 percentage points, no mean accomplishment for a country that had become the epitome of the "welfare state."[95] Furthermore, in late 1988 Sweden's government announced a tax reform that would lower income tax rates by as much as 50 percent by 1991, or that would lower the marginal tax rate for nine out of ten Swedes with incomes of less than $26,000 a year from 60 to 30 percent.[96]

Second, tax avoidance and tax evasion, through the "growth of an informal, gray economy with a private exchange of services and do-it-yourself activities," were seriously eroding the tax base.[97] While these problems may not have been serious when compared with similar problems in other countries, the late Swedish economist and Nobel laureate Gunnar Myrdal felt he had good reason to characterize the once-law-abiding Swedes as a people of "cheaters" and "hustlers."[98] Harvard tax expert Lawrence Lindsey reports that "when you negotiate with your employer, wages don't come up. You talk about lifestyle. Once that is settled, you get together to figure out the best way of paying for that lifestyle. The objective is to have the government pick up as much of the cost as possible."[99]

Third, the tax system discouraged saving and encouraged borrowing; as a result the Swedes' low savings rate of the 1970s reached zero and even went below zero in the 1980s (in spite of the lower marginal rates).[100]

Fourth, the tax system had apparently discouraged Swedes from working. In the two decades before 1981, the hours worked by male and female Swedes between the ages of twenty-five and sixty-four had declined by 18 and 25 percent, and two-thirds of the decline was attributed to the high- and rising-income marginal tax rates.[101] (By 1987, five years after tax reform, the total number of hours worked by Swedes had rebounded to the level achieved in 1970.[102])

Fifth, the Swedish tax system had become so complicated that policymakers were apparently willing to sacrifice equity concerns for simplicity in filing.

Finally, as was especially true of the Germans and Japanese, in the 1980s the Swedes took account of the growing integration of world economies and tax developments in other countries, especially in the United States:

> The increasing internationalization of Sweden's economy is making it more susceptible to developments in the rest of the world. . . . Excessive differences in tax rates between Sweden and other countries also involve the risk of production, employment, and capital being transferred to countries where taxes are lower.[103]

Like the United States and its European neighbors, Sweden has sought to offset the influence of marginal rate reductions by broadening its tax base. The ongoing reform process may reduce the top marginal rate to as low as 60 percent.[104] We believe this critically depends upon continued restraint on public expenditures as a percent of GDP (which fell slightly between 1982 and 1985).[105]

### United Kingdom

Margaret Thatcher, who by 1990 had been prime minister of Great Britain longer than anyone else in this century, dominated world economic policy discussions in the 1980s. Probably more than anyone else, too, including Ronald Reagan, she made supply-side incentives matter in policy debates. She had to do so, because government growth in Great Britain was virtually out of control when she came into office. In the middle and late 1970s, the British economy faced stagnation and a future free fall in economic performance. The perceived problem was widely dubbed the "British disease"—the unrelenting grip of union wage demands and work rules and pervasive government-created disincentives to saving and investment, work, and growth.

After all, the marginal tax rate on personal income in Britain reached 83 percent in 1979 and, through inflation, was being leveled against a growing percentage of national income. Tax evasion and avoidance were also increasing, with the British becoming renowned for finding more economic merit in buying Rolls-Royces than investing in productive plants and equipment.

The Thatcher solution was to rely more extensively on private decision-making and private markets, initiated by tax-rate reductions. Tax reform in Britain began in earnest in 1979 (before "Reaganomics"), with a reduction in marginal tax rates from a range of 33 to 83 percent to a range of 30 to 60 percent. Between 1979 and 1987, the income tax thresholds at which each step of the new rate schedule applied were raised in real terms by 22 percent. Capital gains taxes were indexed; a variety of taxes on investment income, national insurance, and land development were abolished; and the corporate income tax rate was reduced from 52 to 35 percent. To compensate for the potential revenue loss from these changes, the VAT was increased from 8 to 15 percent.[106]

In the 1980s total tax collections actually rose as a percentage of GDP (at factor cost), from 38.4 percent in 1979 to 46.2 percent in 1981–82, only to fall slightly to 45 percent by 1987–88.[107] However, the rise in taxes was partially intentional, designed to reduce deficit spending as a percentage of GDP. As we indicated earlier, tax reform was accompanied by a leveling of the growth in government expenditures as a share of GDP. It is also important to note that tax collections have increased, apparently because incentives for the rich to avoid and evade taxes decreased and because people had greater incentive to move up the income scale.[108]

The success of the first tax-reform effort caused the Thatcher government to push for the elimination of the top five tax brackets, as noted, reducing the top marginal rate from 60 to 40 percent in the late 1980s. As Chancellor of the Exchequer Nigel Lawson explained in making the reform proposal in March 1988, "The reason for the worldwide trend towards lower top rates of tax is clear. Excessive rates of income tax destroy enterprise, encourage avoidance, and drive talent to more hospitable shores overseas."[109] Nevertheless, the economic consequences of the decade of income tax reform has been characterized "disappointing," given the magnitude of the rate reductions, primarily because the benefits of rate reform have been undercut by the "increasingly convoluted structure of national insurance contributions, which are now a tax of almost equal significance."[110]

## The General Attributes of Tax Reform

One cannot read through various explanations of tax-reform efforts in different countries without noting the considerable concern with the equity of distribution of the tax burden of the countries. At the same time, concern for improved efficiency seems to be as prevalent, if not more prevalent, a concern as greater equity. Tax

reformers in the 1980s sought improvement in the allocation of resources; less waste of resources because of tax-code manipulation;
and a dampening of tax-induced disincentives for work, saving, investment, and growth. People around the world appeared to be tired of
tax codes that had unnecessary complications and retarded economic
growth. However, people around the world also seemed unable to
simplify their tax codes. On the other hand, they appeared to be
able to trade off, if necessary, some equity benefits in order to achieve
some improvement in efficiency. There has been a clear willingness
to reduce the progressiveness of taxes through a flatter personal income
tax rate structure and through the imposition of (or increases in)
indirect taxes, of which the VAT is an example.

By focusing on improvements in efficiency, we do not seek a
single and exclusive explanation for the widespread tax reform in
the 1980s. There have been a number of important forces at work
in the various tax-reform movements, not the least of which includes
the arrival in the West, and on the world political scene, of key
political movements of a generally conservative stripe.

Tax reform can also be attributed in part to a number of academic
and policy studies that highlighted both the adverse and perverse
consequences for incentives of high marginal tax rates and that emphasized that the tax disincentives could be moderated by reducing the
marginal rates simultaneously with broadening the tax base (which
permits a constancy or increase in the average tax rate). In addition,
by the end of the 1970s, most tax codes around the world had become
such a maze that a growing body of voters could easily see the waste
of resources tied up just in filing tax returns.

But we must return to our central theme: The growing integration
of world economies and the growing mobility of human and physical
capital appear to have carried substantial weight in fortifying the
reform movement. In arguing the merits of reform, too many government officials point to what other governments have done. The facts
that tax reform in the United States followed closely on the heels
of tax reform in the United Kingdom, and that tax reform elsewhere
followed closely on the heels of reform in the United States, confirm
our basic thesis.

This thesis holds with even greater force if the various underground (gray, or subterranean) economies—inspired by high tax rates
and much tax avoidance and tax evasion—are viewed as viable and
expanding (national) competitors to their (national) counterparts above
ground. A common argument for tax reform has been based on the

need of governments to halt the flow of resources, including capital, into their economies' soft underbellies. Policymakers appear to recognize these underground economies as on par with foreign economies. They should, because the underground economies of a number of countries, especially underdeveloped countries, constitute more than a third of gross domestic product.[111] In the case of Israel, the growth of the underground economy, which may account for as much as 20 percent of the country's total production, was a major consideration in the 1988 tax-reform proposal.[112]

Our thesis might be suspect if tax reform were limited to only major advanced countries. However, tax reform, which has with growing frequency been described by policymakers and commentators as "tax competition," has in recent years spread to many other less-developed countries. For example, economist Alan Reynolds reports significant marginal tax-rate reductions in host of other smaller and less-developed countries, including Bolivia, Botswana, Brazil, Chile, China, Colombia, Egypt, Greece, Grenada, Guatemala, India, Indonesia, Israel, Jamaica, South Korea, Malaysia, Mauritius, Mexico, Pakistan, the Philippines, Portugal, Puerto Rico, Singapore, South Korea, Spain, Thailand, Trinidad and Tobago, and Turkey.[113] Why did all these countries lower their top marginal tax rates by an average 25 percent, from an average of 58.9 percent in 1979 to 44.2 percent in 1989?[114] Their reasons are probably as diverse as the ones cited in our review of tax-reform movements in the major advanced countries.[115]

We think it is very important to observe the growing worldwide interest in the efficiency of government expenditures and taxes. That interest is more indicative of the apparent retardation of government expenditures relative to national economies and to the growing tax competition than is the growth in tax revenues measured in terms of so many billions of the national currency or as a percent of GDP. This is true because, as noted, changes in the level of tax collections may be intended to close the deficit gap in national budgets. We emphasized earlier that the crucial tax on the private sector comes in the form of government expenditures. In addition, lower tax rates may stimulate economic growth and give rise to a shift of resources from the underground to aboveground economy. In this way lower rates may cause increases in absolute or relative tax collections.

Although we do observe reversals of past fiscal trends, we do not see a massive shift away from reliance on government institutions. The demonstration of a massive shift is not necessary, however, in order to make our point, which is that the growth in the power of government is being gradually and persistently checked by worldwide economic forces. We do think that the studies and data show government policymakers being compelled to do things in response to domestic political forces that they would not freely choose to do in a less integrated and less mobile world. This point is reinforced by additional changes in the regulatory policies of world governments.

## Regulatory Reform

Government regulation of industry still abounds throughout the world, and governments still control much of their nations' wealth and provide most of the traditional government services. The trend toward reduced government involvement in economic activity is mixed, with successes, failures, and multiple crosscurrents surrounding the efforts of competing political factions. Obviously not all moves to deregulate industries have been successful. The partial deregulation of the U.S. savings and loan industry, without deregulation of the industry's deposit insurance, is a sorry example of how not to deregulate. Furthermore, there are political moves to extend government regulation, for example, in the areas of child care, environment, and worker health insurance, and to reregulate once-deregulated industries, for example, airlines and trucking.[116]

Nevertheless, on balance, markets are progressively being freed, if not at a rapid pace, at least faster than could have been imagined two decades ago, when policymakers gave little thought to holding back expanding government regulation. Others have devoted their attention to the benefits achieved by deregulation. Our concern here is with the global scale of the deregulation movement, in which the United States took the lead (though some may be surprised that it gained its initial momentum in the 1970s under the middle-of-the-road Carter administration and the liberal leadership in the Senate of Edward Kennedy).

Furthermore, the worldwide deregulation movement has been complemented by a worldwide movement to "privatize," or return to private control, many government properties and services. The lead in the privatization movement has been assumed not by the United States (as might be expected) but by many other countries.[117]

Of all the OECD countries, the United Kingdom has probably followed the United States most closely in deregulation. Great Britain has increased competition in much of its transportation industry, including airlines, airports, buses, and railroads.[118] It has also increased competition in the mail, telecommunications, and energy industries. The 1984 Cable and Broadcasting Act permits private cable companies to run cables and lifts the ban on direct reception by individuals of low-powered satellite broadcasts. Britain has ended state control of the British oil industry and has permitted private use of the pipelines of the state-owned British Gas Corporation.[119]

Australia has relaxed controls on domestic air freight and has also refused to enforce the tariffs and rules of the international airline cartel. Canada and West Germany plan to increase the freedom of entry and exit in their airline industries and restructure their flight schedules and routes to meet increased competition. In addition Canada has increased competition in energy by allowing refiners and distributors to buy oil from Canadian or foreign sources with no restrictions on volumes and prices. West Germany has started licensing private broadcasters to operate alongside state-owned stations. The Germans are also in the process of setting a time limit on cartel agreements in the electricity, gas, and water industries.

Even France, one of the two OECD countries whose government expenditures in the 1980s continued to climb as a percentage of GDP, has begun to deregulate, albeit to a modest degree, with retrenchments from "industrial policies" designed in the 1960s and 1970s. These abandoned policies were previously backed by budget and tax support and by protection from imports. They were intended to promote sectors government officials thought likely to become industrial "national champions."[120] Aid to ailing industries increased between 1976 and 1982 to the point that observers worried about "creeping nationalism" under the banner of "Reconquer the domestic market."

Because the industrial policies and the protectionist measures appeared to be ineffective or to have perverse effects (for example, "inhibiting intersectoral factor mobility and ossifying the industrial structure"[121]), the role of the central government in determining France's industrial structure was curtailed in the 1985–88 period. First, government expenditures for "sectoral assistance" were reduced by 20 percent between 1978 and 1984 and stabilized in current-franc terms. Aid to exporters, which had expanded threefold between 1978 and 1981, was cut by more than 50 percent in 1987 from the 1981 level.[122] Second, the government has substituted a lower, nondiscriminatory corporate tax rate for the variety of discriminatory tax relief policies.[123] Third, in 1987 the government eliminated most price controls on most private-sector services and removed many barriers to competition. For example, quotas for trucking began to be phased out, certain parapharmaceutical products can now be sold outside pharmacies, and some deregulation was introduced into telecommunications.[124]

While Spain's tax burden has been raised, the socialist government of Prime Minister Felipe Gonzalez has pressed ahead with its reform program, which has been called "supply-side socialism" or "Thatcherite socialism." Duties on imports and subsidies for industries like steel and shipbuilding have been drastically reduced, and rules for laying off workers have been greatly eased.[125]

Even Indonesia has joined the deregulation movement, by abolishing the country's monopoly on plastics, ending many controls on steel imports, giving foreign investors a role in the distribution of products at the wholesale level, and opening up the country's tightly controlled shipping industry.[126]

Almost everywhere, government regulation of financial markets is being gradually yet persistently dismantled. Without question, the ease with which capital can flow across industries and national boundaries through computer and communication networks has played a substantial role in the deregulation of banks, brokerage firms, and money markets. The movement of financial capital simply became too large and expansive for governments to control effectively. And government impediments, ranging from controls on interest rates to brokerage fees, on the movement of very fluid financial capital can only insure that the flow will go elsewhere. In the United States the government was forced to decontrol interest rates on bank deposits in the 1980s simply because of rising interest rates in securities markets and the resulting difficulty banks were having with "disintermediation," or stopping deposits from moving to nonbank substitutes, for example, money-market mutual funds, which had grown rapidly since 1971.[127]

For several years, concern has been rising over the growing influence of foreign banks in the U.S. economy, all of which has given rise to political demands that U.S. financial markets be closed off to foreign, especially Japanese, banks. However, Federal Reserve Chairman Alan Greenspan recognized the extent to which policymakers' hands are tied. Restrictions on the entry of foreign institutions into domestic markets would take the pressure off domestic banks to become more competitive. Besides, Greenspan observed, "The globalization of financial markets means that most of the business that foreign banks do with U.S. customers could alternatively be done offshore."[128]

## The Privatization Movement

In general the 1970s and 1980s have stood witness to a sustained reexamination of the boundary between the public and private sectors. This reexamination has been spurred in part by an intellectual revolution of no small dimensions.

### Intellectual Trends

The theory of government bureaucracy, which amounts to a harsh critique of the abilities of government to perform efficiently, became an important topic in the 1960s within the emerging subdiscipline of public-choice economics.[129] Later, in the 1970s, it became fashionable for scholars and policymakers alike to question the legitimacy of government programs. The presumption was that their growth was out of control and that they were failing to achieve their stated objectives.[130] Where it was difficult to eliminate grossly ineffective government activities, ways were also sought to improve their efficiency.

One such method that had significant appeal to both the liberal and conservative sides of the political and academic spectrums was the concept of "privatization"—that is, the denationalization of industries, the contracting out of government services to private firms, and the selling off of government assets to the highest bidder.[131] In addition to potential efficiency improvements, privatization afforded conservatives the prospect of getting government out of many activities, and it offered liberals the hope of reducing the growing opposition to many government-sponsored activities.

To one degree or another, many government activities have always been privatized. Government construction projects and defense equipment procurements have predominantly been contracted out to private firms. What was new about the privatization revolution of the 1980s was the greatly expanded range of government activities considered open to provision by the private sector. Many state and local governments in the 1970s moved to contract out garbage collection, water and sewer services, child care, data processing, care of the elderly and handicapped, vehicle maintenance, housing, recreation, traffic signals and lighting, public transportation, utilities, vehicle towing, education, fire protection, road development, tax audits, clinics for spaying and neutering animals, landscaping, janitorial services, hospital care, police protection, and even penal services.[132] Furthermore, privatization continues to grow, according to the chairman of the President's Commission on Privatization in the United States, because "it delivers major savings or improves service quality, or both, to local taxpayers."[133]

### The Growing Popularity of Privatization

*Privatization* is one of those interesting terms that, before the 1980s, was used by only a few economists and policymakers. Yet in the course of a few short years, it has become part of all economists' and policymakers' professional jargon. It has also become an important banner for reform around the world and has achieved support across the political spectrum. Promarket political forces see privatization as a way to extend and fortify the deregulation movement. (After all, privatization implies that government is relinquishing some control of the economy. It also implies, necessarily, more private decision making and responsibility—which can induce greater care and efficiency in economic choices.)

Advocates of expanded government see privatization as a means of "empowering the masses" with ownership rights to public enterprises (which span public utilities, industrial firms, and public-housing projects) and of increasing government revenues, albeit temporarily.[134] Privatization also offers the hope of making government-orchestrated services more cost-effective, and therefore more appealing to electorates that may have grown more conservative after hearing repeated reports on the inefficiency of public bureaucracies.

According to a series of Reason Foundation reports, a computer search of major English-language publications in 1985 found 457 citations to articles dealing with privatization. By 1987 the citation count had nearly quadrupled to 2,195. By 1988 it had nearly doubled again to 3,838.[135]

### Country-by-Country Privatization Efforts

Political substance has apparently followed the growing volume of writings on privatization. In all the years prior to 1987, revenues generated by all governments' efforts to privatize state-owned enterprises amounted to $18 billion. In 1987 alone $117 billion of state-owned enterprises were privatized. In 1988 sales increased 37 percent to $160 billion. Admittedly most of the sales occurred in three countries—the United States, United Kingdom, and Japan—but the privatization movement showed no signs of abating in the late 1980s.[136] Indeed, if anything, the political appeal of privatization was spreading in the late 1980s as a result of the growing number of success stories.

All told, by 1987 the privatization movement had spread to six continents and at least sixty-five countries—including even the Soviet Union, several Eastern European countries, and China.[137] In addition to the $110 billion in state-owned assets that had already been privatized around the world by 1987, $40 billion more were scheduled for privatization in the years after 1987. More than two thousand worldwide state-owned operations have been under serious consideration for privatization until the year 2000.

Privatization in the United Kingdom is not totally new to the 1980s. In the 1960s and 1970s, before the Thatcher government, privatization simply went by another name—*denationalization*. However, what is new to the United Kingdom in the 1980s is the momentum achieved by the privatization movement.[138] Prior to 1987, the Thatcher administration gave the movement a critical political boost by selling off the British Gas Corporation, Rolls-Royce, National Freight Corporation, British Telecommunications, and 850,000 public-housing units.[139] In 1987 the government sold off British Airways and British Petroleum, as well as its British Airport Authority, which owned and/or operated seven major airports in the United Kingdom. Through 1988 the Thatcher government had sold close to $40 billion of its industrial assets.[140] In 1987 the government also agreed to continue with its plans to privatize the Central Electricity Generating Board, British Steel, high-rise public housing, the postal service, and prisons. Furthermore, in a move that potentially expands privatized local services, the national government required all local governments to seek competitive bids on such traditional local-government services as garbage collection, street and building cleaning, vehicle maintenance, ground maintenance, and school meals.[141] Even more recently the Thatcher government has proposed to sell off its huge water industries, which, at the time, were hotly contested.[142]

In France in 1986 and 1987, the privatized companies included the Compagnie Générale d'Electricité; CGCT telephone service; St. Gobain (a glass producer); and a major television network, TFI. The national government also announced plans in 1987 to sell off another $16.4 billion of assets in state-owned financial and industrial companies.[143]

In West Germany in 1986 and 1987, shares in VEBA and VIAG were sold, thereby partially privatizing the firms, both of which were energy and chemical concerns. After a couple of years of delay, in 1988 Germany also sold its shares of the automobile producer Volkswagen and had plans to sell in 1989 or later a portion of the government's interest in the airline Lufthansa and three major financial institutions.[144]

In 1987 Austria sold shares in Oesterreichische Länderbank and OMV, an oil and chemical company, and plans were announced to sell 25 percent of Austrian Airlines in 1988 and 49 percent of the government's interest in eight electric power and distribution companies over the following five years. In Italy, between 1983 and 1985, the government sold more than twenty state-owned companies, including Alfa Romeo to Fiat. The Italian government also planned to sell MedioBanca and SIP, a telephone company, and to build waste-recovery plants to be funded with private money.[145]

In Finland the government reduced its interest in an electric equipment company, and in Sweden a port was privatized and a steel company was partially privatized. Belgium sold off a portion of its interest in a biotechnology firm, and the Netherlands reduced its interest in KLM airlines; NBM, a chemical company; and Dutch State Mines. Spain sold off major shares in several manufacturing firms; among these was SEAT, an automobile company, to Volkswagen, and Repsol Exploration S.A., a state-owned oil company.[146]

Eight airports, an aircraft factory, an arms depot, and several government offices around the world have been put up for sale in Australia. New Zealand has sold part of its interest in Petrocorp and New Zealand Steel. The country also plans to privatize Air New Zealand and the Development Finance Corporation and to sell an additional nine government-owned corporations, including ones that deal in coal, electricity, and forestry.[147]

According to calculations of the Reason Foundation, Japan had already in 1987 raised more funds from its privatization efforts than Great Britain. The Japanese companies totally or partially privatized by 1987 included Japan Air Lines and the Nippon Telephone and Telegraph Corporation, which had lost its monopoly status in 1985.[148] In addition, the government had plans in 1987 to privatize the Japan National Railway, Japan Tobacco, Salt Monopoly corporation, and Okinawa Electric Power Company.[149]

Canada was considering in late 1987 the privatization of companies owned by the national government, including Petro-Canada and the Canada National Hotels.[150] However, British Columbia, a province, has taken the lead among provinces in Canada, privatizing BC Hydroelectric's distribution system, BC Enterprises Corporations (a real estate firm), BC Rail, BC Ferry Corporation, and the Insurance Company of British Columbia.[151]

Significant privatization efforts, in one form or another, are also under way in many Third World countries.[152] According to a World Bank study, in 1980 there were at least 4,137 state enterprises in Africa, Latin America, and Asia. By 1987 at least 136 of them had been closed or liquidated. An additional 553 state enterprises had been targeted for sale in the 1980s, 433 of which had actually been sold by 1987. More than 55 state enterprises were being handled by management contracts with private firms.[153]

In 1990 the privatization movement showed every sign of picking up steam. Canada announced plans to sell off the state oil company Petro-Canada, and Puerto Rico indicated its willingness to sell the state-run telephone company to the highest bidder, which was expected to be in the $2 billion range. Even the recently deposed Marxist-Leninist Sandinista government in Nicaragua went into its 1990 election with a platform that called for privatizing the country's national airline, and Democrats in the U.S. Congress proposed that the U.S. Postal Service and Amtrak be sold—lock, stock, and barrel— to their employees.[154]

At times privatization has also entailed the extension of traditional government services, requiring additional infrastructure, through private development. For example, a tunnel underneath the English Channel, the "Chunnel," will be financed and operated by a private company but will be connected to the London area through a private toll road owned and operated by another company. The Communist government of mainland China has granted a thirty-year lease on a private toll road between Canton and Hong Kong.[155]

One of the most amazing aspects of the privatization movement is that it does not appear inextricably bound to political ideology. As we have noted, even socialist and communist governments have become active privatizers. Many of these governments have been attracted to privatization as a means of expanding rather than contracting the involvement of government in the economy, of tapping an additional source of revenues, and of reducing their reported deficit spending. At the same time, government leaders of all political stripes appear to have recognized the efficiency improvements many privatized services offer. Many leaders see in privatization a means of relieving the effective burden their citizens must bear from government activities. The world's owners of human and physical capital can be expected to continue to pay heed to such improvements. A number of governments have probably been induced to consider privatization because of their need to remain competitive in world capital markets, if not to serve the needs of their constituencies more effectively.[156] If that is the case, more governments are likely to join the privatization movement, and the governments that are already involved can be expected to increase their efforts to stay one ("privatized") step ahead of their government competitors. We suggest this will probably be the case because of the tightening economic constraints on tax policies. When constrained in their ability to raise tax rates, privatization offers political leaders the promise of a one-time cash intake and, therefore, a respite from making difficult decisions over which government benefit program must be cut.

## The Free-market Movement

The late 1980s may go down as something of a watershed in economic history. The rhetoric of market economics was being heard in the most unusual corners of the globe. Poland sought economic aid from the United States in 1989 to bolster its free-market reforms, while Hungary's Communist party renamed itself the Socialist party the same year in an effort to better characterize its political program of greater reliance on markets. Abel Aganbegyan, Mikhail Gorbachev's chief economic adviser, characterized Milton Friedman, prominent defender of the free-market faith, as a "great thinker" whose "concrete theories . . . can be of great use to us," and then gives "quite high marks" to Margaret Thatcher's privatization and tax-reduction policies.[157] Reports repeatedly surfaced in 1989 on market reforms in Latin America, from Mexico to Argentina. Perhaps nowhere in Latin America have market reforms been more fervently embraced than in Nicaragua where, because of the reforms, 16,000 civilian government and 10,000 military jobs were abolished in 1989, cuts that were a part of a 50 percent reduction in government spending.[158] This was followed by the election of a democratic government. While Brazil was still experiencing an inflation rate of over 300 percent a month in 1989, the rhetoric of the presidential election campaign was changing radically. The eventual winner, Fernando Collor de Mello, ran as an antistatist, Reagan-style campaign, arguing that inefficient government companies should be privatized and that subsidies ought to be drastically cut. One Brazilian commentator noted that "people in Brazil have become aware that big government is the sore spot of the Brazilian economy. . . . Their proclamations to privatize government companies, dismiss millions of public servants and jail corrupt officials are non-ideological, calculated responses to the reality of a system caving in on itself."[159]

Babson College economist Laurence Moss probably spoke for

many Western visitors when he surmised upon his return from his trip to China, "Ten years ago no one imagined China would reach out to embrace capitalist economic methods. During Mao Zedong's Cultural Revolution, bands of teenagers had roamed China's countryside, burning books, destroying historical monuments, and dragging reluctant counterrevolutionaries through the streets. Thousands of citizens were forced to renounce their bourgeois-capitalist ways and close their flourishing commercial institutions. Today [1988] the news media are filled with reports of China's return to capitalism."[160]

By Western standards China retains a highly controlled economy, and the Tiananmen Square massacre in 1989 reminded the world that Chinese leaders have not renounced brutal force as a means of control. Nevertheless the leaders have acknowledged that they are not sufficiently powerful to command efficient production in an economy the size of China and that they need to greatly increase their production efficiency to attract foreign capital, not to mention the need to divert Chinese resources, labor and capital, from the indigenous informal economy. If markets are not yet free in China, they certainly are freer. Among the many Western companies that have established joint ventures in China, R. J. Reynolds (tobacco), Gillette (razor blades), Foxboro (automatic controls), and IBM (computers) stand out.[161]

Since the current reform movement started in 1979, much central government authority over industries has been devolved to the provinces, and the realm of individual decision making has been significantly expanded. Before reforms, people were assigned jobs, houses, and ration coupons, since prices were set below market-clearing levels. They often needed to get permission to marry and have children. Peasants were told what to plant and to whom they could distribute their crops.[162]

Since reform, and the adoption of the so-called responsibility system, individuals have been able to change jobs with greater freedom; to buy in black markets that have become "grayer"; and to save through bank deposits, durable goods, farm equipment, and education. University of Michigan economist Roger Gordon reports that farmers have been assigned fixed plots of land for a fifteen-year period at fixed rental payments, and "rural households have been free to make virtually all economic and consumption decisions."[163] As a consequence a quarter of the rural households have shifted out of farming to rural manufacturing, expanding income from rural "community enterprises" (to be distinguished from "private enterprises," which have been discouraged by relatively high tax rates and the subsidies granted state and community enterprises) by 20 percent per year between 1978 and 1986.[164] The remaining farmers have drastically adjusted their crop mixes to meet local climate and soil conditions, official prices paid on quotas, and market prices—often twice the official prices—that could be received on output in excess of the quotas. The result has been a decrease in the production of grains (to minimal levels required by remaining grain quotas) and an expansion in the output of relatively more profitable goods, namely cotton, vegetables, meat, fish, and fruit; an increase in the quality of the produce; and a tripling of farm income between 1979 and 1986.[165]

While the government still assigns jobs in urban centers, free markets have emerged in groceries and consumer goods. The prices, wages, and employment levels of state-owned enterprises remain heavily regulated, primarily through the approval process, but "there appears to be more flexibility than in the past."[166] The ability of these enterprises to reinvest their earnings or to borrow from banks dramatically increased new investment.[167] Given the ebb and flow of decentralization and recentralization movements, the precise direction in which China is heading at this writing remains uncertain. However, the drop-off in foreign investment after the Tiananmen Square massacre suggests that there is strong international pressure for continued liberalization.

## The Competitive Threshold for Government

Our analysis of the economic policies of world governments has no natural ending point. There are simply too many countries and so many government policies relevant to the issue at hand. Instead of seeking to be exhaustive in reviewing government economic policies, we have sought in this chapter to indicate trends in key policy areas. Our research will simply have to be broadened by others.

Obviously the evidence of world policy trends brought to bear in this chapter does not totally support our basic thesis. Inevitable crosscurrents of policies are evident. Some taxes are rising while others are falling. Some governments are increasing their tax take at the same time that they are deregulating private industries and privatizing public services.

But the fundamental point is that during the past twenty years many governments of many political persuasions have sought to become more efficient by adopting new economic strategies. Massive amounts of capital have moved across national borders in response to minute differentials in interest rates, and even more capital has moved in response to significant differences in fiscal and regulatory burdens.

The historical and econometric evidence reviewed in chapter 5, combined with the empirical evidence in this chapter, points inevitably to the full-fledged emergence of modern government markets. Roger Douglas, former finance minister of New Zealand, said it best when he wrote: "The government recognizes that New Zealand must match or better the international trend to lower tax rates if we are to retain skills and investment within our shores."[168]

This is not to say that, in the past, governments have not had to consider their competitive positions. To deny this would be to repudiate the evidence supplied by historians such as North, Polanyi, and Baechler. However, in the last decade or so, governments appeared to have passed through a "competitiveness threshold" that has caused something of a quantum leap in their concern for efficiency and their responsiveness to one another. Governments now appear to be interacting to a degree not fully matched in earlier periods, a point that has not been missed by one economist working for a major international oil company:

> Despite the fear I sense among economists that continuing international economic integration will intensify competition among tax authorities, I expect that such competition will be the salvation of international business in what would otherwise be a grim world of taxes. Such competition will be the only effective restraint on the rapaciousness of the preparers of tax laws and regulations toward those who, by their nature, are not likely to have the political clout, for example, of the "small" local businessman.[169]

We have pointed out that the governments of (at least) West Germany, France, Canada, and Japan took up the tax-reform movement partially because of the reform movement in the United States and the need to remain competitive in capital markets—something that will become more readily apparent after the review of the U.S. policy record in chapters 8 and 9.

The level of competitiveness has escalated to the point that would-be regulators, including distinguished economists, now talk openly about limiting, through international cooperative efforts, the competition among governments. In recognition of growing government competitiveness, Nobel laureate James Tobin has called for more "friction in the system," and Rudiger Dornbusch has suggested that capital controls need to be considered as an ordinary instrument of public finance.[170] The temptation to regulate government competitiveness is ever-present. We suspect, however, that Alan Waters, a former adviser to the Thatcher government, was right when he suggested that the "development of information technology will enable capital owners to outwit the regulators. The bureaucracy will always lag behind the private sector in the use of new methods and techniques of avoiding the network of controls."[171]

# 7

# Quicksilver Commissars

*From the Propaganda of Success to the
Provenance of Competitiveness*

This hen will produce 180 eggs this year,
183 eggs the next, then 185. Why don't we
finally leave this hen alone and let her live
with her rooster. Thanking us for her
independence, this hen will provide us with
enough eggs.

*Moscow City Council Official Gavriil Popov*[1]

THE transformation of government strategies now under
way in the world is not limited to Western countries. Much has
been made of the changing of policies in China, which was, until it
massacred its demonstrating students, experiencing something of a
new economic birth.[2] The same movement is also evident in the
Soviet Union.

President Mikhail Gorbachev and former U.S. President Ronald
Reagan may have disagreed on many issues, but they did have one
thing in common: the belief that economic incentives matter. Accordingly they both recommended sweeping changes in their respective
economies. They both demonstrated that greater prosperity could
be had by reducing the onerous burden imposed by government on
people and by shifting a greater amount of power into decentralized
decision making.

President Reagan's supply-side criticisms of government policies in the United States are well known. He showed how taxes and government subsidies dampened people's inclinations to work, save, and invest. He harbored a well-publicized disdain for welfare cheats.

What is not so well appreciated is that President Gorbachev, in his book *Perestroika*, marshaled criticisms against current policies in the Soviet Union that appear to be transatlantic echoes of Reagan's best critical initiatives.[3] What is astounding about Gorbachev's review of Soviet economic and political problems is his frankness. He openly admits to economic stagnation and to moral decay in the Soviet Union, due in large part to the system's excessive reliance on "officialdom, red tape, patronizing attitudes and careerism."[4] He tells his readers that "the political economy of socialism is stuck with outdated concepts and is no longer in tune with the dialectics of life."[5]

Like many other current leaders commenting on their own countries, President Gorbachev explains that the blame for the Soviet Union's problems is directly attributable to a "specific feature of socialism," namely "the high degree of protection in our society."[6] Although by some standards such a feature may be a mark of achievement, it has also made many people "sponges." Because the state has virtually eliminated unemployment:

> Even a person dismissed for laziness or a breach of labor discipline must be given another job. Also, wage-leveling has become a regular feature of everyday life: even if a person is a bad worker, he gets enough to live fairly comfortably. The children of an outright parasite will not be left to the mercy of fate.[7]

The country's problem, according to Gorbachev, is that:

> dishonest people try to exploit these advantages of socialism; they know only their rights, but they do not want to know their duties: they work poorly, shirk and drink hard. There are quite a few people who have adapted the existing laws and practices to their own selfish interests. They give little to society, but nevertheless [have] managed to get from it all that is possible and what even seems more impossible; they have lived on unearned incomes.[8]

The reader is left to wonder if Reagan or Thatcher were ever so passionate and articulate in criticizing government waste, or whether a Soviet president could have been so blunt a decade ago without being hog-tied and shipped out on the next Siberian express.

In no uncertain terms Gorbachev disclaims as unrealistic and destructive the communist adage, "From each according to ability, to each according to needs." According to him, the new, restructured Soviet economic policy will be guided by a much more practical party line of Lenin, "From each according to ability, to each according to his *work*."[9]

In blunt and subtle twists of Leninist philosophy, Gorbachev claims that renewed economic growth must be based to a substantially greater extent on market principles. He argues that no great nation can produce efficiently when orders are handed down from a central authority. He also maintains that individuals and groups of individuals who are given the authority to make economic decisions formerly made by the state must be held responsible for their decisions. This means that individuals must be subjected to the risk of failure, even to a loss of income and wealth or employment.

Nonetheless Gorbachev recognizes, in full concurrence with the most ardent market supporters, that "amazing things happen when people take responsibility for everything themselves. The results are quite different, and at times people are unrecognizable. Work changes and attitudes to it, too."[10]

Gorbachev's book is important for three principal reasons. First, he explains the logic of his proposed structural changes in the Soviet economy. The similarity between the economic logic undergirding enacted and proposed changes in government policies in the Soviet and U.S. economies, as well as elsewhere, is remarkable. His concern for improving economic efficiency within the Soviet Union is a call being heard in countries around the world.

Gorbachev agrees with the leaders of the West that decentralized decision making is crucial to prosperity. The Soviet president insists that the main dispute between himself and Western leaders is one of degree—that of how much decentralization is politically and economically practical. He asserts that his country will retain a form of socialist economic democracy, wherein workers continue to have a say in how their firms operate. But he also wants those workers to understand that they are both motivated and constrained by the dictates of profit making and financial survival.[11] The Soviet president has backed up his proposals for promarket reforms with action. In 1989 there were 99,300 co-ops in the USSR, of similar legal status to limited partnerships in the West, and these co-ops stood ready to switch to full corporate status once the Supreme Soviet adopted the Corporations Act (which it recently has). A drop in the bucket by Western standards, it is six times the number of Soviet co-ops in existence just a year earlier.[12] In early 1990 much agricultural land in the Soviet Union was effectively privatized, and "citizen property," a Soviet euphemism for private ownership, in the means of production, including factories, was approved.

Second, Gorbachev provides in his book a record of his domestic and worldwide political intentions. He asserts that the Soviet leadership is no longer interested in the persecution of its own people or the domination of others. In effect he says his country must give up many of its missiles and its misadventure in Afghanistan in order to release needed resources for the restructuring process. The country must become more tolerant of criticism of its leaders, its citizens, and its institutions. *Glasnost,* the policy of expanding human rights and political freedoms, is crucial to economic revitalization, or so Gorbachev says.

More important, the Soviet president appears at this time to have the political muscle and will to carry out certain reforms that include, among many others, the return of farming to private control. However, in order to make privatization work, Gorbachev is convinced that some on-the-farm job security must be sacrificed. As he is reported to have said in introducing his reforms in agriculture, "No fool is going to work on a lease contract as long as he can have a salary [on the collective farms] without earning it."[13]

Gorbachev's book is especially intriguing because it spells out his plan for integrating markets with Marxism. In doing so it offers us a great deal of hope—mainly that some of the resources now devoted to military posturing in international disputes soon may be diverted to more productive uses.

What gives substance to the plan of *perestroika* is that it reflects the new perspective of many other socialist leaders of Eastern Europe who have now been labelled "Atari communists" because of their willingness to revise and reinterpret communist doctrine—to allow modern, technologically advanced markets to supplant antique central plans—an ironic reversal of approach on the road from swords to plowshares.

## Battle Stations into Work Stations

The current generation of world citizens is blessed. With the hope of *perestroika* at hand, we stand witness to a remarkable shift in the Soviet Union's military agenda. In a matter of a few years the Soviet Union has gone from actively resisting arms reduction to actively supporting it. Furthermore, it is reversing its past efforts to manipulate the countries of Eastern Europe, thereby indirectly contributing to the expansion of political and economic freedom. The recent dismantling of the Berlin Wall epitomizes the pace of global political events and with it the shift in the Soviet Union's place on the world stage.

However, this reversal in the Soviets' disarmament stance is more directly attributable to the international economic forces embodied in our ongoing discussion of technologically driven forces of communication, capital mobility, and production sophistication than to the rise of Gorbachev and the Atari communists. Indeed, these leadership changes have been strongly influenced by changes in the global economy.

Just over three decades ago, an arrogant Nikita Khrushchev (1894–1971) told the world that communism would bury the West— economically and politically, if not militarily. The ensuing years have been filled with cold and calculated threats and counterthreats between the superpowers reminiscent of ill-mannered schoolboys on the playground. One country built missiles; the other built even more. At times the arms race appeared to have no end. Any reduction in arms seemed like the proverbial pipe dream. The Soviets seldom expressed genuine interest, and the West never trusted them when they did.

Practically since its revolutionary inception, the Soviet Union has forcibly enlisted its citizens into national plans established by party leaders in Moscow. Communist dogma justified the suppression by brute police force of practically all forms of individual expression— speech, religion, and enterprise. People were shot for no greater crime than dissent from the party line. Capital, as in capitalism, was denigrated unless it was owned, managed, and manipulated by the state. Profit made by individuals from the labor of others was, according to Soviet doctrine, the source of capitalism's wickedness and weakness. Economic incentives and disincentives did not exist. Citizens were expected to pursue the state's established goals, and were appropriately schooled in the evils of capitalism and the glories of communism. Military might was always at the ready to extend the Soviet empire where schooling did not.

What a striking difference a death can make! Leonid Brezhnev (1906–1982) was an old school, sword-rattling communist leader. His death may stand as a watershed in the history of human events. He may be remembered for being the last true communist leader, one who looked to communist principles for the defense of national domestic and military policies, even when those policies had been exposed as patent failures.

Mikhail Gorbachev, Brezhnev's successor twice removed, is obviously different, as revolutionary as Lenin in his approach to domestic and international Soviet policies. In terms almost as blunt as those used by Khrushchev, he has told his fellow countrymen that communists will not bury the West but rather themselves, unless they overhaul their political system and adopt the revolutionary economic strategy alluded to at the beginning of this chapter. In words that in the past came only from the detractors of communism, Gorbachev stressed that a part of the "Soviet problem" has been that the Soviet leadership covered up the growing failures of the system with "propaganda of success," which too many of the leaders began to believe and parrot as truth.[14] He has trekked around the world several times, much like Western leaders, in search of capitalists who will invest in his country—with the intent of enabling them, the capitalists, to earn profits through the efforts of the Soviet people.

In fundamental ways the change in the Soviet position on economics reflected in Gorbachev's crusade has altered the Soviet position on armaments. Whereas Soviet leaders once balked at significant moves to disarm, Gorbachev has now co-opted the American lead. Indeed, former President Reagan, who once called the Soviet Union the "evil empire," seemed genuinely befuddled, and understandably so, when first confronted at the Iceland summit in February 1987 with Soviet proposals to eliminate whole classes of missiles and to build down Soviet and American troop strength in Europe. Indeed, there were several American defense leaders—including former Secretary of Defense Caspar Weinberger—who began scrambling to caution the American public against treating the Soviet Union as a newfound ally.[15]

Reagan's confusion could have only been heightened when (on the anniversary of Pearl Harbor, December 7, 1988). Gorbachev announced unilateral reductions in the Soviet forces in Europe. He proposed to pull back from Eastern Europe five hundred thousand Soviet troops (or 20 percent of the Soviet Union's worldwide military manpower) and ten thousand tanks. In addition, Gorbachev's chief cabinet officer, Soviet Prime Minister Nicolai Rizhkov, announced to the newly elected Congress of People's Deputies, "We intend to proceed persistently along the road to disarmament, seeking to reduce the share of national income devoted to defense expenditures by one-third to one-half by 1995."[16] In response, while U.S. defense spending as a percentage of GNP had already been scaled back significantly from its 1985 peak, U.S. Secretary of Defense Dick Cheney has considered $180 billion in cuts over five years after 1990 from a defense budget that was projected to grow by one to two percent per year in real-dollar terms but now will fall slightly in real-dollar terms.[17] If the tendered plan is enacted, it appears that by the middle of the 1990s there will be a 16 percent reduction in active U.S. Army combat divisions, a 20 percent reduction in Air Force fighter wings, and an 11 percent reduction in Navy ships.[18]

## The Political Economy of Disarmament

Why the dramatic shift in Soviet defense policy? Will it continue? Admittedly some conflicting data cast doubt on the Soviet intentions about armaments. According to the Pentagon, despite the announced reductions, the Soviet Union increased defense spending by 14 percent in 1989 alone, and average real growth has been 3 percent since Gorbachev came to power. In addition, before Gorbachev's election, the Soviet military-industrial complex was producing 2,800 tanks a year; in the 1985–88 period, they spewed out tanks 21 percent faster, for an average of 3,400 a year.[19] Further, the shift in Soviet policy may be no more durable than the leaders' political mortality, which former Secretary Weinberger worries is the case.[20] And there remains much to fear if policy trends are viewed as the product of leaders' personalities. However, it is worth noting that the change in direction occurred before Gorbachev. It started with Yuri Andropov, who was Brezhnev's immediate replacement in 1982 but who died in 1984, a year before Gorbachev was elected. Furthermore, citing leadership as the source of change begs the question because it does not explain the shift in Gorbachev's own policy views, and that of all the other loyal Communists who elected him and support his current stances (or that of Gorbachev's political opponents who want more radical reforms).

Obviously Gorbachev was at one time devoted to communist principles of economy and government as reasonably fair and efficient guides for collective decision making. Without such dedication it is doubtful that he could have risen through the ranks of the Communist party, which he joined in 1952, when Stalin was still in control.[21] Indeed, Gorbachev's book *Perestroika* provides ample evidence of the intellectual struggle he experienced in his effort to justify the dramatic shift in government policy he has sought to orchestrate in a few short years.

So what accounts for the shift? We contend that Gorbachev and his policies, like those of other leaders throughout the world, are the product of the times and, ironically, especially in the Soviet case, have emerged as a consequence of the reversal of the "technological dialectic" on which much communist theory is based.

We noted in our discussion of Marxism that, in the mid-nineteenth century, Karl Marx deduced that the ongoing evolution of technology would alter basic economic institutions until the economic system was, at some undefined point, no longer compatible with the prevailing governmental system. Marx revealed that capitalism, founded on private ownership and the profit motive, emerged because of the developing dictates of economies of scale. As a consequence, said Marx, capitalism would create friction between the drive of capitalists to hold wages down (to subsistence levels) and make a profit, and their need to sell the expanding quantities of goods and services they produce. Workers would eventually revolt against the capitalists' exploitation of labor and erect the socialist state.

The Soviet Union has never been a full-fledged textbook example of the communist state. The Revolution occurred when Russia was still a Third World—or, better yet, a Fourth world—country, meaning it still had a grossly underdeveloped capital base. But this did not stop the Soviets, who not only imposed a capital-dependent system on a country with historically little capital base but adopted Marx's other directives to lead a socialist revolution throughout the world. With little economic wherewithal to carry out this plan, they resorted to extreme military means. Foreign policy expert Dimitri Simes defines the primary role played by the military in Soviet politics. He admits that requests by Third World leaders for Soviet military involvement "almost never reflect the belief that Communist Russia is a model for Third World development. Moscow's military power and its willingness to provide arms and geopolitical protection, not the appeal of Soviet ideas and accomplishments, are what normally motivate Third World overtures to the Soviet Union."[22] And as an admiral in the Soviet Navy has noted, "Visits of Soviet navy men make it possible for the peoples of many countries to become convinced with their own eyes of the creativity of the ideas of Communism. . . . They see warships as embodying the achievements of Soviet science, technology, and industry."[23]

Unfortunately for the United States, the Soviet Union has for a long time maintained a comparative cost advantage in the production of a strong military posture in spite of—indeed, partly because of—a domestic economy that works poorly. In the United States expansion of the military budget has been tightly constrained by the need for democratic consensus, which can be foiled by competing political interest groups seeking domestic programs; and, given the productivity of the private sector, armaments have been very costly in terms of domestic goods given up.

On the other hand, the Soviets' highly centralized political structure, which relies extensively on commands issued from Moscow, has facilitated the development of their military. They have simply not had to worry very much in the past about political dissent over military decisions. In addition the lagging performance of the Soviet economy has meant that the economic cost of the military—measured by the number and variety of consumer goods that have to be forgone—has been much lower in the Soviet Union than in the United States and other Western economies. This is because, as Gorbachev and other Soviet leaders now admit, the Soviet people have been deprived of the requisite economic incentives to produce and innovate, and they have been miserably unproductive in civilian goods when compared with the United States and much of the rest of the Western world. In short, measured by domestic opportunities forgone, armaments have been relatively cheap for the Soviet Union.

Accordingly, the Soviets have specialized in the development of a strong military, consistently devoting at least 15 percent, and very likely as much as 25 percent, of their GDP to military expenditures.[24] By comparison the United States has devoted no more than 7 percent of its gross national product to military expenditures at any time since 1972.[25]

From this perspective the Soviets' past recalcitrance in arms negotiation has been understandable. Any U.S. proposal for more-or-less equal contractions of military power must have been seen by Soviet leaders as something approaching a devious Western plot to undermine the Soviet Union's world standing. To paraphrase a former director of the Central Intelligence Agency, "Military might is about all the Soviets have had."[26]

An equal reduction in forces would not only be a better economic bargain for the United States than the Soviet Union, given the relatively greater cost of military hardware measured in terms of civilian goods in the United States, but the arms reduction would also amount to an unequal reduction in each country's respective standing within the world community. With a far more advanced economy, an equal reduction in military spending would mean that U.S. influence and standing in the world could be expected to rise absolutely and (perhaps more important to the Soviet Union) relatively. The Soviet Union would no longer have as much in the way of military power to export to other countries, and the United States would have relatively more economic power to export.

## Explaining the Turnaround

To get back to the question at hand, Why, then, have the Soviets changed their armament position practically 180 degrees? From the perspective just outlined, the turnaround in the Soviet Union's willingness to concede in arms negotiations is somewhat perplexing, at least if the change in the Soviet leadership is discounted. During Gorbachev's short tenure in office, the Soviet economy has continued to spiral downward, relatively, if not absolutely. According to the CIA's data, very likely an optimistic assessment, the Soviet annual rate of real growth in per capita consumption has fallen from 5 percent in the 1966–70 period to .5 percent in the 1983–87 period.[27] In 1990 the Soviet economy was teetering on the brink of collapse; if not, it was stagnating at best and possibly regressing in economic performance while the Western world was progressing at a reasonable pace.

If the Soviet military stance is founded solely on a comparative advantage in military production, it would appear to follow that the Soviet Union might be more, not less, reluctant to forgo military power. The Soviet Union would be expected to be even more dependent on its military clout for its world standing, and the economic cost of the Soviet military might be expected to drop with each downward movement in the Soviet economy—meaning that the country would have an even stronger comparative advantage in military power, which they would naturally exploit.

What has changed in the last decade that might have caused the Soviet leadership to reverse course? The critical change, among others, has been in the value of economic prowess, relative to defense prowess, in determining a country's world standing. More specifically, the change in the Soviet attitude is grounded in the same forces that have worked on other world governments and their economies: namely, the advancing telecommunications and trade technology and the subsequent acceleration of capital mobility and reversal of economies of scale in many industries that have inspired greater openness and, at the same time, greater integration of national economies. This change, combined with the success of Western nuclear deterrence, particularly the Reagan administration's defeat of the Brezhnev campaign of influence over Western Europe in the early 1980s, and the growing resistance of citizen groups not only in the USSR but throughout the Soviet Bloc, have forced Soviet leaders from Andropov on into a new stance. Economic prowess, dependent more on brains than brawn, has been shown to be fundamentally valuable to a country's power and influence in the modern world. Japan, which was brought to its knees militarily in World War II, has proved that point. Over the few short decades since the war, Japan, with little usable land and without firing a shot, has literally gained command of much of the world's resources, simply by hard work and economic shrewdness. The success stories of Hong Kong, Taiwan, and Korea reinforce this point.

Alternatively, those countries, such as the Soviet Union and China, that have remained closed to the rest of the world—or that have failed to adopt policies that would allow them to integrate with the rest of the world through greater international trade and investment—have simply been relegated to the economic sidelines, to watch a fast-paced world-class game in progress. To no small extent, the dictates of communism relegated the Soviet Union to the status of bench warmers in the global economy.[28]

Not too many decades ago the Soviet Union could afford to be effectively closed to outside influences. All they had to do was control immigration and emigration. Since movement across national boundaries was very costly in economic and emotional terms, the immigration and emigration flows could be contained at a relatively modest cost to the state. So long as international information flows could be controlled effectively by the Soviet state, the Soviet people would literally not know what they were missing. That is to say, they, and even their leaders, would not know the true long-run economic cost of the military.

In a truly closed society the economic costs of the military—and, for that matter, the communist system—are perceived to be more or less equal to the domestic goods and services that are forgone within the closed system. However, when the domestic economy is opened to other economies by television and news reports, and residents can see what is produced in other countries, the economic cost of the military, and of the system itself, is the much higher quantity (and quality) of goods and services that are produced and can be obtained abroad. When the Soviet leaders and people realized that they could trade in their collectivist, centrally planned economy for a market economy, the cost of the Soviet military escalated. Measured in terms of forgone consumer goods, at the limit, the cost of the military is equal to those incurred by other market-oriented countries, most notably, the United States, Japan, and West Germany. And the greater economic cost of the military (albeit only perceived via word-of-mouth, newspaper, and television reports) can shift the country's comparative advantage, meaning that the country then can be expected to become more receptive to disarmament proposals and cut backs on military production.

Thus, under the circumstances of open economies and open information flows, which have become virtually impossible to contain, the Soviet military expenditures are simply not the bargain they once were, as perceived by the leaders *or* the citizens. Put bluntly, Soviet citizens want the now-relatively-cheaper butter, not guns, and their leaders are scurrying desperately to respond.

It should be no surprise that Gorbachev has coupled disarmament proposals with proposals to shift toward market and democratic-political institutions and to pull back from control of the Eastern Bloc countries. Disarmament will allow the shift of resources to private production and to the development of the broader capital base needed to increase worker productivity. The adoption of market institutions will also spur productivity in goods and services, enabling the Soviet Union to progress economically relative to the United States and other Western countries and to recapture its lost prestige.

Democratic institutions are inherently designed to disperse—and thus stabilize—political power and to prevent its abuse by mad and bad men, like Stalin, who might ascend to the top of the political hierarchy. In this regard, democratic institutions are designed to stabilize power and to stabilize policies that can flow from expressions of political power. The adoption of more democratic political institutions has been necessary to give foreign and domestic investors the additional insurance that Soviet policy will not be changed at the whim of every new set of leaders.

To build a dynamic economy, a country like the Soviet Union cannot afford to continue to maintain "outright parasites." Gorbachev has served notice that his countrymen must learn to work harder for their keep and that they will no longer be able to count exclusively on state aid for their failures. In a similar vein he effectively told Eastern Bloc countries that they too are a drain on the Soviet state, especially now that they must recoup some of their world standing by developing more dynamic economies. We expect that (if he has not already) Gorbachev will soon be relaying the same notice to Fidel Castro.

In serving such notices, Gorbachev has also recognized that landmass per se—even in the form of whole countries—is no longer as valuable as it once may have been in a country's production or world standing. Technology has made other economic ingredients—specifically, creativity, inventiveness, and dedication—relatively more important than political or military control over land and people. Gorbachev and his advisers have come to realize that modern production, possibly to a greater extent that ever before, must spring from individual (as distinct from collective or state) initiative. This means that individuals must be given economic and political freedoms just to make individual initiative viable. By disarming, pulling back from directly controlling other countries, and by seeking to move toward market institutions, the Soviets are simply trying to recombine resources to take advantage of modern production methods. They are saying, in effect, "Land is out, initiative is in." They are saying that they can cut the controls, permit countries (their own and those in the Eastern Bloc) to prosper, and then recapture more than any benefits from its lost sovereignty through international trade.

Furthermore, it should be noted, the new, more sophisticated and complex modes of modern production and the more sophisticated and complex goods and services that emerge in the modern world have made centrally directed and controlled societies uneconomical. We mentioned earlier that nearly half a century ago Nobel laureate Friedrich Hayek pointed out that centrally directed economies are beset by an information problem. Government leaders, even with hordes of bureaucrats on their staffs, do not and cannot know enough to direct vast resources in their myriad uses efficiently.[29] The persistent, year-by-year arithmetic growth in technology since the wise Professor Hayek made his observation has simply compounded exponentially the central planners' basic information problem.

Finally, containing outflows of citizens becomes more difficult for the state when citizens become aware of the higher wages and consumption levels abroad. Staying put is no longer the economic bargain that it once was to the citizens, because its cost is rising. With the lure of movement all the greater, citizens can be expected to devote more resources to moving out of the country and, if they cannot move out of the country, to opting out of the economic system—doing as little as possible for the state and/or going underground. Either way, the country's economic problems worsen and human and capital outflows are encouraged. In the modern world the centralized state is caught in a fiscal bind. It must incur greater costs to contain its people, and it must impose greater taxes to cover that greater containment cost.

In short, technology has had profound effects on the incentives of Soviet leaders, resulting in their seeking a radically new strategy for economic development. Technological developments have hiked the cost of maintaining a closed system, increasing the relative attractiveness of opening the Soviet system. However, given that technology has increased the transnational mobility of people and capital, the Soviet Union must reduce the relative attractiveness of moving abroad, because the people and their brains, not vast acres of land that can't move, will be the country's ultimate salvation. The Soviets have been forced to accept a Western-style development strategy: Increase people's personal incentives to use the information close at hand that only they, as individuals, can know, and to work, save, invest, and innovate by adopting market institutions and techniques. To do that Gorbachev has had to make Soviet citizens residual claimants to their own diligence, which, in effect, means that he has had to betray his rhetorical dedication to Marx and turn to private property and a modified form of capitalism.

## The Durability of the Turnaround

Are the changes in Soviet military and economic policies permanent? Nothing can ever be said to be irreversible (a play on the wisdom of Greek philosopher Heracleitus, who observed about 540 B.C. that "nothing is permanent except change"). However, we are inclined to believe that the direction of the policy changes taking place in the Soviet Union is more permanent and more durable than Gorbachev. The technological forces at work in the world economy that are making capital more productive and more mobile are not likely to be reversed in the foreseeable future. Telecommunications, computers, and information flows are here to stay. Capital will continue to become more mobile as it becomes progressively smaller and more powerful. The complexity of economic life will only escalate.

The changing economic world is fundamentally transforming the strategy national leaders must follow to enhance their own welfare. It used to be that national leaders had to work to enslave their people with severe political and economic restrictions, as the Soviet Union has done, or manipulate them with heavy taxes and regulations of all sorts, as Western countries have done. Today national leaders are forced to consider a new strategy—one of relinquishing control, lowering taxes, and lessening the burden of regulations—all for the purpose of making the national climate more hospitable to capital, human and physical, that can give rise to economic development. Such a strategy can afford leaders the opportunity to prosper personally and to retain influence in the eyes of the world.

## Quicksilver Commissars

Without doubt, changes in a country's policy agenda as broad as those under way in the Soviet Union are the product of many forces. Again, we have sought not to proffer a single explanation but to explore one aspect of a range of explanations, given the limits of space.

We recognize Gorbachev's considerable talents in initiating and directing change, and we have not overlooked the possibility that Ronald Reagan's defense buildup may have played a role in causing the Soviets to rethink their disarmament policy—to learn that they were playing an armament game they could not hope to win, except at substantially greater cost to incentives and production in their domestic economy.

We acknowledge that change in the Soviet Union may also have been motivated by political concerns: the growing divisions among the ethnic groups in the Soviet Union and the fear of revolt if state decision-making powers were not passed to lower levels of the Soviet political structure. Change has also been inspired by a very practical concern: In many blatantly obvious ways, Soviet communism has not worked very well.[30] The stark contrast between the performance of market-oriented and communist-dominated economies has given rise to an inevitable reexamination of Soviet economic institutions and to an equally inevitable search for reforms that offer hope for improvement in the welfare of the Soviet people.

Having introduced the appropriate caveats, however, we hasten to add that the power of international technological and economic forces to shape policy agendas of both communist and capitalist countries should not be overlooked. We have suggested that technology has increased the cost of military expenditures for all countries, but especially for the Soviet Union. Soviet leaders and people can now see—on their visits abroad and on their television screens—what they have been missing, because of their substantial military expenditures and the economic and political system they regrettably inherited. They can sense that technology has opened up tremendous opportunities to attract capital goods, and a better way to organize their political economy, from abroad.

But to become a part of this modern world, political and economic reforms are necessary. The Soviets are unlikely to attract capital when the political system may be guided by the whims of a small band of tyrants or planners, when private profits cannot be made, when the people have few incentives to work hard and effectively, or when the domestic economy is burdened by military posturing.

We suggest that this new "technological dialectic" has led to consequences not imagined by Marx himself. It has undermined the all-encompassing power of the Soviet state by making military and police power too costly. It has made economic development by market and democratic institutions imperative, and official government policy endorsed by the Soviet Congress in June 1990.

Gorbachev and his advisers have apparently seen the need to conform Soviet policy-making to the new world realities. They have written as much and more. Whether they will be able to bring about the needed reforms in a timely manner remains the unsettled issue. The Soviet military brass are notoriously resistant to reductions in their power. Soviet planners are no more interested in being planned out of out their subsidized existence than their military brethren. Many new Soviet voters will have strong incentives to reform—so long as their jobs, benefits, and security are not jeopardized. Nevertheless, the pain that will inevitably accompany the shift to a market economy has been reduced by the speed that capital can move internationally. Today, "amazing things," to use Gorbachev's words, can happen when market institutions are adopted. The growing complexity of modern production and capital mobility have simply made the Soviet's shift to a market economy all the more attractive and imperative.

The lack of serious substantive reforms, including the adoption of market prices, in Gorbachev's five-year plan proposed in late 1989, speaks eloquently of the political difficulties that will be encountered. As quoted at the head of this chapter, Gavriil Popov, the mayor of Moscow and a member of the new Soviet Congress of People's Deputies, characterized the new five-year plan as a continuance of Soviet efforts to tell chickens how many eggs they must lay.

Nevertheless, the one great hope for the emergence of a new Soviet consensus lies in the fact that the cost of the current system has become so great and obvious the Soviet leaders will take Popov's advice and leave the hen alone.

# 8

# Perestroika, American Style

## The Newly Competitive U.S. Economy

Hack, chop, crunch!

*Time* magazine

AMID all of the rhetoric about unchecked government expansion, one fact stands out: In the past decade the growth of many governments around the world has slowed, at least as measured by several statistical series widely used to chart relative change in government size. In several cases it has been halted altogether. And in the Soviet Bloc it has been thrown into convulsions. This chapter pays special attention to government growth in the United States. As acknowledged previously there are unavoidable imperfections in the data for major industrial countries, even for the United States. Yet the available evidence shows that governments in the United States are charting fiscal and regulatory paths akin to those observed elsewhere in the world.

## Total Government Expenditures

Support for the claim that technologically driven capital mobility and economic complexity is circumscribing the power of government can be found in the rhetoric of government policymakers in Washington and around the world. They talk a great deal about "competitive-

175

ness," which, as we have pointed out, often means the competitiveness of their own government's policies. Additional supporting evidence can be found in the decreasing rate of growth of government expenditures in the United States.

An important measure of the cost of government in the economy is the size of government outlays. This is true because government expenditures reflect the value of resources diverted from private-sector uses. Governments at virtually all levels in the United States—federal, state, and local—have continued to grow in dollar terms, albeit irregularly, along a virtually unbroken upward trend. Together, governments in the United States, in current-dollar terms, spent slightly more than $10 billion in 1929, $137 billion in 1960, and nearly $1.8 trillion in 1989—a 180-fold increase in sixty years. Even after adjusting for inflation, real (constant, 1982-dollar) total-government expenditures rose by almost thirteenfold in this period—from just under $110 billion in 1929 to $1.4 trillion in 1987.

However, the growth in such absolute-dollar measures of governmental influence in the economy is deceptive because the whole U.S. economy grew during the period—with more people, increased income, and greater capital that needed to be supported by these growing real-dollar government expenditures. Accordingly, growth in the real-dollar size of government can conceal declines in government influence per dollar of income and production, and per capita.

Consider figure 8.1, which depicts the combined growth of all governments in the United States relative to gross national product (GNP). The bars in record total outlays of all governments as a percentage of GNP.[1] This measure of government influence shows significant growth over the entire 1960–89 period.

However, as mentioned, the trend over the 1960–89 period can hide changes in the rate of government growth relative to the national economy. To see what has happened to the growth rate, trends for shorter periods are needed. The top, longer straight line plots the trend in the ratio of government expenditures to GNP, based on data from 1960 to 1970. The other, lower, straight line plots the trend in the ratio based on data from 1970 to 1989.

Obviously total government expenditures as a percentage of GNP grew throughout most of the period, but it is equally obvious (from the lower slope of the bottom trend line) that the growth of total government relative to national production began to slow in the 1970s. Indeed, in the 1970–89 period, the average annual rate of growth (0.7 percent per year) was less than half the rate of growth

FIGURE 8.1    Total Government Expenditures in the United States as a
Percentage of GNP, 1960–1989

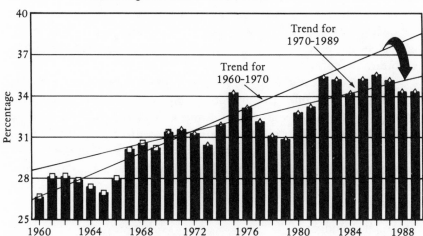

Source: Author's calculations from the *Economic Report of the President* (1990), pp. 294,
387.

in the 1960–70 period (1.5 percent per year).[2] Furthermore, the trend
in government expenditures relative to GNP during the 1980s has
been practically horizontal (that is, practically 0.0 percent per year),
or slightly downward sloping (or negative) from 1982 onward.

The pace of government growth, evident above in total expenditures, also shows up in total government employment. In 1960 all
governments in the United States employed 8.3 million civilian workers. By 1980 the employment level had almost doubled, breaking
16 million. By 1989 government added almost 2 million more workers.
Again, however, the economy, including the civilian labor force, was
also expanding during the period—but at a slightly faster pace. Total
government employment rose from 12.7 percent of total civilian employment in 1960 to 17.1 percent in 1975. After 1975 a steady decline
in government employment share set in, reaching 15.1 percent of
civilian employment in 1989 (a loss of nearly 12 percent in employment
share between 1975 and 1989).

Obviously government in the United States is not yet getting
smaller in absolute-dollar or employment terms. Furthermore, the
decline in the growth of government outlays as a percent of national
production, and in the growth of government employment as a share
of civilian employment, may be consistent with alternative hypotheses. For example, the slower pace of growth in government may

have been due to a shift to a more conservative ruling majority within the electorate or in Congress, or to a shift from government's reliance on expenditures to reliance on regulations, which require consumers and businesses to incur greater costs not reflected in government budgets. Nonetheless, we must wonder why the electorate or Congress became more conservative.

The available data on U.S. government expenditures, taxes, and regulations do offer preliminary evidence that competitive pressures on governments may be building and in fact be contributing to a continuing decline in government relative to the overall size of the economy. This evidence suggests that governments in the United States collectively have relatively fewer resources to control the economy and the people in it.

## The Federal Budget

Government expenditures over the 1960–89 period became more centralized in the federal government, a fact that might indicate growth in government's monopoly power. Growth in federal government expenditures as a percentage of GNP was actually higher in 1989 than in 1960. However, two points must be kept in mind in interpreting the available data. First, growth in federal expenditures relative to GNP leveled off and started on a slight downward trend after 1982. The upward trend in federal expenditures as a percentage of GNP in the 1970s was being driven by the expansion of federal government expenditures at the same time the rate of growth in GNP began to fall.

Second, the expansion of federal expenditures, relative to state and local expenditures, in the late 1960s and 1970s actually supports our point concerning the constraining influence of capital mobility. We have maintained all along that an increase in capital mobility can be expected to constrict government growth. Expansions in capital mobility affect, first, the shorter-distance moves of people and capital among state and local governments, and thereby constrain their growth first. To overcome the influence of escalating capital mobility, policymakers tried to override these growing competitive constraints first appearing at the state and local levels by shifting many government responsibilities from local governments to state governments, and then to the federal government.

Thus, the increase in the growth rate of federal expenditures relative to national production in the 1970s reflects the influence of capital mobility on government. Since the 1980s the growth rate of federal expenditures as a percentage of GNP has declined and appears to have stopped growing altogether during the last half of the 1980s. Furthermore, it is clear from the slower growth in total government expenditures during this period that the impact of quicksilver capital has been felt throughout the U.S. government.

The growth of state and local government expenditures as a percentage of GNP was curtailed long ago, as far back as the early 1970s. State and local government expenditures (excluding net interest)—supported by taxes from their own (as distinct from federal) sources—rose more or less steadily from 4.6 percent of GNP in 1947 to 7.5 percent in 1960 to 10.1 percent in 1971. Then, after a temporary decline, state and local expenditures peaked at 10.2 percent of GNP in 1975. After 1976 state and local expenditures fell and leveled off, varying within a range of 8.9 to 10 percent of GNP through 1988.[3]

A part of the fall in state and local expenditures can be attributed to federal programs such as revenue sharing, which was instituted in the early 1970s. However, the cause and effect may have been the other way around. Strapped for resources to continue their growth in the face of increasing competition among themselves, state and local governments turned to the federal government for assistance. Stated differently, all state and local governments, taken together, can tap practically the same aggregate tax base that is available to the federal government. By going to the federal government for help, they succumbed to the limiting force of intergovernmental competition on their own capacity to tax.

As noted, changes in federal budgetary priorities may actually have compensated for the waning growth in total expenditures in the 1980s. Put differently, government may have directed a greater portion of its expenditures toward regulatory agencies, away from budget categories that have little influence on the economy. However, it is questionable whether changes in budget composition had an offsetting impact, mainly because the growth in federal expenditures in the 1980s emanated extensively from one source: national defense. Slightly more than half of the increase in real federal outlays from 1980 to 1989 was on defense.[4] Much of the rest can be accounted for by greater interest payments on the escalating federal debt and greater payments to a larger number of older individuals under Social Security (who, on average, received practically no increase in real payments).

Granted, governments can influence the economy through defense, interest payments, and Social Security outlays. However, it is hard to see how growth in those budget components could mean greater government control in the economy when growth in the budget totals, as a percent of national production, is slowing and when those three components are driven extensively by forces external to the government budget process. Defense expenditures were driven extensively by international political considerations, mainly how much the Russians were spending and the threat of military hostilities. Interest rates were determined by international market forces over which the federal government has virtually no control, and total Social Security payments were rising because of the growth in the size of the elderly population. As a consequence, the components of the federal budget over which Congress and the administration retained discretionary control fell in total real (1982) dollars from $187 billion in 1980 to $151 billion in 1988, or from 5.9 percent of the federal budget in 1980 to 3.6 percent in 1988, a 39 percent decline in budget share. As the 1990s approached Congress and the administration simply had less budgetary flexibility than they had had a decade or two earlier.

## Federal Regulations

If budgetary composition is difficult to interpret, government expenditures on regulations are a totally different matter. Such expenditures can certainly increase the influence of government in the economy beyond the budget dollars they represent. Each dollar of regulatory expenditures has a "multiplier effect," giving rise to more private expenditures to deal with, for example, environmental pollution or workplace hazards. However, as table 8.1 indicates, the pace of growth in the administrative costs of most categories of regulations slowed drastically in the 1980s. From 1970 to 1980, the real (1982) administrative costs to government of so-called social regulations, including consumer product and job safety, environment, and energy regulations, rose by 157 percent, from $2.4 billion to $6.2 billion—an average annual increase of nearly 16 percent. From 1980 to 1989, the administrative costs of social regulations rose 9 percent, for an average annual increase of 1 percent, reaching a real-dollar level of only $6.7 billion in 1989. The administrative costs of so-called economic regulations, including banking and finance and industry-specific and general business regulations, rose by 84 percent from 1970 to

TABLE 8.1  Administrative Costs of Federal Regulatory Activities in Constant (1982) Dollars (Fiscal Years, Millions of 1982 Dollars)

| Area of Regulation | 1970 | 1975 | 1980 | Percentage of Change 1970–80 | 1985 | 1989 | Percentage of Change 1980–89 |
|---|---|---|---|---|---|---|---|
| Social Regulation | | | | | | | |
| Consumer Safety | 1,523 | 2,462 | 2,676 | 79 | 2,408 | 2,513 | – 8 |
| Job Safety | 274 | 598 | 873 | 219 | 771 | 757 | –13 |
| Environment/Energy | 596 | 1,832 | 2,553 | 328 | 2,669 | 3,435 | 35 |
| Total | 2,394 | 4,893 | 6,156 | 157 | 5,849 | 6,705 | 9 |
| Economic Regulation | | | | | | | |
| Finance/Banking | 186 | 254 | 419 | 125 | 559 | 842 | 101 |
| Industry specific | 195 | 263 | 323 | 66 | 259 | 238 | –27 |
| General Business | 246 | 338 | 410 | 67 | 454 | 547 | 33 |
| Total | 628 | 856 | 1,154 | 84 | 1,273 | 1,627 | 41 |
| Grand Total | 3,023 | 5,750 | 7,310 | 142 | 7,122 | 8,332 | 14 |

Source: Melinda Warren and Kenneth Chilton, *Regulation Rebound: Bush Budget Gives Regulation a Boost* (St. Louis: Center for the Study of American Business, Washington Univeristy, 1990), p. 4.

1980, for an average annual increase of over 8 percent. These costs rose by less than half, or 41 percent, from 1980 to 1987, an average annual increase of 4 to 5 percent. As revealed in table 8.1, the grand total of all administrative (social plus economic) regulatory costs rose by 142 percent from 1970 to 1980 and by 14 percent from 1980 to 1989.[5]

As a percentage of GNP, administrative regulatory costs declined in the 1980s. In the 1970s and 1980s the administrative costs of economic regulations remained more or less steady as a percentage of GNP, varying from .03 percent to .04 percent. The administrative costs of social regulations, however, nearly doubled as a percentage of GNP in the 1970s—rising from .10 percent in 1970 to .19 percent in 1980—only to fall, albeit slightly, in the 1980s. The total of all administrative regulatory costs as a percentage of GNP followed much the same general pattern of social regulatory costs but, of course, at a higher percentage level. Total costs as a percentage of GNP first rose in the 1970s and then declined slightly, 13 percent in relative size in the 1980s.

Employment in U.S. regulatory agencies rose with the growth in the budget in the 1970s, from just over 73,000 in 1970 to just under 119,000 in 1980, or an increase of 62 percent. However, employment in the agencies actually fell by 11 percent in absolute numbers in the 1980s, dropping to almost 106,000 by 1987.[6] Because of the continuing growth in the U.S. labor force, regulatory employment has not grown relative to the labor force since the mid-1970s. In fact, employment in economic regulatory agencies fell as a percentage of the employed civilian labor force, from .03 percent in 1980 to .02 in 1989. However, because of the drop in social regulatory employment, total regulatory employment in the United States declined from .12 percent of the labor force in 1980 to .09 percent in 1987.

The figures are quite small in absolute terms. Still, the ratio of employment in federal regulatory agencies dropped 25 percent as a share of total employment from 1980 to 1989. Furthermore, such decreases in the percentages are not what one would expect after hearing so much political rhetoric about the "unbridled growth of government," especially in the area of regulations. Of course, the regulators may have more than made up for their lost numbers by improvements in the efficiency with which they impose regulations. This is a proposition we find dubious.

Unfortunately, there are few good ways of measuring the proliferation of regulations. We can only use the imperfect measures at hand. The *Federal Register*, established in 1936, is the one place where Congress and every department and agency of the federal government must announce all pending and enacted laws, rules, and regulations. The number of pages in the *Register* is obviously a very rough—and mildly comical—measure of changing federal influence in the economy. Many pages of the *Federal Register* deal with matters that have little or nothing to do with economic activities in either the public or private sectors. For example, pages may deal with the particulars of organizational structures of agencies or nuclear test-ban treaties (when such matters are being considered). In other instances single lines can carry considerable private costs. This might have been the case when the federal government announced in the 1970s that Tris, a chemical compound, must be used as a flame retardant on fabrics for infant clothes (and later found it to be a carcinogen). Some pages also deal with the elimination of federal rules and regulations.

However, the *Federal Register* page count is a ready measure of government tinkering in the economy through actual or threatened regulations, and it has value if for no other reason than that no better measures exist. Furthermore, many journalists, policymakers at the highest levels of government (including former President Ronald Reagan), and scholars have used the *Federal Register* page count as a barometer of intrusive government growth in the 1960s and 1970s.[7] Consider what the page count shows.

In 1936 the *Federal Register* had a measly (in subsequent historical context) 2,800 pages.[8] The number of annual pages did not begin to escalate dramatically until the Nixon years, during which the annual page count more than doubled, from approximately 25,000 in 1968, the last year of the Johnson administration, to almost 56,000 in 1974, the year Richard Nixon left office.

The page count reached its peak at just over 87,000 in 1980, the last year of the Carter administration. However, the rate of growth began to taper off in 1975. Jimmy Carter significantly slowed it; furthermore, in the late 1970s, many of the pages dealt with *de*regulation.[9] Ronald Reagan, with nontrivial help from Congress, clearly reversed the direction of the trend in the page count; in 1989 it was down to just under 54,000, 38 percent below the 1980 peak. The suggestion here is clear: Total government regulation is at least expanding at a significantly slower rate.

This is the case. Between the late 1960s and 1980, twenty new regulatory agencies were created by Congress, which meant there were more than fifty in existence.[10] The major regulatory agencies created between 1965 and 1980 included the Consumer Product Safety Commission (1972), the Environmental Protection Agency (1970), the National Highway Safety Administration (1966), and the Occupational Safety and Health Administration (1970).[11]

Contrary to popular belief, the deregulation movement began not under Ronald Reagan but under Richard Nixon, who, given growing concern over the cost of federal regulations, especially environmental regulations, set up an interagency regulatory review process. The Ford administration sought to strengthen the regulatory review process and developed, with the support of Senator Edward Kennedy (D., Mass), the first plans to deregulate the airline, trucking, and railroad industries. Their efforts, understandably, fueled years of congressional debate.[12] It was left to the Carter administration to finalize drives to deregulate airlines (Airline Deregulation Act of 1978), trucking (Motor Carrier Act of 1980), railroads (Staggers Rail Act of 1980), and banking and financial institutions (Depository Institutions Deregulation and Monetary Control Act of 1980). Before the advent of the Reagan administration in 1981, Congress had partially decontrolled natural gas (Natural Gas Policy Act of 1978) and set a one-year deadline for the elimination of price controls on oil, which had been established earlier in response to the first OPEC oil embargo in 1973.

Ronald Reagan supposedly embraced with gusto the deregulation movement with what *Time* reporters described as "energetic zeal": "*Hack, chop, crunch!* were the sounds during the early 1980s as Reagan's regulatory appointees stripped away decades' worth of business restraints like so much prickly underbrush on the President's ranch."[13] Reagan began his quest to control the growth of regulations ten days after taking office by putting on hold 170 pending regulations.[14] Within a few days of taking office, the Reagan administration terminated all oil price controls and "voluntary" wage and price guidelines, abolishing the Council on Wage and Price Stability and centralizing the regulatory review process in the newly established Office of Information and Regulatory Affairs within the Office of Management and Budget. All this was done by the end of January 1981.

More important, the Reagan people sought to retard the growth in government regulations by requiring that all new and newly reviewed government regulations pass a "maximum net benefit criterion."[15] For all proposed major regulations—those with an esti-

mated annual cost of more than $100 million—agencies were directed
to prepare a " 'regulatory impact analysis,' to include an estimate of
the benefits and costs of the proposed rule and an explanation of
the legal reason why some alternative rule with higher net benefits
could not be adopted."[16] The Reagan administration also succeeded
in phasing out remaining natural gas controls, deregulating intercity
bus traffic (Bus Regulatory Reform Act of 1982), setting aside many
program restrictions on broadcasters through the abandonment of
the "fairness doctrine," increasing the speed with which new drugs
were approved (partially by permitting greater reliance on test data
from abroad), shifting safety inspections from low-hazard to high-
hazard work sites, expanding firms' flexibility to meet established
pollution standards, facilitating trades of "pollution rights," and eliminating many restrictions on prices and services of shipping (Shipping
Act of 1984).[17]

The Reagan administration's greatest deregulation success may
have been in the area of antitrust law. The administration terminated
the seemingly endless suit against the supposed monopolistic practices
of IBM in 1982; completed the breakup of AT&T in 1984; reduced
the Justice Department objections to mergers by broadening the definition of relevant markets to include foreign competition;[18] reduced
the range of antitrust cases in which treble damages could be awarded;
and terminated investigations within the Federal Trade Commission
against the automobile, cereal, and oil industries.

In addition, the Reagan administration supported a number of
changes in state laws that would eliminate state-sponsored local monopolies. It also pressed for legislation that would permit export trading
companies (joint ventures of competing domestic firms organized to
increase their exports) and joint ventures among competing firms in
research and development projects. In general, the Reagan administration, mainly through the appointment of William Baxter as assistant
attorney general for antitrust enforcement and James Miller as chairman of the FTC, "changed antitrust enforcement from a rather general
harassment of American business to a more vigorous prosecution of
potential monopoly cases under existing laws."[19]

Nonetheless, the *Time* reporters fell prey to their own brand
of "energetic zeal" in giving more credit (or blame) to Reagan for
spurring the deregulation movement than the former president de-
served. Critics outside the administration clearly give the Reagan
Administration more credit for continuing and accelerating the deregu-

lation revolution than do his supporters and officials.[20] William Niskanen, who had one of the longest tenures as a member of the Council
of Economic Advisors during the Reagan presidency, described the
administration's efforts to eliminate "social regulations" as a "near-
complete failure."[21] Furthermore, he stressed that the Reagan administration was unable to reform most basic (and, as we will see, very
costly) environmental regulatory laws. Its Office of Information and
Regulatory Review turned back or revised only one out of every
nine proposed regulations.[22]

Granted, AT&T was finally broken up during Reagan's first
term, but the legal and political assault on the AT&T telephone
monopoly had begun much earlier, under President Gerald Ford.
The budget of the Justice Department declined sharply in real-dollar
terms during the first two years of the Reagan administration, but
that decline in Justice Department outlays was a continuation of
the real-dollar decline begun back in 1975. Given significant increases
in the budget of the Justice Department after 1982, the most that
can be said is that the department suffered real-budget reductions
during most of the 1980s (as well as all of the late 1970s). The
Justice Department budget fell as a percentage of the federal budget
and as a percentage of GNP after 1975.[23]

In general Niskanen was probably correct when he concluded
that, on balance, "The regulatory momentum was clearly slowed,
but it was not reversed."[24] Brookings Institution scholar Robert Crandall agrees: "On the surface at least, it appears that the Reagan
appointees have only prevented the return of regulation where deregulation was under way, slowed the pace of new rule-making, and
repulsed most emotional calls for new regulations."[25] In general,
this conclusion is also endorsed by Murray Weidenbaum, Reagan's
first chairman of the Council of Economic Advisors. Still, there is a
bright side to what has not happened. Since 1980, writes Weidenbaum:

> The most significant development on the regulatory front is along
> the lines of that Sherlock Holmes story in which the decisive point
> was the fact that the dog did not bark. During the past eight years
> [1981–88], not a single major new regulatory law has been enacted
> (although several have been toughened). Nor has a new regulatory
> agency been established. This has been the first such extended period
> in the past half century when the federal rule-making dog did not
> bark. The state is not withering away, but some high-cost resources
> are being reoriented to more productive pursuits.[26]

Assessing the overall cost of government regulations on the economy is difficult at best. Available year-to-year cost figures for individual regulatory programs are very limited, especially given the coverage of the programs. However, we do have some cost data on three major programs—environmental regulations, occupational safety and health regulations, and highway safety.

As table 8.2 shows, the economic costs of environmental controls are by far the greatest.[27] These costs rose slightly in real (1982) dollars during the 1972–85 period: from $26.8 billion in 1972 to $40.8 billion in 1985.[28] Occupational safety and health regulatory costs peaked at $8.5 billion in 1978 and stayed below $6 billion thereafter.[29] Highway safety costs peaked at $7.2 billion in 1974 and were below $5 billion during the 1980s.[30]

However, these regulatory costs were being imposed on a grow-

TABLE 8.2   Environmental and Safety Expenditures for Three Major Programs, 1972 to 1985 (Billions of 1982 Dollars)

| Year | Environment | Occupational Safety and Health | Highway Safety | Total |
|------|-------------|--------------------------------|----------------|-------|
| 1972 | 26.8 | 6.4 | 3.8 | 37.0 |
| 1973 | 30.6 | 6.5 | 6.7 | 43.8 |
| 1974 | 30.0 | 7.8 | 7.2 | 45.0 |
| 1975 | 31.5 | 5.8 | 5.7 | 43.0 |
| 1976 | 33.2 | 5.0 | 6.8 | 45.0 |
| 1977 | 35.2 | 5.8 | 7.1 | 48.1 |
| 1978 | 36.6 | 8.5 | 6.7 | 51.8 |
| 1979 | 38.4 | 5.4 | 6.1 | 49.9 |
| 1980 | 37.9 | 4.8 | 4.7 | 47.4 |
| 1981 | 37.5 | 5.6 | 4.4 | 47.5 |
| 1982 | 35.6 | 4.6 | 3.4 | 43.6 |
| 1983 | 36.5 | 5.0 | 4.1 | 45.6 |
| 1984 | 39.4 | 6.3 | 4.4 | 50.1 |
| 1985 | 40.8 | 6.9 | 4.4 | 52.1 |

Source: Robert W. Crandall, "What Ever Happened to Deregulation?" in *Assessing the Reagan Years*, ed. David Boaz (Washington, D.C.: Cato Institute, 1988), p. 286. Crandall cites the following sources: Kit D. Farber and Gary L. Rutledge, "Pollution Abatement and Control Expenditures," *Survey of Current Business* (July 1986), pp.94–105; (May 1987), pp. 21–25; Data Resources, Inc., "Real Capital Expenditures on Occupational Safety and Health"— figures given include only capital expenditures; and Robert W. Crandall, *Regulating the Automobile* (Washington, D.C.: Brookings Institution, 1986), pp. 36–38—figures given represent total costs of safety and regulation, including fuel penalties, deflated by the consumer price index.

ing economy. Consequently, the costs as a percentage of GNP declined, albeit very slightly, after the late 1970s, and were still below
the 1978 peak percentage in 1985. The total of the three regulatory
costs amounted to 1.7 percent in 1978 and 1.4 percent in 1985.
This ratio, which might be dubbed the "average regulatory tax rate"
for the three programs, fell by almost 18 percent in a seven-year
period (although it may have been rising after 1985).

Of course, the regulatory accomplishments, or lack thereof, during the 1980s cannot be totally attributed to Ronald Reagan. Congress,
both houses of which were controlled by the Democrats for almost
the entire decade, can be given some of the blame or credit, which
suggests that political outcomes were being influenced by forces that
were operating on both the Congress and the presidency.

## Trade Policy

Probably nowhere did the Reagan administration, as well as
Congress, fall off the deregulation bandwagon more than in the area
of international trade. Although the administration talked continually
about the value of free trade, it repeatedly conceded to protectionists'
demands for more tariffs, quotas, and "voluntary export restraints"
(commonly cited as VERs).

Prior to the 1980s protectionism appeared to be in retreat. The
average U.S. tariff on imports fell dramatically from an index of
100 just after World War II to under 5 in the 1973–79 period.[31]
However, during the 1980s, the Reagan administration approved a
number of protectionist measures. At the behest of Reagan officials,
the Japanese in 1981 established the first VER on their automobile
exports to the United States at 1.68 million cars during the first
year (with unspecified adjustments in the number of exported cars
in the subsequent two years). That restraint program was followed
by a VER on European, Japanese, Korean, and Brazilian steel.[32]

The Reagan administration also supported a renewal of the Multifiber Agreement in 1981, which limited the importing of textile and
apparel products from Third World countries and which may have
imposed an annual cost of $3 billion on the American economy.[33]
Under the banner of securing "fair trade," the Reagan Administration
in the 1981–85 period instituted 252 "countervailing duties" and
took twenty "anti-dumping actions,"[34] whose net effect may have
been to raise the percentage of U.S. imports receiving special protection from 12 percent in 1980 to 23 percent in 1987.[35]

Finally, while the Reagan administration rebuffed several attempts by representatives of special domestic interests in Congress
to increase protectionism (for example, efforts to impose quotas on
imported shoes) and also negotiated the Canada Free Trade Agreement in 1988, it eventually endorsed efforts to manage trade in computer chips and the Omnibus Trade Act of 1988, which gives the
president greater powers to retaliate against unfair trade practices of
foreign countries.[36]

"On balance," writes Professor Weidenbaum, "it is clear that
the United States has become more protectionist since Ronald Reagan
moved into the Oval Office. By 1985, the Reagan Administration
had openly adopted the 'fair trade' term that traditionally has been
the protectionists' euphemism for trade restrictions."[37] The only possible virtue to be found in the administration's trade position over its
eight years may be that the administration was not as protectionist
as many in Congress might have liked it to be. In addition, from
the growth in trade as a percentage of GNP, it is obvious that the
administration provided domestic industries only modest protection
from foreign competition. The administration's reliance on quantitative restrictions, which have been circumvented with relative ease—
perhaps with the administration's blessings—explains why trade restrictions have been porous. If the government was more diligently
trying to control international trade with more resources, the unprecedented expansion of trade has demonstrated government's fading
powers of control in face of mounting transnational economic forces.[38]

## Federal Labor Policy

One of the growth areas in government policies was in labor
relations. And the most obvious turnaround in labor policy trends
in the 1960s and 1970s was probably in minimum-wage legislation.
The first minimum wage, set at $.25 an hour, was passed in 1938.
Subsequently the minimum wage has been raised in steps, through
the passage of seven amendments to the Fair Labor Standards Act,
to $3.35 an hour in 1981, where it remained until 1989 when another
amendment was passed to raise the minimum wage to $3.80 an hour
in 1990 and to $4.25 an hour in 1991.

In the 1987–89 congressional struggle to raise the minimum
wage, many observers blamed the Reagan administration for undermining the incomes of millions of American low-income workers because the administration failed to support further increases in the

nominal minimum wage. In 1989, however, the real value of the minimum wage had been trending downward for two decades. The real minimum wage peaked in 1968 at $5.78 an hour (in 1989 dollars). The value had decreased $1.16, or 20 percent, by 1981, the year President Reagan took office. The real minimum wage dropped another $1.27, or 27 percent, from 1981 to 1989, and by 1989 had returned to the real level first achieved in the early 1950s. The real minimum wage did decline more rapidly (on a per-year basis) in the 1980s than it had in the previous decade.[39] Yet, except for slightly more than three million workers, the minimum wage had by 1990 become a "non-binding labor-market constraint." That is a sophisticated way of saying the law no longer served as a wage floor for the vast majority of low-wage workers.

This history of the real minimum wage raises the question, What caused Congress to retreat on the minimum wage? Could it have been international pressures to make American labor policies more competitive? The history of the public debate over the minimum wage indicates that two major considerations were guiding Congress and the president. First, a large volume of econometric research showed that the minimum wage was significantly reducing the employment opportunities of disadvantaged workers, especially low-income minority teenagers. Second, previous supporters of the minimum wage, including that bastion of eastern liberalism, the *New York Times*, began opposing increases out of the recognition that American workers had to compete in the global economy, and foreign workers could be paid far less than the U.S. minimum.[40] Even with the increases passed in late 1989 to become effective in 1990 and 1991, the long-run trend in the minimum wage remains decidedly downward.[41]

The history of other forms of government involvement in labor markets is difficult to judge. This is true primarily because so much of the influence of labor laws is achieved through the threat of legal action against violators, and the impact of threats is hard to measure. Federal labor laws control many aspects of employment that require administrative and judicial enforcement, not the least of which are what age a person must be in order legally to work full-time; what types of discrimination in employment will be permitted; what can and cannot be produced at home; what wages can be paid on federally funded projects; which foreign workers will be granted employment rights; and how and when labor unions will be recognized as the representatives of worker groups.

Antagonists of federal intervention have much to criticize. And few new deregulation laws, which would reduce government involvement in labor markets, have even been proposed, much less passed. Indeed, laws have recently been enacted that move the country in the opposite direction, including measures to restrict immigration (through alien identification procedures, 1986) and to restrict plant closings (through a sixty-day prenotification requirement at plants that have more than 100 workers, 1988). In addition, Congress passed, but failed to override President Bush's veto, to mandate leave for child or parental care (up to twelve weeks annually).

Nonetheless, there is much empirical evidence of at least *some* decline in federal entanglement in labor markets. From 1962 to 1976, the outlays of the U.S. Department of Labor expanded in constant (1982) dollars by 232 percent, reaching $45 billion in 1976. Since then, however, the real-dollar budget of the Labor Department has trended downward, standing at $18.5 billion in fiscal 1988. The total number of employees of the Labor Department followed a similar pattern, rising in the 1960s and early 1970s and falling in the late 1970s and 1980s.

Of course, given the growth in the economy, the budget of the Labor Department has contracted even more in relative terms. The relative contraction began during the first year of the Carter administration—not with the advent of the Reagan administration. The department's budget amounted to 1.6 percent of GNP at its peak in 1976, but only .5 percent in 1988. Some of the decline in the department's budget since the early 1980s can be attributed to a reduction in unemployment and unemployment compensation payments. However, even if the impact of recessions on the department's budget is excluded, a decline is still evident, reflecting ongoing changes in basic budget priorities.[42]

Growth in union membership has been attributed to congenial labor laws.[43] If that is the case, the history of union membership may be an indirect, albeit very imperfect, measure of the extent of government involvement in labor markets.[44] By that measure government influence has seriously eroded. Union membership peaked in 1975 at approximately 22.2 million, and was more than 5 million, or 24 percent, below that in 1987.

As a share of the labor force, union membership rose very slightly during the 1950s and 1960s, and from 1967 to 1970 stayed close to its peak of 24.7 percent of the labor force, after which a steady decline set in. By 1987, union members accounted for only 13.9 percent of the total labor force, a decline in unions' labor-market share of nearly 45 percent.[45]

However, such statistics on unions' decline within the total labor force obscures their even more precipitous decline the private sector. This is because unions' total share of employment has been augmented by gains in public-sector unions.[46] Many researchers expect union membership to continue its decline, possible falling to 5 percent of the total labor force, by the turn of the century.

By the late 1980s the annual number of work stoppages and days idled due to those work stoppages had also been reduced to a fraction of what they were in the 1970s and early 1980s, possibly reflecting the weakened position of unions in the economy and the weakened ability of the federal government to fortify their position.

Many union supporters are convinced that a major explanation for the alleged decline of the middle class (which has not really occurred[47]) has been the government's hostile attitude toward unions, best epitomized by the Reagan administration's firing of the federal air traffic controllers in 1981.[48] The loss of many high-paying union jobs has supposedly lowered many workers' incomes to the point that these workers are in fact no longer in the middle class.

But unions have fallen on hard times for the same reason that governments have—the general fluidity of the global economy and their inability to extract their usual share of rents. The relative decline in the resources available to government to "protect" workers or their rents is a reflection of the international forces at work on Congress and the presidency. If labor markets were more highly regulated in the late 1980s than in earlier decades, it is hard to see how. The federal government had fewer real dollars and fewer Labor Department workers to control a growing labor force that was expanding total domestic product.[49] In addition, labor unions were rusting internally, unable to avoid making wage concessions, much less achieving wage gains for their shrinking membership.

Tax Policy

In the 1980s Congress and the Reagan administration joined efforts to further enfranchise Americans through reductions in tax rates and the broadening the tax base.[50] President Reagan's first supply-side tax bill, the Economic Recovery Act of 1981, served to reduce income tax rates by approximately 23 percent over three years, and to index taxes to inflation thereafter—all with the intent of giving taxpayers greater incentives to work, save, and invest.[51] His second major tax bill, the Tax Reform Act of 1986, went further, reducing rates again and eliminating various loopholes and exemptions in the federal tax code. While Congress and the administration failed to simplify the tax code in 1986, they did reduce tax rates and did arrest, at least temporarily, the growth in federal tax collections in constant dollars and also as a percentage of gross national product.[52] The maximum federal marginal income tax rate was 70 percent in 1980 but stood at only 28 (or, for some taxpayers, 33) percent in 1989.[53]

In general, according to one estimate, the 1981 Economic Recovery Act lowered the average tax rates (including Social Security) for families with one-half the median income from 15.5 percent to 13.4 percent; for families with the median income from 20.1 percent to 17.0 percent; and for families with twice the median income from 25.8 percent to 20.8 percent.[54] Another researcher estimates that the 1981 act lowered the effective average tax rate of the upper tenth of the income distribution from 27.1 percent in 1980 to 25.3 percent.[55] The 1981 act also lowered the average tax rates on corporations; the 1986 tax-reform act further lowered tax rates on plants at the same time as it raised tax rates on equipment, primarily through the elimination of acceleration of depreciation and the investment tax credit, the net effect of all corporate tax revisions being an increase in direct taxation of business.[56]

A point that may be obvious is the fact that the federal tax-law changes in the 1980s have probably not abated the growth in federal receipts nearly as much as might have been presumed, given all the hoopla surrounding the passage of the various pieces of tax legislation. Aside from the decrease in federal receipts in 1982 and 1983, due in part to the recession, federal tax receipts have continued along an upward trend. All the Reagan administration and Congress may have done is to move taxpayers off the much-steeper tax revenue path established under the Nixon, Ford, and Carter administrations.[57] Many of the benefits from reductions in federal tax rates were partially offset by increases in Social Security. At the same time the continuing growth in revenues has been due, at least partially, to greater efficiency in the economy; greater taxpayer incentives to work, save, and invest; and to fewer taxpayer incentives to avoid and evade taxes. To this extent the tax-reform packages of the 1980s had their intended supply-side effect.

According to Harvard economist Lawrence Lindsey, there remains no doubt that the 1981 tax changes had a powerful effect on
the U.S. economy. Indeed, because of the 1981 law, tax revenues
in 1985 were $33 billion less than they would otherwise have been,
but GNP in that year was 2 to 3 percent higher than it would otherwise
have been. In addition, "rich" Americans, those with incomes in
the top .1 percent of all income earners, or earning more than $200,000
a year, paid more in taxes because of reductions in the marginal tax
rates they faced, which induced them to increase their earnings and
reduce their efforts to avoid and evade taxes. Income earners in the
top .1 percent increased their share of all federal taxes paid from 7
percent in 1981 to 14 percent in 1985. Income earners in the top 2
percent of all income recipients saw their tax share rise from 26
percent in 1981 to 34 percent in 1985.[58] Again, these changes are
directly attributable to the 1981 tax changes.

The evidence has accumulated and leads to important general
conclusions. Federal tax laws are important, in and of themselves.
Tax-code provisions can powerfully affect people's incentives to work,
save, and invest and to avoid and evade taxes. In Professor Lindsey's
words,

> The Reagan tax cuts put supply-side economics on the map intellectu-
> ally and politically. The evidence certainly favors the fundamental
> supply-side proposition that taxes matter: they distort taxpayer behav-
> ior, limit the supply of productive factors, and hold the economy
> below its potential. The effects of the 1981 tax changes shift the
> burden of proof to those who claim government can raise taxes with
> impunity.[59]

As a matter of fact, it appears that "tax rates over 50 percent are
counterproductive from the view of collecting tax revenue,"[60] which
implies that "governments that play soak-the-rich to win votes do
so at the treasury's expense."[61]

However, gains at the federal level can be nullified by changes
in receipts of state and local governments. Somewhat surprisingly,
the total of real-tax receipts of all governments (federal, state, and
local) has continued to rise. Yet, the growth in total receipts as a
percentage of GNP began to fall dramatically in the early 1970s.[62]

There is, of course, some cause for concern. But the capacity
of governments to increase their combined revenues is slipping. So

too is their capacity to increase their expenditures. Some growth in revenue is still evident, but the pace of growth in taxes has slowed, particularly in relation to the growth of the economy. The overall growth in the U.S. economy may have been spurred by the waning capacity of governments to capture a higher percentage of people's incomes.

Perhaps the most important turnaround in governmental tax policy took place in the nature and the substance of tax-policy discussions. In the 1960s, few tax debates were openly concerned with the incentive effects of tax increases or reductions. Indeed, rates were considered only as devices for achieving prescribed revenue levels. The revenue levels were important because many economists heeded the teachings of the late British economist John Maynard Keynes, according to which, national income could be raised by increasing aggregate demand in the economy. One way aggregate demand could be increased was through a reduction in tax revenues, leaving more money in the hands of taxpayers to spend. How revenues were reduced—either by lower rates or across-the-board tax credits—was not a particularly important issue. By the 1980s, however, Keynesian economics had fallen into disrepute for its apparent inability in the 1970s to cope with the growing problems of "stagflation," a condition of high rates of inflation and unemployment.

In the 1970s people everywhere began talking about incentives and the impact of policies on people's behavior. Prices of all kinds, including "tax prices," began to be recognized as an important factor in determining the magnitude of investments and production. Policymakers began to be alert to what other countries were doing.

Though we cannot be certain why market (and tax) prices began to enter into policy discussions in the 1970s rather than earlier, one likely cause is that people and capital had become more mobile and could respond with greater ease and rapidity to prices of all kinds, including tax and regulatory prices. In short, prices could no longer be excluded from consideration by economic theorists and policymakers. They mattered a great deal. Indeed, Reagan may have won the presidency in 1980 at least partly because his views on taxes and regulations more closely mirrored the growing importance of tax and regulatory incentives and disincentives in determining national production, employment, and government revenues than did those of all of his political rivals.

The experience of major countries like the United States with tax-rate reductions can no longer be ignored by others. Tax-rate reductions obviously work, especially where tax rates are high, in the sense that they can spur economic development from both domestic and foreign sources. To achieve the same results and to prevent their own capital bases from moving out, other countries have had to follow the U.S. lead, just as the United States understood that it would have to co-opt the lead in tax reform from Britain.

## Privatization

To date the federal government has done little to privatize many of its activities.[63] However, plans were underway in late 1989 for expanding privatization to low-income housing, federal loans, air-traffic control and other Federal Aviation Administration functions, education (through vouchers and tax credits), prisons, petroleum reserves, segmentation of the frequency spectrum for radio and television, some real estate, military commissaries, urban mass transit, and the postal service.[64]

The growing reliance on the private provision of federal programs is probably most dramatic in federally constructed housing for low-income people. There has been a marked reduction in federally constructed public housing and a marked increase in housing for low-income residents through rent, mortgage, and building subsidies provided in facilities constructed and maintained by the private sector.[65]

For our purposes the privatization movement is significant not for what has actually been accomplished, but because it reveals the growing need all levels of governments have felt to become more efficient by responding to market pressures and by spinning off many inefficient public ventures and misadventures. We personally believe that much scholarly and policy research has proved the value of privatization.[66] However, policymakers have been receptive to the research because of the growing competitive pressures being imposed upon them. By seeking private methods for providing government services, governments have been able to reduce taxes and/or expenditures—thereby reducing the drag governments impose on their economies and enhancing their competitive positions.

## The Underground Economy

Nowhere are the growing constraints on the economic powers of government more self-evident than in crime control. Over recent decades criminal activity—much of which has economic foundations—has mushroomed. The annual rates of increase in shoplifting, prostitution, burglaries, loan-sharking, muggings, embezzlements, bank robberies, and a host of other economic crimes speak eloquently to slippages in the power of societal norms but also to government's lost grip on the illegal economy. The dramatic growth in the nation's drug trade corroborates the widely held view that the government can no longer be counted on to suppress effectively economic activities considered undesirable. The level of activity in the illegal economy also speaks volumes about the importance of economic incentives to the movement of the nation's capital stock, not so much internationally—although international trade is definitely involved—as between the aboveground, legal economy, often heavily taxed and regulated, and the underground, illegal economy, which is devoid of government taxes and regulation.

Of course, the underground economy is no longer restricted to the employment of stereotypical common criminals banishing guns and clubs. Indeed, according to one estimate, income from strictly illegal sources accounts for less than half of the total economic activity in the "underground economy."[67] The underground now includes people down the block who sell a variety of goods and services—from firewood to scarves to housecleaning to haircuts to fence posts—all on the condition that payment must be made in cash and is, therefore, difficult for taxing authorities to trace. It also includes the many self-employed people who hide—or fail to report—business income or who engage in barter, for example, the trade of a swimming pool for a new roof, and who avoid tax payments on the profits that would have been made on the separate sales.

Unfortunately, estimates of the relative size of the underground economy in the United States vary greatly and range upward to 15 and even 25 percent of GNP—a significant share of the economy but one that pales in comparison with the underground economies in many other countries.[68] Because of the nature of the businesses in the underground, the estimates of its size are not considered very reliable.[69] However, in spite of the ongoing dispute over its relative size, few doubt that the underground, untaxed, and unregulated segment of the U.S. (and world) economy has been growing in recent decades faster than its aboveground counterpart—possibly giving rise to an understatement in the annual growth rate of the U.S. economy since World War II of at least a quarter of 1 percent.[70]

Understandably, by the late 1970s, the underground economy—

and the ability of people to move from the aboveground to the underground economy—had become a major issue in public demands for
tax reform. Proponents of tax reform argued quite effectively that
marginal tax rates (as noted, these then ranged up to 70 percent)
had to be lowered and the tax code had to be simplified in order to
eliminate the incentive citizens had to take their skills—and their
income-earning and tax-generating capabilities—out of the reach of
the tax authorities. In 1986 the IRS reported some progress in improving voluntary compliance.[71] The fact that the federal government,
including members of the Reagan administration and congress, felt
obliged to couch their tax-reform oratory in terms of shrinking the
underground economy, not to mention tax avoidance and evasion,
suggests the extent to which this alternative economy was undermining the ability of governments to expand.

## Reflections on Containment

The empirical evidence we have reviewed demonstrates that
waning growth in government expenditures and taxes in the United
States is apparent. From both the data sources and the commentaries
of public officials who witnessed the regulatory process in their government work, it appears reasonable to observe that the regulatory movement began to lose its momentum in the early to mid-1970s; the
pace of growth in regulations began to slow in the mid- to late 1970s
and was held in check in the 1980s. The slowing pace of regulation
was accompanied by a growing interest in privatizing government
services. This amounts to a form of deregulating or demonopolizing
government services.

Deregulation of a limited number of industries accompanied
the slowing pace of growth in the regulation of other industries in
the late 1970s. The pace of deregulation, however, appears to have
slowed in the mid-1980s. And, given recent increases in regulatory
costs and the growing congressional demands for employer-paid "mandated benefits" heard in the late 1980s, there are reasons to fear
that the promise of continued regulatory restraint may have "faded"
(to paraphrase Dr. Crandall's assessment[72]).

Both the critics and supporters of the Reagan administration
have reason to be disappointed by what did not happen on the regulatory and deregulatory front in the 1980s. Critics can bemoan the
continuing decline of the influence of government regulation. Supporters can fret that much remains to be done and that the pace of

disentangling governments from the economy has been slowed or even reversed.[73]

The obvious policy crosscurrents, with some trends pointing toward the containment of governmental influence while others point toward greater involvement of governments, reflect the nature of the real world, which is buffeted by a myriad of political forces of varying intensities. In fact, the crosscurrents of policies are necessarily interrelated, given the overall, more tightly drawn limitations on the overall capacity of government to tax, spend, and regulate. These limitations suggest that more costly regulations in one area—say, international trade—must give way to lower taxes and/or the elimination or modification of regulations in another area. Similarly, a reduction in taxes might be undertaken with a view toward offsetting the negative effects of other regulations that have either been or are being imposed.

These problems notwithstanding, the late 1970s and the whole of the 1980s have witnessed a significant containment, at least, of the relative expansion of governmental budgetary and regulatory powers in a growing U.S. economy. Indeed, given the abundance of evidence, one conclusion is safe: the economy did grow more rapidly in the 1980s partly because of the growing overall constraints on governmental regulatory and fiscal powers.[74]

Many remain convinced that government in the United States is still far too large. However, it is difficult to ignore the fact that government growth has slowed. The only question is, Why has it done so? Critics of the Reagan administration are convinced that the dominant reason is the ideological swing of the electorate expressed in the Reagan presidency. These ideological changes can never be summarily dismissed. However, the waning growth of governmental power in the United States did not start abruptly with the arrival of the supposedly ideologically rigid Reagan administration in Washington anymore than *perestroika* arrived in Moscow the day Gorbachev took charge. Furthermore, as noted, the Reagan administration needed the cooperation of both houses of Congress, which were controlled by Democrats during most of the 1970s and 1980s.

Economic analyses of ineffective and inefficient government fiscal and regulatory policies proliferated during the 1960s and 1970s. People learned much about what not to try to do through government from the raw experience of rapidly expanding (and failing) government programs. People became aware that most government programs do not always match promises and many are even counterproductive.

The path of government growth with a decreasing upward slope in the United States has amounted to a political learning curve.

If that is the whole story, government growth may be choked, more or less "naturally," at some predetermined level of governmental involvement in the economy. International comparisons of government growth can help sort out the influence of such "learning by doing." If countries with different levels of governmental involvement in their respective economies begin curtailing the growth of government simultaneously, then other common forces, not just a shared learning curve on which countries held different positions in the 1970s and 1980s, must have coaxed the coordination of transnational policies and the dampening of the growth rates of their governments. The success the United States and other countries have had with constricting government involvement in their respective economies has only served to hasten the spread of supply-side policy solutions, once derided as "voodoo economics."

The waning growth of many dimensions of government in the United States and of the many governments around the world is largely therefore the power of the growing competitiveness of the world economy. If technology and capital mobility are significant causative factors in this competitiveness, we would expect government growth rates across nations to continue to fall at more or less the same rate and in response to each other's economic policy adjustments. Thus, policy changes that make governments reduce the burden on quicksilver capital will keep spreading relatively rapidly among nations.

# 9

## The Fall of the Fat Cats

### An Unorthodox Challenge to the Decline Theorists

No single reason adequately explains what has occurred. But I believe there is one circumstance which overshadows all else and has set the current period apart: unprecedented, deep, and continual technological change. In the 1970s and 1980s extraordinarily rapid technological change has thrust upon us new and as yet unresolved problems of governance in the national and international spheres.

*W. Michael Blumenthal*[1]

IN the late 1980s the American economy was experiencing its longest peacetime recovery since World War II.[2] Nonetheless despair abounded. In those years, a chorus of scholars, policymakers, and critics worried, as they had so often before, that the continuing rebound in economic activity amounted to nothing more than temporary relief from a longer-term downward slide in U.S. standing in the world economy.

These observers enlisted a plethora of economic facts to indicate that the so-called American Empire was in decline because the economy on which it ultimately rested was in decline.[3] Additionally, many observers contended that this decline was inevitable—unless remedial public policy actions were undertaken, and undertaken soon. In order to prevent this we were told that the economy needed to be managed more carefully from Washington. Even then, these observers feared, it was doubtful that policy changes could do anything more than ease America's transition to a less-influential position in the world.

However, economic data on the relative health of the U.S. economy have been fundamentally misinterpreted by advocates of the decline thesis, as we will show in this chapter. Contrary to the proponents of the thesis, the U.S. economy continues to hold its own in the expanding global economy. Nevertheless, we think the urgency of recent commentaries on America's presumed decline do reflect dramatically changing world events. Our basic disagreement with the proponents of the decline thesis is that they fail to perceive the real decline that is taking place and, consequently, have recommended policies that are out of sync with world trends. Granted, American business was confronted with real challenges during the 1980s to adjust to world competitive forces, but it appears to have met the challenges reasonably well. On the contrary it is not American business but American government that is in decline. Ironically, this decline in the power of the U.S. government has come about because U.S. business has been smarter than government; it has looked beyond its own borders for more hospitable and competitive locales and has been prepared to drain government of its capital base.

That is the hidden message in the clarion calls for reform. Critics who thirst for government involvement in the economy are mistakenly equating the decline of government power to the decline of America. Calls for reform are often nothing more than calls for attempts to reassert the power of government to control, tax, and grow. Such attempts go against global trends and can only be successful at the expense of the economy's ability to respond appropriately to these trends. The surest way to fulfill the predictions of those who see the United States in decline is to take public action to prevent the decline in the power of government.

## Competing Visions of Decline

Recent theories of decline come in all shapes and sizes. We begin our analysis by noting several of them in brief and then provide more throughgoing presentations of the criticisms of Mancur Olson, Walter Russell Mead, and, especially, Paul Kennedy.

Daniel Sharp, president of the American Assembly, said flatly,

"America can't compete."[4] The chief evidence he cites is the huge balance of trade deficits and the failure of the falling value of the dollar on international money markets to materially reduce those deficits. Joel Kurtzman, an economic consultant and futurist, warned that the United States needs to alter its economic course, principally through national planning, in order to end the "steep decline" of the country and "to recover our lost ground. There is still time to reassert our leadership, recapture our markets, and create new wealth."[5] He argued that if the country had remained on the path of economic dominance established in the 1950s, poverty might now be eliminated from the face of the earth and Americans would be enjoying far more industrial power and personal wealth.[6] "The saddest outcome of all," wrote Harvard University economist Benjamin Friedman, "would be for America's decline to go on, but to go on so gradually that by the time the members of the next generation are old enough to begin asking who was responsible for their diminished circumstances, they will not even know what they have lost."[7]

Former Colorado governor Richard Lamm advised that "the United States is not structured for long-term success. It is structured for long-term decline."[8] This is true because, "The United States is not on the cutting edge of competition any more, and while the problem has many roots, to a large extent the United States is a victim of its own institutions."[9] The institutional factors Governor Lamm considered to be major drags on growth span virtually the entire American economy: the country's overly generous health care system, excessively complicated and inefficient legal and tax codes, an ineffective education system, the low saving rate and resulting high cost of capital, and the government and consumer "debt bomb"—to mention just half his list.[10]

Former Secretary of the Treasury Michael Blumenthal worried:

On economic matters, we seem to be governing ourselves less adequately than at any time since World War II; sometimes we seem to be confronted by factors and forces that we cannot quite understand, let alone predict or correct. We find ourselves more and more in an environment of unaccustomed economic uncertainty and instability, both at home and abroad, and with no real consensus on what is happening, what is causing it, or what should be done next.[11]

The October 19, 1987, stock market crash reminded us all that "the system appears no longer to be working as it should."[12] Blumenthal believes our problems stem from federal deficits of "unprecedented proportions;" "huge" trade deficits; excessive indebtedness to the rest of the world; dependence on foreign oil; low saving rate; tolerance of poverty and distress "amid a national binge of borrowing and consumption"; and "unprecedented securities market uncertainties, with excessive, sometimes violent, up and down swings that threaten the stability of the system."[13]

Others warned with equal conviction that the global economy is in "deep trouble," mainly because of U.S. excesses: excessive budget deficits, excessive trade deficits, excessive inattentiveness to domestic social ills, and excessive reliance on military strength.[14] "American policy in recent years," these authors tell us, "has been more and more addicted to wishful thinking. Economically, . . . the era of comfortable self-indulgence appears near its close. Today the United States is on a collision course with history. The American fiscal dilemma must be resolved, and the perpetual instability of the dollar that is the consequence must cease."[15] Why is this so? We are forewarned that a breakdown of international monetary and trading arrangements is "so grave a danger that no responsible American government can ignore our own heavy responsibility for the present disarray."[16]

However, the logic of various decline theorists differs. For example, Mancur Olson, whom we have mentioned before, was one of the first academics to remind us that history teaches an important principle: Long periods of political stability invariably lead to the decline of nations.[17] Olson concluded that this is because extended political stability enables interest groups to gradually but persistently use the powers of their governments for their own private ends. Government regulatory powers will be used to monopolize markets. Government fiscal powers will be exploited not for the general good, but for subsidies and tax benefits that serve only private interests.

Olson argued that the net affect of private efforts to exploit government powers would be an expansion of inefficient government intrusions in the private sectors and the containment of competitive pressures. Economic growth would be checked, inevitably, by growing private "disincentives" to innovate and produce. Sluggish economic growth in national production would then be foreshadowed by sluggish productivity improvements. Indeed, scholars have recently warned that the United States now faces a productivity "crisis."[18]

The United States has faced the threat of decline, somewhat paradoxically, according to Olson, because it has been blessed (or damned?) by relative political stability for the past two hundred years and the absence of catastrophic natural disasters or all-consuming military disruptions for almost five decades. Thankfully, natural and military calamities are never sought for their own sake; but these disasters have the saving grace of loosening the privately engineered economic constraints imposed on economic growth. As alluded to in chapter 2, according to Olson, Germany and Japan were able to orchestrate their respective postwar "economic miracles" precisely because their defeats included a breaking of the 'hammer-locks imposed by interests groups on their respective economies.[19]

Social analyst Walter Mead examines decline from another angle. He argues that the decline of the United States is a product of the evaporation of its monopoly power with the rebuilding of Europe and Japan following World War II.[20] U.S. firms became monopolists with the destruction of their foreign competition during the war. For two decades or so after the war, U.S. firms were able to charge monopoly prices and to overlook the need to remain competitive. However, as Mead points out, price competition appeared with the emergence of rebuilt economies. The U.S. standard of living has suffered because domestic firms have had to give up their monopoly rents—to seek lower-cost production outlets in Third World economies. In Mead's view, decline has been perpetuated. He noted:

> The failure to protect American jobs [from capital flight abroad and from the inroads of foreign products in domestic markets], however, leads to rising unemployment in the United States and to a steady decline in the wages of those who keep their jobs. This intensifies the price pressure on those who produce consumer goods, because consumers have less money to spend. And this, in turn, strengthens the competitive advantage of low-wage manufacturing countries and thereby accelerates the flight of jobs to off-shore sites.[21]

Through his widely read book, Yale historian Paul Kennedy has probably done more than anyone else to substantiate growing despair over the country's fate. In spite of modern signs to the contrary, Professor Kennedy argues that America is following a well-worn, historically validated road to economic decline, if not ruin.[22] According to Professor Kennedy, history is replete with records of countries rising to the status of world powers, measured by economic and military might, only to overextend themselves and fall relatively, if not absolutely, to their world neighbors. Kennedy tells us that relative

economic standing among nations is important only because relative
economic performance largely determines relative political and military might in the world.[23]

During the nineteenth and early twentieth centuries, according
to Kennedy, the United States rose through the ranks of world powers
partly because of a favored resource base but also partly because of
extensive reliance on market institutions and the absence of world
military responsibilities. However, in the 1980s the United States
began to confront the prospects of decline partly, if not principally,
by seeking to police the world, something that cannot be done without
escalating military expenditures. Kennedy wrote:

> This test of American abilities [to fend off relative decline among
> Great Powers] will be the greater because it, like Imperial Spain around
> 1600 or the British Empire around 1900, is the inheritor of a vast
> array of strategical commitments which had been made decades earlier,
> when the nation's political, economic, and military capacity to influence
> world affairs seemed so much more assured. In consequence, the United
> States now runs the risk, so familiar to historians of the rise and fall
> of previous Great Powers, of what might be called "imperial over-
> stretch": that is to say, decision-makers in Washington must face the
> awkward and enduring fact that the sum total of the United States'
> global interests and obligations is nowadays far larger than the country's
> power to defend them all simultaneously.[24]

Through growing tax demands on the citizenry, the demands of any
escalating military buildup inevitably sap private investment expenditures, which, in turn, retard a country's economic development and
growth.[25] The expanding defense budgets and the lagging saving
and investment rates in the United States (as well as in the Soviet
Union and Western Europe) suggest that the country is following
the established historical pattern.[26] Indeed, the ascendancy of Japan,
China, and other "Pacific rim" countries makes the *relative* decline
of the United States altogether certain. Post–World War II Japan,
in particular, has been blessed with the absence of world military
responsibilities partly imposed by the United States.

According to Professor Kennedy, the relative decline of the
United States is apparent in its declining share of world GDP (especially the manufactured goods component), lost industrial jobs, growing trade imbalance, and the shrinking share of world trade dominated
by United States producers.[27] For example, in 1945, the United
States accounted for approximately half the world's aggregate produc-

tion. By 1953 the expected economic recovery of war-torn countries had lowered the United States' share to 44.7 percent. However, by 1980 the percentage had fallen to 31.5 percent, "and it was still falling" at the time he completed his survey of the available empirical literature.[28]

Future decline is practically assured, according to Professor Kennedy, unless the United States dramatically reforms its ways. At the same time, he doubted the capacity of the United States to buck historical trends. In fact, he was so sure of his gloomy prognosis for the country that he maintained that the main "task facing American statesmen over the next decades, therefore, is to recognize that broad trends are under way, and that there is a need to 'manage' affairs so that the *relative* erosion of the United States' position takes place slowly and smoothly, and is not accelerated by policies which bring merely short-term advantage but longer-term disadvantage."[29]

In general, modern scenarios of U.S. decline point to one overriding conclusion: The United States must reverse its dwindling savings and investment rates in order to remain a world-class economic, political, and military power. Much disagreement exists over exactly what policies should be implemented. Disagreement over reform strategies is probably never more intense than over protectionist proposals.[30] Typically, however, most proponents of the decline thesis maintain that the United States must first pay attention to reviving its economy. While it is not always true that economic prosperity and world military and political power go hand in hand, "the fact remains that all of the major shifts in the world's *military-power* balances have followed alterations in the *productive* balances; and further, that the rising and falling of various empires and states in the international system has been confirmed by the outcomes of the major Great Power wars, where victory has always gone to the side with the greatest material resources."[31]

The required shift in emphasis in government policy demands that the country rescind, if not renege on, many of its military and political commitments and demands that other countries—most notably, Japan and members of the European Economic Community— take on a greater defense burden. It may also require a reorganization of the fiscal priorities to ensure that "the consequent decline in our capacity to add value to the world economy" does not continue unabated.[32]

The general presumption is that "America's first problem may be that it spends too little on civilian benefits rather than too much."[33]

The only recourse, or so we were told in the late 1980s by virtually every advocate of the decline thesis, is that government must increase its incentives for investment and its spending on job training, nutrition, education, research and development, and infrastructure.[34]

But do the facts of decline square with the rhetoric of decline? We suggest that all of the gloom-and-doom observers have misread and misinterpreted the nature of decline.[35] If the facts are presented fairly and interpreted properly, there is much room for optimism over the fate of American economic power, as distinguished from political power, in the global economy.

## The Facts of the Matter

Few now dispute the fact that U.S. production has continued to rise in the 1980s.[36] Even industrial production and manufactured-output levels have maintained their upward trend in the 1980s. The overall industrial production index (1977 = 100) stood at 48.8 in 1960 and had more than doubled by 1980 to 108.6. By March 1990, the index was above 142, or more than 30 percent higher than in 1980. The expansion of the industrial production index covering only manufacturing was significantly greater (over 38 percent) than the expansion of all categories of industrial production.

U.S. GNP has also continued to grow in real terms. In fact, real GNP in 1989 was almost two and a half times its size in 1960. It rose by 32 percent between 1970 and 1980 and by another 30 percent between 1980 and 1989. Many, but certainly not all, proponents of the decline thesis freely acknowledge the rise in the absolute level of production—industrial and otherwise—in the United States. Their main claim is that U.S. production *relative* to the world is on the decline. In this regard, it is unfortunate that Professor Kennedy truncated his empirical research in 1980 or a couple of years thereafter. Extension of his data calls into question his central conclusion, which is that the United States continued in the 1980s to decline in total production relative to the rest of the world.

Between 1960 and 1986, world GNP (excluding the United States) grew by 183 percent, from $4.5 to $12.6 trillion, whereas U.S. GNP grew by 118 percent, from $1.9 to $4.1 trillion.[37] A long-term decline of sorts is evident in those comparisons. However, when U.S. GNP is computed as a percentage of GNP in the rest of the world (world GNP minus U.S. GNP), assessments of long-term economic decline become far more tenuous, if not totally premature. U.S. GNP as a percentage of GNP for the rest of the world fell from 1960 through the mid-1970s, from 42.7 percent in 1960 to 36.1 percent in 1970 to 32.8 percent in 1975. But, somewhere between 1975 and 1978, U.S. GNP relative to the rest of the world began to level off, staying between 32.8 percent in 1975 and 31.6 percent in 1982. (In fact, U.S. GNP relative to world GNP was higher in 1984 than 1980, albeit ever so slightly. It was .1 percent lower in 1986 than it was in 1975.)[38]

The stable relationship between U.S. GNP and the combined GNPs of major, developed countries is confirmed by data on GDP (computed by purchasing-power-parity methods) from the OECD.[39] Oscillation in the percentages is apparent, and if the percentage figures for 1970 were compared with those for 1980 alone (which was done by Professor Kennedy), some slight downward trend would be detected (although incorrectly). U.S. GDP fell from 67.8 to 63.6 percent OECD GDP between 1970 and 1980. However, if any trend is evident in the entire stretch of data in the series, it is a flat one. The trend in U.S. GDP relative to Japan is, however, decidedly downward throughout the 1970s and at the start of the 1980s—*until 1982 or 1983*. U.S. GDP fell from 346 percent of Japan GDP in 1970 to 279 percent in 1986. This implies that the trend in U.S. GDP relative to OECD (with Japan's GDP excluded) is lightly upward in the 1970–86 period.[40]

As with non-Communist countries, U.S. GNP fell in the 1960s relative to the combined GNP of the represented collection of Communist countries (including the USSR) and to the GNP of the USSR alone.[41] However, in both comparisons the downward trend flattened out some time in the late 1970s. U.S. GNP was 206 percent of the USSR GNP in 1960, down to 170 percent in 1975 but up to 177 percent in 1986. However, the actual increase in the U.S. output relative to the output of the Soviet Union may have been substantially greater than is indicated by the statistics, which are drawn from CIA sources. This is because reports surfaced in early 1990 that the CIA had been overestimating Soviet production by as much as a third for decades. According to one report from the Institute for Contemporary Studies, "Soviet average annual gross national product growth from 1961 to 1985 was overstated 112 percent by government statistics and at least 50 percent by the CIA," and the difference between estimated and actual Soviet production grew larger over the period.[42]

## Relative Wealth

Proponents of the decline thesis also maintain that data reveal that the wealth of the United States is on the decline. That is clearly not the case for the absolute level of the country's wealth as measured, say, by the Bureau of Economic Analysis (BEA). The measured "gross stock of fixed reproducible tangible wealth" grew in constant (1982) dollars from $10.7 trillion in 1970 to $18.5 trillion in 1987, a 72.8 percent increase.[43] In spite of this evidence, however, final conclusions about what is happening to the absolute level of wealth in the United States must be postponed. This is because there is obviously much "wealth"—most prominently, human skills—that the BEA does not (and cannot) measure. In addition, prices used to compute actual wealth may not appropriately measure the potential contribution of the wealth. For example, the real prices of computers have decreased while the power of computers has increased.

Whether or not total wealth in the United States is declining relative to other countries is not completely clear. Reliable data on wealth around the world are not available. However, the wealth of countries might be inferred, at least tentatively, from their productive capacity. The present monetary value of productive assets is a direct function of the (present discounted value) of the real income (and output) generated by the assets over time. Since we have already assessed the relative productive power of the United States vis-à-vis other countries, we might tentatively conclude that through the mid-1970s the wealth of the United States has fallen relative to the combined wealth in the rest of the world. This is because U.S. measured output fell relatively. However, since the mid-1970s, U.S. GNP has remained more or less stable relative to the rest of the world. It follows that, since the mid-1970s, U.S. wealth might have remained stable relative to world wealth.

We have stressed the tentativeness of these interpretations because we can only assess the issues from available measurements, which, as noted, have strict limitations. The *actual* wealth of European countries and Japan very likely did not fall nearly as much as their *measured* wealth during World War II. Even in the postwar years, European countries and Japan were blessed with much human (capital) wealth that no government agency has ever attempted to measure. Accordingly, in the postwar years the increase in the actual wealth of those countries was not nearly as dramatic as the increase in their measured wealth. Of course, the debate is further complicated by the fact that human wealth is extended over time with expenditures on education and health care. Many countries may outspend the United States on education on a per capita basis, but none spends more on health care.

Finally, much has been made of the low and declining savings and investment rates in the United States. For example, two researchers concerned with the savings trend maintain, "For more than a decade, Americans have been saving at rates low enough to cheat our future," a presumed fact that caused the researchers to call for federally devised "national saving guidelines."[44] Personal savings in the United States as a percentage of disposable income did fall from about 8 percent in 1970 to less than 5.5 percent in 1989, and the United States has one of the lowest personal savings rates among major economic powers.[45] There are many explanations for the decline in the savings rate—some have been discussed so often that they need not be considered here. However, it must be stressed that Americans appear to save a great deal indirectly by way of business savings. Over the years the sum of personal and business savings has varied from year to year as a percentage of national income, but there has been no dramatic downward trend since 1970. Total personal and business savings were 19.8 percent in 1970 and were down only a little, to 18.9 percent, in 1989.[46]

In addition it should be noted that a declining savings rate, as conventionally measured, is not necessarily "all bad." People can save, in effect, through increases in their wealth, not solely through "nonconsumption" out of disposable income. Indeed, it would not be totally unreasonable to expect people to save a marginally smaller share of their current income when their accumulated wealth portfolios are rising in money or productive value.[47] Lawrence Lindsey, whom we have cited before in connection with his exhaustive study of the economic effects of tax-rate changes of the early 1980s, correctly argues that the crucial variable households consider is change in their net worth, or the difference between their assets and liabilities. He figures that between the end of 1981 and 1986, the liabilities of U.S. households rose by a whopping $1.3 trillion, but their assets increased by several times more, $6 trillion. Measuring the "savings rate" by the annual rise in net worth, Americans on average saved 13.5 percent of their annual personal income between 1982 and 1987, up from an average savings rate of 7.8 percent between 1977 and 1981. Hence, Professor Lindsey reasons that the often-cited decline in savings as a percentage of disposable income is a mark of the renewed vigor of the American economy. With asset prices rising, people simply did not feel as compelled to prepare for the future by reducing current consumption.[48]

Also, even if the U.S. savings rate had fallen dramatically as claimed, it would not matter as much as it would have several decades ago, when the country's future economic health did depend extensively on the domestic savings rate. However, savings has become internationalized through the world's financial markets. When someone from Easton, Pennsylvania, fails to save, the shortfall can be offset by an increase in the savings of someone from Tokyo. The future growth of the United States simply does not suffer as much (through reduced investment) as it once would have when the U.S. and Japanese economies were not as integrated as they are today. Similarly, any upsurge in U.S. savings will not have the same strong impact on U.S. growth as it once would have had. This is the case simply because all savings can be expected to seek its highest return, meaning part of the increase in savings can be expected to go abroad.

The notion of America's relative decline is also founded on a decrease in the rate of investment as a percentage of GNP from the late 1970s. The unusually large budget deficits incurred during the Reagan years supposedly "crowded out" private investment. In fact, when current-dollar gross private domestic investment is divided by GNP, a decline is evident, from above 17 percent in 1978 to about 15 percent in 1988. However, as St. Louis Federal Reserve economist John Tatom points out, the perception of decline is deceptive, attributable largely to a 15 percent decrease in the price of investment goods relative to all other goods included in GNP.[49] When the distorting effects of relative price changes are corrected (by first dividing gross investment and GNP by their respective price indexes), the decline scenario is again called into question. Real investment as a percentage of real GNP trended upward throughout the 1960s and 1970s and was at an all-time high during the first half of the 1980s. The ratio was down slightly, close to 12 percent in 1988, but it was still higher than in any year between 1950 and 1980.[50]

Tatom notes that real net investment (gross investment minus depreciation) as a percentage of real GNP fell in the 1970s and 1980s from more than 4.5 percent in 1966 to about 2 percent in 1987, which is grounds for some concern. However, caution is warranted in interpreting such figures. Net investment can seriously understate the increase in the country's productive capability because, as Tatom notes, "The newer vintage plant and equipment embodies a newer technology and is more productive than the older, discarded plant and equipment, so that output rises despite the absence of net investment."[51] In short, because the facts regarding the relative wealth of the United States are necessarily inconclusive, those who have proclaimed its decline cannot be as confident of their assertions as they seem.[52]

## International Trade

According to most proponents of the "decline thesis," the mounting U.S. international trade deficit is prima facie evidence of the country's lost competitiveness, lost drive, and a declining standing in the world economy. Professor Kennedy tells us:

> The uncompetitiveness of U.S. industrial products abroad and the declining sales of agricultural exports have together produced staggering deficits in visible trade—$160 billion in the twelve months to May 1986—but what is alarming is that such a gap can no longer be covered by American earnings on "invisibles," which is the traditional recourse of a mature economy. . . . On the contrary, the only way the United States can pay its way in the world is by importing ever-larger sums of capital, which has transformed it from being the world's largest creditor to the world's largest debtor nation *in the space of a few years*.[53]

Indeed, over the past decade there has been a marked reversal of U.S. international fortunes, at least as measured by the difference between the dollar value of internationally exported and imported goods. The United States had minor merchandise trade surpluses (measured in constant 1982 dollars) and modest trade deficits during the entire decade of the 1960s.[54] However, as measured by the merchandise trade balance, the economic screws began to tighten in the 1970s. During the first half of the 1970s, deficits, when they occurred, were modest. Yet the late 1970s and early 1980s stood witness to an explosion of the trade deficit, which in constant (1982) dollars reached almost $168 billion in 1987, falling to $109 billion by 1989.

But is the trade deficit the result of lagging exports or rising imports? The answer is both. A portion of the deficit in the early 1980s was due to declining real exports, as well as rising real imports. Constant (1982) merchandise exports grew from $69 billion in 1960 to $121 billion in 1970, rising to $242 billion in 1980 before falling during the recessions of the early 1980s. Exports fell to just under $208 billion in 1983 but reached their historical peak of $387 billion in 1989. All the while, constant-dollar (1982) merchandise imports continued to grow from $68 billion in 1960 to $151 billion in 1970 to $254 billion in 1980. Except for the recession years of the early 1980s, real imports continued to grow, reaching $496 billion in 1989.

Nor can the presumed decline in competitiveness be calculated away by taking into account growth in U.S. GNP. The relationship between exports and imports as a percentage of GNP indicates that merchandise exports expanded as a percentage of U.S. GNP for most of the years in the 1960–80 period, reaching 7.6 percent of U.S. GNP in 1980. However, by 1989 real-merchandise exports were up to 9.3 percent (after falling for several years in between). On the other hand, as a percentage of U.S. GNP throughout most of the 1960–89 period, imports continued to rise, albeit at a slower rate of increase after 1985. U.S. exports as a percentage of world GNP grew through 1980 and have declined from a peak of 1.5 percent in 1980 to 1.3 percent in 1986 (and, given the rise in real exports since 1986, by 1989 they were probably back up to their 1980 relative level).[55]

Does the rise in the trade deficit, however measured, support the more general claim that America is in decline because of its businesses' growing inability to compete on world markets? One of the authors has sought to answer that question in substantial detail elsewhere.[56] Here, two of several lines of argument may be summarized.

First, one of the reasons for the rise in the U.S. trade deficit in the 1980s was the faster pace of economic growth in the United States compared to many other countries around the world.[57] With a more rapid rate of growth, producers need more resources, many of which must be drawn from abroad in the form of imports. Fewer domestic resources are available for the production of goods for export (this is especially true when other countries are not growing as rapidly). The decline in real U.S. exports in the 1980s probably reflects, at least in part, the significant rise in domestic production.

Clearly, imports do not always measure decline in the economic strength of a country. On the contrary, they may retard decline or even contribute to a country's relative growth. On domestic and world markets, many imported products can make U.S. firms more competitive, not less so, directly increasing the productivity of domestic firms.

For example, in the early 1980s American textile firms imported a substantial share of their new machinery (50 percent in 1987) from abroad, but they did so in order to increase their productivity by more than they could have otherwise. The rise in imported textile machinery, spurred by efforts to reduce domestic production costs, may itself have been spurred marginally by the rise in textile imports. Without much question the substantial rise in textile productivity over the past decade and a half has contributed to a reduction in the number of workers in the domestic textile industry.[58] This means that the imported machinery in the textile industry made more workers available for an expansion of domestic industry (the same can probably be said for many other industries). It also means that domestic textile firms could then better fend off foreign competition and extend their penetration of foreign markets—more so than otherwise. In other words, both the imports of textiles and textile machinery very likely contributed to the long-run competitive health of the domestic textile industry.

Second, the balance on capital account necessarily mirrors, more or less, the balance on trade account (with adjustments for other elements in the overall balance of payments). This means that exports are not the only U.S. products foreigners want. As evident in the growing balance of capital account surplus in the 1980s, foreigners also want capital goods that can be put to work in this country. The demand for (competitively produced) capital goods in this country could have been a cause for the appreciation of the dollar during, especially, the first half of the 1980s. American exporters of goods stand at all times in competition with American producers of investment opportunities for the dollars held by foreigners.

Hence the trade deficits could have reflected the fact that American exporters of goods were simply outcompeted, not by foreign producers but by domestic producers of investment opportunities in the United States. Seen from this perspective, the growing balance of trade deficits in the 1980s reflects not some overall demise of American competitive drive, but a shift in competitiveness *among* producers in the United States, not between U.S. and foreign producers.

As indicated, proponents of the decline thesis suggest that U.S. competitiveness can be assessed by U.S. sales of "things" produced domestically as a percent of aggregate world production. When it is recognized that domestic investment opportunities are also "things" sold to foreigners, it does not follow that the aggregate of sales of all "things" (exports and investment opportunities) are on the decline.[59] Indeed, the sales of all things have been on the rise since 1970 and perhaps from before 1970. In 1960 the total of U.S. exports of goods and services and capital inflow represented 6.2 percent of U.S. GNP. The percentage was up to 6.8 in 1970 and to 15 percent in 1980 and, after falling to 8.7 in 1983, was back to 15.7 percent in 1988.[60]

In short, trade deficit statistics, by themselves, are not very good means of assessing the decline thesis, which is partially founded on the proposition that the country's international competitiveness is on the wane.[61] So long as international trades for goods, services, and assets are made voluntarily, it is not unreasonable to assume that they are, generally speaking, beneficial to both parties involved.[62] Whether the parties in the United States gain more or less than those in other countries is impossible to say. As discussed earlier, all we do know is that U.S. domestic production held its own in the world economy after the mid-1970s—at the very time the trade deficits began to emerge. The deficits of the early 1980s were also accompanied by relatively rapid rates of growth in the domestic economy. That fact can be understood by recognizing that U.S. exports fell less rapidly and U.S. imports grew less rapidly with respect to world than to domestic output.

Proponents of the decline thesis might quickly object to the foregoing analysis, arguing that data on trade deficits were accompanied by an enormous expansion in the U.S. federal budget deficit, at times to levels above $200 billion. These proponents might argue that those deficits increased upward pressures on real interest rates and caused capital to flow into this country. The resulting larger capital inflow (and lower capital outflow) caused the U.S. dollar to appreciate on the international money markets. The budget deficits thereby reduced (artificially) the competitiveness of U.S. goods on foreign markets.[63]

Although appealing and widely believed (even by opponents of the decline thesis) to exist, the so-called twin-deficit problem loses some of its force when it is recognized that federal budget deficits—apart from real federal expenditures—do not appear to influence real interest rates very much (if at all), and real interest rates do not appear to be highly correlated with exchange-rate movements.[64] Indeed, in the mid-1980s, real interest rates in the United States appeared to be falling at the time the budget deficits were rising most rapidly and the international value of the dollar was falling.[65]

Further, the trade deficit was falling in the very late 1980s and 1990, when the federal budget deficit was rising.

Besides, the claimed linkages between the budget and trade deficits presume that if the budget deficit is eliminated (say, by a tax hike), interest rates would fall and the dollar would depreciate.[66] However, the elimination of the deficit through tax increases would be accompanied by largely offsetting forces on the nation's money markets. The tax hike might reduce the federal government's demand for loanable funds, but it would also reduce the supply of loanable funds. The net effect on real interest rates would probably be little or nothing.

The line of argument we have developed for the twin-deficit problem does not lead to the conclusion that the federal government has no influence on the country's competitiveness and future economic, political, and military capabilities in the world. Of course it does. However, such an observation directs attention away from the size of the budget deficit to the size of government expenditures, which, because they draw resources away from private-sector activities, are the ultimate form of taxation on the economy. Government expenditures may very well have contributed indirectly to a reduction in the capacity of U.S. businesses to expand exports and fend off imports. However, proponents of the decline thesis often seek more government expenditures that might, in fact, retard the competitiveness of U.S. businesses simply because those expenditures would draw more resources away from private uses. Businesses cannot expand exports and defend their domestic market shares if the government insists on using more of the domestic resources.[67]

Discussions of decline probably never become more confused and misleading than when the specter of the "debtor nation" is raised. We have noted that Professor Kennedy is concerned that the United States has "in the space of a few years" switched from being the largest creditor to the largest debtor nation. Robert Reich also adds, in a different context, that "our failure to invest in future productivity is now reflected in . . . the steady sale to foreigners of shares in our companies and of our prime real estate. . . . Trying to offset our trade imbalance by selling off our assets makes as much sense as selling the house to help pay future rent."[68] Brookings Institution scholar Robert Lawrence also maintains that "even if foreign creditors continue to finance America's borrowing, U.S. debt-servicing requirements will become increasingly burdensome, requiring a larger portion of U.S. output and dragging down U.S. living standards."[69] Such comments may suggest that wealth in the United States is actually falling or is not rising by as much as it otherwise would in the absence of the capital inflows. The wealth of the United States, as noted earlier, is clearly rising, as measured directly by adding up tangible properties and indirectly by charting expansion in national production.

Granted, capital inflows can imply the selling off of assets, but they can also contribute to a net increase in the nation's assets held by Americans as well as by foreigners. So long as the inflows are invested productively, capital inflows can also increase the future flow of income to both Americans and foreigners. In short, it does not follow that capital inflows, debt and asset purchases, per se, represent a threat to America's future living standard. True enough, they will give rise to a future interest and dividend drain on the American economy. However, so long as the foreign security purchases give rise to a domestic capital stock that is greater than it would otherwise be, the interest and dividend drain can easily represent a minor portion of the nation's greater future income flow. In other words, the greater current capital inflow can leave the country with a greater future income flow, after the interest and dividend drain.

No one can commend Congress for spending hundreds of billions of dollars more than it collects in taxes. Much of the accumulated federal debt will, indeed, burden future generations that will have to suffer tax increases and/or program curtailments just to meet the interest payments, regardless of where they are sent. However, given the federal debt (which is determined by Congress, not foreigners), it simply does not follow that the country's future burden is increased by selling federal bonds to foreigners. In fact, the opposite is true. Presumably, by selling the bonds to West Germans, British, or Japanese rather than to Texans or New Yorkers, the federal Treasury can sell them at a lower rate of interest, thus reducing the future interest drain on the Treasury (and the American taxpaying public).[70]

Finally, it must be realized that when imports are covered by exports, the sale of American assets are included. American resources—assets—are included in the make-up of the merchandise exports, and those resources could have been used to produce capital goods in the United States. Furthermore, American capital assets are "consumed" (through wear and tear) in the production of goods for exports. It simply does not follow that had the trade deficit been covered by exports, as opposed to capital inflows, the country's economic future would be any brighter than it is.

## Relative Versus Absolute Decline

Kennedy insists that his factual and conceptual review of the history of the past five centuries leads inextricably to one overriding conclusion: America is in decline—relatively. The decline is more or less natural, dictated by the natural proclivities of "Great Powers" to overextend themselves. Furthermore, he suggests that the decline is not relative to just one or to a few countries, but to most of the developed and undeveloped world. If nothing else, the foregoing review of available data should cast a healthy measure of doubt on the validity of Kennedy's conclusion. Indeed, the limitations of the data are so severe that it might be said that his conclusion is probably ill-conceived. A more reasonable conclusion may be as follows: Without much question there is some truth to Kennedy's observation that powerful countries probably try to do too much. Further, the United States did decline, as measured by various economic criteria, from the end of World War II to the mid-1970s, and the United States remains in relative decline with respect to Japan and maybe a handful of other countries. However, sometime after the mid-1970s, the U.S. decline relative to the "rest of the world" was slowed, if not altogether stopped. This conclusion is based on updated and more complete data from several of the sources used by Kennedy.

This does not mean that the power and influence of America, as a country or as a political entity, have not declined—absolutely. Much factual and anecdotal evidence could be marshaled to demonstrate that the United States government continues to lose influence—economically, politically, and militarily. The inability of the United States to thwart the military efforts of small countries like North Vietnam, Libya, and Iran speaks eloquently to absolute decline. The ability of American producers to transfer their production facilities abroad speaks to a growing inability of the U.S. government to tax and regulate its own production and, thereby, to control production on a worldwide scale. The dependence of the U.S. economy on imports, exports, and capital flows—and the overall growing interdependence of the U.S. economy with the rest of the world—says much about the waning capacity of U.S. governments to control, manipulate, or influence political and economic events around the world. Clearly, the U.S. government retains a great deal of influence around the globe; but just as clearly, its influence is slipping—absolutely.

We emphasize the *absolute* slippage of power and influence because, as we have demonstrated, the power and influence of other countries is slipping as well. The power of countries—the Soviet Union, Japan, China, or any other country—to control events in the world is simply on the wane—absolutely.

## Quicksand Policies

In his essay on the decline of American hegemony, Michael Blumenthal was probably never more perceptive than when he asked, in effect, for an explanation of all the signs of decay and then wrote the words that head this chapter, pointing to the influence of "unprecedented, deep, and continual technological change" that distinguished the 1970s and 1980s. Blumenthal cites specific technological improvements that are at the heart of the "yet unresolved problems" without fully exploring exactly how technology is contributing to those problems.[71]

The central point of this book may be the "single reason" that explains much of "what has occurred": The technological revolution, which Blumenthal identifies, has greatly increased the ability of capital to move internationally. This technology has made the domestic and the world economies far more complex than they used to be. These two facts are what "thrust upon us new and as yet unresolved problems of governance," because they have constricted the ability of governments in general, and the U.S. government in particular, to undertake policies that do anything other than rely more extensively on markets and less extensively on bureaucratic processes.

In short, we contend that it is the American government, not the American economy, that is in decline. The evidence to support this point has been marshaled throughout the book, especially in chapter 8 on the recent record of growing U.S. competitiveness. However, contrary to what Kennedy and others maintain, the U.S. government's power is probably not slipping as badly on a relative basis as on an absolute basis. This view squares with the evidence presented in chapter 6, which shows that the power of other governments to control world events has also waned. This argument for the absolute loss of government power is nowhere better seen than in the Soviet Union, whose influence has slipped because, as chapter 7 starkly shows, it had for so long resisted both market forces and accelerating technological forces. While American and other market economies were exploiting quicksilver capital, the Soviets were choking on their politically created quicksand.

# 10

# U-Turn on the Road to Serfdom

*A Policy Sampler*

---

The complexity of modern finance makes New York dependent upon London, London upon Paris, Paris upon Berlin to a greater degree than has ever yet been the case in history. This interdependence is the result of the daily use of those contrivances of civilization which date from yesterday—the rapid post, the instantaneous dissemination of financial and commercial information by means of telegraphy and generally the incredible progress of rapidity in communication which has put the half-dozen chief cities of Christendom in closer contact financially, and has rendered them more dependent the one upon the other, than were the chief cities of Great Britain less than a hundred years ago.

---

*Norman Angell,*
*The Great Illusion*[1]

PEOPLE with radically divergent ideological perspectives have for centuries predicted the eventual demise of capitalism along with the emergence of a powerful state. We noted in chapter 2 Karl

Marx's admiration for capitalism as the engine of economic development and his prediction that the capitalistic system would, partially because of its success, collapse in a workers' revolution inspired by subsistence-level, exploitive wages.

Though Marx's hope that capitalism would eventually collapse may remain unmatched, he is not the only thinker who has predicted its demise. Early on we stressed that Marx's vision of growth in state power under socialism has been shared by liberal and conservative economists and social philosophers. For example, Friedrich Hayek worried that countries around the world were, in the 1930s and 1940s, on "the road to serfdom" through incremental changes in the scope and authority of government.[2] Such fears have also been reflected in the work of such luminaries as Milton Friedman and James Buchanan.[3]

It is time to entertain the possibility that these dismal tales of a looming all-powerful state are flawed and misguided and to consider a new more optimistic vision of the future. As University of Chicago economist George Stigler, another Nobel laureate, has observed, recent history has failed to confirm a critical element of Hayek's prediction.[4] Over the past fifty years, most, if not all, national governments have clearly grown in size and have abused newly acquired powers. But, contrary to Hayek's prediction, citizens of Western democracies have hardly become serfs in all-powerful states.

Without question, citizens must obey the law, but they still retain considerable economic and political freedoms, not exactly what Hayek may have imagined when he wrote his classic commentaries. While we might quibble over specifics, we concur with Stigler, who observes that the American citizen's "range of economic choices has become wider with the spread of higher education and rise of real incomes, and his main political rights, as enumerated in the first ten amendments to our constitution, have not been seriously impaired."[5] More prominently, communism is in retreat everywhere.

In this chapter we summarize our vision of the way the world works, pushing it to its limits for hints of the types of economic and political policies that will be adopted in the future, mainly in the United States but also elsewhere. We outline the major policy changes implied by greater capital mobility, complexity and sophistication of production, and economic integration of national economies. We hardly think our outline of implications is exhaustive. Indeed, the most important attribute of the arguments presented in this book is that they represent a new way of thinking about government that offers prospects of new and exciting conclusions not yet recognized.

## Optimistic Revisions in Outlook

We all find the lack of formal, central organization inherent in markets at odds with the brain's need for orderliness. It is easy for us to think in terms of "government," a presumed organized body with formal rules for making decisions, doing various things to manage the more volatile market. It is not so easy to think in terms of the market, with its presumed lack of central control and organization, similarly managing governments. Nevertheless, it appears to be the case that the market has once again—in a style that only Adam Smith may have appreciated—worked like an "invisible hand," giving rise to an end that no one—not people in governments or markets, not even many of Smith's most ardent admirers—may have had in mind.

We hardly believe we have written the final word on the progress—or the regress—of governments in the modern global economy. The worldwide shift in governments' taxing and regulatory policies described in chapters 6, 7, and 8 appears to be, by the standards of human history, a relatively recent phenomenon, encompassing the last three decades. The data are sometimes conflicting and sometimes grossly inadequate to tell the full story of what is happening to government.

Nevertheless, our analysis suggests that something unusual is happening on the world scene. Many countries appear to be making something of a U-turn on Hayek's "road to serfdom." Modern technology appears to be serving as a liberating force on the institutional constraints on individual decision making. Markets are emerging everywhere, in developed and less-developed countries, under Communist and non-Communist regimes. The evolutionary, snowballing effects of technology and markets have not completed their work. By the twenty-first century they will give way to more important changes in the way many governments and businesses operate.

## The Changing Justification for Government

At the most fundamental level, technology has reduced, and will continue to reduce, the justification for government actions based on the provision of public goods and services. In the past many activities have traditionally been considered within the proper domain of government action because they were difficult, if not impossible, to accomplish through private initiative. However, because of technological improvements, a number of these activities may soon be undertaken by private individuals or firms. Consider the following short list of examples, which is sure to grow with time:

• The government's monopoly on first-class mail has been directly undermined by the advent of overnight express services, telephones, computer modems, and fax machines. Like it or not, the U.S. Postal Service must now become more efficient because it must now compete. It has had to compete for several decades in parcel post (and now has less than 10 percent of package business as opposed to more than 90 percent in the early 1960s), and it has had to compete for "urgent mail" (overnight) deliveries since the late 1970s, the result of which has been a growing share of the mail market going to private carriers.[6] It will soon have to compete with private carriers for third-class mail deliveries. At this writing, Time, Inc., plans to inaugurate Publishers Express, which will provide deliveries of magazines and other third-class forms of bulk mail.

We would not be at all surprised if, before the turn of the century, Congress gives up trying to maintain the remaining vestiges of a postal monopoly, privatizes the U.S. Postal Service, and permits other firms to provide first-class mail delivery. For a long time the Postal Service has maintained that it needs its monopolistic entry restrictions on first-class mail deliveries because otherwise private carriers will skim off the most profitable deliveries, leaving the Postal Service with only the high-cost mail routes.[7] In fact, telephones, fax machines, computers, and other telecommunication services have already begun to skim the "cream" (which amounts to a euphemism for "monopoly profits") off the Postal Service system.[8] Any future efforts to raise rates and reduce service at the same time—both of which the Postal Service proposed to do in early 1990—can only hasten the collapse of its first-class postal monopoly.

• Economists and policymakers alike have used highways and city streets as grand examples of goods that must be provided by government. This is so because charging for the use of highways and streets (on anything other than limited-access freeways) has been very costly. Technology is gradually making it possible cheaply to monitor and charge for the actual use of streets and highways, increasing the prospects of their being provided and financed in much the same way that telephone service is now.

• Certain industries—for example, electric companies—have been viewed as "natural monopolies." Such industries have high fixed plant and equipment costs. As a consequence, their (long-run) average cost of production declines throughout the relevant range of output, which means that only one firm (a "natural monopolist"), with the lowest average (and marginal) cost of production, serves the entire market. Government regulation of natural monopolists has been justified on the grounds that without regulation, the natural monopolist would exploit its market position, restricting output and raising its prices and profits. Technology is undermining the natural-monopoly justification for government regulation by greatly reducing the fixed-capital requirements necessary to provide goods and services efficiently, or by allowing several firms to monitor their individual use and, therefore, share a common infrastructure of capital, or by expanding the market to the point where it is possible for several firms competitively to serve the market.

• The United States and other countries have extensive antitrust laws to reduce monopoly control of markets or prevent other anticompetitive activities of firms. Accordingly, antitrust cases have been launched against major cereal and computer producers and dozens of others, on the grounds that their respective markets were controlled by a very small number of producers. With the advent of worldwide markets for an increasing array of goods, the traditional justification for antitrust actions is eroding. There are simply more viable competitors and, therefore, less fear that they will collude and monopolize any particular market. The number of important automobile manufacturers in the United States is no longer limited to the "Big Three"; there are more than two dozen relevant automobile competitors when all the foreign manufacturers are counted.

## Government Transfers

While public goods may provide much rhetorical justification for government activity, a substantial share of it is actually motivated primarily by the demands of organized interests—farmers, unions, elderly, government workers (from office paper pushers to teachers to poverty workers), road pavers, and military hardware producers—for income transfers that have little, if anything, to do with the provision of public goods or poverty relief. Technological advances may serve to limit the transfer activity of government because income transfers, like so many other market activities, can be thought of as products of the forces of supply and demand.

The emphasis of this book has been on the supply side of government activity and on how international economic forces are constraining the ability of government to supply goods and services. Technology is making it easy for those who are not represented in the political process, and who would bear the burden of these transfers, to both avoid them through exit and oppose them through voice.

However, it is worth stressing that the supply-side constraints on government may be reinforced by the impact of technology on the demand for government goods and services. The demand for government transfers is part of people's more general demand for wealth. People can acquire more wealth in only two ways: They can engage in activities that produce new wealth or engage in those that take existing wealth from others through government tax collections that are subsequently transferred to identified beneficiaries. Economic theory demonstrates that the lower the costs of producing new wealth, relative to the cost of taking existing wealth from others, the greater will be the demand for productive activity relative to transfer activity. There is little doubt that the technological advances that are taking place are lowering the cost of producing new wealth at the same time as they are increasing the cost of using government to capture existing wealth. The ongoing changing forces of supply and demand in politics therefore will lead to a reduction of government transfers, maybe not in absolute, real-dollar terms, but certainly as a percentage of national income.

## The Plight of the Poor

It is quite possible that the expected future reductions in government transfers will have unfortunate consequences for the poor. Some poor people will probably receive less government welfare. This is especially likely for those poor people who could help themselves and make little effort to do so. The government will be more tightly constrained in its ability to raise taxes and, accordingly, will not be able to tolerate, as much as it has in the past, the continuation of welfare programs that perpetuate poverty.

However, American voters will ensure that a higher percentage of the reduction in transfers will come out of the pockets of the nonpoor—particularly those beneficiaries within the renowned "corporate welfare state"—not those of the deserving poor. The primary reason for government transfers to members of the "corporate welfare state" has always been that the recipients have the necessary muscle to gain political influence. We are confident that voters have always had a soft spot in their hearts for the truly disadvantaged and the poor who, through no fault of their own, do not have an equal opportunity to compete in market settings. Accordingly, we suspect that welfare benefits to the truly poor will not be reduced as much as the welfare benefits of the nonpoor, if at all.

Fortunately for the poor, the technological advances that serve to constrain government transfers will facilitate the production of wealth, which can help practically everyone. For this reason we are inclined to believe that the most effective way to help the poor is for government to do less to provide special-interest advantages to the nonpoor, not to attempt to do more for the poor.[9]

### Public Assistance for the Elderly

In 1989 more than 40 percent of the U.S. federal budget was dedicated to helping the elderly who, on average, had 11 percent more income than adults under twenty-four and a 14 percent lower chance of living in poverty than the nonelderly. In addition, while constituting only 12 percent of the country's population, the elderly, in total, controlled 30 percent of all household net worth and 40 percent of all financial assets.[10] According to Phillip Longman, author of *Born to Pay: The New Politics of Aging in America,* the Medicare benefits of the current generation of elderly are expected to be ten to twelve times the value of their lifetime contributions to the Medicare system, and the Social Security payments are expected to be two and a half to five times what they paid over their lives in Social Security taxes.[11] Criticizing their own generation, two Hoover Institution scholars, who described themselves as elderly, complained, "If you want to achieve greater equity, you can use federal government programs to redistribute wealth. That usually means taking from Peter to pay Paul. The fallacy of much of what we are doing today is taking from Paul (the younger and poorer person) to pay Peter (the well-off, older person)."[12] Many policy analysts share the concern that current demographic trends indicate that there will not be enough nonelderly working adults to maintain the life-styles the elderly have demanded through their considerable political clout and to which they have become accustomed.

The political clout of older people cannot continue to grow or even be maintained at current levels. Granted, in the future the elderly will comprise a greater share of the population, but that will be a reason for their political undoing. The political clout of the elderly in recent decades has been, in part, dependent on their limited numbers and the small fraction of the population they represent. It has also been due to the fact that they have been better organized politically than their younger compatriots.

We suspect that programs for the elderly have been expanded

in part because an expansion in their per capita federal benefits has not been sufficiently great to politically activate the vast number of nonelderly voters, and because there has been much nonelderly income that could be redistributed to the elderly. As the elderly grow in numbers, the cost of increasing their federal benefits on a per capita basis should rise precipitously, and the escalating cost should fuel political opposition among the young, who will then have access to modern technology (and the possibility of direct democracy through votes taken over telephone lines) to organize and make more effective their demands.

In addition, because senior citizens will be more numerous, a declining share of the national income will be earned by the working nonelderly. The elderly, in other words, will have to pay a growing share of their own government benefits, a fact that should temper their own (political) enthusiasm for expansion. Also, just like everyone else, the elderly will have to face the facts of the global economy: Their governments will be less free to expand senior-citizen benefits.

Given expected improvements in health care and life expectancy, the elderly will be able, and some will probably want, to work longer, if for no other reason than to avoid getting bored. Given the slowdown in growth of government benefits for the elderly, however, many will *have* to work longer, which is likely to lead, by the turn of the century, to the elimination of all remaining mandatory retirement rules and disincentives against more work embedded in the Social Security system and the tax laws.[13]

## Assistance to Business

In August 1989, a Memphis, Tennessee, newspaper carried a banner headline story: FEDEX CHOOSES MEMPHIS SITE FOR PLANE MAINTENANCE CENTER.[14] The lead story and background reports told how Memphis had outlasted twenty-five other cities in the competitive struggle to entice Federal Express (whose international headquarters were already in Memphis) to locate its proposed $75 to $100 million maintenance facility along with, eventually, up to two thousand jobs, most of which would pay $35,000 to $45,000 a year, at the Memphis International Airport.[15]

State and local government officials were ecstatic about Federal Express's choice. However, Fred Smith, Federal Express CEO, should have been the one glowing, because he received a bargain.

Memphis, surrounding Shelby County, and the state of Tennessee agreed to:

- Construct a new road to serve the facility site at an estimated cost of $2 million to the city and county
- Provide a sewer connection at an estimated cost of $100,000 to the city and county
- Make the facility site ready to use, which means that the Memphis Airport Authority would have to acquire additional land, close roads, and rezone property at no cost to Federal Express and at a cost of $400,000 to the Airport Authority
- Build at state expense a training facility on airport property at a cost of $4 million and then train, again at state expense, about seven hundred aircraft mechanics at a cost of $3 million to the state
- Finance the facility's construction with bonds issued by the Memphis Airport Authority, which would enable Federal Express to avoid taxes on the property, or concede to a tax freeze if the project could not be financed with bonds issued by the Airport Authority
- Provide a $1 million state grant immediately and work with the state legislature to obtain an additional $4 million grant for taxiway improvements[16]

In making all these concessions, the local and state governments involved were, in effect, conceding to the mounting forces of international capital mobility outlined throughout this book. There is probably no better example of capital mobility than Federal Express, for most of its capital—aircrafts—can literally fly off to a host of other destinations. Federal Express need not have its maintenance facility (or, for that matter, its headquarters) in Memphis; the local and state governments knew that and, accordingly, had to bid for its location. We suspect that Federal Express took two years to make its location decision partly because it realized its mobility represented a threat to Memphis and wanted to hear competitive offers, just to get the best deal it could from Memphis, its major hub. In the process Tennessee and Memphis officials handed over part of their governments' sovereignty to the Federal Express executives, who literally and figuratively were in the driver's seat (or cockpit).

The concessions made by the governments in Tennessee are

no longer unusual. They are noteworthy only because of the amounts of money involved and of major significance only to local audiences. Other governments around the world have become mired in a competitive struggle for capital. This struggle will do nothing but escalate, as it has been in the past, for two reasons. First, capital is getting more mobile and governments will have to compete. Second, when governments make concessions, they alert other businesses to the prospects of making money (via shifting production costs to governments), and as time passes, more businesses should bargain for concessions. When Tennessee bargained in the early 1980s for its Honda plant by making substantial concessions, it alerted Federal Express to the benefits of putting its expansion plans up for sale.

In the short run there is some risk that immobile capital will be hit by the tax burdens that will not be paid by mobile capital with substantial bargaining power. However, in the long run, most capital is mobile. Any state that concedes to the demands of firms that bargain over new facilities can be expected to confront demands for concessions by existing firms who will threaten to move out. A government that pays to have new jobs come in should be just as willing to pay to avoid existing jobs from leaving. For example, Detroit had to bargain with General Motors and make tens of millions of dollars in concessions to keep GM from moving a Cadillac plant (which was to replace an existing plant) out of Detroit.[17] Time will only compound the trend, which should lead governments to make across-the-board concessions to mobile capital in terms of improved services for their tax dollars.

Over the short term businesses may expand their efforts to manipulate, through lobbying or bargaining, government benefits. They will try to use those benefits to stay competitive with other businesses that get similar packages. However, eventually, government will see that it is having to make concessions on many, if not all fronts, and that it is wasting a lot of its limited resources negotiating so many individual contracts that, when summed, amount practically to across-the-board concessions. It will then give up and lower its tax rates and benefits to competitive levels.

Businesses—and, for that matter, other interest groups—will also have to recognize the growing constraints on government to do their bidding. The days when Chrysler CEO Lee Iacocca or Roger Milliken, head of a major textile firm, could trek to Washington for the type of bailout that Chrysler received in the early 1980s or for the type of import protection the textile industry has received for two decades are now numbered. As a consequence, employment in the lobbying industry in Washington will eventually (after an initial and temporary expansion in a futile attempt to fight governments' newfound constraints) decline, at least as a percentage of the labor force. The CEOs of the future and their immediate subordinates will, to a greater extent, get paid for production and satisfying consumer wants, not for padding politicians' campaign pockets.

## Illegal Drugs

As late as the early 1980s, few dared to suggest that street drugs should be legalized. Nevertheless, by the end of the decade, the legalization of drugs was actively being promoted by conservative and liberal groups alike. Some drugs will probably be legalized in the 1990s. Technology in the form of fax machines, beepers, two-way radios, and electronic fund transfers is simply making effective control of the drug trade too difficult and too expensive—if not altogether impossible. Beepers and two-way radios enable dealers to avoid being caught. In 1989 as much as $100 billion from the sale of cocaine was being channeled from American to foreign banks by way of electronic-fund transfers,[18] all of which caused *Chicago Tribune* columnist Mike Royko to conclude:

> Poor William Bennett, the nation's chief drug warrior [appointed by President George Bush in 1989]. He's outgunned, outnumbered, underfinanced and overwhelmed. In other words, he can't win. The other side—those who use drugs, make drugs, sell drugs and profit from drugs—has become too big and too powerful. . . . There isn't any "drug war" because the war has long been lost for a number of reasons.[19]

Constrained by international forces, governments will probably not be able to afford for very long the luxury of continued efforts at control, which, under President George Bush's proposed drug war, cost the federal government alone nearly $8 billion in 1989 (eight times as much as in 1980).[20] This is especially true when the enforcement efforts seem so futile and even counterproductive.[21] In 1988 more than eight thousand deaths, resulting from murders of competitors and lack of quality control in drug production, could be attributed to drug prohibition; and 37 percent of all federal prisoners were incarcerated on drug-related charges.[22] Strapped for funds (and prison space), state and federal governments will seek rationalizations, if not solid philosophical justifications, for legalizing at least some street drugs by the turn of the century.

Admittedly any partial or complete decontrol of street drugs might produce more addicts. After all, legal drugs are likely to be less expensive and consumed in greater quantities. The addicts of the future, however, will probably have to suffer most, if not all, of the cost of their addiction themselves, meaning they will probably not be able to appeal to government for much assistance. Faced with its own constraints, which will contribute to the decriminalization of drugs, the government will very likely have already made the decision to preclude assistance or, at the most, limit it to something less than the prior levels of expenditures on drug control.

## The Opening of Borders

American workers must also learn that the government is becoming less able to keep out foreign workers and that immigration restrictions are no longer the economic barriers to worker mobility they once were. Workers from around the world can immigrate to this country via modern electronics. We noted that New York Life now has its insurance claims sent to a post office box at Kennedy Airport and then ships the claims by overnight courier to Ireland, where they are keyed into a computer and then, before the day is over, transmitted back to the States via satellite. In effect, the Irish workers have gotten American work permits without becoming citizens or landing on our shores. "Electronic immigration and emigration" will escalate. As a consequence immigration restrictions will be looked upon more and more as policy relics of a bygone era, no longer worth very much in terms of protecting domestic workers. Immigration restrictions will be loosened.[23]

## The Continuing Liberation of Trade

Although beset by the imposition of creative restrictions on international trade—most importantly, the United States VERs—in the 1980s, international trade escalated. This trend can be expected to continue because the United States and other countries will be forced back to the long-run trend of trade liberalization. Three principal forces will be at work.

First, countries will learn a lesson from their experience of the

1980s: Trade restrictions cannot be very effective in keeping foreign goods out of the country. Prevented from expanding their imports, foreign companies such as Honda can shift production to domestic plants. This means that domestic producers who might favor trade restrictions will then have to compete with foreign firms in markets for both consumers and suppliers. In addition foreign firms can readily shift production around the world to circumvent trade restrictions. Joseph Nye reports that for years France limited the importation of Japanese automobiles to 3 percent of French sales and also restricted Japanese investment in the French industry. However, the French government had to withdraw its import restrictions when Japanese automobile makers started building plants in other European countries that could still export to France.[24]

Second, a growing number of domestic jobs will be directly or indirectly tied to expanding international trade. These employees will cause the ranks of the antiprotectionists to swell, and government legislators will have to pay progressively more attention to their political interests.

Third, efficiency in production will necessitate growing specialization—on a world scale. Capital will not flow to areas of the world where it cannot be used in the most effective manner without artificial, government-created trade impediments. The expected fall of trade barriers in Europe by 1992 forced the United States and Canada to increase the potential efficiency of their capital base by eliminating their mutually debilitating trade barriers. To counter the policy competition from Europe, the United States–Canada free trade area will have to be extended to Mexico, if not far beyond. When President George Bush proposed a free trade zone in 1990 for the entire Western Hemisphere, he was conceding to the practical, liberating forces at work in world trade.

## Education

The ongoing changes in the world economy have exposed the soft underbelly of the American economy, the American public school system, which by all accounts has failed the market tests of cost-effectiveness and efficiency and has left the "nation at risk."[25] In comparing the mathematical proficiency of eighth-grade students, a recent study found that the United States finished next to last of twelve economically advanced democracies. In another recent comparison of mathematical knowledge, South Korean students were found

to be achieving levels of performance four times greater than those
of U.S. students.[26] According to its survey undertaken in the mid-
1980s, the U.S. Department of Education found that:

- Only about three-fifths of whites, two-fifths of Hispanics, and
  a quarter of blacks could locate information in a news article
  or an almanac
- Only a quarter of whites, 7 percent of Hispanics, and 3 percent
  of blacks could decipher a bus schedule
- Only 44 percent of whites, 20 percent of Hispanics, and 8
  percent of blacks could correctly determine the change they
  were due from the purchase of a two-item restaurant meal[27]

Other researchers have found that while the average Scholastic
Aptitude Test (SAT) combined score may have been rising recently,
it has recovered only 14 of the 90 points lost between 1963 and
1980.[28] Furthermore, the decline in student performance cannot be
attributed totally to an increase in the number of students taking
the test, as many educators believe. The number of students scoring
600 or above (out of a possible 800) on the verbal section of the
SAT is currently rising but is still 30 percent below the 1972 level.
Half as many students scored 750 or above in 1988 as in 1981. Although
the number of students scoring 600 or above on the math section
has risen somewhat (9 percent between 1972 and 1988), educators
are understandably concerned that the "gains have been confined
primarily to lower-order skills," to the increase in the number of
Asian-American students taking the test, and to greater emphasis
on "teaching for the test."[29] And even educators have lamented
the fact that, "Only 7 percent of the nation's 17-year-olds have the
prerequisite knowledge and skills thought to be needed to perform
well in college-level courses. . . . While average science proficiency
is on the rise, students in the upper range of science proficiency
did not show any improvement—nor are there increasing numbers
of these students."[30]

The business community is becoming painfully aware of the
deficiencies of U.S. public schools. A recent report based on a survey
of 134 employers found that two-thirds felt that applicants for entry-
level jobs lacked basic skills in reading, writing, mathematics, and
communications.[31] For each person Chemical Bank of New York
hires to be trained as a teller, it has to interview forty applicants.
After IBM installed expensive computers in its Burlington, Vermont,

factories, it discovered that thousands of workers had to be taught high-school algebra in order to operate them.[32] Chrysler recently reworked its assembly-line training manual from the ninth-through-twelfth-grade reading level to the sixth-grade level, and Lee Iacocca still had reason to complain that even that was not low enough for many of the employees. For example, the written instruction "bad hood fit" had to be relabeled with graphics because many workers could not understand the concept of those three single-syllable words.[33]

The National Commission on Excellence in Education was probably not exaggerating when it concluded, in *A Nation at Risk*, "If an unfriendly foreign power had attempted to impose on America the mediocre educational performance that exists today, we might well have viewed it as an act of war."[34]

The dictates of economic efficiency will no longer permit a country like the United States the extravagance of maintaining an unfettered monopoly public school system in a competitive world economy. Whether the public schools in the United States should be privatized is no longer a pressing or even a relevant question. With the rapidly expanding expenditures of the business sector on remedial education and retraining expenditures and the personal expenditures of parents on home-based-education products and on private schools as substitute for inadequate public education, education is *being* privatized.[35] In our view the only relevant questions the nation faces are, When will our political leaders recognize the trends and when will they aggressively give parents greater choice in how their children will be educated, thus overtly encouraging the privatization process?

State governments—if not in unison, then one by one—will be forced to privatize education because of the dictates of efficiency and because they will not, in the quest to make their respective state economies more competitive, have the resources to waste on a monopoly-based educational bureaucracy. To develop their capital bases and expand their revenues, states need investment from both private and foreign sources, and few states can afford to let the poor ratings of their public schools turn off potential investors.

In fact, competition is beginning to play a role in the restructuring of public education. In the late 1980s the Minnesota and Arkansas legislatures gave parents in those states the right to choose the public schools their children will attend, and Minnesota went one step further, giving the state's junior and senior high-school students the option of taking courses at state universities. Under both systems tuition would be covered by payments from state funds according to the choices of parents and students.

Boston has had a similar "parental choice" program since the early 1980s, and the system has resulted in higher test scores, especially among minorities. Vermont has for years used the so-called voucher system, under which students in two hundred of the state's towns that do not have high schools are given "vouchers" worth $3,000 (the average per-pupil expenditure on education in the state) that can be used to "buy" a year of education at any high school in Vermont or any surrounding state. Washington State uses private education firms to help students who have dropped out of school. In early 1990 the city of Milwaukee approved what amounted to a voucher plan that would allow about one thousand low-income students to use $2,500 in state funds to attend private, nonsectarian schools.[36]

Chicago's public school system, described by former Secretary of Education William Bennett as approximating "educational meltdown" because its students' average test scores were in the lowest 1 percent of all school districts, has moved in the direction of turning over the reins of educational power to parents. A wide range of school policies, including those surrounding the hiring and firing of principals, can now be made at each school by councils dominated by parents, not educational professionals in the system's vast bureaucracy. The expectation is that the newly empowered parents will be more interested in their children's educational welfare than the professionals and that the parents will be in a better position to adapt policies to the particular circumstances of various schools—a line of logic so sensible that we can only imagine that other schools, not yet ready to undertake more radical reforms, will follow suit.

In 1989 alone bills were introduced in twenty-three state legislatures that would grant a greater degree of parental choice; three of the proposals passed.[37] All told in 1989 the country had an estimated ten thousand schools where attendance was a matter of choice, not assignment—a fact that caused a *Fortune* magazine reporter to declare that educational choice "is simply the hottest item on the education reform agenda today."[38] More states and local communities will follow the demonopolization and decentralization trend in education. Then, those that have led the reform movement will have to become more serious about privatizing and decentralizing education and will expand further parental choice.

In short, the choice of where, what, and how students are taught will gradually but relentlessly be wrested from the public school establishment, whose foundations are the "union cards" known as "education degrees." With the shift in control, we don't believe that teachers' conventional university education will meet the demands of parents and students or will stand the test of competition. In selecting teachers states will progressively emphasize the candidates' competence in the subject matter, not the education courses taken, and will recognize that education administrators should know how to run school systems as businesses that have global competitors.

Thirty-three states have already officially adopted "alternative teacher certification" programs, which have permitted a relatively small number of college graduates to teach without having taken the requisite education courses.[39] Although resistance to the implementation of these certification procedures abounds, states will be forced to make growing use of them because states will be strapped for funds and will need to get competent teachers any way they can and because they will have to improve the quality of their school systems by hiring the most knowledgeable people available.

The world economy will demand that graduates' skills meet the world's work demands; after all, the graduates in any country will have to compete for the world's business with the graduates in Japan. We expect that countries, the United States included, will have to shift a larger share of education expenditures to private individuals and companies. This is likely to be the case because, as trade expands and economies become more integrated, the benefits of future education will spill over to other countries. Countries will gradually become more resistent to incurring the cost of education for the benefit of other people from whom they cannot collect taxes but with whom their taxpayers must compete.

It will always be important that teachers know how to teach (whether the skills come naturally or through course work), but demanding course content, especially in verbal and math skills, will rise in importance. Teachers will necessarily have to be better prepared in teaching subject matter, which means that education degrees will have to be drastically remodeled with less emphasis on teaching skills and more room for subject content.

Many education departments that specialize in teaching skills (and providing credit hours and easy grades for mediocre students at the undergraduate or graduate levels) will contract as student schedules become clogged with more meaningful, content-based courses. Some education departments and degrees can probably plan on closing down as states begin to accept teachers without the prerequisite education courses, and stop giving raises to teachers who get advanced degrees for no other purpose than to have them on their vitae and to meet bureaucratic standards for raises that have little or nothing to do with meritorious teaching.

## Changing Policy Agenda

In 1989, his first year in office, President Bush proposed a reduction in the capital-gains tax from 28 percent (or 33 percent for some high-income taxpayers) to 15 percent. House and Senate critics of the tax cut howled and objected with a collective knee jerk. They stressed that the Bush proposal amounted to a tax cut for the rich, which the middle- and low-income classes would pay in the form of higher taxes. When President Bush made the proposal, policy analysts all over Washington said it was "dead on arrival"—as if Congress had a choice in the matter. Dan Rostenkowski, chairman of the House Ways and Means Committee, said in early 1989 that the Bush proposal was a "tax break for the wealthy that will significantly increase the deficit. I can't imagine any member of Congress willing to take such a step."[40] By the middle of the summer, Rostenkowski was holding firm to his prediction that a reduction in the capital gains tax would be a "financial disaster for this country," but others were beginning to find the proposal's "political pulse," as evidenced by the fact that it had been voted out of committee over Rostenkowski's objections.[41]

However, the political issue has never been whether the capital-gains tax would be lowered, but when and by how much. If a lower capital-gains tax has not been passed by the time this book is in print, it soon will be. When President Bush proposed lowering the capital-gains tax rate, Congress did not really have much choice, mainly because the tax was unfair and uncompetitive.

The capital-gains tax (a tax on the difference between the purchase and sell price of assets—for example, stocks and real estate) is unfair primarily to small entrepreneurs who take the substantial risks associated with investing everything they have in business ventures and then reinvesting all earnings back into their businesses. The value of the business may rise, and if the business is sold, the financial gain may be taxed at the high marginal rate of 28 (or 33) percent—as if all the gains, which may be substantial, were earned like income in one year, and as if all the increase in financial wealth represents an improvement in the entrepreneurs' real wealth. But in fact much, if not all, of the gain may represent nothing more than inflation.

For example, consider an investor who bought a few acres of land in 1967 for $50,000 and has a relatively modest income that puts him or her in the 20 percent tax bracket. If the investor sells the land for $200,000, the Internal Revenue Service will treat the capital gains of $150,000 in the same way all earnings are treated, which means that the investor will pay a top marginal rate of 33 percent (since he or she will be viewed as a high-income earner for the year).

The IRS will take about $50,000 in taxes, leaving the investor with an after-tax financial gain of $100,000. However, the $100,000 must be adjusted for the effects of inflation, and prices in 1990 were almost 290 percent higher than they were in 1967, which means that the investor's after-tax real wealth has actually deteriorated during the ensuing twenty-three years, from $50,000 in 1967 to just under $39,000 in 1990 (using 1967 prices).

At the same time the small investor, who doesn't have enough wealth to "spread the risk" by investing in a number of projects, can be assured that the government will not cover any of his or her losses, which are inevitably a part of risky ventures. Large investors and companies are able to spread their risks by investing widely and then deducting the capital losses from the capital gains before taxes are computed. Of course, such tax rules encourage mergers. They also encourage bigness in business simply by suppressing the emergence of competition from new, aggressive, innovative, and necessarily small firms.

Capital-gains tax rules are simply out of line with the U.S. government's competition around the world. According to Alan Reynolds of the Hudson Institute, Hong Kong, South Korea, Malaysia, Singapore, Germany, Italy, Belgium, and the Netherlands either impose no tax on capital gains or exempt a substantial portion of capital gains from taxation. France and Sweden have rates of 16 to 18 percent on long-term capital gains, and Canada exempts the first $500,000 (Canadian dollars) in capital gains from taxation. More important, Japan has a capital-gains tax rate of a mere 5 percent.[42] In short, the after-tax cost of raising equity capital was much higher in the United States than elsewhere in the world, and the government will have to do what it can to offset the cost advantage other countries currently have.

President Bush had to make his proposal out of respect for the growing international mobility of capital. And Congress must follow, eventually, the drummer President Bush has heard, not just to take away disincentives to invest that are built into the current capital-gains tax rules, but to discriminate *in favor* of capital, which now carries the political leverage that comes with mobility. In the end Congress will lower capital-gains taxes not because it wants to but out of the same respect for international competitive forces that limited President Bush's tax-policy options and that make a lower capital-gains tax rate "revenue enhancing."[43]

Every few years political leaders in Washington seek to make a name for themselves by proposing an increase in the minimum wage or an array of work-related benefits that should be mandated by government: child care and health insurance were the most frequently talked about "mandated benefits" in the late 1980s. Congress will sooner or later legislate additional nominal increases in the minimum wage (above the increase to $4.25 scheduled for 1991) and, in the process, continue to claim that it is helping low-wage workers. Nevertheless, we noted in an earlier chapter the decline in the real (inflation-adjusted) minimum wage since 1968. In spite of what Congress may claim is "right" for covered workers, the trend in the *real* minimum wage is likely to continue on its current downward course.[44] All Congress will be able to do, given international competitive forces, is moderate the rate of the fall.

In the years to come, debate over mandated benefits will lose much of its political steam simply because the costs of the benefits in terms of lost money wages, other benefits forgone, or lost employment opportunities will become painfully obvious to American workers. There will always be political rhetoric about doing something for workers, but workers will see rhetoric for what it will become— just so much vacuous talk by leaders who are losing their power to back up their words with meaningful action.

All in all, policy agendas will continue to change over coming decades because the array of *viable* policy options is being constricted. Politicians will have fewer degrees of freedom, while the rest of us have more.

## Emerging Problems

We have noted from time to time that not all the changes resulting from "globalism" are likely to be positive.

*Environmental Decay*

As emphasized in chapter 5, one of the fundamental functions of government is to provide certain public goods and services that are not, and cannot be, provided effectively by the private sector. One such public service is the control of pollution of the environment. Unless prevented or discouraged from doing otherwise, firms will seek to lower their production costs and hold their prices down by polluting, using the country's airways and waterways as dumping grounds for their waste, which might be more costly to dispose of in other ways. In this way, firms "externalize" (or impose on others) their production costs. Each firm may want to maintain a clean environment, but because of competitive pressures, each may be forced to pollute as much as it can economically justify. If it tries to control its own pollution while other firms do not, its production costs and prices will most likely be above competitive levels.

Capital mobility will continue to set loose conflicting world forces that will affect the quality of the natural environment. On the one hand, the new world economy will motivate governments to address domestic pollution problems more effectively and at lower cost. For example, governments will tend to shift, as they have already begun to, the emphasis of their antipollution policies from setting pollution standards, which require all firms to meet legally defined limits on pollution, to selling "pollution rights" (or, the more technical phrase, "tradable emission permits"). This means that only firms that do not buy the available pollution rights must curb their pollution. Such a shift in policy can be beneficial to society because, as economists have long recognized, pollution can be reduced to any given level at lower cost by the sale of pollution rights.[45]

In addition, capital mobility is making the world a richer place because of the competitive discipline it is imposing on both business and government. And expanding wealth tends to increase the demand for environmental quality. When people are cold, hungry, and poor, they worry little about the environmental consequences of the fuel they burn, the agricultural techniques they use, or the sewage disposal systems they employ. The wealth effect of capital mobility will encourage greater environmental care.

On the other hand, the ability of many governments to reduce pollution or just control its growth may be impaired, especially in the short run, by the growing competition among governments. Each government may fear that the actions it takes to control pollution (via pollution standards, the sale of pollution rights, or special taxes designed to reduce the economic incentives firms have to emit pollutants) will increase production costs in its jurisdiction and increase the actual level or threat of "capital flight" to other jurisdictions that do not seek to control pollution to the same degree. Hence, with the increased threat of capital flight and resulting loss of tax revenues, governments are likely to impose fewer and less onerous controls.

Governments can be expected to be especially reluctant to control pollution that transcends national boundaries. Clearly many government leaders harbor honest, well-meaning intentions to do their part in keeping the world environment in good shape, and they will probably always be willing to do some things to improve the world's environment. However, there are competitive limits to what they can do. In the face of growing capital mobility, each government has to pay more attention to the costs of its governmental policies, because the owners of capital do not have to accept the greater costs, even though they may result from well-meaning environmental policies. Each government is likely to be more inclined to shirk any responsibility they may feel to control domestic pollution (or to produce other public goods and services, the effects of which are transnational). Naturally transnational pollution will become a more pressing social and economic problem, attributable partially to more production and the emission of more pollutants, but also to growing capital mobility on a world scale.

### Taxation of Mobile Versus Immobile Capital

As governments seek to cope under tighter fiscal and regulatory constraints and seek to recapture some of their lost capacity to grow and draw revenues from the private sector, conflicts among political interest groups will become more intense.

Pressed for more tax revenues, governments can be expected to shift a greater share of their countries' tax burden away from capital (and people) that is relatively mobile to capital (and people) that is relatively immobile. The capital that is mobile can threaten governments with movement if its tax burden is not lowered or if government concessions in the way of publicly provided services (for example, water lines and access roads) are not granted. The reductions in the tax burden and increases in concessions will have to be financed by increases in tax collections from the immobile capital, which cannot as effectively threaten its governments with movement. Mobile capital will simply be in a better bargaining position vis-à-vis its government;

immobile capital will find its bargaining position impaired, at least marginally. Much future social strife will result from political battles over which—mobile or immobile capital—bears its "fair" share of the tax burden.

Of course, faced with a growing share of their governments' fiscal burden, owners of immobile capital will not "play dead" and just take the greater burden imposed on them. They will try to do what they can to become *more* mobile. They might, for example:

- Downsize their firms and plants, making themselves more "mobile and hostile"
- Contract out the production of many of their needed intermediate parts and the provision of business services, facilitating the shift of more of their work to firms in other governmental jurisdictions
- Reduce the "payout period" (or the time over which the original investment is returned) on their plants, which will enable them to redeploy their investments more quickly and to move out from under adverse governmental policies
- Rely more extensively on equipment (rather than plant) in their production processes, which can be more easily moved to, or repurchased in, a new location
- Establish more production facilities in different governmental units so that production can be moved in response to changes in government policies.

All these changes would facilitate movement or, just as important, create the threat of movement. Those firms that cannot increase their mobility or develop a believable threat of mobility will be saddled with an even heavier share of their countries' fiscal burdens.

## Economic Determinants of Military and Foreign Policies

In adjusting to the realities of the new world economic order, government may face its greatest challenge and reap the greatest benefit in foreign and military policy. As noted, governments are used to controlling "territory," defining national boundaries, defending them from aggression, and extending them by way of military action against other governments. They are adept at continuing the "cool (if not Cold) War," and the economic interests of many depend on neither side claiming victory or calling a stalemate.

## The Lost Value of Military Power

The Allies won in World War II, and they remain prepared to fight a similar war in the future. The Soviet Union extended its geopolitical power after World War II by military domination of the countries of Eastern Europe. Later it increased its world power by subverting the political systems of country after country to communist ideology. North Korea, North Vietnam, and Cuba are prominent examples of extended communist influence in the world in recent decades.

In the future, military might will obviously play a role in directing world affairs. However, it is likely to lose much of its usefulness. Today the Japanese would probably have second thoughts about bombing Pearl Harbor simply because so much of Japan is already in Hawaii via the buildup of Japanese investments. In a sense, because of the integration of the American and Japanese economies, Japanese leaders would have to realize that they would be bombing a part of themselves by attacking Pearl Harbor. Of course, the United States would have similar concerns in any proposed counterattack over Nagasaki. Thoughts by government leaders of counterproductive conquests will, in the future, be likely to put the brakes on attacks and make obsolete much military power.

Obviously it does not follow that such actions will be altogether eliminated in the future. Fighting among countries can be expected to continue, and a defensive posture will always be necessary. But world economic integration will make the fights less frequent, with more concern for national wealth held abroad.

These expected economic checks on military expenditures in the Soviet Union and the United States and among U.S. allies can be expected to result in more arms-reduction treaties, which, in turn, should mean that military spending will become less of a drag on the world economy. In other words, more of the world's resources will be freed to be reemployed in the global private sector. Because it has carried the greatest defense burden, the United States may benefit more than its allies from a worldwide reduction in military spending. The United States' relatively higher military spending may mean that the country's growth rate will climb relative to the growth rates of other noncommunist countries, most notably Japan. The United States can possibly look forward to recapturing its leadership in the world economy, but only because governments have become less powerful, less able to shape events by military or economic policies.

Of course, if military expenditures in the United States are scaled back in response to reduced military threat, there will be (as there has already been) pressure from a host of special-interest groups to declare a "peace dividend" by having government spend more on their favored programs. It is widely expected that military spending will be quickly converted to social-welfare spending. That is unlikely. Indeed, the very forces that are working to make a peace dividend possible are also working against its use for many social programs.

Capital mobility has done far more than reduce international tensions. One overarching theme in this book is that the ability of wealth, and of wealth-producing assets, to flow through the global marketplace with little concern for their country of origin has reduced the ability of governments to respond to the demands of organized interest groups. This suggests that the forces that are making possible a reduction in military spending are reducing the ability of special-interest groups to garner the saving for their particular programs. There may well be a peace dividend, but not the type of peace dividend organized groups with offices in Washington will be clamoring for.

## The Allure of Cooperation

Other political analysts have recognized "the spectacular decline in the cost of moving goods. The movement of people, resources, and information across national borders has left governments with little room for unilateral action and little choice but to find changed forms for mutual accommodations."[46] In addition, these analysts have acknowledged that:

> as the economic interests of the United States have become more deeply intertwined with those of other countries, a policy of tit-for-tat has begun to approach the practice of self-flagellation. Ironically, the United States cannot punish Japanese exporters without improving the position of Japanese interests already located in the United States. And it cannot punish Mexico without endangering American interests, including investment interests, export interests, and the interests of retirees.[47]

We could not agree more with this assessment of the U.S. predicament, but we could not agree less with the implied assessment of the solution, which amounts to a declaration that "the U.S. government cannot get very far in responding to its present problems unless it can develop much more extensive cooperative arrangements with other countries"[48] or that "as distances shrink and national economies become increasingly sensitive to outside forces, the need for coopera-tion in international economic affairs continues to grow."[49]

Cooperation in the establishment of domestic policies will no doubt work—in some cases, for a limited period of time. However, as we explained earlier, analysts are daydreaming if they think govern-ments can use "cooperation" or "coordination" in policy matters as a means of thwarting international competition in the move toward more efficient, price-sensitive fiscal and regulatory policies. Any coop-erative effort across nations, for example, to keep tax rates from falling will be likely to meet with competitive realities faced by all collusive organizations. Those countries not party to the cooperative arrangement will have a greater competitive advantage in attracting capital by way of lower tax rates. Those countries that are party to the cooperative arrangement will have a hefty economic incentive to cheat on the agreement by lowering tax rates in a variety of covert ways or by more than offsetting the tax disadvantage by eliminating costly regulations.

### The Economic Value of Coups

Political instability inhibits economic development. When govern-ments change frequently, capitalists run the risk that the property rights to their investments will be usurped by the new regimes. In other words, political instability increases the "risk cost" and lowers the return on investments.

Coups have many motivations, not least of which is to increase the power and prestige of the coup leaders. When capital is immobile, coup leaders can expect that the political instability resulting from their planned takeovers will not reduce very much the power and prestige of the jobs they seek. However, when capital is highly mobile, the leaders' calculations must be adjusted. The leaders of planned coups must consider that the capital base will erode as plant, equip-ment, and production are moved to safer, more hospitable territories. To that extent coups may be discouraged.

Our line of argument does not lead to the conclusion that over-throws of governments are a thing of the past. Hardly. Coups occur for more (noneconomic) reasons than we can consider here. Neverthe-less we would expect the continuing increase in capital mobility to lead to marginally fewer, possibly less violent and destructive coups—especially those that are hostile to the maintenance and expansion of private property rights.

*The Special Case of Hong Kong*

The leaders and people of mainland China must look upon Hong Kong as a major economic prize. Mainland China is itself highly controlled and backward—a Third World economic power at best. On the other hand, Hong Kong, which is only a dot on the coast of any map of China, is industrious, vibrant, a haven of entrepreneurship. The per capita income of this port city may be as high as 50 times the per capita income of the mainland.[50] China is understandably pleased that it will gain control of Hong Kong in 1997.

However, what China gets at the time of the transfer of control is now uncertain. In anticipation of the transfer, the "brain drain" from Hong Kong continues and, after the Tiananmen Square massacre in June of 1989, has accelerated to a total annual outflow of more than one hundred thousand people (from Hong Kong's population of 5.7 million),[51] most of whom are skilled craftsmen and professionals.

Unless China liberalizes its domestic economy and gives assurances, by words and deeds, that it does not intend to appropriate—through confiscation, taxation, or regulation—the property rights of the Hong Kong people, it can expect to receive in 1997 a city that is only marginally more productive than other cities on the coast of China. The entrepreneurial talent and other forms of human capital, which give Hong Kong so much economic life, will be long gone. The financial capital will have been deposited in other banks outside Hong Kong. About the only significant capital assets that will be left will be the buildings and sewer systems, which cannot be moved, and the pace of their depreciation will be accelerated due to lack of maintenance and an infusion of replacement capital from Hong Kong and foreign sources. Early in the twenty-first century, Hong Kong should be no more productive than the rest of the coast. China will then have more territory to control, but not much to gain from it.

We doubt that this dismal scenario will come to pass in full force. We expect China's leaders to recognize its prospect and to institute additional market reforms on the mainland. Hong Kong's economic growth may be dampened because of the takeover, the outflow of capital, and the threat of greater taxation and regulation, but it will be dampened less than it could be precisely because the Chinese leaders want more than mere territory to govern. As a consequence of the reforms motivated by the acquisition of Hong Kong, China's economy will likely grow marginally more rapidly than if the Hong Kong takeover were not possible. The greater growth in

China can be attributable not so much to the acquisition of Hong Kong's capital, but to China's reforms encouraged by the prospects of capital flight from Hong Kong.[52]

## The New Outlook

After reading an initial draft of this book for a symposium, Robert Tollison, our good friend and former colleague at George Mason University's Center for the Study of Public Choice, wrote with tongue in cheek:

> Holy Cow! Just when the gloom and doom theorists have convinced just about everyone that the world is going to hell in a handcart, McKenzie and Lee (hereafter M-L) have found a silver lining in the clouds of the future. I should feel better after reading this book, but I don't. The M-L theory says that government is practically going to disappear, which means that public choice scholars will no longer have anything to study, which means that we will have to find other jobs, which is even more complicated than ordinary because there won't be any government jobs left. We might even have to teach more. This is a depressing book in terms of its personal implications for a public choice scholar.[53]

We realize that our optimism is in stark contrast to the commentaries of many "gloom and doom theorists," and we are aware that many others long before us have made optimistic (perhaps too optimistic) assessments of the future of government power.[54] Nevertheless we think it is important to assess trends and to tell it as we see it, if for no other purpose than to critique previous less-optimistic assessments.

In addition, we hasten to add that Tollison and many other scholars who study the workings of governments do not have all that much to fear. We have never said that governments will disappear, or that war was totally obsolete, or that we are at the "end of history," as other writers have maintained.[55] Our claims are far more modest. We have only argued that greater capital mobility and production sophistication have constrained the growth of governments. Though there is a good chance that governments will actually start contracting on many fronts, the prospects of that outcome are uncertain. To date, the evidence only supports constrained growth relative to national income. The evidence presented nonetheless suggests that there has been something of a U-turn in government growth, from escalating growth to constrained, if not negative, growth.

As we have said repeatedly, governments will retain considerable economic powers for decades and centuries to come. There will therefore be much for Tollison, his public-choice colleagues—including us—and other scholars to study about government, even if governments never change sizes.

In addition we suggest that constrained growth in the powers of governments increases the range of research topics. We need to know a great deal more about how the policy making process has changed, or will change, in an era of constrained growth; that is to say, what types of political systems will be needed and what types of policies will be selected in the adjusted political systems. We need to know a great deal more than we now do about how international economic forces will influence the survivability of the different political systems, and political interest groups within any given political system. We need to know more about the efficacy of constitutional provisions, such as the balanced budget/tax limitation amendment, in constraining government when, in fact, governments are becoming more constrained by economic forces. We suspect that technology will increase reliance on direct votes by the citizenry on major public issues and will decrease reliance on votes by representatives in government capitals. Yet we know little about how the shift in the way votes are taken will affect the size, scope, and effectiveness of governments.

We noted earlier in the chapter that the growth in competitiveness of governments might worsen the world's environmental problems. Furthermore, people's allegiance to their countries and local communities can be expected to fade. As opposed to being governed by geography, allegiance will increasingly become influenced by international economic opportunities and electronic hook-ups. Much work needs to be done on how governments can be expected to solve the world's environmental problems, adjust to the buildup of transnational communities, and evolve with developments in telecommunications.

The people out there in the world who work for their governments, however, *do* have something to fear—if they have an innate disdain for competition. This is because the world is simply becoming more competitive for everyone. Government workers will have to learn to compete, or give way to those who do. They will face the loss of their country's capital base and their government's revenue base if they do not learn to compete, to produce their government's services more efficiently. They will have to make their government's policies less nettlesome and more constructive—or they and their countries and constituencies will suffer the consequences of international resource flight at quicksilver speeds.

In general we have offered in this book a new way of thinking about policy developments. This new way of thinking has an important moral to which Americans especially must pay heed. Global forces *are* at work, consequences *will* occur. Policymakers and pundits of all political persuasions have acknowledged many of these forces with more or less clarity. However, some recommend that the United States should tilt like a windmill against the winds of change. They would have the country return to policies of control—reregulation, higher taxes, and more spending. Such a policy course would be tantamount to a slide-rule company hiking its prices in face of competition from hand calculators. That is to say, the recommended recontrol policy would be totally out of context with the new and unfolding competitive constraints. The country will not recapture its former greatness in the world until its policymakers seek to lead—not follow—the competitive trend.

# Notes

Preface

1. "New Jersey's Taxes: Why Don't They Love Them," *The Economist*, August 4, 1990, p. 23.

2. Much of this evidence is covered in this book. For a recent review of the impact of taxes on people economic decisions in the United States, see David Littman, "High-Tax States Are Low-Growth States," *Wall Street Journal*, August 6, 1990, p. A12.

3. Paul Kennedy, *The Rise and Decline of Great Powers: Economic Change and Military conflict from 1500 to 2000* (New York: Random House, 1987); Robert B. Reich, *The Next American Frontier* (New York: Times Books, 1983); and Kevin Phillips, *The Politics of the Rich and Poor* (New York: Random House, 1990).

Chapter 1.   Government's Dilemma in a Competitive Economy

1. Norman Macrae, "Workplace Flexibility: Past, Present, and Future" (copy of a speech, received June 1988), p. 5.

2. As reported in John H. Fund, "Czechoslovakia's Free Market Minister," *Wall Street Journal*, March 2, 1990, p. A10.

3. Vaclav Klaus and Thomas Jezek, "The Evolutionary Approach," *Financial Times*, December 13, 1989, p. 15.

4. As reported in Fund, "Czechoslovakia's Free-Market Minister."

5. See, for example, Martin Anderson, *Revolution* (San Diego: Harcourt Brace Jovanovich, 1988).

6. See Zbigniew Brzezinski, *The Grand Failure: The Birth and Death of Communism in the Twentieth Century* (New York: Charles Scribner's Sons, 1989).

7. We have written at length about government failures and the difficulty of containing the growth of government into areas in which frequent failures are assured. See Dwight R. Lee and Richard B. McKenzie, *Regulating Government: A Preface to Constitutional Economics* (Lexington, Mass.: Lexington Books, 1987).

8. See, for example, Rosabeth Moss Kanter, *When Giants Learn to Dance* (New York: Simon & Schuster, 1989); Robert B. Reich, *The Next American Frontier* (New

York: Times Books, 1983); and Robert B. Reich, *The Resurgent Liberal (and Other Unfashionable Prophecies)* (New York: Random House, 1989).

9. See Barry Bluestone and Bennett Harrison, *The Deindustrialization of America: Plant Closings, Community Abandonment, and the Dismantling of Basic Industry* (New York: Basic Books, 1982).

10. Bluestone and Harrison, *The Deindustrialization of America*, p. 18.

11. Bennett Harrison and Barry Bluestone, *The Great U-Turn: Corporate Restructuring and the Polarization of America;* Reich, *The Next American Frontier.*

12. See Lester C. Thurow, *The Zero-Sum Solution: Building a World-Class American Economy* (New York: Simon & Schuster, 1985); Robert Kuttner, *The Economic Illusion: False Choices between Prosperity and Social Justice* (Boston: Houghton Mifflin, 1984); Paul Kennedy, *The Rise and Fall of the Great Powers: Economic Change and Military Conflict from 1500 to 2000* (New York: Random House, 1987); Benjamin M. Friedman, *Day of Reckoning: The Consequences of American Economic Policy under Reagan and After* (New York: Random House, 1988); and Joel Kurtzman, *The Decline and Crash of the American Economy* (New York: W. W. Norton, 1988).

13. David S. Broder, "Getting the Government Its Due," *Washington Post National Weekly Edition*, February 26, 1990, p. 4.

14. Reich, *The Resurgent Liberal*, p. xiv.

15. Ibid.

16. One of the authors has questioned the validity of the case for industrial policies (Richard B. McKenzie, *Fugitive Industry: The Economics and Politics of Deindustrialization* [San Francisco: Pacific Institute, 1984]; and Richard B. McKenzie, *Competing Visions: The Political Conflict over America's Economic Future* [Washington, D.C.: Cato Institute, 1985]).

17. George Gilder, *Microcosm: The Quantum Revolution in Economics and Technology* (New York: Simon & Schuster, 1989), p. 15.


Chapter 2.   From Captive Capital to Quicksilver Capital: A Short History of Technology and Its Influence on Modern Government

1. Karl Marx, *The Poverty of Philosophy*, quoted in M. M. Bober, *Karl Marx's Interpretation of History* (New York: W. W. Norton, Company, 1965), p. 6.

2. See Bober, *Karl Marx's Interpretation of History*, chap. 2.

3. Friedrich Engels, *Herr Eugen Duhring's Revolution in Science (Anti-Duhring)*, trans. Emile Burns (New York: International Publishers, 1939), quoted in Bober, *Karl Marx's Interpretation of History*, p. 39.

4. Marx, *The Poverty of Philosophy*, quoted in Bober, *Karl Marx's Interpretation of History*, p. 6.

5. In *The Communist Manifesto*, Marx and Engels claim that "the bourgeoisie cannot exist without constantly revolutionizing the instruments of production, and thereby the relations of production, and with them the whole relations of society." *The Communist Manifesto* [Chicago: Henry Regnery, 1954], pp. 19–20).

6. Karl Marx and Friedrich Engels, *The Holy Family* (Moscow: Foreign Languages Publishing House, 1956), p. 168.

7. Karl Marx, *Capital: A Critique of Political Economy*, (Chicago: Charles H. Kerr, 1909), quoted in Bober, *Karl Marx's Interpretation of History*, p. 40.

8. Oskar Lange, *On the Economic Theory of Socialism* (New York: McGraw-Hill, 1964), p. 116.

9. While Marx was hostile to the continuation of capitalism, he reasoned that capitalism was a necessary, if regrettable, step in the historical development of the ideal communist state. Capitalism incorporated the necessary incentives people needed to build the capital base that would permit the creation of the socialist state. Marx once praised capitalism:

> The bourgeoisie, during its rule of scarce one hundred years, has created more massive and more colossal productive forces than have all the proceeding generations together. Subjection of Nature's forces to man, machinery, and application of chemistry to industry and agriculture, steam navigation, railways, electric telegraph, clearing whole continents for cultivation, canalization of rivers, whole populations conjured out of the ground—what earlier century had even a presentiment that such productive forces slumbered in the lap of social labor? (*Communist Manifesto* [Chicago: Henry Regnery, 1954], p. 23).

10. For an extensive critique of Marxian economics, see Thomas Sowell, *Marxism: Philosophy and Economics* (New York: William Morrow, 1985).

11. Douglass C. North, *Structure and Change in Economic History* (New York: W. W. Norton, 1981), p. 146.

12. For a history of the motivations that led to development of computer technology, see George Gilder, *Microcosm: The Quantum Revolution in Economics and Technology* (New York: Simon & Schuster, 1989).

13. Joseph A. Schumpeter, *Capitalism, Socialism, and Democracy*, 2nd ed. (New York: Harper & Brothers, 1947).

14. Ibid., p. 83.

15. F. A. Hayek, *The Road to Serfdom* (Chicago: University of Chicago Press, 1944).

16. As a contemporary example, Congress might legislate subsidies for farmers and tariffs on imported textiles in separate bills even though, taken together, the farm subsidies and the textile tariffs might make both groups worse off. Granted, the farmers may gain in the case of the subsidies, and the textile owners may gain because of the import restrictions. However, textile manufacturers would have to pay higher taxes to finance the subsidies, while the farmers might have to pay higher prices for their clothes and not be able to export as many farm products because of the restrictions on imports.

17. Aaron Wildavsky, *How to Limit Government Spending* (Berkeley: University of California Press, 1980), p. 46.

18. Economies of scale imply that output, in percentage terms, expands more rapidly than the scale of production or the use of all factors, capital included. For example, with economies of scale, if the use of all resources, including capital, increases by 10 percent, then production should expand disproportionately more, say by 15 or 20 percent, lowering the minimum average of all production costs. In more concrete terms, the development of the steam engine might have been capital

using—that is, it required the purchase of more and larger plant and equipment dedicated to the production of, for example, textile products. However, what made the steam engine a technological wonder is that it increased the output of textile plants (and many other lines of production) by more than it increased the overall cost of production.

19. See John Kenneth Galbraith, *The New Industrial State* (Boston: Houghton Mifflin, 1967); and Barry Bluestone and Bennett Harrison, *The Deindustrialization of America: Plant Closings, Community Abandonment, and the Dismantling of Basic Industry* (New York: Basic Books, 1982).

20. Former Harvard University economics professor John Kenneth Galbraith writes that if society continues to follow the objectives of private industries:

> Our wants will be managed in accordance with the needs of the industrial system; the policies of the state will be subject to similar influences; education will be adapted to industrial need; the disciplines required by the industrial system will be the conventional morality of the community. (*The New Industrial State*, p. 398)

21. John Kenneth Galbraith, *American Capitalism: The Concept of Countervailing Power* (Boston: Houghton Mifflin, 1956), p. 111.

22. John Kenneth Galbraith, *Economics and the Public Purpose* (Boston: Houghton Mifflin, 1973), p. 315.

23. See Galbraith, *American Capitalism*, chap. 10; Martin Carnoy, Derek Shearer, and Russell Rumberger, *A New Social Contract: The Economy and Government after Reagan* (New York: Harper & Row, 1983), chap. 9.

24. These problems include, for example, so-called paper entrepreneurship, a contemporary financial fad that is driven by the technology of computers and communications and that diverts productive efforts from making profits via production to making profits from reshuffling the ownership of firms.

25. Robert B. Reich, *The Next American Frontier* (New York: Times Books, 1983), p. 20.

26. Robert B. Reich, *The Resurgent Liberal and Other Unfashionable Prophecies* (New York: Times Books, 1989), p. xiv.

27. Reich, *The Next American Frontier*, chap. 11.

28. We are very familiar with this public-choice line of analysis, because we have helped develop elements of it [Dwight R. Lee and Richard B. McKenzie, *Regulating Government: A Preface to Constitutional Economics* (Lexington, Mass.: Lexington Books, 1987)]. However, as will become evident in following footnotes, this line of argument has been extensively developed by many others, including Milton and Rose Friedman, *Free to Choose: A Personal Statement* (New York: Harcourt Brace Jovanovich, 1980); and Milton and Rose Friedman, *Tyranny of the Status Quo* (San Diego: Harcourt Brace Jovanovich, 1984).

29. A supply-and-demand theory of regulation has been developed by George J. Stigler, "A Theory of Regulation," *Bell Journal of Economics and Management Science* (Spring 1971), pp. 3–21.

30. See James M. Buchanan and Gordon Tullock, *The Calculus of Consent: Logical Foundations of Constitutional Democracy* (Ann Arbor, Mich.: University of Michigan Press, 1962); and James M. Buchanan, *The Limits of Liberty: Between Anarchy and Leviathan* (Chicago: University of Chicago Press, 1975).

31. See Jonathan R. T. Hughes, *The Governmental Habit: Economic Controls from Colonial Times to the Present* (New York: Basic Books, 1977); and Terry L. Anderson and Peter J. Hill, *The Birth of the Transfer Society* (Stanford, Calif.: Hoover Institution Press, 1980).

32. Gale Ann Norton, "The Limitless Federal Taxing Power," in *Public Choice and Constitutional Economics*, ed. James D. Gwartney and Richard E. Wagner (Greenwich, Conn.: JAI Press, 1988), pp. 253–84.

33. See Roger Pilon, "Property rights, Takings, and a Free Society," in *Public Choice and Constitutional Economics*, pp. 151–80; Richard Epstein, "Taxation, Regulation and Confiscation," in *Public Choice and Constitutional Economics*, pp. 181–206; and Terry Anderson and P. J. Hill, "Constitutional Constraints, Entrepreneurship, and the Evolution of Property Rights," in *Public Choice and Constitutional Economics*, pp. 207–28.

34. See James M. Buchanan and Richard E. Wagner, *Democracy in Deficit: The Political Legacy of Lord Keynes* (New York: Academic Press, 1977).

35. See Hayek, *The Road to Serfdom* (Chicago: University of Chicago Press, 1944).

36. James T. Bennett and Manuel H. Johnson, *The Political Economy of Federal Government Growth: 1959–1978* (College Station, Tex.: Center for Education and Research in Free Enterprise, Texas A & M University Press, 1980).

37. See Norman J. Ornstein and Mark Schmitt, "The New World of Interest Politics," *The American Enterprise* (January/February 1990), pp. 46–51.

38. Mancur Olson, *The Rise and Decline of Nations* (New Haven, Conn.: Yale University Press, 1983).

39. See William A. Niskanen, Jr., *Bureaucracy and Representative Government* (Chicago: Aldine, 1971); Thomas E. Borcherding, ed., *Budgets and Bureaucrats: The Source of Government Growth* (Durham, N.C.: Duke University Press, 1977); James M. Buchanan, Robert D. Tollison, and Gordon Tullock, eds., *Toward a Theory of the Rent-Seeking Society* (College Station, Tex.: Texas A & M University Press, 1980); and Richard E. Wagner, *To Promote the General Welfare* (San Francisco: Pacific Research Institute for Public Policy, 1989).

40. See James M. Buchanan and Geoffrey Brennan, *The Power to Tax: Analytical Foundations of a Fiscal Constitution* (Cambridge: Cambridge University Press, 1980); and Geoffrey Brennan and James M. Buchanan, *The Reason for Rules: Constitutional Political Economy* (Cambridge: Cambridge University Press, 1985).

41. The theory of voter interest is developed in Anthony Downs, *An Economic Theory of Democracy* (New York: Harper & Row, 1957); and the theory of voter ignorance is further refined in Gordon Tullock, *Toward a Mathematics of Politics* (Ann Arbor, Mich.: University of Michigan Press, 1967).

42. Robert E. McCormick, William F. Shughart, and Robert D. Tollison, "The Disinterest in Deregulation," *American Economic Review* (December 1984), pp. 1074–79.

43. "Welfare Paradise Lost," *Wall Street Journal*, February 22, 1990, p. A12.

44. Gary Anderson, Dolores Martin, William F. Shughart, and Robert D. Tollison, "Behind the Veil: The Political Economy of Constitutional Choice," *Predicting Politics: Essays on Political Economy* (Ann Arbor: University of Michigan Press, 1990).

45. See Olson, *The Rise and Decline of Nations*.

46. Thomas Babington Macaulay in a letter written from London (May 23, 1857) to Henry Stephens Randall, author of *Life of Thomas Jefferson*.

Chapter 3.    Economics, Meet Electronics: The Technology of Decreasing Scale

1. Alan Greenspan, "Goods Shrink and Trade Grows," *Wall Street Journal*, October 24, 1988, p. A14.

2. For a perspective on how the U.S. manufacturing base may have declined by more than standard statistics indicate, see Lawrence Mishel, *Manufacturing Numbers: How Inaccurate Statistics Conceal U.S. Industrial Decline* (Washington, D.C.: Economic Policy Institute, 1988).

3. For more particulars on this debate, see Richard B. McKenzie, *The American Job Machine* (New York: Universe Books, 1988), chap. 3.

4. See Mack Ott, "The Growing Share of Services in the U.S. Economy—Degeneration or Evolution?" *Review* (Federal Reserve Bank of St. Louis, June/July 1987).

5. Data from the U.S. Small Business Administration, Office of Advocacy, as reported in "The Growing Importance of Small Manufacturers, 1980–1986," *Wall Street Journal*, December 8, 1988, p. B2. Only small firms in food, kindred products, and tobacco products lost employment share in the 1980–86 period.

6. David L. Birch, *Job Creation in America: How Our Smallest Companies Put the Most People to Work* (New York: Free Press, 1987), p. 14. The Small Business Administration estimates of growth in "small" business employment are not nearly as large as Birch's. Still, the SBA found that in the 1980–86 period more than half of the nation's new jobs occurred in firms with fewer than one hundred employees (U.S. Small Business Administration, *The State of Small Business: A Report to the President* [Washington: U.S. Government Printing Office, 1988], p. 38). The growth of small firms has also accelerated in other countries, most notably Great Britain. In Britain, the number of self-employed people expanded by 59 percent between 1979 and 1987, reaching 2.9 million in 1987. The number of businesses registered for tax purposes in Britain grew by an average of nine hundred a week in 1987, a rate triple the 1980 growth rate; this gave rise to claims that Britain was going through an "entrepreneurial renaissance," as much reflected in a change in attitude as it is a matter of a change in statistics (Steve Lohr, "A Small-Business Boom in Britain," *New York Times*, November 29, 1988, p. 31).

7. Birch, *Job Creation in America*, p. 9.

8. Apparently, in spite of the tremendous success small businesses have had in creating most of the new jobs in the United States, the public is largely unaware of that fact. A 1988 survey found that only 19 percent of the people surveyed by telephone were aware of it, even though two-thirds of the respondents had worked at a small business (Buck Brown, "Enterprise," *Wall Street Journal*, October 6, 1988, p. B1).

9. As reported in Ben Wattenberg, "CEOs Optimistic about Future of Business," *Greenville* (S.C.) *News*, March 5, 1988, p. 4A.

10. Albert P. Carr, "Labor Letter: Downsizing Continues Unabated, as Worries about the Economy Grow," *Wall Street Journal*, August 15, 1989, p. A1. See also Cindy Skrzycki, "Downsizing Isn't Just for Downturns," *Washington Post National Weekly edition*, August 28, 1989, p. 20.

11. Skrzycki, "Downsizing Isn't Just for Downturns," p. 21.

12. Robert Crandall, "The Regional Shift of U.S. Economic Activity and Its

Implications for Economic Welfare" (working paper, June 22, 1988, draft) (Washington, D.C.: Brookings Institution), table 13.

13. Manufacturing firms with fewer than 1,000 workers also increased their share of value added in manufacturing from 64.3 percent in 1958 to 68.4 percent in 1982 (ibid.).

14. For an opposing view, see Charles Brown et al., *Employers: Large and Small* (Cambridge, Mass.: Harvard University Press, 1990).

15. As reported in Rosabeth Moss Kanter, *When Giants Learn to Dance: Mastering the Challenges of Strategy, Management, and Careers in the 1990s* (New York: Simon & Schuster, 1989), p. 129.

16. Ibid., p. 118.

17. Ibid., p. 36.

18. Paul B. Carroll and John R. Wilke, "Computer Firms Find Service Is What Sells, Not Fancier Hardware," *Wall Street Journal*, August 15, 1989, p. A1.

19. The integrated circuit was invented in 1958 and patented in 1959 by two people, Jack Kirby of Texas Instrument and Robert Noyce of the Intel Corporation, working independently of one another (John Markoff, "The Chip at 30: Potential Still Vast," *New York Times* [September 14, 1988], p. 33). The technological history of the computer is developed in detail in Kenneth Flamm, *Creating the Computer: Government, Industry, and High Technology* (Washington, D.C.: Brookings Institution, 1988).

20. W. Michael Blumenthal, "The World Economy and Technological Change," *Foreign Affairs* 66, no. 3 (1987/1988), p. 532.

21. A description of the impact of the computer on world markets is covered in Maurice Estabrooks, *Programmed Capitalism: A Computer-Mediated Global Society* (New York: M. E. Sharpe, 1988).

22. In early 1990 IBM announced plans to begin pilot production within eighteen months of a sixteen-million-bit computer chip, which has the capacity to store sixteen hundred double-spaced pages of typewritten text ("IBM Pioneers Chip with Big Capacity," *Commercial Appeal* [Memphis, Tenn.], February 14, 1990, p. B3).

23. Markoff, "The Chip at 30," p. 33. In the 1980s computer speeds were increased principally by making circuits and transistors smaller. However, in early 1989, Nippon Telegraph and Telephone Company announced a new method of making transistors that combines two or more materials in "atomic" layers on a single chip. The new process will enable the transistors to switch electronic signals hundreds of times faster than current methods do. The new transistors switch on and off in "2 trillionths of a second, or 2 picoseconds, compared with several hundred picoseconds for conventional silicon transistors" (Andrew Pollack, "New Chips Offer the Promise of Much Speedier Computers," *New York Times*, January 4, 1989, p. Y1).

24. Blumenthal, "The World Economy and Technological Change," p. 533.

25. George Gilder, "The Revitalization of Everything: The Law of the Microcosm," *Harvard Business Review* (March/April 1988), pp. 59–60.

26. Blumenthal, "The World Economy and Technological Change," p. 535.

27. Ibid., p. 533.

28. The number of mainframe computers rose from eleven million in 1981 to 18 million in 1986 (Bureau of the Census, *Statistical Abstract of the United States* [Washington, D.C.: U.S. Government Printing Office, 1988], p. 727).

29. Gilder, "The Revitalization of Everything," p. 57.

30. In 1988 NEC introduced a 4.4-pound lap-top computer with two megabytes of internal memory but without an internal disk drive. In 1989 Atari announced plans to produce a lap-top computer about the size of a videocassette and weighing one pound ("Atari Weighs in with a One-Pound PC," *New York Times*, April 12, 1989, p. Y26), and Poget announced its one-pound palmtop that is 1 by 8.75 by 4.75 inches, has 512K of internal RAM, runs for as many as 100 hours on two double-A batteries, and uses credit card RAM and ROM cards for programs and storage (Jonathan Matzkin, "Tiny, Powerful Poget PC Tips the Scales at 1 Lb.," *PC Magazine*, November 14, 1989, pp. 33 and 35). In addition, in 1989 Compac introduced a laptop based on the 286 chip that, with a twenty-megabyte hard disk and a backlit screen, weighed just under seven pounds.

31. See "1988 Technology Forecast: Memories Gain in Smarts, Density, and Speed As Feature Sizes Shrink," *Electronic Design*, January 7, 1988, p. 126.

32. A prediction made by Ralph Gomery, chief scientist at IBM, as reported in Gilder, "The Revitalization of Everything," p. 58. Gilder also reports that according to the former head of Stanford Electronics Laboratories, by the year 2000 a billion components will be packed on a single chip: "A billion transistors will offer the computing power of 20 Cray 2 CPUs on one chip, or 20 VAX minicomputers together with all their memory" (ibid.).

33. Ramchandran Jaikumar, "Postindustrial Manufacturing," *Harvard Business Review* (November/December 1986), pp. 69–76.

34. Bruce Stokes, "The 21st-Century Factory," *National Journal*, February 13, 1988, p. 383.

35. As estimated for the authors by Chris Jarvis, professor of textiles, Clemson University, personal communication August 24, 1988.

36. For example, the *Ole Miss Spirit*, an independent weekly tabloid on sports at the University of Mississippi, with only 3,500 subscribers, is written and published by one person.

37. Kenneth Wright and David Bourn, *Manufacturing Intelligence* (Reading, Mass.: Addison Wesley, 1988).

38. Tracy O'Rourke, "A Case for CIM," lecture delivered at the Conference on Manufacturing, Stanford University, May 1988, as reported in Paul Milgrom and John Roberts, "The Economics of Modern Manufacturing: Technology, Strategy, and Organization," *American Economic Review* (June 1990), p. 511.

39. Thomas Moore, "Make or Break Time for General Motors," *Fortune*, February 15, 1988, pp. 32–50.

40. Otis Port, "Smart Factories: America's Turn," *Business Week*, May 8, 1989, p. 142–48.

41. As reported by Kevin Hanlon, purchasing manager of the Jacobs Manufacturing plant in Clemson, South Carolina, personal communication October 15, 1988.

42. Greenspan, "Goods Shrink and Trade Grows."

43. These points were stressed by Greenspan, although his calculations of the percentage declines in the weight per real dollar of exports and imports are slightly higher than our figures (ibid.).

44. For a critique of George Gilder's discussion of the benefits of small scale production, see Charles H. Ferguson, "From the People Who Brought You Voodoo Economics," *Harvard Business Review* (May/June 1988), pp. 55–62.

45. See G. Warren Nutter and Henry Adler Einhorn, *Enterprise Monopoly in the United States: 1888–1958* (New York: Columbia University Press, 1969); and Douglass C. North, Terry L. Anderson, and Peter J. Hill, *Growth and Welfare in the American Past: A New Economic History* (Englewood Cliffs, N.J.: Prentice-Hall, 1983), especially chaps. 12 and 13.

46. Arthur E. Sherman, "Trends in Telecommunications Technology," *Journal of the American Society for Information Science* (June 1986), p. 417.

47. *Statistical Abstract of the United States* (1988), p. 524.

48. One government report notes:

> "Plain Old Telephone Service" (known in the industry as POTS) is rapidly becoming archaic, as both individual and business consumers are confronted with a variety of long-distance services (i.e., services offering different qualitative characteristics for the rate at which data can be transmitted, privately-owned switching systems within firms, and packet switching that can combine many relatively low-data rate services). (Henry C. Kelly, project director, Office of Technology Assessment, U.S. Congress, *Technology and the American Economy in Transition: Choices for the Future* [Washington: U.S. Government Printing Office, 1988], p. 261)

49. The data on telephone calls were obtained from three editions of the *Statistical Abstract of the United States:* 1975, p. 515; 1981, p. 561; and 1988, p. 525. The data do not include calls made on telephone systems not regulated by the Federal Communication Commission (FCC). According to an FCC official, the figures became more difficult to obtain after the breakup of AT&T. As a result the reliability of the reported figures has suffered. Also, the number of calls reported directly by the FCC tends to be lower than the numbers reported in the *Statistical Abstract* (telephone conversation with Katie Rangos, Federal Communication Commission, Washington, D.C., Spring 1988).

50. Trish Hall, "With Phones Everywhere, Everyone Is Talking More," *New York Times*, October 11, 1989, p. Y1.

51. Lesley Gillis, "Critical International Issues Must Be Resolved if the Promise of an ISDN Future Is to Be Kept," *Communications News*, January 1987, p. 52.

52. Ibid.

53. Lisa Torvik, "Fax Machines Generate 'Faxplosion' in US," *Journal of Commerce*, March 24, p. 3A.

54. Peter H. Lewis, "The Facts on the Fax," *New York Times*, January 10, 1989, p. Y18. During the first half of 1988, sales of fax machines were not expected to double 1987 sales until 1990 (Calvin Sims, "Coast-to-Coast in 20 Seconds: Fax Machines Alter Business," *New York Times*, May 5, 1988, p. 1). Another report estimates that fax sales in the United States will exceed 1.5 million by 1991 (Richard Lipkin, "Fax Fever Slams Business Hard, *Insight*, August 22, 1988, p. 8).

55. R. H. Coase, "The Nature of the Firm," *Economica* 4 (November 1937), pp. 386–405. In another seminal article, Professor Coase more completely describes the problems he had in mind when writing about the "costs of market transactions." He enumerates: "In order to carry out a market transaction it is necessary to discover who it is that one wishes to deal with, to inform people that one wishes to deal and on what terms, to conduct negotiations leading up to a bargain, to draw up the contract, to undertake the inspection needed to make sure that the terms of the contract are being observed, and so on." (R. H. Coase, "The Problem of Social

Cost," *The Firm, the Market and the Law* [Chicago: University of Chicago Press, 1988], p. 114)

56. AT&T found in a 1985 survey that as many as 23 million Americans work at home as a part of a home-based business (as reported in Joanne H. Pratt, *Legal Barriers to Home-Based Work* [Dallas, Tex.: National Center for Policy Analysis, September 1987], p. 9). See also "Telecommuting: Staying Away in Droves," *The Economist*, April 4, 1987, p. 88; Sandra Atchinson, "These Top Executives Work Where They Play," *Business Week*, October 27, 1986, pp. 132–34; Karen A. Fortin and Shirley Dennis-Escoffier, "Telecommuting Adds a New Dimension to Office in the Home," *The Woman CPA*, (October 1986), pp. 21–25; Jay Koblenze, "Telecommuting: Traveling to Work Via Your Computer," *Black Enterprise*, November 1986, p. 34; and Carol-Ann Hamilton, "Telecommuting," *Personnel Journal* (April 1987), pp. 91–101.

57. As reported in Kathleen Christensen, "A Hard Day's Work in the Electronic Cottage," *Across the Board*, April 1987, p. 19.

58. Jane Morrill Tazelaar, "Working at Home with Computers," *Byte*, March 1986, p. 156.

59. See Hamilton, "Telecommuting."

60. According to one survey of eleven hundred cities and counties, 90 percent of them had restrictions on home-based work. These restrictions include how many people can work in the home business, how much of the home can be devoted to home-based work, the types of materials that must be used to separate the business from the residence portion of the house, and what kinds of work can and cannot be performed in the home. For example, as reported in one study, Ohio and Michigan require that home-based places of business must have an entrance that is separate from the ones used by the members of the household, while other ordinances forbid entrances used exclusively for businesses. In Pennsylvania products produced in the home must carry a label identifying them as "home produced." In Massachusetts home-produced goods and services produced under contract with an outside employer are illegal. The only people allowed to work in the home are those who cannot leave it (Pratt, *Legal Barriers to Home-Based Work*, pp. 24–39). And in Chicago there is a "virtual ban on all home-based work, including a ban on linking a home computer with an office computer" (ibid., p. i). As suggested by the growth in home-based industries, these restrictions may not be very formidable and may be easily circumvented with new technology. In addition the restrictions may be dissipating. In early 1989 the U.S. Labor Department eased long-established bans on producing knitted garments in the home.

61. Lad Kuzela, "When Going to Work Means Staying Home," *Modern Office Technology*, June 1987, p. 30.

62. Workers also have an economic incentive to participate in telecommuting. One study estimates that telecommuting in the Columbus, Ohio, metropolitan area can save the average worker 2.5 to 6 hours a week in commuting time, plus a reduction in gas and car expenses of at least fourteen hundred dollars a year (Steven L. Gordon and Andrea Van Arsdale, "Simulating Some of Telecommunications/ Transportation Substitution," *Technological Forecasting and Social Change* 29 [1986], p. 291). By reducing the commuting costs of their employees, businesses can expect to reduce their wage bills (since so-called "distance workers" would be willing to work for less at firms that provide telecommuting options).

63. Norman Macrae, editor of *The Economist*, has made this point with more punch:

> So in the twenty-first century an information worker—say, a market re-searcher or investment banker—will be able to live on the beach at Tahiti if he wants to and telecommunicate daily to the office in New York, Frank-furt, or the Timbuctoo tax haven through which he works. I can't understand why those downwardly mobile young people called investment bankers still congregate in bigger and bigger units on far too expensive sites in Tokyo and London at rents 50 times higher per square foot than rents six blocks away. They'll all be undercut by small people with personal computers telecommuting from a tent in Tahiti. (Norman Macrae, "Work-place Flexibility: Past, Present, and Future" [copy of a speech, received June 1988, pp. 3 and 4]).

64. Steve Lohr, "The Growth of the 'Global Office,' " *New York Times*, October 18, 1988, p. D1.

65. As reported by Edward Yardeni, "The Triumph of Capitalism," *Topical Study of Prudential-Bache Securities* 17 (August 1989), p. 16.

66. Lohr, "The Growth of the Global Office."

67. William J. Baumol, Sue Anne Batey Blackman, and Edward N. Wolff, *Productivity and American Leadership: The Long View* (Cambridge, Mass.: MIT Press, 1989), p. 147. These authors conclude that relatively low productivity increases in the information economy account for a major portion of the relative employment growth in the information economy and that increases in demand for information account for a relatively minor portion of the employment growth. We suspect that demand forces in the information economy had a stronger effect than calculated, primarily because of the difficulty of disentangling demand and cost forces in the two broad sectors of the economy. Workers could have been released from the goods economy because of that sector's relatively high productivity growth and reduced demand for labor. However, the relatively high productivity growth in the goods economy could have been encouraged to a significant degree by the increased demand for information that drove up labor costs in the goods economy. And because the goods economy in the 1960s and 1970s may have been more directly affected by international competitive constraints, the increase in labor costs in the goods economy could have stimulated productivity growth in the goods economy. In addition, as the authors recognize, productivity growth in the information economy could have en-hanced the ability of producers in the goods economy to increase productivity.

68. As reported in "The Soaring Payoff from Higher Education," *The Margin* (January/February 1990), p. 22. The same article notes that estimates of the high school/college earnings gap differ but generally show an increase in the 1980s. For example, University of Maryland economist Frank Levy estimates that in 1979 male college graduates aged twenty-five to thirty-four earned 18 percent more than their high school counterparts did. However, by 1986, the estimated earnings gap had more than doubled, to 43 percent. See also Marvin H. Kosters, "Schooling, Work Experience, and Wage Trends," *American Economic Review* (May 1990), pp. 308–312.

69. Ronald Henkoff, *Fortune*, December 19, 1988, pp. 69–76.

70. Russell Mitchell, "Masters of Innovation: How 3M Keeps Its New Products Coming," *Business Week*, April 10, 1989, pp. 58–63.

71. This example is drawn from Robert Abler, Donald Janelle, Allen Philbrick, and John Sommer, eds., *Human Geography in a Shrinking World* (North Scituate, Mass.: Duxbury Press, 1975), p. 4.

72. For a new theory of how new technologies have affected the way firms must do business, see Milgrom and Roberts, "The Economics of Modern Manufacturing," pp. 511–29.

73. Walter Kiechel III, "Corporate Strategies for the 1990s," *Fortune*, February 29, 1988, p. 42.

74. Michael C. Jensen, "Eclipse of the Public Corporation," *Harvard Business Review* (September/October 1989), p. 64.

75. Ibid., p. 67.

76. Ibid., p. 64.

77. Furthermore, there is not much that world governments would want to do, given that the redirection of the funds was intended to develop previously underdeveloped economies, to increase the profitability of Western investments, and to add to the long-term income stream of the whole world, but especially of the countries that redirect investment toward those more profitable opportunities, even if they are in Eastern Europe.

78. Fernand Braudel, *Civilization and Capitalism: 15th–18th Century*, vols. 1–3 (New York: Harper & Row, 1981).

79. Macrae, "Workplace Flexibility," p. 5.

## Chapter 4. Workers of the World Unite—At Last!

1. As quoted in Myron Magnet, "Stars of the 1980s Cast Their Light," *Fortune*, July 3, 1989, p. 67.

2. For example, Harvard University's Robert Reich argues that in order to thwart economic decline in the face of growing international capital mobility, policymakers must first determine what they want corporations to do (e.g., train workers). They can then organize a set of government subsidies that would entice corporations (foreign or domestic) to achieve the established goals ("Corporations and Nations," *Atlantic Monthly*, May 1988, pp. 76–81).

3. Martin and Susan Tolchin, *Buying into America: How Foreign Money is Changing the Face of Our Nation* (New York: Times Books, 1988), p. 15.

4. Ibid.

5. See W. Michael Blumenthal, "The World Economy and Technological Change," *Foreign Affairs* 66, no. 3 (1987/88), pp. 538–50. See also Norman S. Fieleke, "Economic Interdependence between Nations: Reason for Policy Coordination?" *New England Economic Review* (May/June 1988), pp. 21–38; and Richard N. Cooper, "The United States as an Open Economy," in *How Open is the U.S. Economy?* ed. Richard N. Cooper (Lexington, Mass.: Lexington Books, 1986), pp. 3–24.

6. In spite of the evidence presented, Nobel economist Milton Friedman believes that the world economy is becoming more fragmented, at least as measured by international trade's share of U.S. gross national product (GNP) over the past one hundred years, or even since the Great Depression. As reported by *Wall Street*

*Journal* columnist Lindley Clark ("Our World Is More Fragmented Than a Century Ago," *Wall Street Journal* [April 13, 1989], p. A20), Friedman believes that the average of U.S. exports and imports of goods and services as a percent of GNP peaked in 1980 and has been coming down since. The recorded fall can be attributed to the reemergence of protectionism in the United States, which has negated the effects of technology. However, careful analysis of the facts of U.S. world trade since World War II, or even since 1980, suggests just the opposite

Clearly, if U.S. exports and imports of goods and services measured in current dollars are summed and divided by GNP measured in current dollars, the resulting ratio declines for the time period studied by Friedman. In 1980 the sum of current-dollar exports and imports represented 24.5 percent of GNP. In 1987 international trade represented 21.6 percent of GNP—an 11.8 percent decline. (However, by 1989, the combined total of current-dollar exports and imports were back up to 24.8 percent of current-dollar GNP.)

However, if the international economy did become more competitive during the 1980–87 period, then internationally traded goods and services might be expected to rise in price less than domestically traded goods and services, which in fact did happen. Between 1980 and 1987, the implicit-price index for all of GNP rose by 37.3 percent, while the implicit price index for exports rose 10.9 percent and the implicit-price index for imports rose 3.1 percent. Thus, a comparison of the ratio of current-dollar exports and imports to current-dollar GNP understates the relative growth of international trade.

The proper comparison is between the sum of U.S. exports and imports in constant dollars (as adjusted by the implicit-price indexes for exports and imports) with U.S. GNP in constant dollars (as adjusted by the implicit-price deflator for GNP). The sum of constant-dollar U.S. exports and imports as a percentage of constant-dollar GNP has been on a decisive upward trend since 1947. That upward trend was only temporarily abated by the two recessions of the early 1980s. Measured properly, the sum of U.S. exports and imports represented 11.4 percent of GNP in 1947, 22.6 percent in 1980, and 25.8 percent in 1987—a 14.2 percent increase in share between 1980 and 1987. Such data suggest that the world economy is becoming progressively less fragmented.

7. Cooper, "The United States as an Open Economy," p. 4. He also reports a decline in the percent of domestically used chromium, nickel, and tin (ibid.).

8. All figures for OECD-Europe and Japan have been obtained from the Organisation for Economic Cooperation and Development's *National Accounts, 1960–1986* (Washington: OECD, 1988). Where appropriate, as noted in the text, exports and imports are valued in U.S. dollars, measured at 1980 price levels and exchange rates. This method of evaluation incorporates a significant risk that the year-to-year figures are not strictly comparable. At the same time, the figures are mainly used to establish the fact of substantial growth in exports and imports, both in real absolute terms and in relation to growth in national production. The observed growth, using 1980 price levels and exchange rates, is in line with measures of growth using OECD volume indexes (see *National Accounts* and compare the relative values on pages 124–25 with the relative values on pages 136–37).

9. OECD-Europe includes Belgium, Denmark, France, Germany, Greece, Ireland, Italy, Luxembourg, the Netherlands, Portugal, Spain, United Kingdom, Austria, Finland, Iceland, Norway, Sweden, Switzerland, and Turkey.

10. U.S. real exports grew by slightly less than fourfold during the 1960–86 period.

11. The GNP implicit-price deflator for fixed private investment was used to adjust the capital flow levels for the effects of inflation.

12. U.S. Department of Commerce figures as reported by David Wessel, "U.S. Debt to Rest of World Increased 40% to $532.5 Billion Last Year," *Wall Street Journal*, June 30, 1989, p. A2.

13. Ibid. Actually, such statistics on the United States as a "debtor nation" can be grossly misleading. Investment assets are computed on the basis of accumulated historical costs, not current economic values. For example, many U.S. foreign assets were acquired many years ago and are now worth far more than their purchase price. One study, which seeks to adjust capital assets for changes in real values over time, suggests that as late as 1987, the United States may have still been a "creditor nation," with net claims on foreigners of between $31 and $231 billion (Michael Ulan and William G. Dewald, "The U.S. Net International Investment Position: The Numbers are Misstated and Misunderstood," U.S. State Department mimeo, February 1988, as reported in Mack Ott, "Is America Being Sold Out?" *Review* [Federal Reserve Bank of St. Louis, March/April 1989], p. 62).

14. The percentage of fixed wealth controlled by foreigners was computed by dividing total foreign assets in the United States ($1,331 billion in 1986) by the gross stock of fixed reproducible tangible wealth ($19,793 billion in 1986). The actual control by foreigners may have been greater in percentage terms, given that foreign assets are assessed at purchase price rather than current market value, that much foreign-owned wealth is held in the names of Americans, and that the methods used in reporting foreign-owned assets are imprecise. Martin and Susan Tolchin complain that "nobody knows the full extent of foreign investment in the United States. Much of it comes across the U.S. borders with the stealth and anonymity of illegal aliens. Lax reporting requirements, hidden ownership, and other circumventions of the laws have made it virtually impossible to keep track of the flood of foreign money" (Tolchin, *Buying into America*, p. 6). See also Linda M. Spencer, *American Assets: An Examination of Foreign Investment in the United States* (Arlington, Va.: Congressional Economic Leadership Institute, July 1988).

15. Spencer, *American Assets*, p. 12.

16. Tolchin, *Buying into America*, pp. 6–8; and Daniel Yergin, "America, a Wholly Owned Subsidiary of . . . ," *New York Times*, March 30, 1988, p. A27.

17. Norman J. Glickman and Douglas P. Woodward, *The New Competitors: How Foreign Investors are Changing the U.S. Economy* (New York: Basic Books, 1989), p. 4.

18. Spencer, *American Assets*, pp. 12–13. Foreign-owned real estate extends beyond "commercial property," but noncommercial ownership is not covered by the surveys undertaken by the Bureau of Economic Analysis of the Department of Commerce. In addition, foreign investments made via joint ventures with U.S. firms are also not included in totals of foreign-owned real estate (ibid., pp. 13–14). However, it must be noted that estimates of foreign ownership in urban areas vary from data source to data source. Relying on data from Washington/Baltimore Regional Association, nationally syndicated columnist Jack Anderson reported in 1989 that "about 64 percent of the real estate in downtown Los Angeles" was owned by foreigners ("Who Owns America?" *Parade* [April 16, 1989], p. 4).

19. Ibid.

20. Roger Kubarych, an economist with Henry Kaufman & Company, estimates that foreign mergers and acquisitions were running at an annual rate of $75 billion in the first six months of 1988, constituting about a quarter of the total merger and acquisition activity in the country (as noted in Leonard Silk, "Economic Scene: "Buying America 'On the Cheap,' " *New York Times*, October 7, 1988, p. 34). No one should assume that the data suggest that the country is being overwhelmed by foreign investment or foreign takeovers of domestic firms. As one Federal Reserve economist has noted, "The number of [U.S.] companies acquired by foreign investors has been on the rise, but it is an inroad rather than an invasion. The number of takeovers in 1987 is not substantially different from the average number of mergers over the last decade. With the increase in global trade, it is likely that foreign acquisitions will be more important to U.S. firms as well as foreign firms" (Eric S. Rosengren, "Is the United States for Sale? Foreign Acquisitions of U.S. Companies," *New England Economic Review* [November/December 1988], p. 55).

21. See Cooper, "The United States as an Open Economy," pp. 15–22.

22. Jeffrey A. Frankel, "International Capital Mobility and Crowding-Out in the U.S. Economy: Imperfect Integration of Financial Markets or of Goods Markets?" in *How Open Is the U.S. Economy?* pp. 34–67; and Fieleke, "Economic Interdependence between Nations."

23. Fieleke, "Economic Interdependence between Nations," pp. 36–37.

24. Spencer, *American Assets*, pp. 19–38.

25. Jagdish Bhagwati, *Protectionism* (Cambridge, Mass.: MIT Press, 1988), pp. 3–4. See also "Why Trade Barriers Will Fall," *The Economist*, April 30, 1988, p. 65.

26. See John C. Goodman and Ramona Marotz-Baden, *Neo-Mercantilism in Latin America* (Dallas: National Center for Policy Analysis, 1988).

27. As reported in Cooper, "The United States as an Open Economy," p. 12. The reported costs of flights are only rough indicators of the actual change in the total cost of travel across the Pacific Ocean. The figures include air fares for different departure (San Francisco and Los Angeles) and arrival (Hong Kong and Tokyo) points and are not always for the exact same type of flights. (For more details on the flights that are being compared, see Cooper.)

28. Bureau of the Census, *Historical Statistics of the United States* (Washington, D.C.: U.S. Government Printing Office, 1975), p. 770; and Bureau of the Census, *Statistical Abstract of the United States* (Washington, D.C.: U.S. Government Printing Office, 1989), p. 593.

29. *Statistical Abstract of the United States* (1989), p. 545.

30. "Business Goes Body Shopping," *Newsweek*, July 10, 1989, pp. 46–47, as cited in Edward Yardeni, "The Triumph of Capitalism," *Topical Study of Prudential-Bache Securities* 7 (August 1989), p. 16.

31. According to one study, more domestic joint ventures were formed per year in the 1980s than in the 15 to 20 years prior to the advent of the 1980s (Kathryn R. Harrigan, *Strategic Flexibility: A Management Guide for Changing Times* [Lexington, Mass.: Lexington Books, 1985], as reported in Rosabeth Moss Kanter, *When Giants Learn to Dance: Mastering the Challenges of Strategy, Management, and Careers in the 1990s* [New York: Simon & Schuster, 1989], p. 120).

32. Kanter, *When Giants Learn to Dance*, p. 120.

33. For more details on the presumed "decline of the American Hegemony," which has been supposedly founded on an erosion of America's industrial base in the postwar decades, see Paul Kennedy, *The Rise and Fall of the Great Powers: Economic Change and Military Conflict from 1500 to 2000* (New York: Random House, 1987), chap. 7.

34. Kenichi Ohmae, "No Manufacturing Exodus, No Great Comeback," *Wall Street Journal*, April 25, 1988, p. 26.

35. Ibid. Using a different approach, in their study for the National Bureau for Economic Research, Robert Lipsey and Irving Kravis also found that U.S. exports of manufacturers from the rest of the world declined from 17.5 percent of world exports in 1966 to 13.9 in 1983. However, the sales of manufactures by U.S. multinational firms from all countries remained stable, between 17 and 18 percent of world trade throughout the 1966–83 period. The shares of world trade of majority-owned U.S. companies from developed countries increased from 6.8 to 8.6 percent of world trade (Robert E. Lipsey and Irving B. Kravis, *The Competitiveness and Comparative Advantage of U.S. Multinationals, 1957–1983* [New York: National Bureau of Economic Research, 1986], as summarized in Robert E. Lipsey, "Changing Patterns of International Investment in and by the United States," *The United States in the World Economy* [Chicago: University of Chicago Press, 1988], pp. 494–95).

36. Reich, "Corporation and Nation," p. 79. For 1985, the U.S. trade deficit with Japan was $43 billion.

37. Bureau of Economic Analysis, unpublished data, as reported in Spencer, *American Assets*, p. 65.

38. Ibid.

39. Murray Weidenbaum, "Government Economy and Government," *Los Angeles Times*, May 7, 1989, op-ed page.

40. As reported in Magnet, "Stars of the 1980s Cast Their Light," p. 67.

41. Ibid.

42. Ned G. Howenstein, "U.S. Affiliates of Foreign Companies: Operations in 1986," *Survey of Current Business* (May 1988), p. 68. According to Howenstein's survey, in 1986 foreigners also paid Americans $87 billion in wages and compensation, exported $51 billion in goods and services, imported $124 billion, owned 15 million acres of U.S. land, and held mineral rights to another 52 million acres (ibid., pp. 59–75).

43. Tolchin, *Buying into America*, p. 17.

44. Exports represented 9.5 percent of GNP in 1986. If employment in the exporting industries is approximately the same percentage of the total employed workers, then the welfare of more than 10 million workers is tied to exports, and the welfare of millions more is tied to imports.

45. I. M. Destler and John S. Odell, *Anti-Protection: Changing Forces in United States Trade Politics* (Washington, D.C.: Institute for International Economics, 1987), chap. 3.

46. Robert L. Rose, "Currency Squeeze: Caterpillar Sees Gains in Efficiency Imperiled by Strength of Dollar," *Wall Street Journal*, April 6, 1990, p. A1.

47. James Madison, *The Federalist*, nos. 9 and 10, (New York: Modern Library, n.d.), pp. 47–61.

48. Tolchin, *Buying into America*, p. 18. For example, in 1984 Shell Oil, a British firm, contributed almost two hundred thousand dollars to congressional campaigns (ibid., p. 279).

49. Spencer, *American Assets*, p. 2.

50. As quoted in Silk, "Economic Scene," p. 34.

51. Anderson, "Who Owns America? p. 6.

52. Tolchin, *Buying into America*, p. 15.

53. Walter B. Wriston, "On Track with the Deficit," *Wall Street Journal*, January 6, 1989, p. A10.

54. This is true because in cartels comprising many members, cheating is more difficult to detect, and each firm stands to gain more by taking customers away from the large number of other firms.

55. One caveat needs to be added: Private cartels have never worked well unless there exists an external agent that enforces, through penalties, the cartel rules. Ongoing competitive markets are trading arenas in which the number of competitors and the cost of collusion are both so large that the formation of a cartel is patently impractical to all firms in the market. Freedom of entry into markets enhances the continuing competitiveness of markets by increasing the number of "potential" cartel members and the cost of forming and maintaining cartels. The market is so large, relative to the productive capacities of individual producers, that no one producer even has an incentive to enlist the services of an outside enforcer (for example, government).

## Chapter 5.   The Empire Cuts Back: From Coercive Government to Competitive Government

1. Paul Kennedy, *The Rise and Fall of the Great Powers: Economic Change and Military Conflict from 1500 to 2000* (New York: Random House, 1987), p. 20. Copyright © 1987 by Random House, Inc., and with permission of Unwin Hyman Ltd.

2. Ibid.

3. Our concerns about Kennedy's claims that America has declined relatively in the world economy are briefly covered in chapter 8. See also Joseph S. Nye, Jr., *Bound to Lead: The Changing Nature of American Power* (New York: Basic Books, 1990); and William J. Baumol, Sue Anne Batey Blackman, and Edward N. Wolff, *Productivity and American Leadership: The Long View* (Cambridge, Mass.: MIT Press, 1989).

4. Adam Smith, *An Inquiry into the Nature and Causes of the Wealth of Nations* (New York: Modern Library, 1937).

5. Ibid., p. 800. Later, Smith emphasized that capital would respond to tax changes because of the impact the changes would have on the comparative rates of return on investment in different countries:

> When, by different taxes upon the necessaries and convenience of life, the owners and employers of capital stock find, that whatever revenue they derive from it, will not, in a particular country, purchase the same quantity of those necessaries and conveniences which an equal revenue would in almost any other, they will be disposed to remove to some other. And when, in order to raise those taxes, all or a greater part of merchants and manufacturers, come to be continually exposed to the mortifying and vexatious visits of the tax-gatherers, this disposition to remove will soon be changed into an actual removal. (ibid., p. 880)

6. At the same time, they understood that economic forces alone would be insufficient constraints. Hence, they laid out precise, written restraints in the Constitution.

7. See Herbert J. Storing, *What the Anti-Federalists Were For: The Political Thought of the Opponents of the Constitution* (Chicago: University of Chicago Press, 1981).

8. James Madison wrote, "By a faction, I understand a number of citizens, whether amounting to a majority or minority of the whole, who are united and actuated by some common impulse or passion, or of interest, adverse to the rights of other citizens, or to the permanent and the aggregate interests of the community (James Madison, *The Federalist*, no. 10 [New York: Modern Library, 1937], p. 54).

9. Ibid., pp. 61–62.

10. Because of the potential for "factions," Madison also argued for a "compound republic," one made up of "distinct and separate departments," as a means of providing a "double security" for the "rights of individuals." If the decision-making process were made sufficiently complicated and if there existed a "multiplicity of interests," then "the rights of individuals, or of the minority, will be in little danger from interested combinations of the majority" (Madison, *The Federalist*, no. 51, pp. 338–39).

11. Again, this is a primary thesis of Madison in *The Federalist*, no. 51.

12. Vincent Ostrom, *The Political Theory of the Compound Republic: A Reconstruction of the Logical Foundations of American Democracy as Presented by the Federalists* (Blacksburg, Va.: Center for the Study of Public Choice/University Books, 1971).

13. In 1986 local taxes in the United States averaged a modest $604 per person. State taxes, however, were 72 percent higher, or $1,039 per person. Still, federal taxes at $3,131 were three times state taxes, and more than five times local taxes on a per capita basis. This means that, in 1986 as a percentage of personal income, local tax receipts averaged slightly more than 4 percent, state tax receipts represented about 7 percent, and federal tax receipts amounted to just over 21 percent.

Furthermore, to compensate for the greater mobility at the lower government levels, we would expect local governments to resort to obtaining a sizable share of their taxes from sources that are not readily moved. For this reason it should be understandable why in 1986 local governments obtained nearly three-quarters of their revenues garnered from their own sources (excluding state and federal revenue sources) from property taxes. By taxing real property relatively heavily, local governments did not have to worry as much about their tax base walking away as they would have had to worry if they had sought to obtain the same amount of revenue from income or sales (which are obviously more mobile than real property). On the other hand, property taxes represented less than 2 percent of state revenue from own sources, and property taxes provide no revenue to the federal government (Tax Foundation, *Facts and Figures on Government Finance: 1988–1989* [Baltimore: Johns Hopkins University Press, 1988]).

The divergence of the average tax rates at the various levels of government cannot be attributed, as has often been suggested, to the federal government's "larger tax base." To see why this supposition represents a misunderstanding of fiscal facts, suppose the tax base is income that can be subject to taxation. The aggregate of incomes received by all residents within all local government jurisdictions combined equals the aggregate of incomes within all state governments combined. Similarly, the aggregate of incomes of all people in the country necessarily equals the aggregate of incomes of all people within the state and local governments.

One of the reasons people may think the federal government has a "larger" tax base than the aggregate of state or local governments is that the federal government has more monopoly power to tap the income and wealth base at its disposal. State and local governments naturally look to the federal government for help in financing programs because such help alleviates their competitive bind.

14. The basic modern theoretical discussion of competitive governments is built around the "Tiebout hypothesis," which is built on idealized assumptions about the ability of people to move among governments but which suggests that highly competitive governments will produce public goods and services efficiently (Charles M. Tiebout, "A Pure Theory of Local Expenditures," *Journal of Political Economy* [October 1956], pp. 416–24). This basic approach to the study of intergovernmental competition is further developed in James M. Buchanan and Richard E. Wagner, "An Efficiency Basis for Federal Fiscal Equalization," *The Analysis of Public Output*, ed. J. Margolis (New York: National Bureau of Economic Research, 1970); James M. Buchanan and Charles J. Goetz, "Efficiency Limits of Fiscal Mobility: An Assessment of the Tiebout," *Journal of Public Economics* (April 1972), pp. 25–43; and Walter E. Oates, "The Effects of Property Taxes and Local Public Spending on Property Values: An Empirical Assessment of Tax Capitalization and the Tiebout Hypothesis," *Journal of Political Economy* (November/December 1969), pp. 957–71.

15. Geoffrey Brennan and James M. Buchanan, *The Power to Tax* (Cambridge: Cambridge University Press, 1985).

16. See Douglass C. North and Robert Paul Thomas, *The Rise of the Western World: A New Economic History* (New York: Cambridge University Press, 1973).

17. When a person purchases a melon at a fruit stand, he or she is actually exchanging government-protected rights to the money for the store owner's rights to do certain things with the melon. Such rights are not all-inclusive. They include eating or selling the melon but not throwing it at passing motorists. Government-enforced property rights enable markets to function in modern democratic societies.

18. Douglass C. North, *Structure and Change in Economic History* (New York: W. W. Norton, 1981).

19. Ibid., pp. 126–27.

20. Ibid., p. 129.

21. Ibid., pp. 133–34.

22. Ibid., pp. 134–35.

23. Ibid., p. 148.

24. Ibid.

25. Ibid., p. 150.

26. Ibid., p. 151.

27. North attributes the France's impaired economic growth to the fiscal drag of taxation and the resulting expansion in the French bureaucracy: "The French economy remained regional in nature and as a result the gains from a growing market were sacrificed. The benefits of competition were lost to numerous local monopolies that not only exploited their legal position but also discouraged innovation" (ibid., p. 150).

28. Ibid., pp. 154–57.

29. Karl Polanyi, *The Great Transformation: The Political and Economic Origins of Our Times* (Boston: Beacon Press, 1944).

30. Ibid., p. 10.

31. Ibid., p. 14.
32. Ibid., p. 19.
33. Ibid., p. 19.
34. Ibid., p. 24.
35. Jean Baechler, *The Origins of Capitalism* (Oxford: Basil Blackwell, 1975), p. 78.
36. Ibid.
37. Ibid., p. 77.
38. Ibid., p. 79.
39. Ibid., pp. 80–82.
40. Ibid., p. 82.
41. Ibid., pp. 82–86.
42. See Barry Basinger, Robert B. Ekelund, Jr., and Robert D. Tollison, "Mercantilism as a Rent-Seeking Society," *Toward a Theory of the Rent-Seeking Society*, ed. James M. Buchanan, Robert D. Tollison, and Gordon Tullock (College Station, Tex.: Texas A & M University Press, 1980), pp. 235–68. This revised perspective on the rise and fall of mercantilism has been expanded in Robert B. Ekelund and Robert D. Tollison, *Mercantilism as a Rent-Seeking Society: Economic Regulation in Historical Perspective* (College Station, Tex.: Texas A & M University Press, 1982).
43. Ibid., p. 244.
44. "Rent seeking" is usually distinguished from "profit seeking." Profit seeking tends to be productive in the sense that, as a consequence of efforts to obtain more profit, the production of goods and services is expanded, resulting in more net value (benefits minus cost) that is divided among buyers and sellers. For example, the creation of new and improved products is normally assumed to be motivated by profit seeking. Like profit seeking, rent seeking is motivated by private gain. However, rent seeking tends to result in restrictions on or curtailment of production and a loss of net value that are normally thought to be the result of the political process. Accordingly, profit seeking is viewed as a positive-sum game, whereas rent seeking is viewed as a negative-sum game. The first two classic studies on rent seeking are Gordon Tullock, "The Welfare Cost of Tariffs, Monopolies, and Theft," *Western Economic Journal* (June 1967), pp. 224–32; and Anne O. Kruger, "The Political Economy of the Rent Seeking Society," *American Economic Review* (June 1974), pp. 291–303. These and other major works on rent seeking are collected in James M. Buchanan, Robert D. Tollison, and Gordon Tullock, eds., *Toward a Theory of the Rent-Seeking Society* (College Station, Tex.: Texas A & M University Press, 1980).
45. Ibid., p. 245.
46. Ibid.
47. For a review of this literature, see Richard J. Cebula, *The Determinants of Human Migration* (Lexington, Mass.: Lexington Books, 1979); and Richard J. Cebula and Milton Z. Kafoglis, "A Note on the Tiebout-Tullock Hypothesis: The Period 1975–1980," *Public Choice* 48, no. 1 (1986), pp. 65–69.
48. Gary J. Miller, *Cities by Contract* (Cambridge, Mass.: MIT Press, 1981), chaps. 6 and 7.
49. B. W. Hamilton, E. S. Mills, and D. Puryear, "The Tiebout Hypothesis and Residential Income Segregation," in *Fiscal Zoning and Land Use Controls*, ed. Edwin S. Mills and Wallace E. Oates (Lexington, Mass.: Lexington Books, 1975), pp. 101–18; V. G. Munley, "An Alternative Test of the Tiebout Hypothesis,"

*Public Choice* 38, no. 2 (1982), pp. 211–17; R. W. Eberts and T. J. Gronberg, "Jurisdictional Homogeneity and the Tiebout Hypothesis," *Journal of Urban Economics* (September 1981), pp. 227–39; and E. M. Gramlich and D. L. Rubinfield, "Micro Estimates of Public Spending Demand Functions and Tests of the Tiebout and Median-Voter Hypothesis," *Journal of Political Economy* (June 1982), pp. 536–60.

50. Robert T. Deacon, "The Expenditure Effect of Alternative Supply Institutions," *Public Choice* 34, no. 3/4 (1979), pp. 381–98.

51. See S. L. Mehay, "The Effect of Government Structure on Special District Expenditures," *Public Choice* 44, no. 2 (1984), pp. 339–48; and S. L. Mehay and R. A. Gonzalez, "Economic Incentives under Contract Supply of Local Government Services," *Public Choice* 46, no. 1 (1985), pp. 79–86.

52. Steven A. Morrison and Clifford Winston, "Deregulated Airline Markets: The Dynamics of Airline Pricing and Competition," *American Economic Review* (May 1990), pp. 389–93.

53. A more complete statement of the theory of the connection between mobility and the cost-effectiveness of government services is covered by one of the authors in Dolores T. Martin and Richard B. McKenzie, "Migration Costs, Bureaucratic Profits, and the Consolidation of Local Governments," *Public Choice* 31, no. 3 (1975), pp. 95–100.

54. Dolores T. Martin and Richard E. Wagner, "The Institutional Framework for Municipal Incorporation: An Economic Analysis of Local Agency Formation Commissions in California," *Journal of Law and Economics* (October 1978), pp. 409–25.

55. This is the conclusion drawn from an extensive review of the relevant literature by Dennis C. Mueller, *Public Choice II* (Cambridge: Cambridge University Press, 1989), pp. 267–68.

56. See S. L. Mehay, "The Effect of Government Structure on Special District Expenditures," *Public Choice* 44, no. 2 (1984), pp. 339–48; and Thomas J. Dilorenzo, "The Expenditure Effects of Restricting Competition in Local Public Service Industries: The Case of Special Districts," *Public Choice* 37, no. 3 (1981), pp. 569–78.

57. See Elchanan Cohn, "Economies of Scale in High School Operations," *Journal of Human Resources* (Fall 1968) pp. 422–34; Werner Z. Hirsch, "Expenditure Implications of Metropolitan Growth and consolidation," *Review of Economics and statistics* (August 1959), pp. 239–40; Werner Z. Hirsch, "Determinants of Public education expenditures," *National Tax Journal* (March 1960), pp. 29–40; Donald D. Osburn, "Economies of Size Associated with High Schools," *Review of Economics and Statistics* (1967); and John Riew, "Economies of Scale in High School Operations," *Review of Economics and Statistics* (August 1966), pp. 280–87.

58. Byron W. Brown, "Achievement Costs, and the Demand for Public Education," *Western Economic Journal* (June 1972) pp. 198–219; and William A. Niskanen, "Student Performance and School District Size," *Florida Policy Review* (Summer 1990), pp. 1–5.

59. Robert J. Staaf, "The Public School System in Transition: Consolidation and Parental Choice," *Budget and Bureaucrats: The Sources of Government Growth* (Durham, N.C.: Duke University Press, 1977), ed. Thomas E. Borcherding, pp. 143–44.

60. See D. R. Cameron, "The expansion of the Public Economy: A Comparative Analysis," *American Political Science Review* (December 1978), pp. 1243–61; Philip

Saunders, "Explaining International Differences in Public Expenditure: An Empirical Study" (Paper presented at a conference of economists, Clayton, Victoria, Canada, 1986); and M. Schneider, "Fragmentation and the Growth of Local Government," *Public Choice* 48, no. 3 (1986), pp. 255–63.

61. Of course, the national tax base could rise but, because of the country's relatively higher tax rates, still be lower than it would otherwise have been because of higher capital outflows or lower capital inflows.

62. These points have been developed by the authors with greater precision in Dwight R. Lee and Richard B. McKenzie, "The Political Economy of Declining Marginal Tax Rates," *National Tax Journal* (March 1989), pp. 79–84.

63. For a review of recent decreases in marginal tax rates of major industrial countries, see Vito Tanzi, "The Response of Other Industrial Countries to the U.S. Tax Reform Act," *National Tax Journal* (September 1987), pp. 339–55. For a review of tax reform efforts in many other world governments, see Joseph Pechman, *World Tax Reform: A Progress Report* (Washington: Brookings Institution, 1988); and Alan Reynolds, "International Tax Competition" (Paper presented at a conference on taxes and growth sponsored by the Manhattan Institute for Public Policy Research, Frankfurt, West Germany, May 30, 1988).

64. F. A. Hayek, *The Constitution of Liberty* (Chicago: University of Chicago Press, 1960), pp. 24–25.

65. Thomas Sowell, *Knowledge and Decisions* (New York: Basic Books, 1980), pp. 217–18.

66. Hayek, *The Constitution of Liberty*, p. 26.

67. These points were at the core of the lifework of Nobel laureate F. A. Hayek; consider only two of Professor Hayek's books, *The Road to Serfdom* (Chicago: University of Chicago Press, 1944); and *Law, Legislation, and Liberty: Rules and Order*, vol. 1 (Chicago: University of Chicago Press, 1973).

68. Mancur Olson, *The Rise and Decline of Nations* (New Haven, Conn.: Yale University Press, 1983).

69. Hedrick Smith, *The Power Game: How Washington Works* (New York: Random House, 1988), pp. 234–36.

70. The positive relationship between politically-inspired rents (or profits) and rent-seeking political activities, and between rent-seeking political activities and legislated redistributive policies is developed in a series of empirical studies collected in Robert E. McCormick and Robert D. Tollison, *Politicians, Legislation, and the Economy* (Boston: Martinus Nijhoff Publishing, Inc., 1981).

71. Of course, it may be that rent-seeking initially expands with a contraction in the power of government, simply because the interest groups may be forced into a more intense struggle over a shrinking (or less-rapidly-expanding) government budget "pie."

72. Researchers have found in cross-country studies a statistically significant inverse relationship between the relative size of the public sector (government expenditures as a percentage of gross domestic product) and the rate of national economic growth and economic efficiency of national economies. Indeed, one study of 115 "market economies" found that after statistically adjusting for factors like the use of capital and labor, a one percentage point increase in government expenditures as a fraction of gross domestic product reduces the country's "technical efficiency" by 1.8 percentage points and the annual average growth rate by approximately

one-tenth of a percentage point (Gerald W. Scully, "The Size of the State, Economic Growth and the Efficient Utilization of National Resources," *Public Choice* [November 1989], pp. 149–64. This general conclusion is reinforced by the work of Daniel Landau in "Government Expenditure and Economic Growth: A Cross-Country Study," *Southern Economic Journal* [January 1983], pp. 783–92; and Michael L. Marlow, "Private Sector Shrinkage and the Growth of Industrialized Economies," *Public Choice* 49 [1986], pp. 143–54).

73. At one time, economists were hard pressed to show that differences in taxes—whether in the form of sales, property, licensing, or corporate income taxes—or public services across regions of the country explained, to any statistically significant degree, business births and location decisions. However, research partly based on improved data sources and econometric techniques is beginning to support the common-sense presumption that taxes do matter to businesses. We cannot help but suspect that these new findings are also a product of the forces identified in this chapter. See Timothy J. Bartik, "Business Location Decisions in the United States: Estimates of the Effects of Unionization, Taxes, and Other Characteristics," *Journal of Business and Economic Statistics* (January 1985), pp. 14–22; Timothy J. Bartik, "Small Business Start-Ups in the United States: Estimates of the Effects of Characteristics of States," *Southern Economic Journal* (April 1989), pp. 1004–18; L. Jay Helms, "The Effect of State and Local Taxes on Economic Growth: A Time-Series-Cross Section Approach," *Review of Economics and Statistics* (November 1985), pp. 574–82; Robert Newman, "Industry Migration and Growth in the South," *Review of Economics and Statistics* (February 1983), pp. 76–86; Leslie E. Papke, "The Location of New Manufacturing Plants and State Business Taxes: Evidence from Panel Data," *Proceedings of the Seventy-Ninth Annual Conference of the National Tax Association* (November 1986), pp. 44–55; and James A. Papke and Leslie E. Papke, "Measuring Differential State-Local Tax Liabilities and Their Implications for Business Investment Location," *National Tax Journal* (September 1986), pp. 357–66.

74. Of course, capital mobility need not affect, to the same degree, the regulatory and fiscal powers of governments. In addition, in response to growing economic constraints, governments, under some circumstances, may seek to substitute more covert regulations for more overt taxes. However, it could still be the case that government regulatory powers have been suppressed; regulatory powers may have only been suppressed less than government fiscal powers.

75. "China Globalized," *Wall Street Journal*, May 22, 1989, p. A14. Reprinted by permission of Dow Jones, Inc.

76. Julia Leung, "Chinese Modernization Drive Flagging: Waning Foreign Confidence Hurts Showcase Province of Jiangsu," *Wall Street Journal*, August 14, 1989, p. A6.

Chapter 6.   The Invisible Hand of Global Competition Contains the Visible Hand of Government Fiscal and Regulatory Powers

1. Alan Reynolds, "A Baedeker to Better Living," *Wall Street Journal*, February 23, 1989, p. A8.

2. The competitive market process is often discussed among professional economists in terms of "perfect competition," the absolute maximum degree of openness

of markets and of efficiency in the allocation of resources. Critics of the market system have quite correctly pointed out that real-world markets have never met the conditions of "perfect competition" (which requires numerous sellers engaged in the production of an identical good in a market that is subject to costless entry and exit). Accordingly, these critics have used the failures of markets to meet the tests of perfect competition to recommend the replacement of markets with government controls and central planning (see Oskar Lange, *On the Economic Theory of Socialism* [New York: McGraw-Hill, 1964]). We are not suggesting that the type of imperfect, real-world competition we are describing requires the strictures of the perfectly competitive market structure, only that the real-world competitive process improves the allocation of resources and thereby helps alleviate pressing wants. Any suggestion that markets should be replaced by government controls overlooks the prospects that the government institutions may allocate scarce resources no better, and perhaps worse, than the market they replace.

3. All figures relating to government outlays as a percent of GDP were obtained from Organisation for Economic Cooperation and Development, *OECD Economic Outlook* (December 1989), p. 179.

4. French government outlays as a percentage of GDP rose from 46.4 in 1980 to 52.4 percent in 1985. Alan Reynolds reports that Australia is in the process of backtracking on gains made in the early 1980s (Alan Reynolds, "Australia Misses the Supply-Side Boat," *Wall Street Journal*, May 23, 1988, p. 23).

5. Vito Tanzi, "The Response of Other Industrial Countries to the U.S. Tax Reform Act," *National Tax Journal* 40, no. 3 (September 1987), p. 344.

6. Ibid.

7. From a table comparing the maximum marginal tax rates on individual income in forty countries between 1979 and 1989, prepared by Alan Reynolds for Polyconomics, Inc., Morristown, N.J., January 1989; and Nicholas McInnes, "U.K.'s Tax Rate Cuts," letter to the editor, *Wall Street Journal*, September 18, 1989, p. A19.

8. The highest marginal tax rate in Australia had been as high 66.7 percent in 1974–75. However, that highest marginal tax rate applied to income equal to nearly six times average worker earnings in 1974–75. The 60 percent marginal tax rate in the 1980s applied to income above twice average worker earnings (as reported in Michael G. Porter and Christopher Trengove, "Tax Reform in Australia," in *World Tax Reform: Case Studies of Developed and Developing Countries*, ed. Michael J. Boskin and Charles E. McLure, Jr. [San Francisco: International Center for Economic Growth and Institute for Contemporary Studies Press, 1990], p. 55).

9. Notice that in the case of the United States, the lowest marginal tax rates rose from 11 percent in 1985 to 15 percent in 1988. One reason is that the amount of income *not* subject to taxation received by those in the lower tax brackets rose between 1985 and 1988.

10. Tanzi, "The Response of Other Industrial Countries to the U.S. Tax Reform Act," pp. 344–45.

11. Tanzi cites several studies on the perverse disincentive effects of high marginal tax rates that may be indicative of concerns of policymakers: David J. Pyle, *The Political Economy of Tax Evasion* (David Hume Institute, 1987); Vito Tanzi, *The Underground Economy in the United States and Abroad* (Lexington, Mass.: Lexington Books, 1982); M. J. McKee, J. J. C. Visser, and P. G. Saunders, "Marginal Tax

Rates on the Use of Labour and Capital in OECD Countries," *OECD Economic Studies* (Autumn 1986); and M. Killingsworth, *Labor Supply* (Cambridge: Cambridge University Press, 1983).

12. At the time of the tax surveys, only two countries expected corporate tax rate increases (Tanzi, "The Response of Other Industrial Countries to the U.S. Tax Reform Act," p. 348). The tax competition among governments is also evaluated, with similar but not identical findings, by Joseph Pechman, ed. *World Tax Reform: A Progress Report* (Washington, D.C.: Brookings Institution, 1988), especially chap. 1. Pechman also found widespread reductions in corporate income taxes, mainly to reduce the disincentive effects on investment of "double taxation" of corporate income taxes.

13. Joseph A. Pechman, "Introduction," in *World Tax Reform: A Progress Report*, p. 4. Pechman's table summarizes the findings of several researchers whose works are included in his edited volume.

14. Ibid.

15. Ibid., p. 5.

16. Canada raised its top marginal rate on corporate income from 51 percent in 1984 to 53 percent in 1986.

17. Pechman, "Introduction," p. 4.

18. Ibid., p. 1.

19. Ibid., p. 7.

20. Tanzi, "The Response of Other Industrial Countries to the U.S. Tax Reform Act," pp. 339–40.

21. Tax collections equal tax rates times people's incomes, which can be affected by government expenditures and regulatory policies.

22. Edward A. Evans, "Australia," in *World Tax Reform: A Progress Report*, p. 17. For even more details on the escalation of marginal tax rates on progressively lower levels of income, see Porter and Trengove, "Tax Reform in Australia," pp. 54–55.

23. Porter and Trengove, "Tax Reform in Australia," pp. 55–57.

24. Ibid., p. 49.

25. The changes in the Australian tax code are outlined in Evans ("Australia," p. 20).

26. Ibid., p. 21. See also Tanzi, "The Response of Other Industrial Countries to the U.S. Tax Reform Act," pp. 347–48.

27. Evans, "Australia," pp. 28–29.

28. Ibid., p. 15.

29. Ibid., p. 38.

30. Between 1981 and 1986 total federal revenues from the wealthiest 1 percent of income earners in the United States rose from 18.1 to 26.1 percent. Between 1979 and 1988, the wealthiest 5 percent in the United Kingdom rose from 24 to 30 percent (Reynolds, "Australia Misses the Supply-Side Boat").

31. David A. Dodge and John H. Sargent, "Canada," in *World Tax Reform: A Progress Report*, p. 49.

32. John Bossons, "The Impact of the 1986 Tax Reform Act on Tax Reform in Canada," *National Tax Journal* 40, no. 3 (September 1987), p. 334.

33. Dodge and Sargent, "Canada," pp. 50–52.

34. Ibid., p. 43.

35. Ibid., pp. 51–52. John Whalley, a Canadian economist, also acknowledged that Canadian tax reforms were "less that outcome of a conscious strategy for improving the Canadian tax system that they [were] a response to pressures generated by falling corporate and personal tax rates around the world and the perception that the Canadian tax system has undermined the economy's international competitiveness" (John Whalley, "Recent Tax Reform in Canada: Policy Responses to Global and Domestic Pressures," in *World Tax Reform*, p. 73).

36. Indeed, observers of the Canadian tax reform movement felt that "harmonization" of the Canadian tax code with the new U.S. code was mandatory, just to eliminate the opportunities for international corporate tax arbitrage:

> The many Canadian and U.S. companies with operations in both countries can utilize transfer pricing to redistribute taxable income between the two countries, and it is exceedingly difficult to devise effective administrative rules to counter transfer pricing that redistributes taxable incomes. Moreover, where pure transfer pricing by itself is insufficient to redistribute taxable income, it is often possible to redistribute operations in order to improve local interest deductions in the higher-tax jurisdictions. Where this is insufficient, borrowing can be redistributed across jurisdictions in order to locate interest deductions in the higher-taxed country. *All of the opportunities for corporate tax arbitrage could result in a significant erosion of the Canadian corporate tax base if Canadian corporate tax rates did not follow U.S. tax rates down* [emphasis added] (Bossons, "The Impact of the 1986 Tax Reform Act on Tax Reform in Canada," p. 333).

37. The key provisions of Canadian tax reform are summarized in Dodge and Sargent, "Canada," pp. 63–68.

38. Whalley, "Tax Reform in Canada," pp. 79, 81.

39. Sargent, "Canada," p. 69.

40. Jens Drejer, "Denmark," in *World Tax Reform: A Progress Report*, p. 79.

41. Total tax revenues from all sources in Denmark constituted 48.5 percent of GDP in 1985. Of the OECD countries, only Sweden had a higher percentage: 50.5. By contrast, total taxes in the United States amounted to 29.2 percent of GDP in 1985 (Pechman, "Introduction," p. 2).

42. The details of the tax reforms that became effective in 1987 are covered in Drejer, "Denmark," pp. 79–92; and Tanzi, "The Response of Other Industrial Countries to the U.S. Tax Reform Act," pp. 350–51.

43. By lowering personal income taxes in Denmark's monetary unit by Kr 5.8 and raising company taxes by Kr6.8, total taxes went up by Kr1 billion (Drejer, "Denmark," p. 89).

44. As cited by Robert Koch-Nielsen, "Denmark: Comment," in *World Tax Reform: A Progress Report*, p. 92.

45. Ibid., p. 93.

46. Jean-Claude Milleron and Didier Maillard, "France," in *World Tax Reform: A Progress Report*, p. 97.

47. Pechman, "Introduction," p. 2.

48. Milleron and Maillard, "France," p. 99.

49. Ibid., p. 98.

50. Ibid., pp. 98–99.

51. "Tax on Wealth Sought by French Government," *New York Times*, July 14, 1988, p. Y28.

52. Milleron and Maillard, "France," p. 102.

53. Ibid., p. 102.

54. *OECD Economic Surveys: France* (Washington, D.C.: Organisation for Economic Cooperation and Development, 1989), pp. 76–77.

55. As quoted in Seth Lipsky, "France's Socialists Still Dangerous, Balladur Says," *Wall Street Journal*, November 12, 1988, p. A15.

56. Adalbert Uelner and Thomas Menck, "Germany," in *World Tax Reform: A Progress Report*, p. 120.

57. Ibid., pp. 121–22.

58. Gerold Krause-Junk, "Germany: Comment," in *World Tax Reform: A Progress Report*, pp. 127–40.

59. "West Germans Deserve a Tax Break," *The Economist*, July 18, 1988, pp. 13–14.

60. "West German Financial Markets," *The Economist*, October 17, 1987, pp. 94–95; and "A Strange German Logic," ibid., p. 14.

61. Aldo Cardarelli and Michele Del Giudice, "Italy," in *World Tax Reform: Progress Report*, pp. 141–42.

62. Ibid., p. 146.

63. In 1984 tax avoidance accounted for 30.5 percent of unreported income; tax evasion accounted for 12.4 percent; and exemptions accounted for 6.9 percent (L. Bernardi and A. Marenzi, "Il Sistema Tributario, Alcune Evidenze per un Intervento Sugli Imponibili," in Banco d'Italia, *Recerce Quantitative e Basi Statistiche per la Politica Economica* [Rome 1987], as reported in Emilio Gerelli and Luigi Bernardi, "Italy: Comment," in *World Tax Reform: A Progress Report*, p. 148).

64. Gerelli and Bernardi, "Italy: Comment," p. 149.

65. Adolfo Battaglia, "Italy's Industrial Policy Challenged by 1992," *Wall Street Journal*, June 27, 1988, p. A15.

66. See Tanzi, "The Response of Other Industrial Countries to the U.S. Tax Reform Act," pp. 349–50. For a longer treatment of tax-reform issues in Japan, see Yukio Noguchi, "Tax Reform Debates in Japan," in *World Tax Reform: Case Studies of Developed and Developing Countries*, pp. 112–25.

67. Keimei Kaizuka, "Japan: Comment," *World Tax Reform: A Progress Report*, p. 163.

68. In 1950 the richest fifth of all households earned 5.8 times more than the poorest fifth of all households. In 1985 the ratio of the richest to poorest fifths of households was down to 2.9 (Atsushi Nagano, "Japan," in *World Tax Reform: A Progress Report*, p. 155).

69. Ibid., p. 160.

70. Ibid., p. 156.

71. Tanzi, "The Response of Other Industrial Countries to the U.S. Tax Reform Act," p. 349.

72. Nagano, "Japan," p. 159.

73. Tanzi, "The Response of Other Countries to the U.S. Tax Reform Act," p. 350.

74. The two reports used to develop this section on Japan disagreed on the

percentage of the reduction in the corporate income tax rate. Pechman figures that the corporate tax rate will fall from 53 percent in 1986 to 52 percent thereafter (Pechman, "Introduction," p. 5). Tanzi indicates that the overall rate will fall from 53 percent to 50 percent (Tanzi, "The Response of Other Industrial Countries to the U.S. Tax Reform Act," p. 350).

75. Nagano, "Japan," p. 156.

76. Tanzi, "The Response of Other Industrial Countries to the U.S. Tax Reform Act," p. 350.

77. Ibid.

78. Susan Chira, "Major Tax Bills Passed in Japan in Long Session," *New York Times*, December 25, 1989, pp. 1Y, 7Y.

79. Ibid., p. 7Y.

80. Flip de Kam, "Netherlands: Comment," in *World Tax Reform: A Progress Report*, p. 181.

81. Hendrik Elle Koning and Dirk Witteveen, "Netherlands," in *World Tax Reform: A Progress Report*, pp. 171–72.

82. Ibid., p. 177.

83. de Kam, "Netherlands: Comment," p. 181.

84. Koning and Witteveen, "Netherlands," p. 177.

85. William McGurn, "New Zealand's Painful Economic Cure," *Wall Street Journal*, October 11, 1988, p. A22.

86. Michael Walker, "Introduction," *The Economic Policies of New Zealand's Labour Government* (speech delivered by Roger Douglas, Vancouver, B.C., Fraser Institute, July 1988), p. 3. The philosophy behind the microeconomic reforms undertaken by New Zealand's Labour Government is covered in some depth in *OECD Economic Surveys: New Zealand* (Paris: Organisation for Economic Cooperation and Development, 1987), and the actual reforms are covered in outline form in *OECD Economic Surveys: New Zealand* (Paris: Organisation for Economic Cooperation and Development, 1989), p. 16.

87. Roger O. Douglas, Minister of Finance, *Statement on Taxation and Benefit Reform* (Wellington, N.Z.: New Zealand Government, 1985), p. 3.

88. Tanzi, "The Response of Other Industrial Countries to the U.S. Tax Reform Act," p. 355.

89. Douglas, *The Economic Policies of New Zealand's Labour Government*, p. 4.

90. Tanzi, "The Response of Other Industrial Countries to the U.S. Tax Reform Act," pp. 351–52.

91. McGurn, "New Zealand's Painful Economic Cure."

92. Ibid.

93. After a bitter and continuing fight with Prime Minister David Lange, who objected to many of the supply-side reforms, Douglas left the cabinet in 1988, after which a spokesman for the National Party suggested that "the intellectual coherence that marked the party's brief flirtation with economic liberalism has disappeared" and that "New Zealand has ceased to be a fashionable anecdote of libertarian experimentation" (Simon Upton, "Douglas Is Back, But Rogernomics Is Not," *Wall Street Journal*, September 13, 1989, p. A17). That does not mean that the New Zealand Labour government has recanted on the Douglas reforms; it only means that the steam was taken out of the reform movement when Douglas left the cabinet. However, it must be noted that Douglas was reelected to the cabinet

as minister of police and immigration in mid-1989, at which point Prime Minister Lange resigned. At this writing Douglas's influence on New Zealand's future economic policy is unclear.

94. Claes Ljungh, "Sweden," in *World Tax Reform: A Progress Report,* p. 187.

95. Ibid., pp. 192–93.

96. Sweden's government also announced that it would attempt to recoup part of the lost revenues from the lower rates by broadening the tax base to include certain heretofore untaxed fringe benefits, raising taxes on financial income and capital gains, and extending the value-added tax. Overall the government planned to lower tax revenues to 56 percent of GDP ("Supply-Side Sweden," *Wall Street Journal,* November 30, 1988, p. A22).

97. Ljungh, "Sweden," p. 193.

98. As repeated in Leif Muten, "Sweden: Comment," in *World Tax Reform: A Progress Report,* p. 211; and "Supply-Side Sweden," *Wall Street Journal.*

99. Lawrence Lindsey, *The Growth Experiment: How the New Tax Policy Is Transforming the U.S. Economy* (New York: Basic Books, 1990), p. 131.

100. Ljungh, "Sweden," p. 197.

101. As reported in Ingemar Hansson and Charles Stuart, "Sweden: Tax Reform in a High-Tax Environment," in *World Tax Reform: Case Studies of Developed and Developing Countries,* pp. 133–34.

102. Ibid. (see fig. 8.5).

103. Ljungh, "Sweden," p. 193.

104. Ibid., p. 200. According to one observer, by the early 1990s the tax schedule may be reduced from a range of 35 to 75 percent to 30 to 50 percent, with the highest marginal rate paid by most full-time workers from 50 to 30 percent (Hansson and Stuart, "Sweden: Tax Reform in a High-Tax Environment," p. 145).

105. Swedish government outlays as a percent of GDP peaked in 1982 at 66.6 percent. In 1985 they were down to 64.5 percent of GDP (see Table 6.1).

106. Ian C. R. Byatt, "United Kingdom," in *World Tax Reform: A Progress Report,* pp. 220–22. According to one estimate, however, the combined marginal tax rate (after all income-based taxes and the VAT are summed) for the "average" worker declined by less than might be thought, from 48.8 percent in 1978–79 to 46.5 percent in 1987–88. The combined marginal tax rate for a worker paying top rates declined from 83.8 percent in 1978–79 to 66.5 percent in 1987–88 (Kent Mathews and Patrick Minford, "Mrs. Thatcher's Economic Policies, 1979–1987," *Economic Policy [October 1987], p. 73).*

107. John Hills, "United Kingdom: Comment," in *World Tax Reform: A Progress Report,* p. 241.

108. This may have been true despite a possible increase in the tax burden of low-income taxpayers (ibid., pp. 241–43).

109. As quoted in "Supply-Side Britain," editorial, *Wall Street Journal,* March 17, 1988, p. A24.

110. Andrew W. Dilnot and J. A. Kay, "Tax Reform in the United Kingdom: The Recent Experience," *World Tax Reform: Case Studies of Developed and Developing Countries,* p. 175. Dilnot and Kay add that the cuts in tax rates "were little more than political gestures and never touched more than a small minority of the population—and in reality, because avoidance was readily possible and endemic, touched even that minority more lightly than might be thought. None of these comments

are meant to deny that the reform process is a welcome one, but its significance can be, as has been, exaggerated" (ibid.).

111. For example, Mexican economist Oscar Vera Ferrer estimates that in 1985 Mexico's underground economy represented 38 percent of GNP and caused the government to lose 1,278 billion pesos in tax revenue from "legal-activity sectors of the underground economy" (as reported in Marvin Alisky, "Tapping the Resources of Mexico's Underground Economy," *Wall Street Journal*, December 30, 1988, p. A7). Hernando de Soto estimates that Peru has come to be a "country in which 48 percent of the economically active population and 61.2 percent of work hours are devoted to informal activities which contribute 38.9 percent of the gross domestic product recorded in the national accounts" (Hernando de Soto, *The Other Path: The Invisible Revolution in the Third World* [New York: Harper & Row, 1988], p. 12).

112. As reported in Eytan Sheshinski, "The 1988 Tax Reform Proposal in Israel," in *World Tax Reform: Case Studies of Developed and Developing Countries*, p. 95.

113. For example, when Rajiv Gandhi became prime minister of India, the highest marginal tax rates were reduced from 65 to 50 percent. Colombia lowered its highest rates from 56 percent in 1979 to 30 percent in 1988. In 1986 Bolivia substituted a 10 percent flat tax and a 10 percent VAT tax (deductible against the income tax) for the progressive income tax rate system. Israel has reduced its highest marginal tax rate from 66 to 48 percent since 1985. Turkey reduced its income tax rate range from 40 to 75 percent before 1985–86 to 25 to 50 percent today. In 1986 Jamaica lowered its marginal tax rate, which was 57.5 percent on $700 of earned income, to 33 percent on $1,500 of earned income. See Alan Reynolds, "International Tax Competition," (paper prepared for delivery at a conference on taxes and growth sponsored by the Manhattan Institute for Policy Research, Frankfurt, West Germany, May 30, 1988); and "A Baedeker to Better Living."

Reynolds's survey of national tax rates has been supported by an even more complete survey of the reduction in national tax rates undertaken by the U.S. Treasury. It found that of the eighty-six industrial and less-developed countries for which data were available, fifty-five (or 64 percent) lowered their highest marginal tax rates between 1985 and 1989, and only two countries (Luxembourg and Lebanon) increased their highest marginal tax rates. The top marginal rate reduction averaged 16 percent for all eighty-six countries (including those countries that did not change their rates and the two that increased them). The average top rate fell from 56 percent in 1985 to 47 percent in 1989 (Bruce Barlett, "The World-Wide Tax Revolution," *Wall Street Journal*, August 29, 1989, p. A16).

114. Considerable caution is required in interpreting the percentage drop in the average tax rates of the countries listed. This is because the income level at which the maximum marginal tax rate becomes effective, which also declined in many countries' tax reform efforts, is also an important determinant of the incentive impact of the marginal tax rate reduction. See Reynolds, "A Baedeker to Better Living."

115. India has engaged in extensive tax reform to stimulate domestic investment and to woo foreign investors. Top rate on earned income was, accordingly, reduced from 65 to 50 percent after Prime Minister Rajiv Gandhi took over ("India's Tax Reform Seeks to Lure More Investment," *Far Eastern Economic Review* [January 7, 1988], pp. 48–49).

116. The potential for reregulation under the Bush administration is covered in Melinda Warren and Kenneth Chilton, *Regulation Rebound: Bush Budget Gives Regulation a Boost* (St. Louis: Center for the Study of American Business, Washington University, 1990).

117. The material on deregulation practices of OECD members has been drawn from "Deregulation and Privatization," *OECD Observer* 140 (May 1986), pp. 14–17.

118. The microeconomic, supply-side policy changes instituted under the Thatcher government are reviewed in *OECD Economic Surveys: United Kingdom* (Paris: Organisation for Economic Cooperation and Development, 1988).

119. In several instances profits of the deregulated and privatized British industries soared, at times doubling and tripling (Mathews and Minford, "Mrs. Thatcher's Economic Policies, 1979–1987," p. 69).

120. *OECD Economic Surveys: France* (Paris: Organisation for Economic Cooperation and Development, 1988), p. 63.

121. Ibid., p. 69. The OECD researchers also concluded that "job-saving measures in ailing industries in many cases have served only to postpone layoffs which, in the end, took place in much worse conditions and at a considerably greater budgetary cost"; that the aid "produced distortions that have adversely affected external performance"; and that the policies "may have encouraged a 'wait-and-see' attitude, based on the idea that aid is a right" (ibid., pp. 65–69).

122. Ibid., p. 64 (table 25).

123. Ibid., pp. 70–71.

124. Ibid., pp. 71–73.

125. Steven Greenhouse, "Spain's Daring Experiment in 'Supply-Side Socialism,'" *New York Times*, February 13, 1989, pp. Y19, Y30.

126. "Indonesia Announces Steps to Deregulate Its Economy," *Wall Street Journal*, November 22, 1988, p. A6.

127. For a history of the deregulation of financial markets in the United States, see Thomas F. Cargill and Gillian G. Garcia, *Financial Reform in the 1980s* (Stanford, Calif.: Hoover Institution Press, 1985).

128. Alan Greenspan, in a statement (April 4, 1990) before a task force of the Subcommittee on Financial Institutions Supervision, Regulation and Insurance of the House of Representatives Committee on Banking, Finance and Urban Affairs, as published in *Federal Reserve Bulletin* (June 1990), p. 439.

129. Two important treatises of bureaucratic theory that influenced much subsequent public-choice thought are Gordon Tullock, *The Politics of Bureaucracy* (Washington, D.C.: Public Affairs Press, 1965); and William A. Niskanen, *Bureaucrats and Representative Government* (Chicago: Aldine-Atherton, 1971).

130. See Thomas E. Borcherding, ed., *Budgets and Bureaucrats: Sources of Government Growth* (Durham, N.C.: Duke University Press, 1977).

131. The theory, economic benefits, and political efficacy of the privatization movement are developed by Stuart Butler, one of the leading proponents of privatization, in *Privatizing Federal Spending: A Strategy to Eliminate the Deficit* (New York: Universe Books, 1985).

132. For a review of the growth in privatization in the United States, especially at the state and local levels, and around the world in the 1980s, see Philip E.

Fixler, Robert W. Poole, and Lynn Scarlet, *Privatization 1989: Third Annual Report on Privatization* (Santa Monica, Calif.: Reason Foundation, 1989).

133. David F. Linowes, *Privatization: Toward More Effective Government* (Washington, D.C.: Executive Office of the President, 1988), p. 3.

134. The political appeal of privatization is developed in Butler, *Privatizing Federal Spending*, and Robert W. Poole, Jr., "Stocks Populi: Privatization Can Win Bipartisan Support," *Policy Review* (Fall 1988), pp. 24–29.

135. Philip E. Fixler, Jr., and Robert W. Poole, Jr., *Privatization 1988: Second Annual Report on Privatization* (Santa Monica, Calif.: Reason Foundation, 1988), p. 4; and *Privatization 1989, p. 5.*

136. Ibid.

137. *Privatization 1988*, p. 20.

138. John Redwood, "Privatization: The Case of Britain," in *Privatization and Development*, ed. Steve H. Hanke (San Francisco: International Center for Economic Growth, 1987), pp. 181–88.

139. L. Gray Cowan, "A Global Overview of Privatization," in *Privatization and Development*, p. 8.

140. Hoann S. Lublin, "U.K. Steams over Water and Electricity," *Wall Street Journal*, October 12, 1989, p. A13.

141. Cowan, "A Global Overview of Privatization," pp. 23–24.

142. Barbara Toman, "Thatcher Government Plans Legislation to Ease Takeovers, Sell State Utilities," *Wall Street Journal* (November 23, 1988), p. A11. See also Lublin, "U.K. Steams over Water and Electricity," p. A13.

143. Cowan, "A Global Overview of Privatization," p. 25.

144. *OECD Economic Surveys: Germany* (Washington, D.C.: Organisation for Economic Co-operation and Development, 1989), pp. 55–57.

145. Cowan, "A Global Overview of Privatization," pp. 25–26.

146. Greenhouse, "Spain's Daring Experiment in 'Supply-Side Socialism,'" p. 30.

147. Cowan, "A Global Overview of Privatization," p. 27.

148. "Meeker Mandarins," *The Economist*, December 7, 1985, p. 26.

149. Cowan, "A Global Overview of Privatization," pp. 27–28.

150. Ibid., p. 32.

151. Ibid., p. 32. See also Ted M. Ohashi, "Privatization: The Case of British Columbia," *Privatization and Development*, pp. 189–94.

152. Fixler and Poole, *Privatization 1988*, pp. 28–32. The privatization efforts of several developed and less-developed countries are covered in *Privatization: Policies, Methods, and Procedures* (Manila, Philippines: Asian Development Bank, 1985).

153. The numbers are approximate because of missing data on the number of state enterprises in several underdeveloped countries. According to the World Bank study, Guinea had 65 state enterprises in 1980. It liquidated or closed 16 and targeted for sale 43 in the 1980s. Brazil had 527 state enterprises in 1980, closed or liquidated 12, targeted 155 for sale, and sold 27 by 1987. Chile had 421 state enterprises and sold 133. For information on more countries, see Elliot Berg and Mary M. Shirley, *Divesture in Developing Countries* (Washington, D.C.: World Bank, 1987), tables 1, 2, and 3.

154. "A Private Sale" *Wall Street Journal*, March 1, 1990, p. A18.

155. Ibid., p. 3.

156. In the summer of 1988, Jamaica was hit by two deadly and very destructive hurricanes. The government avoided many of the usual bottlenecks in the relief efforts by relying more extensively than it had in the past on the profit motive and private distribution system. The former prime minister of Jamaica reported that under the new privatized system, problems persisted, but "the government is thus spared the considerable additional administrative expense, and the recipients are spared the bureaucratic entanglements that might otherwise be involved" (Edward Seaga, "Jamaica Privatizes Disaster Relief," *Wall Street Journal*, October 28, 1988, p. A15).

157. Abel Aganbegyan, *Inside Perestroika: The Future of the Soviet Economy* (New York: Harper & Row, 1989), as quoted in "Soviet Economists' Call for Radical Reform," *Wall Street Journal*, October 2, 1989, p. A22.

158. James F. Smith, "Latin America Converts to Salvation of Free Market," *Commercial Appeal* (Memphis, Tenn), October 10, 1989, p. A4.

159. Roberto Maksoud, "Brazilian Politicians: Changing the Old Populist Line," *Wall Street Journal*, October 6, 1989, p. A11.

160. Laurence S. Moss, "A Traveler's View of Emerging Capitalism in China," in *Economics*, 2nd ed., ed. David R. Kamerschen, Richard B. McKenzie, and Clark Nardinelli, (Boston: Houghton Mifflin, 1989), p. 946.

161. Ibid., p. 947.

162. For a review of the economic reforms in China, see Roger H. Gordon, "Economic Reform in the People's Republic of China: 1979–1988," in *World Tax Reform: Case Studies of Developed and Developing Countries* (San Francisco: International Center for Economic Growth and the Institute for Contemporary Studies Press, 1990), pp. 190–203.

163. Ibid., p. 191.

164. Ibid., p. 194.

165. Ibid., p. 193.

166. Ibid., p. 198.

167. Ibid., p. 203.

168. Douglas, *The Economic Policies of New Zealand's Labour Government*, p. 6.

169. Jack F. Bennett, "A Plea for Stable Principles," in *Tax Policy in the Twenty-First Century*, ed. Herbert Stein (New York: John Wiley and Sons, 1988), p. 179.

170. As reported in Alan A. Waters, "Political Realities in the New Century," in *Tax Policy in the Twenty-First Century*, ed. Herbert Stein (New York: John Wiley and Sons, 1988), p. 196.

171. Ibid.


Chapter 7.   Quicksilver Commissars: From the Propaganda of Success to the Provenance of Competitiveness

1. Popov, characterizing the Soviet Union's reluctance to forgo central planning over the next five years, as quoted in Francis X. Clines, "Soviet Deputies Fault Gorbachev: Plan Is Called the Old 5-Year System in a New Guise," *New York Times*, December 14, 1989, pp. Y1, Y9.

2. See Alvin Rabushka, *The New China* (San Francisco: Pacific Institute, 1987).

3. Mikhail Gorbachev, *Perestroika: New Thinking for Our Country and the World* (New York: Harper & Row, 1987). Gorbachev's criticisms of the warped incentives under the Soviet economic system have been amplified by his chief economic adviser Abel Aganbegyan in *Inside Perestroika: The Future of the Soviet Economy* (New York: Harper & Row, 1989).

4. Gorbachev, *Perestroika*, pp. 54–55.

5. Ibid., p. 49.

6. Ibid., p. 30.

7. Ibid.

8. Ibid., p. 31.

9. Ibid.

10. Ibid., p. 97.

11. In 1988 Gorbachev sought constitutional changes that would permit more true democracy and, as a result, would increase the reliance on decentralization of political decision making. He proposed the creation of a new national parliament composed of elected members from throughout the Soviet Union, which would assume decision-making powers once held by the Communist party (Philip Taubman, "Gorbachev Plans Approved by Party," *New York Times*, November 29, 1988, p. A6).

12. As reported by Andrei Kuteinkov (a Soviet economics correspondent) "The Emerging Private Sector," *Wall Street Journal*, August 15, 1989, p. A14.

13. As quoted in Bill Keller, "Gorbachev Urges Freeing of Farms from Collectives," *New York Times*, October 14, 1988, p. Y1.

14. Ibid.

15. Caspar W. Weinberger, "Too Soon to Slash Defense," *New York Times*, November 28, 1989, p. Y27.

16. "Soviet Premier Says Cutback Could Reach 33% for Military," *New York Times* (June 8, 1989), p. Y1, as quoted in Edward Yardeni, "The Triumph of Capitalism," *Prudential-Bache Topical Study* 17 (August 1989), p. 6.

17. Paul Blustein and John M. Berry, "Unemployment, but Also a 'Peace Dividend,' " *Washington Post National Weekly*, December 4, 1989, p. 8.

18. Molly Moore and George C. Wilson, "The Pentagon's Quick Weight-Loss Program," *Washington Post National Weekly*, December 4, 1989, p. 7.

19. As reported in "Still an Empire," *Wall Street Journal*, October 3, 1989, p. A26.

20. Weinberger, "Too Soon to Slash Defense."

21. Gorbachev went from secretary of the Komsomol Committee in the 1950s to the Supreme Soviet of the USSR in 1970 and then to a member of the Politburo of the Central Committee of the Communist Party in 1980.

22. Dimitri K. Simes, "The New Soviet Challenge," *Foreign Policy* (Summer 1984), p. 124.

23. As reported in Joseph L. Nogee and Richard H. Donaldson, *Soviet Foreign Policy Since World War II* (New York: Pergamon Press, 1981), p. 149.

24. Yardeni, "The Triumph of Capitalism," p. 6. According to a recent report from the Institute for Contemporary Studies, the CIA has historically overestimated Soviet national income by as much as a third. As a result, the impact of defense expenditures on the economy has been historically underestimated (see Henry S. Rowan and Charles Wolf, Jr., eds., *The Impoverished Superpower: Perestroika and the*

*Soviet Military Burden* [San Francisco: Institute for Contemporary Studies, 1990]).

25. U.S. defense outlays represented 13.5 percent of GNP in 1952, 9.5 percent in 1960, and 6.9 percent in 1972 (down from 9.6 percent in 1968). Defense expenditures were scheduled to represent 5.5 percent of GNP in the 1990 federal budget (Executive Office of the President, Office of Management and Budget, *Historical Tables: Budget of the United States Government: Fiscal Year 1990* [Washington, D.C.: U.S. Government Printing Office, 1989], table 6.2). Two years earlier, defense expenditures were projected to represent 6.1 percent of GNP in the 1990 budget (Executive Office of the President, Office of Management and Budget, *Historical Tables: Budget of the United States Government: Fiscal Year 1988* [Washington, D.C.: U.S. Government Printing Office, 1987], table 6.2).

26. Interview with Stansfield Turner, former director of the CIA, *U.S. News & World Report*, May 16, 1977, p. 24. See also Dwight K. Lee, "Arms Negotiation, the Soviet Economy, and Democratically Induced Delusions," *Contemporary Policy Issues*, October 1986, pp. 22–37.

27. Based on data computed by the authors from Central Intelligence Agency, *Handbook of Economic Statistics, 1988* (Springfield, Va.: National Technical Information Service, September 1988), p. 65.

28. As Gorbachev's chief economist, Abel Aganbegyan, has acknowledged, "Other countries have raced ahead in their standard of living. . . . The most characteristic aspect of our economy are totally distorted production costs and norms of industrial investment, huge losses and unutilized possibilities." (*Inside Perestroika*, p. 227).

29. F. A. Hayek, *The Road to Serfdom* (Chicago: University of Chicago Press, 1944).

30. Padma Desai, *Perestroika In Perspective: The Design and Dilemma of Soviet Reform* (Princeton, N.J.: Princeton University Press, 1989).

Chapter 8.    Perestroika, American Style: The Newly Competitive U.S. Economy

1. The outlays of *all* governments are depicted because of the ability of outlays to be shifted among the various levels of government. An increase in federal outlays may be offset by a decrease in state outlays due to a shift in the responsibility of programs, with no necessary change in the net burden of government on the economy.

2. When the time periods for the two trend lines are changed from 1960 to 1975 and 1975 to 1989, much the same findings are revealed. Also note that there was virtually no growth in the outlays as a percentage of GNP in the 1980s, as evidenced by the fact that the bars in figure 10.1 are more or less level.

3. State and local government expenditures from their own sources stood at 10 percent of GNP in 1988. See Executive Office of the President, Office of Management and Budget, *Historical Tables: Budget of the United States Government: Fiscal Year 1990* (Washington, D.C.: U.S. Government Printing Office, 1989), pp. 365–66.

4. Total real-dollar (1982) federal outlays increased by $203 billion, or 29 percent, between 1980 and 1989. National defense expenditures rose by $86 billion, or 52 percent, during the same time period [Executive Office of the President, Office of

Management and Budget, *Budget of the United States Government: Fiscal Year 1989* (Washington, D.C.: U.S. Government Printing Office, 1989), pp. 6g–42].

5. See Melinda Warren and Kenneth Chilton, *Regulation Rebound: Bush Budget Gives Regulation a Boost* (St. Louis: Center for the Study of American Business, Washington University, 1990), p. 4.

6. Ibid., p. 5.

7. See Milton and Rose Friedman, *Free to Choose: A Personal Statement* (New York: Harcourt Brace Jovanovich, 1980), pp. 190–91. See also Richard B. McKenzie, *Bound to Be Free* (Stanford, Calif.: Hoover Institution Press, 1982), p. 27.

8. The page counts reported in the text are not the actual number of pages, but the number of pages that would have been included if all pages in the 1936–1987 volumes were the same in terms of words per page as the 1988 volume. The actual page count for 1936 was 2,411. The number of words per page was reduced by approximately 24 percent in 1978.

9. The growth of the actual number of government regulations probably slowed by more under Carter than is indicated in figure 8.6. This is because many of the pages in the volumes of the late 1970s were probably taken up with the deregulations of several key industries.

10. For a vivid, graphical account of the growth in federal regulatory agencies, see Murray Weidenbaum, "The Benefits of Regulatory Reform," in *Regulation and Deregulation*, ed. Jules Blackman (Indianapolis: Bobbs-Merrill, 1981), p. 54.

11. The history of the regulation movement is developed in Larry Gerston, Cynthia Fraleigh, and Robert Schwab, *The Deregulated Society* (Pacific Grove, Calif.: Brooks/Cole, 1988), chap. 2.

12. Ibid., p. 42.

13. Stephen Koepp, "Rolling Back Regulation," *Time*, July 6, 1987, p. 51.

14. Ibid.

15. William A. Niskanen, *Reaganomics: An Insider's Account of the Policies and the People* (New York: Oxford University Press, 1988), p. 117.

16. Ibid.

17. Under the so-called bubble policy concept, firms were allowed to alter the levels of pollution emitted at various locations as long as they met overall emission standards for the whole area. Emission standards, to a limited degree, were converted into "rights to pollute," which could be traded within defined limits. See Bruce Yandle, "The Emerging Market in Air Pollution Rights," *Regulation* (July/August, 1978), pp. 21–29; and Michael H. Levin, "Building a Better Bubble at the EPA," *Regulation* (March/April 1985), pp. 32–42.

18. Between 1979 and 1988 the number of mergers between direct competitors was six times the number recorded between 1970 and 1979, according to Robert Pitofsky, dean of the Georgetown University Law Center and professor of antitrust law. However, the number of federal government challenges in the 1979–88 period was reduced to one-third the number in the earlier period (as reported in Stephen Labaton, "Business and the Law: New Leadership's Antitrust Policy," *New York Times*, October 17, 1988, p. Y26).

19. Niskanen, *Reaganomics*, p. 136.

20. For a critical review of the Reagan administration's deregulatory efforts, see Susan J. Tolchin and Martin Tolchin, *Dismantling America: The Rush to Deregulate* (Boston: Houghton Mifflin, 1983), chap. 3.

21. Niskanen, *Reaganomics*, p. 125.

22. Ibid., p. 133.

23. Justice Department outlays rose rapidly in constant (1982) dollars from $1.3 billion in 1968 to $3.6 billion in 1976, after which they fell equally rapidly to $2.6 billion in 1982. By 1987 real Justice Department outlays had recovered to $3.8 billion. As a percentage of the federal budget, Justice Department outlays peaked at .7 percent in 1974 and were down to .4 percent of the budget from 1980 to 1987. As a percentage of GNP, Justice outlays peaked at .14 percent in 1975, then dropped to .1 percent or below for the 1980–87 period.

24. Niskanen, Reaganomics, p. 131.

25. Robert W. Crandall, "What Ever Happened to Deregulation?" in *Assessing the Reagan Years*, ed. David Boaz (Washington, D.C.: Cato Institute, 1988), p. 271.

26. Murray Weidenbaum, *Rendezvous with Reality: The American Economy after Reagan* (New York: Basic Books, 1988), p. 9.

27. These costs are summarized in table form in Crandall, "What Ever Happened to Deregulation?" p. 286.

28. Kit D. Farber and Gary L. Rutledge, "Pollution Abatement and Control Expenditures," *Survey of Current Business* (July 1986), pp. 94–105; (May 1987), pp. 21–25.

29. Cost figures include only capital expenditures (Data Resources, Inc., "Real Capital Expenditures on Occupational Safety and Health," as reported in Crandall, "What Ever Happened to Deregulation?" p. 286).

30. Robert W. Crandall et al., *Regulating the Automobile* (Washington, D.C.: Brookings Institution, 1986), pp. 36–38.

31. See Jagdish Bhagwati, *Protectionism* (Cambridge, Mass.: MIT Press, 1988), chap. 1; or "Why Trade Barriers Will Fall," *Economist*, April 30, 1988, p. 65.

32. All of the Reagan administration's protectionist actions are outlined in Sheldon L. Richman, "The Reagan Record on Trade: Rhetoric Vs. Reality," *Cato Policy Analysis* (Washington: Cato Institute, May 30, 1988). The impact of the VER for steel is evaluated in Arthur Denzau, *How Import Restraints Reduce Employment* (St. Louis: Center for the Study of American Business, Washington University, June 1987); and the impact of the VER for automobiles is considered in Arthur Denzau, "The Japanese Automobile Cartel: Made in the USA," *Regulation* 1 (1988), pp. 11–16. Denzau shows in both studies that the VERs have destroyed significantly more jobs in the rest of the domestic economy than they saved in the protected industries.

33. The Multifiber Agreement (MFA) may also be imposing an annual additional $3 billion on European economies and $11 billion on underdeveloped economies (John Whalley and Irene Trela, *Do Developing Countries Lose from the MFA?* [Cambridge, Mass.: National Bureau of Economic Research, 1988]).

34. As reported in Bhagwati, *Protectionism*, p. 49.

35. "As reported in "America's Trade Policy: Perestroika in Reverse," *The Economist*, February 1989, p. 59, and cited in Joseph S. Nye, Jr., *Bound to Lead: The Changing Nature of American Power* (New York: Basic Books, 1990), p. 206.

36. The Canada Free Trade Agreement eliminates by the start of 1999 virtually all trade barriers to the flow of goods and services between the United States and Canada. The Omnibus Trade Act extends the president's authority to negotiate

trade agreements, expands presidential authority to retaliate against "unfair" trade practices, and provides relief for U.S. industries hurt by imports if they improve their "competitiveness." It also authorizes $1 billion for worker-retraining programs.

37. Murray Weidenbaum, "International Trade: Better than Congress," in *Assessing the Reagan Years*, p. 260.

38. By making the restrictions very product- and country-specific, importers have been able to change the nature of their products and the countries of origin. For example, restrictions on imported coats from Hong Kong can be circumvented by using "vests" (coats without sleeves that are attached after they arrive) that are produced in Hong Kong and shipped to Korea before being sent to the United States. This argument is developed in Bhagwati, *Protectionism*, pp. 54–59.

39. If the Reagan administration had had its way with Congress, the minimum wage would have decreased even faster for young workers. The Reagan administration advocated but failed to obtain from Congress its a "subminimum" or "youth opportunity" wage of $2.50 an hour for teenage workers, and the Bush administration got its proposed "training wage," which meant that new employees could be paid $3.35 an hour for up to six months if they were in a training program.

40. See Richard B. McKenzie, *The New York Times and the Minimum Wage: A Turbulent History* (unpublished manuscript, Economics and Finance Department, University of Mississippi, 1990).

41. Ibid.

42. In 1976 the Labor Department's outlays as a percentage of total federal outlays peaked at 6.9 percent. They were down to 2.1 percent of total federal outlays in 1988.

43. Morgan O. Reynolds, *Making America Poorer: The Cost of Labor Law* (Washington, D.C.: Cato Institute, 1987).

44. We say "may be" because a decline in union membership could be attributable to greater governmental involvement in labor markets. When government provides workers with benefits or mandates that employers must provide those benefits, the government may make unions less useful. Also, the decline in unions' presence in labor markets may be attributable to many of the same forces that cause a decline in government power. Union supporters have argued forcefully that "capital flight" from the United States is partially a product of capital mobility (Barry Bluestone, Bennett Harrison, and Lawrence Baker, *Corporate Flight: The Causes and Consequences of Economic Dislocation* [Washington, D.C.: The Progressive Alliance, 1981]).

45. Union membership in numbers and as a share of the labor force has been estimated based on the U.S. membership/civilian labor ratios using data from Bureau of the Census, *Statistical Abstract of the United States: 1989* (Washington, D.C.: U.S. Government Printing Office, 1989); and from Barry T. Hirsch and John T. Addison, *The Economic Analysis of Unions* (Boston: Allen & Unwin, 1986), p. 47. The Hirsch/Addison ratios for union membership are higher than the ones reported because the whole U.S. labor force, which includes the military, is larger than the civilian labor force.

46. Union membership in private firms (as opposed to government bureaucracies) has fallen dramatically and continuously since the early 1950s, from more than 38 percent of the private-sector labor force in 1952 to 14 percent in 1986. Total union membership as a percentage of the total labor force continued to rise through much of the 1960s because of the growth in public-sector union membership growth.

(For a review of the data on growth and decline, see Richard B. Freeman, "Contraction and Expansion: The Divergence of Private Sector and Public Sector Unionism in the United States," *Journal of Economic Perspective* [Spring 1988], pp. 63–88; and Melvin W. Reder, "The Rise and Fall of Unions: The Public Sector and the Private," *Journal of Economic Perspective* [Spring 1988], pp. 89–110.)

47. For a review of these arguments, see Richard B. McKenzie, *The American Job Machine* (New York: Universe Books, 1988), chap. 5; and Richard B. McKenzie, *The Mythical U-Turn in Worker Pay* (St. Louis: Center for the Study of American Business, Washington University, 1990).

48. Barry Bluestone and Bennett Harrison, *The Great American Job Machine: The Proliferation of Low Wage Employment in the U.S. Economy* (Washington, D.C., Joint Economic Committee, U.S. Congress, 1986).

49. The number of employees of the Labor Department fell by 22 percent, or from 22,400 to 18,200, between 1980 and 1985 (Reynolds, *Making America Poorer*, p. 325).

50. The political, more popular cases for the tax-rate reductions and for tax reform were developed in Jude Wanniski, *The Way the World Works* (New York: Simon & Schuster, 1978); George Gilder, *Wealth and Poverty* (New York: Basic Books, 1980); and Robert E. Hall and Alvin Rabushka, *Low Tax, Simple Tax, Flat Tax* (New York: McGraw-Hill, 1983).

51. The benefits of the rate reductions in the 1981 tax act were partially offset by the Tax Equity and Fiscal Responsibility Act of 1982, which increased federal receipts by approximately $100 billion.

52. John Makin contends that the Economic Recovery Tax Act of 1981 had much the same effect on tax revenues as a percentage of GNP as did the Tax Reform Act of 1969. Both lowered the inflation-induced jump in tax revenues as a percentage of GNP back to the long-run upward trend (or at least to within one standard deviation of the upward sloping trend). This is especially true after adjustments are made for the 1981–82 recessions ("The Reagan Years: A Fiscal Perspective," *The AEI Economist* [April 1988], p. 3).

53. The Tax Reform Act of 1986 introduced two top marginal rates, 28 and 33 percent, with 33 percent applied to a limited range of income. For example, for married people, filing joint returns, all income between $71,900 and $149,250 was taxed at a marginal rate of 33 percent in 1989. All income above $149,250 was taxed at a top marginal rate of 28 percent (*U.S. Master Tax Guide: 1989* [Chicago: Commerce Clearing House, 1988], p. 21).

54. As computed by C. Hulten and J. O'Neill, "Tax Policy," in *The Reagan Experiment* (New York: Urban Institute, 1982); and reported in Olivier Jean Blanchard, "Reaganomics," *Economic Policy*, (October 1987), p. 22.

55. However, it needs to be noted that the downward trend in taxes on the rich did not start with the Reagan administration. In 1970 the average tax rate of the highest tenth of the income distribution paid average tax rates of 30.7 percent (Joseph Pechman, *Who Paid the Taxes?* [Washington, D.C.: Brookings Institution, 1986], as reported in Blanchard, "Reaganomics," p. 42).

56. The reduction in the differential treatment of structures and equipment under previous tax laws may have improved economic efficiency somewhat (Blanchard, "Reaganomics," p. 23).

57. The actual net impact of the 1981 tax law on national earnings and aggregate

federal tax collections through 1985 has been computed by Harvard economist Law-rence Lindsey, using an economic model of the National Bureau of Economic Re-search, in *The Growth Experiment: How the New Tax Policy Is Transforming the U.S. Economy* ([New York: Basic Books, 1990], pp. 53–80).

58. Ibid., p. 83. Lindsey's findings have been endorsed by the Congressional Budget Office ("CBO Responds to Lindsey," *Tax Notes* [(May 1987]).

59. Lindsey, *The Growth Experiment*, p. 76.

60. Ibid., p. 85.

61. Ibid., p. 90.

62. Total receipts as a percentage of GNP remained within a very narrow band—30.1 to 32.2 percent—from 1972 to 1987. The so-called Tax Freedom Day—created by Milton Friedman and computed annually by the Tax Foundation to pinpoints the day of the year on which the average taxpayer is, in effect, free of working for the government—vacillated within an equally narrow range from 1970 to 1987, from April 28 to May 4 (Tax Foundation, Inc., *Facts and Figures on Government Finance* (Baltimore: Johns Hopkins Press, 1988), p. 19). State and local government receipts from own sources (except net interest) grew from 4.6 percent of GNP in 1947 to 10.2 percent of GNP in 1975. State and local receipts stayed between 8.9 and 10 percent of GNP from 1977 through 1988 (in which state and local receipts were 10 percent of GNP) (Executive Office of the President, Office of Management and Budget, *Historical Tables: Budget of the United States Government* [Washington, D.C.: U.S. Government Printing Office, 1990], pp. 365–66).

63. The only major privatization success scored by the Reagan administration was the sale of Conrail in 1987. However, in 1988 the federal government agreed to the sale of the Great Plains Coal Gasification plant, and in the 1987–1988 period, the federal government sold federal loan assets for $4.6 billion (Philip E. Fixler, Robert W. Poole, and Lynn Scarlett, *Privatization 1989: Third Annual Report on Privatization* [Santa Monica, Calif.: Reason Foundation, 1989], p. 6).

64. See David F. Linowes, *Privatization: Toward More Effective Government* (Wash-ington, D.C.: Executive Office of the President, Presidents' Commission on Privatiza-tion, 1988). Several of these proposals were actually included in the 1988 federal budget.

65. Slightly more than 1,000 federally-funded housing units were constructed in 1950. The count was nearly 21,000 in 1960 and more than 92,000 in 1971. Since the early 1970s, the count of housing units, in most years, has been less than a third of the peak in 1971. (See Linowes, *Privatization*, pp. 7–10.)

66. For other recent works that make the academic and policy case for privatiza-tion, see Steve H. Hanke, ed., *Privatization and Development* (San Francisco: Institute for Contemporary Studies, 1987); E. S. Savas, *Privatization: The Key to Better Govern-ment* (Chatham, N.J.: Chatham House Publications, 1987); and Michael A. Walker, ed., *Privatization: Tactics and Techniques* (Vancouver, B.C.: Fraser Institute, 1988).

67. Michael Cusack, "Economics in Our Lives," *Senior Scholastic*, October 1, 1982, pp. 6, 7, and 13.

68. See Edgar Feige, "How Big Is the Irregular Economy?" *Challenge* (November/December 1979), pp. 5–13; Frank de Leeuw, "An Indirect Technique for Measuring the Underground Economy," *Survey of Current Business* (April 1985), pp. 64–72; Kevin F. McCrohan and James D. Smith, "A Consumer Expenditure Approach to

Estimating the Size of the Underground Economy," *Journal of Marketing* (April 1986), pp. 48–59; and Vito Tanzi, "The Underground Economy in the United States: Annual Estimates, 1930–1980," *International Monetary Fund Staff Papers* (June 1983), pp. 283–305.

Hernando de Soto, the president of the Instituto Libertad y Democracia in Peru, maintains that Peru is "a country in which 48 percent of the economically active population and 61.2 percent of the work hours are devoted to informal activities which contribute 38.9 percent of the gross domestic product (GDP recorded in the national accounts . . . [and which] will continue to grow and by the year 2000 can be expected to generate 61.3 percent of GDP recorded in the national accounts" [*The Other Path: The Invisible Revolution in the Third World* (New York: Harper & Row, 1989), p. 12]).

69. The statistical methods used for assessing the size of the underground economy, and the understatement of reported income and employment in the aboveground economy, are challenged in Richard J. McDonald, "The 'Underground Economy' and the BLS Statistical Data," *Monthly Labor Review* (January 1984), pp. 4–18; and Gillian Garcia, "The Currency Ratio and the Subterranean Economy," *Financial Analysts Journal* (November/December 1978), pp. 64–69.

70. De Leeuw, "An Indirect Technique for Measuring the Underground Economy."

71. The Internal Revenue Service estimated that in the early 1980s, the federal government was losing close to $100 billion in tax revenue due to the increasing level of underground economic activity and to tax evasion and avoidance (Cusack, "Economics in Our Lives," p. 7). According to the IRS's "Compliance Measurement Program," of the four income groups in which voluntary compliance had increased in 1986, three were high-income groups, which had received significant tax-rate reductions (see Charles N. Stabler, "Underground Economy May Start Shrinking," *Wall Street Journal*, August 25, 1989, p. 1).

72. Crandall, "What Ever Happened to Deregulation?" p. 289.

73. On the issue of lost gains from tax reductions due to the 1986 tax-reform package, see Norman B. Ture, "The Tax Reform Act of 1986: Revolution or Counterrevolution?" in *Assessing the Reagan Years*, pp. 29–43. For a long list of protectionist measures adopted by the Reagan administration, see "The Reagan Record on Trade: Rhetoric Vs. Reality."

74. The net economic benefits of deregulation are probably most easily assessed in the transportation industries. See Steven Morrison and Clifford Winston, *The Economic Effects of Airline Deregulation* (Washington, D.C.: Brookings Institution, 1986); Thomas Gale Moore, "Rail and Truck Reform—The Record So Far," *Regulation* (November/December 1983), pp. 33–41. Growth in the economy from reform of the tax code is supported by Lindsey, *The Growth Experiment*, chap. 4.

Chapter 9.   The Fall of the Fat Cats: An Unorthodox Challenge to the Decline Theorists

1. W. Michael Blumenthal, "The World Economy and Technological Change," *Foreign Affairs* 66, no. 3 (1987/1988), pp. 531–32.

2. Thirty-five of thirty-eight forecasters polled by the *Wall Street Journal* in June 1988 believed that a recession was unlikely within the following twelve months. The predicted average rate of growth in real GNP for all thirty-eight forecasters was 2.7 percent for the second half of 1988 and 2.2 percent for the first half of 1989. The anticipated growth rates for the second half of 1988 ranged from 3.3 percent to −0.2 percent (Tom Herman, "Economists Expect Expansion to Continue for at Least a Year," *Wall Street Journal,* July 5, 1988, p. 3).

3. Walter Russell Mead observes:

> That great empires should fall as well as rise seems perfectly natural when we consider the land of the pharaohs or ancient Babylon. That the American Empire should suffer such a fate is more disturbing. And that the decline, and ultimately the fall, of the American Empire is the basic political fact of the present period in world history is more disturbing still. We cannot sit back and observe the fall of the American Empire with the detachment with which we view Rome; our hope and fears are too closely bound up in the fate of the American Empire. (*Mortal Splendor: The American Empire in Transition* [Boston: Houghton Mifflin, 1987], p. 10)

4. Daniel A. Sharp, "America is Running Out of Time," *New York Times,* February 7, 1988, as reprinted in *The World Trade Imbalance: When Profit Motives Collide* (Washington, D.C.: Executive Council on Foreign Diplomats, U.S. Department of State, 1988), p. 25.

5. Joel Kurtzman, *The Decline and Crash of the American Economy* (New York: W. W. Norton, 1988), p. 212.

6. Ibid., pp. 25–34.

7. Benjamin M. Friedman, *Day of Reckoning: The Consequences of American Economic Policy under Reagan and After* (New York: Random House, 1988), p. 300.

8. Richard D. Lamm "Crisis: The Uncompetitive Society," in *Global Competitiveness: Getting the U.S. Back on Track*, ed. Martin K. Starr (New York: W. W. Norton, 1988), p. 13.

9. Ibid.

10. Ibid., pp. 17–39.

11. Blumenthal, "The World Economy and Technological Change," p. 528.

12. Ibid.

13. Ibid., pp. 529–31.

14. David P. Calleo, Harold van B. Cleveland, and Leonard Silk, "The Dollar and the Defense of the West," *Foreign Affairs* 66, no. 4 (Spring 1988), p. 845.

15. Ibid.

16. Ibid.

17. Mancur Olson, *The Rise and Decline of Nations* (New Haven, Conn.: Yale University Press, 1982).

18. Brookings Institution researchers Martin Baily and Alok Chakrabarti found that the productivity crisis is evident in statistics on growth of GDP per hour and growth of manufacturing output per hour. In the United States in the 1950–73 period, GDP per hour increased at an average annual rate of 2.44 percent, while manufacturing output per hour grew at a slightly higher average annual rate, 2.62 percent. However, GDP per hour in the 1979–84 period grew at one-half its earlier rate, 1.09 percent per year. Manufacturing output per hour grew more rapidly in

the more recent period, 3.10 percent per year (*Innovation and the Productivity Crisis* [Washington, D.C.: Brookings Institution, 1988], p. 5 [see also p. 9 for alternative measures of productivity growth relative to other countries]).

19. Olson maintains:

> The everyday use of the word *miracle* to describe the rapid economic growth in these countries [Japan and West Germany] testifies that this growth was not only unexpected, but also outside the range of known laws and experience. In Japan and West Germany, totalitarian governments were followed by Allied occupiers determined to promote institutional change and to ensure that institutional life would start almost anew. In Germany, Hitler had done away with independent unions as well as all other dissenting groups, whereas the Allies, through measures such as the decartelization decrees of 1947 and denazification programs, had emasculated cartels and organizations with right-wing backgrounds. In Japan, the militaristic regime had kept down left-wing organizations, and the Supreme Commander of the Allied Powers imposed the antimonopoly law of 1947 and purged many hundreds of officers of zaibatsu and other organizations for their war-time activities. (In Italy, the institutional destruction from totalitarianism, war, and Allied occupation was less severe and the postwar growth "miracle" correspondingly shorter. . . .) (*The Rise and Decline of Nations*, pp. 75–76)

20. Mead, *Mortal Splendor*, especially pp. 54–57.

21. Ibid., p. 56.

22. Paul Kennedy, *The Rise and Fall of the Great Powers: Economic Change and Military Conflict from 1500 to 2000* (New York: Random House, 1987).

23. Kennedy admits that he is not arguing that economics is the sole cause of the rise and decline of great powers: "There simply is too much evidence pointing to other things: geography, military organization, national morale, the alliance system, and many other factors can all affect the relative power of members of the states system. . . . What does seem incontestable, however, is that in a long-run-drawn-out Great Power (and usually coalition) war, victory has repeatedly gone to the side with the more flourishing productive base—or, as the Spanish captains used to say, to him who has the last escudo" (ibid., p. xxiv).

24. Ibid., p. 515.

25. This theme is also fundamental to the analysis of David P. Calleo, *Beyond American Hegemony: The Future of the Western Alliance* (New York: Basic Books, 1987), especially chap. 7.

26. Because of the breadth of the audience he has reached through his best-seller, Professor Kennedy's thesis regarding the importance of military spending in fostering economic and political decline has occasionally drawn sharp, sometimes acid, criticism in the media. For example, Joseph Nye, a professor of international security at Harvard, asks that readers "look again before drawing gloomy conclusions. The United States is nothing like Phillip II's empire, where, as Kennedy said, three-quarters of all government expenditures were 'devoted to war or to debt repayments for previous wars.' Even under President Reagan's buildup, our defense outlay is only 6.5 percent of the gross national product and is lower than those of the Eisenhower and Kennedy Administrations, which each spent more than 10 percent" ("America's Decline: A Myth," *New York Times*, April 10, 1988, p. 31).

27. Kennedy, *The Rise and Fall of the Great Powers*, pp. 413–37. "Gross Domestic

Product," or GDP, is similar, but not identical, to GNP; GDP equals "the total of the gross expenditures on the final use of the domestic supply of goods and services valued at purchasers' values *less* imports of goods and services valued c.i.f." (Organisation for Economic Cooperation and Development, *National Accounts, 1960–1986*, vol. I [Paris, 1988], p. 6).

28. Kennedy, *The Rise and Fall of the Great Powers*, p. 432. Kennedy cites (as his primary source for his data on world production shares) P. Bairoch, "International Industrialization Levels from 1750 to 1980," *Journal of European Economic History* 11 (1980), p. 304. Kennedy also points out that CIA figures show that the United States' share of world output dropped from 25.9 percent in 1960 to 21.5 percent in 1980 (Central Intelligence Agency, *Handbook of Economic Statistics* [Washington, D.C.: 1984], p. 4). However, he acknowledges that CIA figures may be influenced by exchange-rate considerations (Kennedy, *The Rise and Fall of the Great Powers*, p. 608, n. 248).

29. Kennedy, *The Rise and Fall of the Great Powers*, p. 534.

30. Consider, for example, the conflicting protectionist positions of Senator Lloyd Bentsen (D., Tex.) and Harvard economist Robert Reich, both of whom worry that the U.S. economy is, at the very least, not working very well and may be in long-term decline without remedial policies. Senator Bentsen is an old-style protectionist, while Professor Reich opposes protectionist measures, except when they are part of a broader industrial policy to shape the future course of the economy (Lloyd Bentsen, "National Press Club Speech," *Congressional Record* [May 20, 1987]; and Robert B. Reich, "The Economics of Illusion and the Illusion of Economics," *Foreign Affairs* 66, no. 3 [Winter 1987/1988], pp. 516–28).

31. Kennedy, *The Rise and Fall of the Great Powers*, p. 439.

32. Reich, "The Economics of Illusion and the Illusion of Economics," p. 523.

33. Calleo, Cleveland, and Silk, "The Dollar and the Defense of the West," p. 852. The authors continue, "Equally unrealistic, in our view, is the strategy that would eliminate the deficit by heavy cuts in our country's comparatively undeveloped welfare spending, as the Reagan Administration has always advocated rhetorically, or by large cuts in America's comparatively low level of 'middle-class entitlements,' as advocated by many of the Administration's critics" (ibid., p. 852).

34. Ibid., pp. 526–28. See also Sharp, "America is Running Out of Time" and Starr, *Global Competitiveness*, pp. 299–310.

35. The statistical details are provided in Richard B. McKenzie, *The Decline of America: Myth or Fate?* (St. Louis: Center for the Study of American Business, Washington University, 1988).

36. In the early 1980s, the trend of U.S. industrial power was in considerable dispute. Many commentators then claimed, with much statistical support, that the United States was "deindustrializing" in the sense that manufacturing or industrial production was in absolute decline. See Barry Bluestone and Bennett Harrison, *The Deindustrialization of America* (New York: Basic Books, 1982); and Robert Reich, *The Next American Frontier* (New York: Times Books, 1983).

37. We use data on GNP as computed and reported by the CIA, a principal data source of the studies cited by Kennedy.

38. U.S. GNP as a percentage of world GNP actually is sensitive to the source of the data. In using the *Statistical Abstract of the United States* for data on world and U.S. GNP, the percentage rises modestly over the 1970–84 period. U.S. GNP was

36.3 percent of the rest-of-the-world GNP in 1970; 38.6 percent in 1975; 38.8 percent in 1980; and 39.7 percent in 1984 (authors' calculations based on data from *Statistical Abstract of the United States: 1988* [Washington, D.C.: U.S. Government Printing Office, 1988], pp. 805, which cites U.S. Arms Control and Disarmament Commission, *World Military Expenditures and Arms Transfers*, annual). These data are probably sensitive to exchange-rate changes, which is why the percentage statistics reported in the text are based on CIA data founded on the OECD purchasing-power-parity calculations, methods designed to minimize the distorting influences of exchange rates.

The same patterns of decline in the 1960–75 period and then stabilization in the 1975–86 period are evident in comparisons of U.S. GNP with the GNPs of other "developed countries" and "less developed countries" (LDCs). U.S. GNP was 75 percent the GNP of the developed countries in 1960 but had fallen to 58.3 percent by 1975. However, U.S. GNP was still 59.1 percent of the GNP of the developed countries in 1986. U.S. GNP was more than four times the GNP of the LDCs in 1960, but was down to 251 percent of the GNP of the LDCs in 1975 and then to 226 of LDC GNP in 1980. However, after 1980, further decline abated, more or less. For details on these international comparisons, see the tables and charts in Richard B. McKenzie, *The Decline of America*.

39. Data drawn from Department of Economics and Statistics, OECD, *National Accounts*, p. 145.

40. The same general pattern on U.S. gross domestic output relative to OECD countries is observed in ratios of OECD volume indexes for GDP between 1960 and 1986 (OECD, *National Accounts*, pp. 134–35).

These general trends are confirmed by data on the ratio of the industrial production index in the United States to the industrial production index in Japan and for all member countries of the European Economic Community. For the EEC as a whole, the trend in the ratio is slightly upward, meaning that U.S. industrial production tended to grow relative to European countries. For Japan, on the other hand, the trend is downward, once again confirming earlier deductions. However, it is important to notice that the trend began to flatten out in the early to mid-1970s. After 1985 the ratio between the industrial production indexes of the United States and Japan stayed at or above .85. The ratios for individual countries varied, of course. The ratio between the U.S. and West Germany followed the upward trend of the EEC. Industrial production in Canada grew slightly relative to industrial production in the United States. However, the industrial production in France, Italy, and the United Kingdom fell significantly.

41. The Communist countries include the USSR, Bulgaria, Czechoslovakia, East Germany, Hungary, Poland, Romania, China, and Yugoslavia. Data obtained from CIA, *Handbook of Economic Statistics*, pp. 34–35.

42. As reported in Warren T. Brooks, "CIA Missed Soviet Decline," *Commercial Appeal* (Memphis, Tenn.), February 20, 1990, p. A7. See also Henry S. Rowan and Charles Wolf, Jr., *The Impoverished Superpower: Perestroika and the Soviet Military Burden* (San Francisco: Institute for Contemporary Studies, 1989).

43. The country's fixed reproducible tangible wealth includes all equipment and structures of government and private individuals and firms, plus consumer durable goods (automobiles, furniture, household appliances, and "other"). See *Statistical Abstract* (1989), table 744. The United States' net stock of wealth increased from

$6.6 trillion (in 1982 dollars) in 1970 to $10.8 trillion in 1987, a 63.6 percent increase (ibid.).

44. Frank Levy and Richard C. Michel, "The Curse of the Comfort Zone Sapped America's Saving Grace," *Washington Post National Weekly Edition*, February 12–18, 1990, p. 23.

45. Saving as a percentage of net national income in the 1980–87 period averaged 20.3 percent in Japan, 12.8 percent in Italy, 10.8 percent in West Germany, 9.9 percent in Canada, 8.6 percent in France, 6.3 percent in Great Britain, and 4.2 percent in the United States ("Mr. Bush's Piggy Bank," *New York Times*, February 2, 1990, p. A14).

46. *Washington Post* and *Newsweek* columnist Robert Samuelson has focused on the average savings rate over a longer stretch of time. He found that total private savings averaged 16.7 percent between 1980 and 1988 and 16.8 percent between 1950 and 1979 ("The Great Saving Debate: A Smoke Screen," *Washington Post National Weekly Edition*, February 12–18, 1990, p. 29).

47. The rate of appreciation of U.S. real stock of wealth as measured by the BEA actually increased between the 1970s and the 1980s. Between 1970 and 1980, the stock appreciated by an average annual increase of 1.4 percent. Between 1980 and 1986, the rate of increase was slightly higher, 1.5 percent (authors' calculations from data in the *Statistical Abstract* [1989], p. 744).

48. Lawrence Lindsey, *The Growth Experiment: How the New Tax Policy Is Transforming the U.S. Economy* (New York: Basic Books, 1990), pp. 121–22.

49. The relative decline in investment goods prices means that the investment/GNP ratio understates the relative growth of real-investment goods. See John A. Tatom, "U.S. Investment in the 1980s: The Real Story," *Review* (Federal Reserve Bank of St. Louis, March/April 1989), pp. 3–15.

50. Ibid., pp. 8–10 (especially figure 5). Tatom attributes the relative rise in investment in the early 1980s to tax breaks for investment—principally the investment tax credit and accelerated depreciation allowance—incorporated in the 1981 tax reform bill and the relative decline in investment after 1985 to the elimination of tax breaks for investment included in the 1986 tax reform bill.

51. Ibid., p. 12.

52. Kennedy implicitly and correctly assumes that relative production levels and wealth across countries are inextricably linked. Because he believes U.S. relative production continued to fall into the 1980s, its relative wealth level (and relative military power) must have continued to fall. He repeatedly makes passing references (without adding the supporting data) to the decline in U.S. wealth, for example: "The United States' relative share of global production and *wealth* [italics added] was at that time [during the Eisenhower and Kennedy administrations] around *twice* what it is today" (*The Rise and Fall of the Great Powers*, p. 532).

53. Ibid., p. 526.

54. Surpluses in the trade in both goods and services were more frequent and larger than the surpluses in the trade of goods alone.

55. Exports of the United States as a percentage of the exports of the rest of the world also fell significantly during the 1960–80 period, from 18.9 percent in 1960 to 12.4 percent in 1980—a 34 percent reduction in world export share. The U.S. export share remained relatively stable through 1985, then fell from 12.5 percent in 1985 to 11.2 percent in 1986 (authors' calculations based on CIA, *Handbook of*

*Economic Statistics*, pp. 22, 78). However, these changes in U.S. export shares (and lack thereof) could have been greatly influenced by exchange-rate changes and by the growth in world exports to the United States (which reflects the growth in U.S. imports).

56. Richard B. McKenzie, "American Competitiveness: Do We Really Need to Worry?" *Public Interest* (Winter 1988), pp. 66–80.

57. For an elaboration of this line of argument, see Council of Economic Advisors, *Economic Report of the President* (Washington, D.C.: U.S. Government Printing Office, 1987), pp. 101–7.

58. See Baily and Chakrabarti, *Innovation and the Productivity Crisis*, chap. 3; Richard B. McKenzie, *The American Job Machine* (New York, Universe Books, 1988), chap. 7.

59. To this point, it must be recognized that domestic investment opportunities sold to foreigners represent "things" not shipped out of the country. They are, however, no less goods that are produced. For example, if a foreigner buys a Mack truck for use in construction in a foreign country, the sale will be classified in the U.S. balance of payments as an export and will reduce the trade deficit. If the Mack truck is, on the other hand, retained in the United States for use in construction in the United States, it is no less a capital good produced domestically. At the same time, the truck sale will be classified as a capital inflow and will not reduce the trade deficit. The classification system in this and many other cases is largely arbitrary.

60. Authors' calculations based on data from the *Economic Report of the President* (1990), pp. 294, 411.

61. On this point, see the extended discussion by Allen J. Lenz, "U.S. International Competitiveness: Conceptual and Measurement Problems," in *United States Trade: Performance in 1985 and Outlook* (Washington, D.C.: U.S. Government Printing Office, 1986), pp. 97–101.

62. For additional points on this line of argument, see Herbert Stein, "A Primer on the Other Deficit," *AEI Economist* (March 1987), from which Stein drew his exceptionally incisive columns ("Leave the Trade Deficit Alone," *Wall Street Journal*, March 11, 1987, p. A36; and "Don't Worry about the Trade Deficit," *Wall Street Journal*, May 16, 1989, p. A14).

63. This line of argument is developed in Robert Z. Lawrence, "International Dimension," in *American Living Standards: Threats and Challenges* (Washington, D.C.: Brookings Institution, 1988), pp. 23–65.

64. This is hardly a settled issue in the econometric literature. There are two basic econometric problems. The first has to do with separating the impact on trade deficits of real federal expenditures and the impact of the budget deficits on real interest rates. The second problem has to do with the fact that trade deficits can affect budget deficits, as well as the other way around. For studies that report an uncertain, if at all detectable, connection between government deficits, interest rates, and trade deficits, see John Tatom, "A Perspective on the Federal Budget Deficit," *Review* (St. Louis Federal Reserve Bank, June/July 1984), pp. 5–17; and David Bowles, Holley Ulbrich, and Myles Wallace, "Default Risk, Interest Differentials, and Fiscal Policy: A New Look at Crowding Out," *Eastern Economic Journal* (July/September 1989), pp. 203–12; and Nathan Childs, *International Trade Explanations for Farm Troubles in the 1980s* (Ph.D. dissertation, Agriculture Economics and

Rural Sociology Department, Clemson University, 1987). A statistically significant correlation between the budget and trade deficits may eventually be found. However, the computed effect may not explain a substantial share of the variation of the trade deficit. For a study that assesses the interactive effects of trade and budget deficits, see Alis Darrat, "Have Large Budget Deficits Caused Rising Trade Deficits?" *Southern Economic Journal* (April 1988), pp. 879–87.

65. See the discussion on this point with accompanying charts in McKenzie, *The American Job Machine*, chap. 6.

66. Harvard Professor Robert Reich recommends a tax increase to partially solve the deficit problem ("The Economics of Illusion and the Illusion of Economics," p. 527). Almost everyone recommends a scaling back of defense expenditures (Calleo, "The Dollar and the Defense of the West," pp. 853–56).

67. See Calleo, Cleveland, and Silk, "The Dollar and the Defense of the West." Proponents of the decline thesis often look to reductions in defense expenditures to finance their proposed expansion of domestic programs.

68. Robert Reich, "The Economics of Illusion and the Illusion of Economics," p. 524.

69. Lawrence, "International Dimensions," p. 26.

70. The only way that foreign capital inflows could add to the future burden of Americans is by increasing Congress's proclivity to increase its wasteful (or nonproductive) expenditures by using debt, which, admittedly, may be the case.

71. For example, Blumenthal notes that "through miniaturization it has been possible, on the average, to double the number of transistors on one tiny chip each since . . ." (Blumenthal, "The World Economy and Technological Change," p. 533). This means that between 1961 and 1981, the number of arithmetic operations that could be handled by computers rose from 34,000 per second to 800 million per second. This increased computational ability has been accompanied by tremendous reductions in the sizes of machines and in the costs of calculations.

## Chapter 10.   U-Turn on the Road to Serfdom: A Policy Sampler

1. As reported in David Frum, "The Great Delusion," *Wall Street Journal*, October 11, 1989, p. A18.

2. F. A. Hayek, *The Road to Serfdom* (Chicago: University of Chicago Press, 1944).

3. See Milton and Rose Friedman, *Tyranny of the Status Quo* (San Diego: Harcourt Brace Jovanovich, 1984); and James M. Buchanan, *The Limits of Liberty: Between Anarchy and Leviathan* (Chicago: University of Chicago Press, 1975).

4. George J. Stigler, *Memoirs of an Unregulated Economist* (New York: Basic Books, 1985), chap. 9.

5. Ibid., p. 147.

6. Federal Express's overnight delivery business expanded by more than 26 percent in 1987 alone to a daily average of 925,000 overnight deliveries (James Bruce, "Fax Machines Generate 'Faxplosion' in US," *Journal of Commerce*, March 24, 1988, p. 3A.

7. Obviously, the U.S. Postal Service will be around for a long time to come. Ongoing federal subsidies will ensure its continued survival. At the same time, it

is not unreasonable to expect the concept of a "post office" and "post office box" to change dramatically. The post office box of the future will, to a growing extent, be a personal computer or a fax machine; the latter will weigh five to ten pounds (or even less), be about the size of an answering machine, and double as a household telephone, personal copier, and text and image scanner for computerized desktop publishing in homes, as well as offices.

8. See James Bovard, "The Slow Death of the Postal Service," *Policy Analysis* (Washington, D.C.: Cato Institute, 1988).

9. These points are more fully developed in a forthcoming book by the authors, *Failure and Progress: The Virtue of Economic Failure and the Failure of Political Virtue*.

10. June Marotta and George Marotta, "Yippies from Yuppies," *Commercial Appeal* (Memphis, Tenn.), August 25, 1989, p. A12.

11. Phillip Longman, "Elderly, Affluent—and Selfish," *New York Times*, October 10, 1989, p. Y27.

12. Marotta, "Yippies from Yuppies."

13. The expected reduction in the growth of benefits for the elderly is documented in Richard B. McKenzie, *The Retreat of the Elderly Welfare State* (St. Louis: Center for the Study of American Business, Washington University, 1990). In 1989 many elderly who worked and earned more than several thousand dollars had to give up fifty cents in Social Security benefits for every extra dollar earned. In addition, a greater share of their Social Security benefits was taxed, and they had to make additional payments for their federal catastrophic health insurance. Many found that their actual purchasing power went down when their earned income went up, a decided disincentive to work. See John Goodman, *The Elderly: The People the Supply-Side Revolution Forgot* (Dallas: National Policy Center, 1989).

14. Deborah White, "FedEx Chooses Memphis Site for Plane Maintenance Center," *Commercial Appeal* Memphis, Tenn., August 18, 1989, p. A1.

15. Ibid.

16. Ibid., p. A10.

17. Detroit bought the necessary property for the GM plant for $200 million ($150 million of which was covered by a federal grant) and sold the site to GM for slightly more than $8 million. See Sheldon Richman, "The Rape of Poletown," *Inquiry* (August 3 and 24, 1981).

18. Stephen Labaton, "High Tech Helps Drug Dealers Export Cash," *Athens* (Ga.) *Banner/Herald*, August 14, 1989, p. 1.

19. Mike Royko, "Drug War Was Lost a Long Time Ago," *Commercial Appeal* (Memphis, Tenn.), August 25, 1989, p. A13.

20. Alan L. Otten, "Severity of Crisis May be Due to U.S. Trait," *Wall Street Journal*, September 6, 1989, p. A10.

21. "War on Drugs Has Failed: Drug Prohibition Criticized at Cato Conference," *Cato Policy Report* (July/August 1989), p. 3.

22. James Ostrowski, "Thinking about Drug Legalization," *Policy Analysis* (Washington, D.C.: Cato Institute, 1989).

23. The intellectual case for liberalizing immigration restrictions has been made by Julian L. Simon in *The Economic Consequences of Immigration* (Cambridge, Mass.: Basil Blackwell, 1989).

24. Joseph S. Nye, Jr., *Bound to Lead: The Changing Nature of American Power* (New York: Basic Books, 1990), pp. 184–85.

25. National Commission on Excellence in Education, *A Nation at Risk: The Imperative for Educational Reform* (Washington, D.C.: U.S. Government Printing Office, 1983).

26. John E. Chubb and Terry M. Moe, "Give Choice a Chance," *Florida Policy Review* (Summer 1989), pp. 17–24.

27. As reported in William B. Johnson and Arnold E. Packer, *Workforce 2000: Work and Workers for the Twenty-First Century* (Indianapolis: Hudson Institute, 1987), p. 103.

28. Lawrence A. Uzzell, "Education Reform Fails the Test," *Wall Street Journal*, May 10, 1989, p. A18.

29. Ibid.

30. As quoted from a federally funded report by the committee on the National Assessment of Educational Progress in Uzzell, "Education Reform Fails the Test."

31. U.S. Departments of Labor, Education, and Commerce, *Building a Quality Workforce* (Washington, D.C.: U.S. Government Printing Office, 1988), p. 13.

32. "Needed: Human Capital," *Business Week*, September 19, 1988, p. 102.

33. Stanley J. Molic, "No. 1 Resource Far Short of Potential, *Industry Week*, April 17, 1989, pp. 74–76.

34. National Commission on Excellence in Education, *A Nation at Risk*.

35. For a recent discussion of the extent to which businesses have become involved in providing their workers with basic education, see Joseph Berger, "Companies Step in Where the Schools Fail," *New York Times*, September 26, 1989, p. Y1.

36. Amy Stuart Wells, "Milwaukee Parents Get More Choice on Schools," *New York Times*, March 28, 1990, p. B8. However, the public educational establishment and Wisconsin teachers' union sued in spring 1990 to have the voucher plan declared unconstitutional ("Teachers Vs. Kids, *Wall Street Journal*, June 6, 1990, p. A14).

37. Susan Phillips, "Education Choice Emerging Trends?" *Family, Law & Democracy Report* (July 1989), pp. 1–3.

38. Jaclyn Fierman, "Giving Parents a Choice of schools," *Fortune* (December 4, 1989), p. 147.

39. C. Emily Feistritzer, "Break the Teaching Monopoly," *Wall Street Journal*, June 29, 1990, p. A10.

40. Jeffrey H. Birnbaum, "Rostenkowski Buttered by Bush and Battered by Democrats Erred Badly on Capital Gains," *Wall Street Journal*, September 19, 1989, p. A30.

41. Ibid.

42. Alan Reynolds, "Time to Cut the Capital Gains Tax," *Supply-Side Analytics* (March 15, 1989), p. 15.

43. Lawrence Lindsey argues that the 1978 and 1981 reductions in the capital-gains tax rate resulted in increased revenues and that the Congressional Budget Office also concluded in 1988 that a capital-gains tax rate of 25 percent would produce the same revenue as a 28 percent rate [Lawrence Lindsey, *The Growth Experiment: How the New Tax Policy Is Transforming the U.S. Economy* (New York: Basic Books, 1990), pp. 142–43]. See also Congressional Budget Office, *How Capital Gains Affect Revenue: The Historical Evidence* (Washington, D.C.: U.S. Congressional Budget Office, 1988).

44. In 1989 Congress passed a bill that would have raised the minimum wage to $4.55 by 1992, which was vetoed by President George Bush, who supported an

increase to $4.25 an hour with a provision that would allow employers to continue to pay $3.35 an hour for a "training period" of up to six months.

45. In the case of the pollution standards, all polluters—regardless of the cleanup costs they incur—must reduce their pollutants. In the case of pollution rights, those firms that have relatively high clean-up costs will buy the pollution rights. Those that have relatively low cleanup costs will not buy the rights and will, therefore, do the most cleaning up. A shift from pollution standards to pollution rights will lower the total cleanup cost. For more details on this line of argument, see Hugh H. Macaulay and Bruce Yandle, *Environmental Use and the Market* (Lexington, Mass.: Lexington Books, 1977), chaps. 1–6; or Richard B. McKenzie and Gordon Tullock, *The Best of the New World of Economics* (Homewood, Ill.: Irwin, 1989), chap. 12. The Environmental Protection Agency under the Bush administration is seeking to expand the market for pollution rights, while Congress may obstruct its ability to do so. For a discussion of the theory behind tradable emissions rights and of recent congressional efforts to retard the development of pollution-rights markets, see Anne Sholtz with Kenneth Chilton, *Acid Rain and Tradeable Permits: How Congress Hobbles the Marketplace* (St. Louis: Center for the Study of American Business, Washington University, 1990).

46. Raymond Vernon and Debora Spar, *Beyond Globalism: Remaking American Foreign Economic Policy* (New York: Free Press, 1989), p. 3.

47. Ibid., p. 196.

48. Ibid., p. 15.

49. Ibid., p. 193.

50. Alvin Rabushka, *The New China: Comparative Economic Development of Mainland China, Hong Kong, and Taiwan* (San Francisco: Pacific Institute, 1987). Rabushka stresses that the relative income of people in China and Hong Kong depends crucially on which exchange rate is employed. However, no one would estimate the per capita income of Hong Kong to be less than six times that of China.

51. Data drawn from a memorandum sent to friends of the Heritage Foundation, based on a tour of Pacific Rim countries, by Edwin J. Feulner, Jr. (August 14, 1989), p. 1.

52. We recognize that at the time of this writing, signs abound that the reform movement in China has been partially halted (Ada Ignatius, "China's Economic Reform Program Stalls: Political Crackdown Threatens Free-Market Policy," *Wall Street Journal*, September 26, 1989, p. A18). However, because of the economic forces at work on China's politics, we expect only a delay in the reform movement.

53. Robert D. Tollison, "The Twilight of Government Power: Commentary," a paper prepared for a symposium on "International Competitiveness and Government Power," sponsored by the Liberty Fund (Charlotte, N.C.: August 3–6, 1989), p. 1.

54. For example, consider the quotation at the head of this chapter from Norman Angell's *The Great Illusion*. In his book, published in 1910, Angell suggested that technology had caused a substitution of economic for physical forces in the guidance of public international policies. War was, therefore, not as likely because financial disaster would fall upon any country that sought to conquer another.

55. See the preface and Francis Fukuyama, "The End of History?" *National Interest* (Summer 1989), pp. 3–18.

# Index

303